The Practice of Rhetorical Criticism

The Practice of Rhetorical Criticism

James R. Andrews
Indiana University

Macmillan Publishing Co., Inc.
New York

Collier Macmillan Publishers
London

Macmillan Publishing Co., Inc.
866 Third Avenue, New York, New York 10022

Collier Macmillan Canada, Inc.

Library of Congress Cataloging in Publication Data

Andrews, James Robertson,
  The practice of rhetorical criticism.

  Includes bibliographies and index.
  1. Rhetorical criticism. I. Title.
PN4096.A5   808   82-15271
ISBN 0-02-303490-4   AACR2

Printing: 1 2 3 4 5 6 7 8   Year: 3 4 5 6 7 8 9 0

Acknowledgments

The author gratefully acknowledges permission to reprint material from the following sources: (1) Central States Speech Association (CSSA), (2) Speech Communication Association (SCA), and (3) Wadsworth Publishing Company, Inc.

1.

Auer, J. Jeffery. "The Image of the Rt. Hon. Margaret Thatcher." *Central States Speech Journal*, 30 (Winter 1979), 289-310.

Patton, John H. "The Eagleton Phenomenon in the 1972 Presidential Campaign: A Case Study in the Rhetoric of Paradox." *Central States Speech Journal*, 24 (Winter 1973), 278-287.

2.

Andrews, James R. "The Passionate Negation: The Chartist Movement in Rhetorical Perspective." *Quarterly Journal of Speech*, 59 (April 1973), 196-208.

Black, Edwin. "The Second Persona." *Quarterly Journal of Speech*, 56 (April 1970), 109-119.

Bormann, Ernest G. "The Eagleton Affair: A Fantasy Theme Analysis." *Quarterly Journal of Speech*, 59 (April 1973), 143-159.

Campbell, Karlyn Khors. "The Forum: "'Conventional Wisdom—Traditional Form': A Rejoinder." *Quarterly Journal of Speech*, 58 (December 1972), 451-460.

Hill, Forbes. "Conventional Wisdom—Traditional Form—The President's Message of November 3, 1969." *Quarterly Journal of Speech*, 58 (December 1972), 373-386.

Hill, Forbes. "Reply to Professor Campbell." *Quarterly Journal of Speech*, 58 (December 1972), 451-460.

Jamieson, Kathleen Hall. "The Metaphoric Cluster in the Rhetoric of Pope Paul VI and Edmund G. Brown, Jr." *Quarterly Journal of Speech*, 66 (February 1980), 51-72.

Leff, Michael, and G. P. Mohrmann. "Lincoln at Cooper Union: A Rhetorical Analysis of the Text," *Quarterly Speech Journal*, 60 (October 1974), 346-358.

Mohrmann, G. P., and Michael Leff. "Lincoln at Cooper Union: A Rationale for Neoclassical Criticism." *Quarterly Journal of Speech*, 60 December 1974), 459-467.

Newman, Robert P. "Under the Veneer: Nixon's Vietnam Speech of November 3, 1969." *Quarterly Journal of Speech*, 56 (April 1970), 113-128.

Stelzher, Herman G. "The Quest Story and Nixon's November 3, 1969 Address." *Quarterly Journal of Speech*, 57 (April 1971), 163-172.

3.

Campbell, Karlyn Kohrs, "An Exercise in the Rhetoric of Mythical America" From *Critiques of Contemporary Rhetoric* by Karlyn Kohrs Campbell. © 1972 by Wadsworth Publishing Company, Inc., Belmont, California 94002. Reprinted by permission of the publisher.

ISBN   0-02-303490-4

For Alistair James Noel Andrews

Preface

George Campbell wrote in his introduction to *The Philosophy of Rhetoric* that without "eloquence, or the art of speaking . . . the greatest talents, even wisdom itself, lose much of their lustre, and still more of their usefulness." By wisdom, Campbell observed, "a man's own conduct may be well regulated," but, the art of speaking "is absolutely necessary for diffusing valuable knowledge, and enforcing right rules of action upon others."[1]

For centuries past, as in our own time, men and women have communicated with each other in order to transmit what they have learned and to influence each others' actions. This communication has taken many forms, but undoubtedly much of it has been through public discourse. Campbell's *Philosophy of Rhetoric* was published in London in 1776, a time when some of the greatest orators of the English language—Edmund Burke, William Pitt, Charles James Fox—debated the great questions of empire, and when Americans like James Otis, Patrick Henry, and Samuel Adams brought their persuasive powers to bear on the creation of a new nation. Throughout history, and certainly in the present day, issues of great monument have been and are argued publicly. Living as we do in a rhetorical world, heirs

---

[1] George Campbell, *The Philosophy of Rhetoric*. Lloyd F. Bitzer, ed. Carbondale and Edwardsville: Southern Illinois University Press, 1963, xlix.

Preface

as we are of a rhetorical tradition, it is essential that we understand the operations of public persuasion.

This book is designed to orient the beginning student to the nature and function of rhetorical criticism, to acquaint the student with those elements in the rhetorical situation that warrant serious attention, and to teach the student a useful strategy with which to begin to practice criticism.

Scholars and teachers will recognize a "traditional" perspective in this book. Its focus is clearly on public speeches and it recommends careful critical attention be paid to those aspects of the rhetorical act that have long been recognized as comprising the fundamental ingredients of public persuasion. This work is not, however, a call to return to some past critical age; the author's assumption is that the beginning student should start first with a discreet object for critical scrutiny and with a practical way of examining that object. There should be no methodological or philosophical restraints on the critical imagination other than those of sound scholarship, and this book does not seek to impose any. But there must be some place to begin. As the painter first learns to draw the human figure, to suggest perspective, to appreciate the uses of color, and the like, so the rhetorical critic begins by studying basic factors in persuasion and by practicing the technique of explicating the ways in which those factors interact.

This, then, is not a handbook to guide or direct all critical inquiry. It is meant to launch a critical voyage and not to chart its eventual course: for the rest of his or her life the serious critic, through the study of discourse, of theory, and of the critical works of others, and through the practice of the critical art, will continue to develop abilities, to refine judgment, and to create more perspective methods and approaches. This book, it is hoped, is a beginning.

This book reviews the nature of rhetorical criticism paying particular attention to the critical functions. It explores the role of rhetorical variables—the context, the audience, and the speaker—and how these variables interact with the text itself. Analytical categories are explained and interpretive and judgmental processes are discussed.

Included are examples of critical studies. First, in Part II, Richard Nixon's "Address on the Vietnam War, November 3, 1969" is presented. Students may read the text and then study critical essays on that speech by four distinguished contemporary critics. These four studies exhibit variety in approach, interpretation, and judgment. The exchange between Professors Hill and Campbell highlights important issues for critics and provides some insight into the basic assumptions and methods of practicing critics. The examples of other critical studies that appear in Part III offer the student a small sample of varieties of contemporary critical practice; they demonstrate the results of combining imagination and scholarship to reach critical conclusions. These studies are, of course, the work of mature critics, and beginning students are unlikely to emulate them. But the studies do provide points of departure for discussion and might serve as stimulants to students' own critical work.

In a work of this kind it is impossible to single out those who have contributed to it—either directly or indirectly—since it is the result of what I began to learn as a graduate student and what I have continued to learn over the years from my students and colleagues. What shortcomings this book may have are the result of defects in my learning and certainly not in the excellence of their teaching.

I wish to acknowledge with gratitude those who greatly assisted me in the preparation of this work: Ms. Bernadine Psaty, Ms. Peggy Arter, Ms. Judy Granbois, and Ms. Sandra Lieberman. I also wish to thank Indiana University for granting me a sabbatical leave during which much of the work for this book was completed.

James R. Andrews
Bloomington, Indiana

Contents

Contents

_____ **PART III   CRITICAL EXAMPLES 129**

Part I

An Introduction to the Practice of Rhetorical Criticism

1

The Nature of Criticism: An Overview

Everyone reacts to things produced by others, but is everyone a critic? The student who responds to a question about a political speech with, "It was boring"; the seven-year-old who pronounces the latest offering in the *Star Wars* saga "great"; the parent whose comment on the music that his or her child enjoys is, "It's too loud"; the visitor to an art gallary who observes that a new painting "doesn't look like anything"—all are reacting to products of human talent and imagination in a personal and idiosyncratic way. In our common, everyday use of the word, some of these comments might be labeled "critical."

In common parlance, criticism has become associated with carping, with tearing down, with the pointed, negative comment. We tend to label one as "too critical" when we mean that that person appears to be harping on insignificant details, or objecting for the sake of objecting, or looking for something that is wrong; in this sense, the "critic" is the builder of roadblocks, the troublemaker, or the cynic. In our more egocentric moods we see praise as justified evaluation and blame as unwarranted "criticism."

But such popular notions of criticism are certainly not the basis for defining the activity of serious critics. In this connection, Marie Hochmuth Nichols points to John Dewey's observation that "criticism . . . is not fault-finding. It is not pointing out evils to be reformed. It is judgment engaged in discriminating among values. It

3

is taking thought as to what is better and worse in any field at any time, with some consciousness of *why* the worse is worse."[1] One way to define criticism succinctly would be as the systematic process of illuminating and evaluating products of human activity.

As a *process* of illumination and evaluation, criticism does not result solely in ultimate pronouncements. The critical impulse is not one that leads to destruction, but, rather, is one that builds understanding. The serious study of criticism should be free of the misleading conceptions of "destructive" criticism and "constructive" criticism; criticism in the sense that the term is used here can never be destructive, and to say that it is constructive is redundant. At its best, criticism leads us to a fuller and richer understanding of a particular work as it exists within the context of human endeavor. The critic of rhetoric focuses his or her attention on human efforts to be persuasive.

Students of the art of rhetoric have not achieved universal agreement on what the critic of rhetoric should be studying. Nevertheless, both common sense and the evidence presented by what critics actually study suggest that persuasive public discourse is an obvious and sensible object for critical examination. Whereas mature scholars and critics may argue that a variety of phenomena may be studied rhetorically, certainly the best place to *begin* to deal with the problems of rhetorical criticism is with persuasive public discourse. Indeed, such an overwhelming number and variety of persuasive messages are a crucial part of the human experience that most critics devote their sustained attention to them.[2]

RESPONDING CRITICALLY

It is necessary early on to distinguish between responding critically and being a critic. Learning to respond critically is one of the possible, and very important, outcomes of the study of criticism. Persuasion invites response, and the nature of the responses to any given message can vary widely. Responses can be personal, impressionistic, or global. Many times the response tells more about the person responding than about the message. For example, in a group of people listening to an address by the President of the United States, one listener might respond favorably because that listener happened to be of the same political party as the President, or because the listener found certain of his or her own frustrations echoed in the speech, or because the President sounded so sincere, or because that listener found himself or herself agreeing with what the President said. Another listener might respond negatively to the speech because he or she never did trust the President, or because the speech sounded slow and monotonous, or because the listener found nothing in the speech with which he or she could directly identify, or even because the speech preempted the latest episode of "Buck Rogers in the Twenty-fifth Century."

All of us occasionally respond to the appearances of things rather than to the substance. One can read newspaper columns in which one is told how to dress in order to *appear* successful and confident on the probably valid assumption that potential associates will make a judgment about what we know and what we can do on the basis of how we look. Political advertisements may show a candidate with his shirt sleeves rolled up and his tie loosened, talking with factory workers so as to imply not only that the candidate has a real concern for the problems of ordinary people but also to suggest that somehow he knows how to cope with those problems. Actors or athletes who are famous, or even notorious, for their macho images are made to imply that the secret of their prowess somehow lies in the kind of scented alcohol they splash on their faces after they shave. All of us, no matter how well educated or intelligent we may be, can be influenced in some way by the appearance of things.

To respond critically to a message, however, is to be able to distinguish between what is relevant and what is irrelevant in that message. It is to know what the speaker was trying to do, what the speaker said, and what the speaker meant. It is to make some sense out of the speech by comparing the problem as it is addressed by the speaker with the problem as it is seen by the listener and by others who have experienced the problem; by comparing the solution offered by the speaker with other solutions; and by matching the solution with the dimensions and subtleties of the problem as the listener evaluates them. The listener, responding critically, can ask many questions, such as: Who is the speaker and what does he or she have to gain by giving this speech? What are the circumstances that gave rise to the speech? Did the speaker articulate some purpose or goal in giving the speech? What were the speaker's major points? How did he or she support these points? The listener who responds critically is the listener who tries to decide what the speech is all about, what it means, and what there is in the speech that should lead the listener to make some kind of decision or take some kind of action. The critical listener will realize that ideas and not gray hair denote wisdom; that clear thinking is not dependent on a youthful, handsome profile; that being smooth and glib is not an indication of sound reasoning.

Learning to respond critically is, in part, learning to apply the perspective and the methods of a critic. Some students will become rhetorical critics, serious and continuing students of rhetoric and of the way rhetoric influences and is influenced by human events. Other students who read this book, however, will seek to make intelligent responses to public discourse by adopting a critical stance toward communication. They will *do* criticism not because they hope to become professional critics, but because they hope to acquire the point of view and the skills that will help them to respond critically.

In the final analysis, developing the ability to respond critically will be extremely useful on a personal level. The critical listener will be able to make more informed judgments that will improve the quality of his or her response to public messages. Just as one who studies music can respond to certain musical works with more pleasure and appreciation, and just as one who studies poetry can read works of poetry with a deeper sense of personal satisfaction and identification, one who learns to respond critically to public communication can develop a sound basis for his or her own actions.

CHARACTERISTICS OF A CRITIC

A critic is a specialist and must be able to communicate to others the results of his or her critical observation and inquiry. A critic combines knowledge with a systematic way of using that knowledge and constantly seeks to refine his or her practice of criticism.

In the most fundamental sense the critic is an educator. He or she confronts a message; his or her reaction to that message is not the same as the reaction of the casual or even the critical listener. The critic seeks to understand what is going on in order to interpret more fully the rhetorical dynamics involved in the production and reception of the message and to make certain judgments aout the quality of the message.

All critics do not go about their work in the same way, nor do all critics reach the same conclusions about a particular message. The critical impulse—the impulse to illuminate and evaluate—may be similar in all critics; the demands for system and rigor likewise obtain for all criticism; and whereas all critics seek to ask significant questions and go about answering those questions in a methodical fashion, the questions themselves and the means of answering them are not the same for all critics.[3]

For the beginning critic two considerations are primary. First, it is necessary to understand the kinds of questions that appropriately can be raised about a rhetorical message, and, second, it is crucial to develop a methodical way of answering those questions. The remainder of this chapter is devoted to a discussion of the possible function of rhetorical criticism as a way of pointing out the major questions that a critic may address. The remainder of the book presents a framework within which the critic may go about answering these questions systematically.

CRITICAL FUNCTIONS: SEARCHING FOR EFFECT

In what is probably the most influential essay on rhetorical criticism written in this century, Herbert Wichelns observes that rhetorical criticism "is not concerned with permanence nor yet with beauty. It is concerned with effect. It regards a speech as a communication to a specific audience, and holds its business to be the analysis and appreciation of the orator's method of imparting his ideas to his hearers."[4] Certainly the purpose of any rhetorical message is to persuade, to influence human feelings or beliefs or actions in some specific way. When any speaker faces an audience he or she wants members of that audience to *do* something. We think of an "effective" speaker as one who is able to accomplish his or her rhetorical purposes. It is logical and eminently understandable that one possible function of rhetorical criticism is to assess rhetorical effect.

At first glance this function may seem a somewhat simple one, a matter of determining what the auditors did after a speech was given. But just to count the votes at the end of a debate or the number of orders at the end of a sales pitch, or even to consult national polls hardly illuminates a rhetorical message. Nor does it tell us in reality very much about the causal relationship between the message and the actions that followed the message.

In trying to understand effect, the basic question that the critic needs to raise is more complex than simply, "What was the effect of the speech?" The crucial question focuses on the interaction between the message and its total context and is best stated: What potential did the message have to influence what audience or audiences in what ways? Answering such a question involves careful analysis, interpretation, and evaluation—processes that are developed in some detail in following sections of this book. At this point, however, it is appropriate to consider the most relevant factors that engage critics' attention.

To understand rhetorical effect, it is crucial to understand the dimensions of purpose and possibility. A speech functions within a larger context and happens because of things that are happening in the world. A speaker may wish to rally public opinion behind a proposal, create goodwill for an organization or a group in society or a country, or induce members of the audience to take some specified action such as giving money or signing a petition or buying a product. Great oratory often grows out of a series of events that either precipitate a crisis which calls for immediate action or delineates a serious problem which demands a solution. Whatever the circumstances, a rhetorical message is a purposive message; its aim is to get a response from an audience. *The critic who would search for effect must try to discern the purpose of the message*, that is to say, *what effect is desired by the speaker*. In discovering this purpose the critic will need to know what events brought the speech about, what was or is in the speaker's present position or background that caused him or her to speak at this time, what the speaker actually says in the speech that explicitly defines the purpose, and what there is in the speech that may reveal an unstated purpose.

A speaker's purposes are not always apparent or easy to determine. The speaker may have an underlying purpose that is more pressing and important than the apparent one. It has been argued persuasively, for example, that during a political campaign a speaker's real purpose is to "ingratiate" himself or herself with an audience.[5] Whereas the topic of a speech might be foreign policy and the speaker's purpose may seem to be to convince the audience that the NATO alliance should be strengthened, the speaker's "real" purpose might be to convince that audience that he or she is a well-informed and capable leader.

Once the best case possible for his or her reconstruction of the speaker's rhetorical purpose has been made, the critic will consider the possibilities for effecting that purpose. Here the critic must understand the constraints that are likely to affect the outcome of a speech. For example, political, personal, and social realities may shape or limit the achievement of rhetorical goals. A member of Congress might listen to a particularly well-crafted speech—clear, well-organized, amply documented, and supported—but still vote against the speaker's proposal because of his or her own party's commitment to an opposing point of view. A listener may hear a speech given by someone he or she distrusts and dislikes, and, even though the speaker's ideas may match those of the listener, the listener may respond negatively because of his or her overpowering personal antipathy to the speaker. A speaker favoring a Constitutional amendment that would prohibit abortion would be unlikely to devise any speech that would win support from an audience of members of the National Organization for Women because the social viewpoints of the speaker and listeners are separated by a deep, unbridgeable chasm. This does not mean, of course, that the speaker and the listener must always be in perfect agreement; if that were the case, there would be no such concept as persuasion—there would be no change and no need for change. But it does mean that *persuasion must take place within the limits of the possible*, and one of the critic's tasks is to try to determine what those limits are and the extent to which the speaker has recognized the limits and operated within them. Given this understanding of context, the critic will look to the text of the speech itself in order to discover clues as to the speaker's identification of an appropriate audience or audiences and the ways in which the speaker has sought to move those audiences. Through a careful textual analysis, the critic attempts to understand the ways in which persuasive potential has been exploited.

The critic's search for effect, then, involves him or her in the examination of both external and internal factors. The study of context sheds light on the nature of the issues being addressed, the speaker's relationship to those issues and the speaker's personal potential to exert influence, and the audience's relationship to the issues and its potential to influence change in the direction urged by the speaker. An examination of the internal factors, that is, the text of the message itself, should provide insights into how well the speech was crafted—how well arguments were constructed in order to appeal to influential audiences as the critic can best understand those audiences.

Forbes Hill, arguing for Aristotelian criticism, maintains that Aristotle's rhetoric provides a "comprehensive inventory" of the means whereby a speaker can persuade audiences. He asserts that the end of criticism "is to discover whether the speaker makes the best choices from the inventory to get a favorable decision from a specified group of auditors in a specific situation. It does not, of course, aim to discover whether or not the speaker actually gets his favorable decision. . . . "[6] The critic does not make the absolutely causal assessment embodied in the judgment, "The speech was effective"; rather, rhetorical investigation leads the critic to a conclusion concerning the *probable* effectiveness of the message.

Data of various kinds are available to a critic concerning actions taken or statements made following a speech. But the critic must be extremely cautious in dealing with such data. It would be simplistic and misleading, for example, to say that a candidate for political office who won that office did so as the direct result of a speech or even a series of speeches.

In a relatively limited number of cases, students of contemporary speaking have some poll data, usually gathered only after what are considered to be extremely important speeches, but even these data must be viewed with some suspicion. Polls may register impressions of certain audiences at a particular time, but they will never tell the critic that the speaker's use of certain kinds of evidence changed auditors' minds, or that the organizational pattern of the speech functioned persuasively—indeed, such data will not be able to establish any direct relationship between specific rhetorical behaviors and specific outcomes.

Critics also will be able to find a variety of personal reactions to speeches; some listeners will record their responses in their diaries or in letters to friends or even in public statements. But all such manifestations of behavior that occur after a speech are vague and can be extremely unrepresentative, and would constitute unsound bases upon which to argue direct effect. The critic should not ignore such data, but he or she needs to use them with care and to put recorded reactions to speeches into proper perspective.

As Wayne Minnick has observed, "Contemporary testimony and post-speech behaviors best serve the critic if he treats them as establishing hypotheses to be supported rather than as conclusive evidence of effect itself."[7] For the rhetorical critic who would attempt to assess effect, Professor Minnick's conclusion is a sound one: "A hypothetical effect based on testimony and/or post-speech behavior is supported with evidence that the speaker reached an appropriate audience and employed rhetorical methods which, on the face of it, seemed adequate to produce the effect."[8] Furthermore, the probability that the alleged effect actually took place is increased when the critic can demonstrate that "the speaker presented a broadly distributed, rhetorically adequate case in a context which allows the negation of extra-speech events as major causal factors."[9]

Determining effect in short, is not just finding out what happened after a speech was given; it is a careful examination of the interrelationships between text and context in order to offer the most reasonable explanation for the probable result of any given message.

CRITICAL FUNCTIONS: ILLUMINATING EVENTS, CONTEXT AND SPEAKERS

At various times in human history, public discussion and debate of important issues has been a crucial mode of solving or contributing to the solution of the problems faced by human societies. In the English-speaking countries in modern times public discourse has accompanied political and social change; public argument is a part of the Anglo-American tradition.

By turning its attention to such public argument, rhetorical criticism may function to illuminate specific historical events and the social/cultural context in which these events occur. When a rhetorical critic approaches a historical event, he or she does so from a unique perspective. The careful historical investigation of any set of events or period may well reveal hidden forces at work, or at least reveal submerged forces of which the participants in events might be only dimly aware. Examining historical data by looking back on events may lead the historian to discover patterns of behavior and motivations for behavior of which the participants in those events were not fully cognizant. Historical perspective might lead one in a sense to describe what "really" happened.

But events are not always fully or clearly apprehended by those who participate in them. A prime function of rhetoric is to interpret and make meaningful what is in the process of happening. *The reality of one's world at any given moment is the reality as it is perceived.* Speeches afford concrete evidence of how actors living through history perceive what is going on and how they try to shape the perceptions of others. A speaker may judge events imperfectly or incorrectly or may even interpret events deceptively, but what he or she says is an effort to make sense out of events and to project courses of action consistent with that sense.

The critic does not study speeches carefully only to learn what conclusions the speaker reaches or what positions the speaker holds. Also of essential interest to the rhetorical critic is the way in which the speaker attempts to make issues salient and ideas persuasive. Through a careful examination of rhetorical behaviors, the critic should be able to uncover the issues as they are defined and refined at the time of their importance. The critic should be able to discover the implicit and explicit points of clash between differing views. Much rhetorical activity is devoted to the struggle for control of the issues. A careful reading of speeches that focuses not only on the ideational content but also on rhetorical method will uncover the ways in which issues emerge, the ways in which they jostle each other for supremacy, and the ways in which they assume hierarchical values.

Since the rhetorical critic is concerned with rhetorical method, he or she is compelled to come to grips with the totality of a speaker's argument. A full examination of argument can generate insights into the nature of the society in which that argument flourishes. The critic, for example, will search for the uncontested premises of argument. He or she will attempt to uncover those fundamental premises that the speaker perceives as being so basic that they do not need elaboration or justification.

These premises provide clues as to a culture's value structure. This basic structure can be filled in as the critic begins to look at other rhetorical factors. The critic can find much that is instructive in the forms of evidence used by a speaker to determine what that speaker considers to be compelling. This analysis is more than simply identifying forms of support. If, for example, testimony is a predominant form of evidence, it could be enlightening to know the source of *authoritative* testimony. One might, for example, construct the outlines of the social history of the United States by uncovering the time in our own history in which religious leaders, or the founding fathers, or businessmen, or scientists were considered as the ultimate voices of authority.

To be persuasive, a speaker must involve his or her audience in the message itself; the speaker must make that message meaningful or salient to those who listen and must appeal to what the speaker conceives to be the most motivating of audience needs. As the critic examines the rhetorical methods of achieving salience and determines what hierarchical patterns of audience appeals exist, the critic begins to fit into place some of the tiny pieces that make up the mosaic of a culture. A legitimate function of rhetorical criticism, then, is to try to determine how people argue as a means of describing who those people are.

Within the general context of culture, rhetorical criticism can also provide specific illumination of individuals through the study of their rhetorical practices. Not only does an examination of the various parts of discourse shed light on the society in which that discourse flourishes, it can also tell the investigator much about the ways in which the particular speaker thinks and the way he or she sees his or her world. Rhetorical criticism can thus contribute much to biographical study since it uncovers the rhetor's ideas in action as he or she seeks to persuade those over whom that speaker would exert influence.

CRITICAL FUNCTIONS: SOCIAL CRITICISM

If criticism can illuminate historical and cultural contexts, it surely must be able to contribute to the understanding of contemporary events as they are occurring. The rhetorical criticism of contemporary messages may perform what Karlyn Kohrs Campbell describes as a "social function." According to Professor Campbell, "this function requires that critics appraise both the techniques used and the ends advocated in rhetorical acts, in addition to the immediate and long-range effects of both." Campbell goes on to define social criticism as "criticism that evaluates the ways in which issues are formulated and policies justified, and the effects of both on society at a particular historical moment."[10] What Campbell in effect implies is that critics enter the fray of public discussion, using their ciritical abilities and perspective to become active *participants* in the solution of problems by their careful investigation of rhetoric and its consequences.

The social function of rhetorical criticism is a matter of some controversy.[11] An argument against such criticism might go something like this: The criticism of rhetoric involves the evaluation of *rhetorical* choices. If the function of rhetoric is to persuade, then the critic of rhetoric has as his or her task the discovery of the ways in which, and the extent to which, a message was persuasive. When one begins to make judgments about whether the aims of persuasion are good or bad for our society, or judgments about whether the policies advocated are practical and useful solutions to problems, one ceases to be a *rhetorical* critic and ventures into the realm of other disciplines. This is not to say that the rhetorical critic cannot comment on contemporary affairs; he or she does so, however, as an intelligent, educated observer might do, not as a *rhetorical critic*.

On the other hand, there is a compelling argument that such a view limits too severely the possible functions of rhetorical criticism. When public discussion takes place, *how* the participants in that discussion argue is as important as the conclusions they reach. If rhetoric does, indeed, shape perceptions, then the critic of rhetoric should be able to make evaluative statements concerning the accuracy and the implications of those perceptions as the speaker would have them.

There would be little disagreement that a rhetorical critic may, for example, legitimately focus his or her attention on arguments. The critic can make descriptive statements about the structure of an argument, but the investigation does not end there; an assessment of the quality of an argument is surely within the realm of rhetorical criticism. Quality may be judged upon a variety of standards. The potential effectiveness of the argument is certainly a standard that can be applied, but it is not the *only* standard. Consider the quantity and quality of evidence used to support argumentative conclusions; is the critic's legitimate standard a measurement of how convincing an audience might find the evidence? An argument, after all, is a structure that must be utilitarian as well as pleasing. A house may be well designed, beautiful to look at, and functional; it may sell at a high price and return a substantial profit to the builder, but the firmness of the foundation and the quality of the support beams, which are not readily discernible to the untrained consumer, may be such that the building collapses on the new occupants during the first storm. Building codes are designed to provide some protection for the consumer by demanding expert certification of soundness. Should not the expert in agrument be prepared to expose the shaky premises or the tenuous supporting evidence that underpins a conclusion advocating actions that affect our lives?

Such critical response is not as simple as pointing out a deliberate prevarication on the part of the speaker. It is more subtle than that; it may be raising the question of whether a speaker has adequately "proved" a point. For the critic who is concerned only with effect, "adequate" is defined as what an audience accepts, but for the social critic "adequate" can be defined as convincing enough to establish the probable truth of a claim for the discerning, informed, skeptical observer. In establishing probable "truth," the critic becomes a *participant* in the rhetorical process. The critic who is trained in rhetoric knows what *is* persuasive; when that critic enters into a controversy, it is to argue the question of what *should* be persuasive. The rhetorical critic can argue, for example, that the speaker's selective choice of supporting material ignores relevant data and thus distorts perceptions of events, or that the speaker's argument hinges on acceptance of a premise that conflicts with widely held values, or that there is a discongruity between the problem as the speaker outlines it and the solutions to that problem which he or she proposes.

Critics, like other human beings, have a perspective that shapes their perceptions. When they enter into a controversy, they bring with them their own biases and experiences. Complete objectivity in any critical activity is a quixotic goal; certainly in the realm of social criticism the nature of the critic's subjectivity has the potential to distort his or her judgment. The only possible answer to such a problem is to remind oursleves as critics that we have one prime obligation to those to whom we address ourselves—and that is to apply the same rigorous standards to *all* rhetorical efforts we seek to judge. A good critic scrutinizes the position with which she or he agrees just as carefully as opinions that conflict with the critic's own position. Political judgments are inevitably formed in part on the basis of rhetorical messages; what the critic seeks to avoid is making a judgment of rhetorical soundness on the basis of political conviction.[12]

CRITICAL FUNCTIONS: DEVELOPMENT AND REFINEMENT OF THEORY

Another primary function of criticism, in a sense, subsumes all others: The criticism of rhetoric contributes to the development and refinement of rhetorical theory. All criticism is implicitly theoretical. *Theory*, like *criticism* and *rhetoric*, is a term that has a variety of specialized and popular meanings. Contrasted with *applied* or *practical*, *theoretical* connotes for some kind of idle speculation on the ideal. However, that is not what is meant by the term when we talk of rhetorical theory. *By theory we mean a body of plausible generalizations or principles that explain a complex set of facts or phenomena.* A theory looks at a series of related events and tries to tell us why things happen as they do; and if the explanation of why things happen is accurate, then that explanation should be able to tell us what *will* happen in a similar set of circumstances. Rhetorical theory, then, can be visualized, in the words of Samuel Becker, as an "explanatory-predictive mosaic."[13]

The mosaic image is a very useful one in discussing the relationship between theory and criticism. Pieced together with tiny bits of glass or stone that form patterns, the completed mosaic is a total picture in which the smaller patterns merge into a complete whole. Looked at in that way, all criticism is implicitly theoretical; the more we learn about what happened in one particular situation, that is, the more information bits that can be adduced, the better able we will be to generalize a pattern of rhetorical behavior. As these patterns are formed, and compared and contrasted with other patterns, a basis for predicting what will happen in similar cases is established.

Most students of speech communication have had experience in dealing with theory even though they might not be fully aware of it. Take, for example, the study of public speaking. Any good textbook on public speaking is really an embodiment of theory, no matter how "practical" it is alleged to be or perceived to be. When the author of a textbook advises the student on how to prepare for a speech, for example, that author is really laying down certain principles. The author may recommend rules to be observed when organizing a speech, present the characteristics of a good introduction to a speech, explain the ways in which to test the validity of an argument, or suggest the basis upon which evidence ought to be judged, and so forth. What the author of the textbook is really saying is that if that student organizes well, develops a valid argument with good supporting materials, and follows a whole range of suggestions in the text, then the student is likely to be successful in achieving his or her purpose in speaking. That is, the author implicitly asserts that certain patterns of rhetorical behavior will lead to certain results—from the theory (what we know about public speaking) certain procedures are recommended (the practice of public speaking) which should lead to predictable results (getting the desired audience response).

Criticism plays a vital role in this chain of rhetorical events. The critic focuses intensely on the practice of public discourse, and his or her findings may strengthen or weaken the predictive power of any theory or may generate hypotheses upon which new theories can ultimately be built.

CRITICAL FUNCTIONS: PEDAGOGICAL CRITICISM

Every critic is, in some sense, an educator. Rhetorical criticism teaches all of us something about the nature and operations of the persuasive process. In the classroom, however, the teacher-critic is most clearly concerned with applying his or her critical powers to the task of modifying behavior.

It is hoped that all criticism will have some impact on the way people produce and react to messages. But the critical functions we have been examining thus far do not aim at producing such effects immediately or directly. In the educational setting, criticism functions to improve the quality of messages and to increase audiences' awareness of the ways in which they respond (or *should* respond, or *want* to respond) to messages.

The critic's first task as a teacher is to identify and explain the criteria for judgments as to how poorly or how well a student is communicating. A textbook certainly helps the teacher by presenting, in an organized fashion, basic principles that serve as a guide to behavior. The teacher's job is to see that students understand that these principles are just that: They are *generalizations* to be used by the student when planning and executing his or her message. The teacher-critic should never lose sight of the principles; the student must not be allowed to form the impression that there are a raft of techniques, a series of unrelated "helpful hints" to remember when giving or listening to a speech. The critic, rather, points to standards of excellence and illustrates the ways in which and the extent to which these standards are being met in actual student performance.

It is in the pedagogical role that the critic has the opportunity to discuss most fully not only what was happening but what should be happening. The issue is not so much one of raising standards as of helping the student learn what standards are, and applying those standards in creating and delivering a message or responding to a message. The critic in this situation clearly and explicitly matches standards to performance when making a judgment. The specificity of the matching process is crucial. It simply will not do for a critic to tell a student, "Your ideas were not clear." There are standards relating to organizational patterns, development of argument, use of evidence, and language choice, all of which can impinge on the clarity of ideas. The critic, in his or her pedagogical role, must specify these standards and point directly and explicitly to the ways in which their violation contributed to a lack of clarity.

The teacher-critic then takes the next step: suggesting to the student possible strategies for putting these principles into operation. Strategies will grow out of a careful examination of the principles and what went wrong in previous efforts to implement them. Beginning critics, if they are not consciously attuned to the need for careful analysis and the communication of the results of that analysis to the student, are tempted to respond as casual observers rather than as trained professionals. Instead of relating experience to principles and shaping future behavior by helping the student use these principles in devising strategies, the teacher may end up being "critical" in the popular sense and not in the sense we have been using that term. This teacher will respond to the student with the useless observation: "You weren't clear; be clearer when you give your next speech." The true critic, on the other hand, will relate judgments to standards and will communicate specifically the ways in which standards can be made operational in future communication efforts.

SUMMARY: THE FUNCTIONING CRITIC

In this chapter, we have said that the rhetorical critic is one who is engaged in the systematic process of illuminating and evaluating persuasive messages. As the critic functions, he or she may be searching for the potential effects of messages, investigating messages to discover the light they shed on events that have occurred or the society that gave rise to the messages, evaluating the social utility or worth of messages, relating the practice of persuasion exemplified in particular messages to theoretical constructs, or seeking to modify the behavior of persuaders and their audiences.

As should be apparent, these functions are not mutually exclusive. The search for effect, for example, may lead to modifications in, or implications for, rhetorical theory; theoretical conceptions may serve as a starting point for the critic who would study persuasive discourse in order to illuminate the underlying values of a society. Certainly one of the best ways to understand the functions of criticism is to see how critics really work. This volume provides the beginning student the opportunity to study the ways in which mature critics have approached this process and to understand the variety of ways in which they have put the functions discussed into critical practice.

Whatever function, or functions, apply in any given critical work, the practicing critic needs to pursue them systematically. What follows in the remaining chapters is an attempt to construct a system. That is to say, the constituents of the rhetorical act that are invariably present are examined in order to explain what is essential for the beginning critic to know about them in order to move to analysis and judgment. Then, the specific elements to be subjected to analysis and a procedure for carrying out the analysis are presented. What the critic must know in using the results of the analysis in making interpretations and judgments is discussed, and, finally, varieties of ways are suggested in which critics can pattern the results of their investigation in order to illuminate and evaluate different aspects of the total rhetorical process.

Notes

1. Cited by Marie Hochmuth, ed., *A History and Criticism of American Public Address*, III (New York: Longmans, Green, 1955), p. 4.
2. See, e.g., the discussion of appropriate areas of investigation for the rhetorical critic in the "Report of the Committee on the advancement and refinement of rhetorical criticism," from the National Conference on Rhetoric in Lloyd Bitzer and Edwin Black, eds., *The Prospect of Rhetoric* (Englewood Cliffs, N.J.: Prentice-Hall, 1971), pp. 220-227. For a recent statement of what has been—and should be—studied, see G. P. Mohrmann, "Elegy in a Critical Grave-Yard," *Western Speech*, 44 (1980), 265-274.
3. The case study in criticism, which appears later in this book, affords an excellent example. A perusal of the other critical models and of the bibliography of critical studies also suggests this.
4. Herbert Wichelns, "The Literary Criticism of Oratory," reprinted in William A. Linsley, ed., *Speech Criticism: Methods and Materials* (Dubuque, Iowa: Wm. C. Brown, 1968), p. 32.
5. Michael C. Leff and G. P. Mohrmann, "Lincoln at Cooper Union: A Rhetorical Analysis of the Text," *Quarterly Journal of Speech*, 60 (1974), 346-358.
6. Forbes Hill, "Conventional Wisdom—Traditional Forms: The President's Message of November 3, 1969," *Quarterly Journal of Speech*, 58 (1972), 374.
7. Wayne C. Minnick, "A Case Study in Persuasive Effect: Lyman Beecher on Duelling," *Speech Monographs*, 38 (1971), 275.
8. Ibid.
9. Ibid., p. 276.
10. Karlyn Kohrs Campbell, "Criticism: Ephemeral and Enduring," *Speech Teacher*, 23 (1974), 10-11.
11. See the case study in criticism, particularly the exchange between Professor Campbell and Professor Hill, pp. 119-128.
12. A word needs to be said concerning the audience for whom the social critic writes. The principal function of such criticism, since it is by nature a part of the immediate issue, is to have an impact on the outcomes of rhetoric. Accordingly, it is not particularly addressed to other critics and rhetorical theorists. Its publication outlets are not necessarily academic journals. Rhetorical critics, however—for good or ill and for a variety or reasons—rarely publish in popular periodicals; most social criticism of rhetorical acts tends to be undertaken by journalists.
13. Samuel L. Becker, "Rhetorical Studies for the Contemporary World," *The Prospect of Rhetoric*, p. 41.

2

Constituents of the Rhetorical Act: Context and Audience

BEGINNING THE CRITICAL PROCESS

One of the rhetorical critic's first problems is deciding where to begin. If one is going to undertake to explicate and interpret the rhetorical dimensions of a particular message, be it a speech, a pamphlet, an editorial, or a proclamation, it makes obvious and good sense to begin with the message itself. The problem arises when it is realized that all the constituents of the rhetorical act are exerting mutual influence on each other even as the act occurs. What the critic must do, in effect, is to freeze an ongoing process, sort out its various elements, and examine sequentially matters that occur simultaneously.

In a speaking situation, for example, there is always a speaker, a message produced by that speaker, an audience responding to that message, and a complex context made up of a multiplicity of factors ranging from prevailing ethical standards and the importance of the issues involved to the size and temperature of the room and the speaker's energy level. The critic has to deal in some way with all these constituents one by one.

Of course, no critic approaches any rhetorical activity from a completely naive point of view: To be a critic in any discipline presupposes some prior knowledge and background. One would hardly be ready to become a literary critic after reading his or her first novel, nor could one decide to be a music critic and then listen for the first time to a symphony. No student could reasonably expect to become a rhetorical critic after reading one speech.

But the student who would master the critical craft must make a beginning. The nature of that beginning partly depends on the background and knowledge which the student brings to the situation. Whereas the text of the speech is a logical place to start, the student who knows something about the historical, political, and social factors that surround a particular speech obviously will understand better what the speaker is saying and what the speaker is trying to do. It is always advisable for the beginning rhetorical critic to start by reading, carefully and thoughtfully, the text of the message to be studied. The close analysis of that text may come later in the critical process, but initial study of the text must precede a systematic investigation of all the constituents. Following the careful reading of the text, the beginning critic, or the critic who is not already fully versed in the subtle and complex background to, and events surrounding, any communication event, will need to move backward, as it were, in order to understand what gave rise to the speech, how the issues involved emerged over time, what their relevance and importance was, and to whom they were significant. Since messages are designed to influence the way people think and act, the critic must come as close as he or she can to a full comprehension of what those who actually experienced the message thought and felt and believed.[1]

RHETORICAL IMPERATIVES: HISTORICAL AND POLITICAL EVENTS

One of the first factors to be considered by the rhetorical critic is the events that made it possible or necessary for a speaker to address an audience at all. People speak in order to solve problems, to gain adherents, to rouse interest and sympathy, or to compel action because there is something going on in the world around them that is in *need* of modification or is threatened and must be defended. In other words, rhetoric grows out of events that a speaker wants us to see as important. Historical and political events and trends can force certain issues into our consciousness; the situation can make it *imperative* that we somehow come to grips with issues. Let us consider some brief examples of such rhetorical imperatives[2] and how they take on special importance for the critic.

In the 1960s black Americans began a concerted and determined effort to gain for themselves the rights that were guaranteed to them by the Constitution and to reverse the economic and social effects of years of discrimination. Laws in several states barred blacks from eating in restaurants, sleeping in motels, and even drinking from water fountains reserved for whites only. Requirements for registering to vote were so stated and interpreted by white registrars as to effectively disenfranchise large numbers of blacks. While exercising their rights to petition and protest, blacks were often assaulted by police or set upon by dogs. Unemployment among blacks far exceeded that of whites, and the road to improvement through special job training and increased education was blocked to many blacks. Black groups, particularly the NAACP, attempted to work through the courts to redress wrongs, and had secured the landmark Supreme Court decision, in *Brown* v. *Board of Education*, that separate schools for blacks were inherently unequal and thus unconstitutional. Black leaders had lobbied for legislation that would improve the lot of their people, and prior to 1963, Civil Rights Acts had passed Congress. But, in spite of these efforts, the plight of most blacks in the United States was still seen as desperate. The tactics of sit-ins, demonstrations, and civil disobedience were employed to dramatize the problems of blacks, to make clear the extent and depth of black feeling, and to set forth clearly black demands.

In response to this surge of black pressure, white leaders reacted in a variety of ways. Labor leaders like Walter Reuther, religious leaders like Eugene Carson Blake, and political leaders like Hubert Humphrey pressed for congressional action. Other, like Alabama Governor George Wallace, tried to assert the right of the states to determine the nature of black–white relationships, particularly arguing for the right of the state to control such matters as education and voting rights. Many whites became alarmed at the potential for violence and frightened by the frustrated outbursts that erupted in major cities.

In 1963, with major civil rights legislation pending in Congress, at a massive rally, Martin Luther King, Jr., gave his most famous speech, "I Have a Dream." A critic would need to know details of those factors that brought forth and surrounded the speech before he or she could begin to appreciate such matters as King's purpose in giving the speech, his major premise concerning the American dream and the argument derived from it, the hopes and fears of those who heard the speech as they stood massed on the Mall in front of the Lincoln Memorial or watched their television sets at home, and the ways in which King's message might succeed. One would need to know about the challenge to King's leadership from militant blacks who were increasingly embittered by brutal treatment and growing more impatient with the results of what King called "creative suffering." One would also need to know the key provisions of the Civil Rights Bill and what efforts were being made to weaken and strengthen it.

RHETORICAL IMPERATIVES: SOCIAL AND CULTURAL VALUES

In reconstructing rhetorical imperatives, historical and political events obviously must be considered. Social and cultural values and traditions also must be understood as they pertain to a speaking situation. In the civil rights movement, for example, consider the paternalistic myth of the "happy Negro." It was often alleged that blacks were happy with their lot; they didn't want contact with white society; they were content to move in the circles prescribed for them and in accordance with the traditions of white supremacy; the role of whites was to "take care of" blacks; and blacks, when they were not interfered with by "outside agitators," were docile and satisfied. When one recognizes the existence of such a cultural conception, one begins to see the need for black speakers like King to shatter it. And along with the deep-seated racial prejudices and stereotypes embedded in the culture, were conflicting American values that held that all Americans should be treated equally under the law, that ours was a land of equal opportunity, that basic to all religious convictions was the brotherhood of man—values that were available to King and others who sought to awaken the conscience of white Americans. For the critic to understand the rhetorical problems that King had to face, the rhetorical opportunities that were open to him, and the constraints that were placed on him by events in the past and his role in those events and by prevailing attitudes and beliefs, one would have to reconstruct the imperatives that brought King's speech about.[3]

What we are discussing here is much more than a painted backdrop against which the principal scene is played; we are talking about matters that have a direct impact on the very nature of the message itself. The speaker cannot control what is going on in an audience's mind; that is determined by what the listeners have experienced, what they know, and what they believe. The speaker cannot ignore what is important or salient to an audience or assume that what he or she thinks is important will be recognized as such by his or her listeners. So the critic who would assess what the speaker *has* done, working within the limitations imposed by events and by the social and cultural milieu, must know the significant contextual factors that have the potential to influence the message. How could a future critic, for example, hope to render any kind of explanation or judgment about a political speech dealing with foreign policy in 1980 who did not know in detail the impact of the seizure of the hostages in Iran or the Soviet invasion of Afghanistan? Who could hope to shed any light on the rhetorical strategies of Democratic incumbents and Republican challengers who did not appreciate the facts and feelings associated with rising inflation and increasing unemployment?

The rhetorical critic faces certain problems that are somewhat different than those encountered by the historian, although both are engaged in a reconstruction of the past. Whereas the historian may search for an accurate account of what happened, he or she may not be as vitally concerned with *perceptions* of what happened. The historian, for example, may take up the issue of English "tryanny" at the time of the American Revolution and question whether British actions and policy were, indeed, "tyrannical" in regard to political or economic restrictions.[4] The rhetorical scholar is likely to be more interested in how speakers and audiences of the time *interpreted* British actions so that they might be seen and understood as tryannical. Historians looking back at 1980 might be able to discover what was "really" happening to the American economy, whether a "decrease in the rate of increase" of inflation marked a significant economic turning point upon which policies advocated by politicians would have or could have little real impact; the rhetorical critic will focus attention more directly on attitudes and beliefs—whether mistaken or not—that people held toward economic matters. In short, the "imperatives" we are discussing are those that are imperative to speakers and audience at the time discourse is being produced and not unseen forces at work in human affairs. "Nationalism," for example, may be a rising tide, but for the rhetorical critic the ways in which speakers and listeners translate such a conception into concrete reality becomes of primary importance; attempts to stem nationalism or a willingness to be engulfed by it can only be assessed and understood within the context of some public *consciousness* of it. The critic's historical task, then, is the reconstruction of such a consciousness.

DISCERNING ISSUES

Once the critic can master the swirl of events and perceptions of events and can discern some pattern of conflicting and complementary forces—the rhetorical imperatives—that bring matters to a rhetorical head, then the critic needs to turn his or her attention to the emerging issues as they are molded, shaped, distorted, or sharpened in public debate. What really *is* at issue is a matter of serious concern in any controversy. In the civil rights struggle, for example, was the issue legal, social, and educational equality of opportunity for blacks? Or was it the constitutional right of the states to govern themselves in matters beyond the legal right of the federal government to intervene? Was it civil rights or states' rights? Was the issue whether citizens had the right to peaceful protest with the expectation that the forces of the government would protect them in carrying out this right? Or was it whether an orderly society could tolerate protest capable of, or even designed to, provoke violence or to disrupt the normal functioning of those who were unsympathetic to or disinterested in the movement? Was it civil rights or civil wrongs?

What was at issue in the debate over American policy in Vietnam? Was the issue a geopolitical one: Should the United States take whatever steps were necessary to preserve a government friendly to American interests and resistant to the spread of communism? Or was the issue a moral one: Should the United States spend its material and human resources to prop up any government, no matter what its character, in defiance of the wishes of its own people? The issues surrounding the war in Vietnam were seen in terms of patriotism, of defense of freedom, of racism, and of moral and political arrogance. Various sectors of opinion tended to coalesce around what each believed to be the "real" issue, and much of the debate centered on what the debate itself was about.

The rhetorical critic must discern in the context the nature of the issues as various parties see them. Consider this historical example for its relevance to perception of issues. During the American Civil War, both the Union and the Confederate States gave much diplomatic attention to the question of the recognition of the Confederate States by the government of Great Britain.[5] Recognition by England would have greatly benefited the South; the federal blockade could be weakened, the shipbuilding activities of the Confederates in England would have been made easier, the North would likely have become embroiled in a war with Britain, and so forth. In England, the ongoing debate over the Government's stance toward the warring sides touched on a variety of issues: Was it in Britain's best economic interests to encourage the permanent separation of a country that was fast becoming a major trade rival? Should the arrogant, uncouth Yankee industrialists be allowed to bully the more courtly, civilized southerners? And, most pertinently, should the federal blockade of the South be allowed to ruin Britain's important textile industry by creating a "cotton famine" in England? Such formulations of the issues certainly tilted toward the South. But those who were sympathetic to the North put the war in a perspective that was ultimately more captivating to most Englishmen when they described the war as one to eliminate slavery. For a nation that had almost singlehandedly eliminated the African slave trade and had abolished slavery in its own West Indian dominions, a nation whose rising working classes exhibited a strong antipathy to slavery even when the cotton famine brought personal hardship, the issue of slavery for Great Britain was an overriding moral consideration. The promulgation of the Emancipation Proclamation by President Lincoln in 1863 helped define the issue for the English clearly as one that rested on the slavery question and thus tilted the balance in favor of pro-Union spokesmen in England. Once the central issue of the debate was defined, the outcome was no longer in doubt.

AN ARGUMENTATIONAL HISTORY

As the rhetorical critic studies the context, he or she must construct what might be called an argumentational history of issues along with his or her reconstruction of events. As events unfold, people interpret their meaning, argue about their significance, and deliberate on their ultimate effect. Any message occurs at some point in this process that goes on until the issues are resolved, or supplanted by other issues, or diminish in perceived relevance. For a critic to make sense out of the context in which a speech took place, he or she must know what the issues were and were perceived to be *at that point*.

An argumentational history goes further than the definition of the issues. Surely the critic approaching a speech would need to know how others had argued the question in the past since the speaker and the audiences would be likely to have such information or at least have been exposed to it. By studying the ways in which particular matters have been argued, the critic can come to understand what kinds of evidence, what appeals to traditional values, what relationships between ideas have been offered in the past and the extent to which such things persist or fade away. How much better an assessment can be made of a rhetorical event when we know whether the arguments and the support for those arguments are original, or whether they have been used so frequently in the past (and gone unchallenged or only ineffectively combated) as to be conceded as "truths," or whether they have been discarded or discredited long ago.

Take, for example, the debate over the teaching of evolution, an issue that some thought had been laid to rest. In the current controversy, those who oppose on religious grounds what they understand to be evolutionary theory no longer argue the question of whether the Genesis story is "true"; rather, they focus on the concept of "theory." The appeal to the ultimate truth of the literal interpretation of the Bible as opposed to "Godless" science, has faded as an appeal to general audiences. The argument now asserts that there are opposing *theories*, and, in the interests of academic freedom and fair play, both *theories* ought to be taught in the public schools. As a part of the attack on what is called "secular humanism" this argument relies less on proof derived from scriptural quotation and more on the implied opposition of God and Christian principles to secular and human interpretations of events. The critic who would understand how such arguments have evolved must understand the social and cultural context *and* the way the arguments have developed to reflect that context. As another example, Ronald Reagan, in a somewhat offhanded comment in the 1980 presidential campaign, raised the whole issue of American relations with China and Formosa. The reason that this comment caused such consternation among Reagan's political advisers and delight among his opponents was that it was a throwback to old argumentational strategies and premises; the nature of the relation of the United States to Formosa and to the People's Republic of China was thought to be settled. When one understands the argumentational history of this issue, one can better understand the potential impact on the audiences who hear the message.

RHETORICAL CONVENTIONS

Another factor to be considered is one of unique importance to the rhetorical critic. In any given time and place there are rhetorical conventions that apply and communication styles that prevail. Sometimes these are the function of a historical period. In England in the eighteenth and nineteenth centuries, for example, it was not uncommon for a speaker to address the House of Commons in a speech lasting several hours, a practice that few would tolerate in twentieth-century America. The change in the length of speeches is an obvious example of a rhetorical convention that operates within a specific context. These conventions, or common practices, are rooted in audience expectations. A Puritan divine in colonial New England could sermonize for three hours because his audience expected such a lengthy talk; a modern preacher whose sermons consistently ran more than twenty or thirty minutes would probably find his congregations melting away. Modern traditional churchgoers expect that church services will not greatly exceed an hour or so.

Beginning rhetorical critics, when studying texts of speeches that were given in the past, are often struck not only by their length but also by what they perceive as the complexity of the style of these speeches. The matter of prevailing historical styles is a complicated one. Much of what a critic knows about the style of a time comes from his or her immersion in the rhetoric of the period. In the present state of the art of rhetorical scholarship, we have little solid, normative data on stylistic practice. What the critic has, largely, is his or her own impressionistic perceptions of the way in which language was used by speakers in a particular period. (This fact should reinforce the notion that the would-be critic must read widely and extensively in the period in which he or she intends to work.)

The matter of audience expectations goes much deeper than conventions concerning such matters as length and style; we consider these issues further in the discussion of audiences. But it is essential for the critic who embarks on the study of historical rhetoric to bear in mind that what sounds right to the contemporary ear or reads right to the contemporary eye, is not what appeared right to the eighteenth- or nineteenth-century listener and reader.

ETHICS AND CONTEXT

Perhaps one of the most difficult elements contributing to a full understanding of context is the ethical one. If we take the ethics of any group to be a set of behaviors that are judged to be acceptable when measured against some prevailing code of conduct, we can see that what is essential is an understanding of the prevailing code, which, however, is not always spelled out in a specific, concrete fashion. There are, to be sure, "codes of ethics" that professional groups adopt and that are supposed to guide the conduct of their members. The Speech Communication Association, the National Association of Broadcasters, the American Psychological Association, the American Medical Association, and others all have written statements of what they, as a group, consider ethical behavior by members of their profession. The Watergate scandal, in which many of those who were judged guilty of gross misconduct or even illegal activity were lawyers, resulted in the criminal conviction of the attorney general of the United States, caused a wave of dismay to spread throughout the legal profession, and led many law schools to institute or revise courses in legal ethics.

Along with various professionals codes are religious codes—the most notable one in the Judeo-Christian tradition being the Ten Commandments—that are designed to prescribe and circumscribe ethical behavior. But anyone who has studied arguments based on religious principles knows that the precise meaning and application of these codes are subject to wide varieties of interpretation and emphasis. "Thou shalt not kill," for example, seems to be a straightforward injunction, but pacifists have never been able to convince large numbers of people that this commandment applies in *all* cases and in *all* situations.[6] There are also laws that define acceptable behavior. "Conflict of interest" laws, for example, attempt to set out procedures governing the behavior of public officials, particularly in regard to financial matters. These laws are based on the precept that those who are elected to public office should not profit economically through the use of the power derived from holding office. But laws alone do not determine ethical behavior; who has not heard the phrase, often employed by whose actions generate public suspicion or outrage, "It may be unethical, but it's not illegal."

Of utmost importance to the rhetorical critic is what might be called the ethical tenor of the times, the feelings that most people have concerning what is right or wrong behavior, whether or not such behavior is specifically articulated in any written code. For example, take a speaker who attacks a political leader for giving public offices with no real duties assigned to friends and relatives who are thereby paid from the public treasury for doing nothing. Surely, such a charge, if proven, would do serious damage to a modern American politician's career. Those precise charges were leveled against leading political figures in England in the early nineteenth century by radical speakers, and they were most decidedly true. Yet the practice of giving political supporters and family members honorary jobs that entailed no duties ("sinecures," as they were called) was common at the time, and it engendered few denunciations on ethical grounds from the governing classes of England.[7]

Determining the ethical climate of a period is never easy. Major problems confound any attempts that one might make to discern the ethical climate. In any society, competing ethical standards seem to be held simultaneously; subgroups within a society may hold conflicting standards or emphasize different standards. Societies, like individuals, may seem to profess standards that do not, in fact, guide their actions.

In contemporary American society, for example, we are repeatedly faced with choices for which there may be conflicting ethical precepts.[8] One of the most persistent strains to which Americans have been subjected is that of dealing with the demands placed on them by professed ethical imperatives while, at the same time, experiencing the strong urge to succeed. We are often considered a people with a strong sense of what is expedient. In the past, we have been proud of our lack of doctrinaire politics. As Erik H. Erikson reminds us, "American politics is not, as is that of Europe, 'a prelude to civil war'; it cannot become either entirely irresponsible or entirely dogmatic; and it must not try to be logical. It is a rocking sea of checks and balances in which uncompromising absolutes must drown."[9] We have avoided the rigid adherence to principle at all costs and have seen the virtue of our pragmatism contrasted with the factious, splintered politics of Europe.

In politics and in life, success has been our touchstone. Some students of American culture have observed that the will to get ahead, the need to compete successfully with our fellows, may be bred into us.[10] In this connection, "Bear" Bryant's aphorism that "football is life" may be a most apt metaphor. Facing the forces that would hold him back, the American combines physical stamina, strategy, determination, and occasionally heroic bursts of enthusiastic drive to reach his goal. To score, to win is essential, and in this process the American may feel compelled, at times, to gouge, kick, and cheat.

For some, this contradiction has been disquieting. In *Young Radicals*, Kenneth Keniston reports on an interview in which a young man describes his family: "It seems to have a lot of tensions in terms of its orientation—what your aspirations are, what they should be or shouldn't be. 'It isn't important that you make money, it's important that you be godly. But why don't you go out and make some money?' A whole series of contradictions. In terms of what I should do, what my life should be like."[11]

On the whole, however, Americans have learned to live with contradiction. As Gabriel A. Almond observed: "Under normal circumstances this conflict does not appear to have a seriously laming effect. It tends to be disposed of by adding a moral coloration to actions which are really motivated by expediency, and an expediential coloration to actions which are motivated by moral and humanitarian values."[12]

An excellent example of this attempt to render these contradictory values compatible appears in John F. Kennedy's Inaugural Address. Why should we help the world's poor who are "struggling to break the bonds of mass misery"? In the words of Kennedy, "not because the Communists may be doing it, not because we seek their votes, but because it is right." The moral coloration is given to what is, after all, expedient policy (the Communists, with whom we are in competition, *are* doing it; we *do* want votes in the sense that we want international support to check and contain our perceived rival and enemy, the Soviet Union). Yet the most interesting thing about this excerpt is that the sentence that immediately follows the one just quoted gives expedient coloration to what has been stated as a moral stance. There can be no doubt of the implication in, "If a free society cannot help the many who are poor, it cannot save the few who are rich." The rich, in this teeming world of the poor, are obviously the Americans, and we are invited to attend to the realization that, although we may be acting out of principle, when the principle operates in such a way as to help save a few—and the few are us—the moral purpose is given a recognizable practical cast.[13]

A critic's examination of the context will also help him or her understand when a debate is perceived as being over moral issues. In such cases, a tolerant examination of opposing arguments is difficult, for certainly virtue cannot tolerate vice; *nothing* is sacred in such a confrontation. "We make no secret of our determination to tread the law and the Constitution under our feet," Wendell Phillips asserted at an abolitionist meeting, at a time when practical political questions were beginning to become overwhelmed and overshadowed by the moral question of slavery.[14] Phillips' fiery colleague, William Lloyd Garrison, in asserting the primacy of the moral issue, epitomized the rejection of moderation. "I *will be* as harsh as truth, and as uncompromising as justice," Garrison told his readers in the Januay 1, 1831, issue of *The Liberator*. "On this subject, I do not wish to think, or speak, or write, with moderation. No! no! Tell a man whose house is on fire to give a moderate alarm; tell him to moderately rescue his wife from the hands of the ravisher; tell the mother to gradually extricate her babe from the fire into which it has fallen;—but urge me not to use moderation in a cause like the present."[15] When a speaker for a cause envisions a kind of Armageddon, his or her rhetoric reflects the moralist's impatience with expediency. As Barry Goldwater reminded the cheering delegates to the Republican National Convention in 1964, "Extremism in the defense of liberty is no vice. And . . . moderation in the pursuit of justice is no virtue."[16]

The conflict between competitive goals and professed moral values seems to be firmly rooted in our American culture, and the rhetorical critic must be aware of it. The value placed on success in a competitive society has within it the seeds of another conflict. The need to succeed implies a kind of individualistic drive to best others in competition. Yet when a child is reared and judged against the actions of his or her peers, when what constitutes success (particularly in its material dimension) is generally agreed upon, when the methods of attaining success are to some degree prescribed, and when the constraints of the society necessitate teamwork and cooperation, individuality itself is tempered by conformity.

These two elements—individuality and conformity—have existed in a state of tension, pulling at us, shaping, in part, our character. De Tocqueville worried about the conformity induced by the tyranny of the majority, and Frederick Jackson Turner hypothesized that the great American frontier bred the independent qualities of self-reliance. We extolled "rugged individualism" on the one hand and developed the "organization man" on the other.

Any student of the American character would agree that we are more than a sum of separate traits and characteristics; the whole is extremely complex. The qualities of the particular American culture that help to shape the rhetorical behavior alluded to here are not ones a critic can uncover. These qualities are, however, noteworthy and might be helpful in understanding what is going on in a given period of American rhetoric.

As is evident, understanding the prevailing ethical code of any given time is a complex matter. In the final analysis, the most gaping pitfall to be avoided by the rhetorical critic is the assumption that the ethical standards of his or her time, or group, or culture can be imposed on the subject of investigation. The critic who believes in the absolute immutability of ethical standards will have difficulty with the conception that ethical standards are relative to the context in which they flourish. But there can be little argument that the ethical climate that permeates a rhetorical situation will vary from setting to setting, if only with the interpretation and manner of putting ethical conceptions into effect in practical affairs. Certainly the critic is at liberty to apply to discourse any ethical standards he or she wishes, to argue that evils are evils no matter where or when they occur. But to act as if others, removed in time and place, would make similar assumptions, would blind the critic to the ways in which rhetoric actually functioned in a particular situation. The critic may be shocked or repelled by ethical practices or norms, but no sound rhetorical judgments can be made about discourse if the critic fails to understand the prevailing codes.

THE SETTING FOR A SPEECH

We have discussed the larger context in which rhetorical activities take place. Any message occurring in this broad context also takes place within a more particularized setting. The speech is not only occasioned by past and immediate events, by elements that make rhetoric imperative, but it happens at a given moment in time, in certain surroundings, on a discrete occasion. A speech is an event, and the event has the potential for impact on the message and its reception.

First, there is the public *nature* of the occasion, which can shape the expectations that the audience will have and which speakers will feel constrained to meet. An audience will have a sense of what is fitting to be said in the circumstances, which will relate both to the substance and the manner of the speech. Some occasions are ceremonial. They tend to be formal, to have persuasive ends of stimulating feelings of unity, heightening common emotions, or extolling shared values; they tend to concentrate on general or abstract principles. Certain occasions are more frankly issue-oriented, calling for arguments that attempt to move audiences to action or to shape their beliefs. Still other occasions demand that persuasion be muted while the dissemination of information takes precedence.

Contrast, for example, the acceptance speech of a candidate for the presidency given to the nominating convention with the inaugural address of a newly elected President. When the candidate appears before partisan supporters, addressing them and, at the same time, the nation, clearly a "political" speech is expected. This is the right occasion for the speaker to laud the virtues of one's own party and to point to the failings of the opposition. Audiences, both those in the convention hall and those in front of their television sets, know that such an occasion does not call for a careful weighing of all the alternative solutions to problems; it does not call for a modest appraisal of one's own political shortcomings. The clarion sounded in such a speech on such an occasion is a call for a political army to unify, to gird itself to fight for American ideals and against the political enemy who would undermine or fail to live up to those ideals. Most listeners who would readily accept such partisanship in an acceptance speech would be shocked by the same sentiments, expressed in the same way, in an inaugural address. Typically, an inaugural address is an effort to rise above the recently ended political battle and instill a sense of national unity and concerted purpose. For example, John F. Kennedy, in his inaugural address, aptly described the inauguration as a "celebration of freedom," and not a victory of party. The ceremonial occasion of the inaugural, then, raises expectations that are different from the frankly political acceptance speech.

The setting of a speech also has a concrete, specific physical surrounding. It can be indoors or outdoors, in a large auditorium or a small meeting room; it can be given before a small group or large masses of people; it can be amplified by a public address system or heard only by those within earshot of the speaker's voice. The audience may be jammed together, elbow to elbow, or spread thinly throughout the room. The physical surroundings can have a real impact on the way a message is constructed and how it is delivered, again, because of what an audience expects in any given setting.

Everyone has experienced the effects of the setting of a speech on listeners or speakers. One might sit in a dormitory room or in a friend's living room and talk about what's going to happen if tuition costs are to continue to rise; the same person might give a speech in a public speaking class about tuition costs; and the same person might speak on behalf of students at a meeting of the university's board of trustees. Some of the differences in the messages will be determined by audience factors, which are discussed later, but the physical factors of the setting will affect the formality/informality of the discourse, including such matters as language choice, whether the speaker speaks extemporaneously or uses a manuscript, and the nature of audience response and participation. The prescribed behavior of the classroom, for example, rarely leads audience members to cheer or to heckle a speaker. In such a setting the audience does not expect a speaker to exceed a certain level of loudness and would be made uncomfortable or embarrassed by a speaker whom they perceived as "shouting" at them, whereas increased volume may be necessary and deemed quite appropriate at an open-air rally. A political candidate who was asked to state his or her position on the issues at a neighborhood gathering in a supporter's home would not be expected to produce a manuscript and read it to that group; but, called upon to speak at a press club luncheon on the same topic, the candidate may be expected to deliver a manuscript speech.

A critic must understand and appreciate the potential significance of a specific setting, which, like the broader context, will be reflected in a variety of ways in the message. The setting can influence the speaker's delivery, his or her style, and the emotional and intellectual responses of his or her listeners. Students, for example, are often concerned about large lecture classes as opposed to small, less formal classes. Many students believe that the opportunity to respond in a smaller class, the feeling of more direct contact with the instructor, and the fact that in smaller classes students know each other better and are known by the instructor better, all contribute to their ability to respond better intellectually. Consider also Martin Luther King, Jr.'s, "I Have a Dream" speech, for which the setting clearly contributed to the heightened emotional response of the audience. Thousands of people gathered in a large crowd on the Mall facing the statue of Abraham Lincoln as King spoke. The author of this book was in the audience for that speech. At the point in King's speech in which he stressed the need for blacks and whites to work together, a black man standing next to me put an arm around my shoulder and said, "We're in this together, brother." This natural, spontaneous emotional act of response to the speaker was prompted not only by the content of the speech but by the physical surroundings; it would not have been likely to occur in an auditorium. And the presence of such feelings in an audience, along with the opportunity to display them, had an influence on King's speech itself that a perceptive critic understands as he or she analyzes and evaluates the message.

The circumstances of Dr. King's speech suggest another important consideration for the critic in studying the impact of setting. While thousands listened to the speech in Washington, millions watched the speech on television throughout the country. The television viewers may or may not have sensed the emotional environment that surrounded the speech, but they certainly could not experience it in precisely the same way as those who were there. The *medium* through which listeners receive a speech is an aspect of the setting that can profoundly affect the listener's reactions. There are situations, such as King's speech or the inaugural address, in which viewers are looking in on an event; their unseen presence will certainly influence what is going on, but their expectations are colored by the total event. This situation differs somewhat from a speech given, for example, by the President of the United States, directly *to* the American people via television. Nevertheless, whichever case obtains, television itself presents a unique setting for a speech.

For one thing, television viewers tend to be in smaller groups and less subject to the moods, attitudes, and actions of those around them, and would probably be more passive than a live audience. The speaker will receive no stimulation from a television audience that might encourage him or her to become more excited or to "tone down" his or her material, or to combat restlessness by moving rapidly to a new point. The medium itself, because it brings the speaker into the living room, encourages a muted presentation that is more conversational in tone. It also provides a more concentrated focus on the speaker, so that other factors of the *speaker's* setting are either eliminated (there are no other people to look at or outside noises to contend with) or highlighted (the American flag may be unobtrusively, but nonetheless obviously, displayed in the background). Audience attention may be directed toward visual materials, and subtle nuances of delivery, such as facial expression, may be more pointedly brought to listeners' attention. On the other hand, the television audience is far less captive than a live one. A viewer can switch to another channel, or begin to read a newspaper, or even get up and leave to fix a snack or answer the telephone.

Perhaps the most important, and obvious, aspect of the television medium is its highly visual nature, which tends to emphasize what is *seen* at the possible expense of what is *said*. Audiences can form judgments about the speaker's competence, compassion, and intelligence based on what the speaker looks and sounds like, close up, and not only on what he or she says. It has often been observed, for example, that the outcome of the televised debates between Richard Nixon and John Kennedy turned on how Nixon looked, that Nixon's make-up man "did him in." Whether or not this bit of conventional wisdom is true, there is no doubt that practical politicians are very much concerned with their appearances as they are projected on television. The rhetorical critic who limits himself or herself exclusively to the text of such a speech is in danger of overlooking a potentially significant part of the setting that could lead to distorted conclusions about what happened rhetorically.

THE CENTRALITY OF THE AUDIENCE

Frequent mention has been made of the expectations of the audience. The audience for any message is one of the most important constituents of the rhetorical act with which a critic must deal. Speeches are, by their nature, audience centered; the understanding of the audience is absolutely vital to any critical inquiry.

As the critic reconstructs the context for a message or series of messages, much information about the nature of the audiences addressed will be uncovered. The critic must organize, systematize, and search out missing information to give as complete a picture as possible of those whom the speaker would influence. In order to do this, the critic must first identify immediate and potential audiences, and then examine the primary variables that have a direct bearing on how audiences might receive and act on messages.

IDENTIFYING AUDIENCES

The critic's first consideration is to identify the audience or audiences. In some cases, this task will not be too difficult; it will be obvious that the primary audience is the one actually gathered to hear the speech. Certainly before the advent of mass media this was more likely to be the case. A speech given in the House of Commons in the eighteenth century, for example, was largely addressed to the members present; a speech given at a state convention called for the purpose of ratifying the new United States Constitution was primarily directed at the assembled delegates. But, even in historical cases, speeches were often designed with those in mind who would read about them later. Robert Emmet, the Irish revolutionary, spoke not for the English court that condemned him to hang, but to the larger Irish audience who would hear reports of what he said.[17] Abraham Lincoln, delivering his first inaugural speech, did not address the crowd assembled in Washington as much as the people and leaders of the southern states who had already begun to secede from the Union and those in the border states who might contemplate doing so.[18] Those who failed to take wider audiences into consideration were sometimes confounded by the results. William Seward's speech on the "irrepressible conflict" in Rochester, New York, had a profound effect on those who were not there and who judged the speech as an "abolitionist" one. It thereby helped to thwart Seward's chances to gain the Republican nomination for President.[19]

For any speech, then, there is an immediate audience and a potentially larger one. This is true of messages given in the past, and it is certainly true of modern times when the mass media have the potential to disseminate a speaker's ideas rapidly, sometimes instantaneously, throughout the world. It is obvious, for example, that a major address by the President of the United States may be an attempt to communicate with the American people at large or with segments of the American public, with legislators who will act to effect presidential policy, with foreign governments in alliance with the United States, and with those who are seen as hostile to American interests and intentions. The immediate audience may be the Congress in joint session, students and faculty in a university convocation, television viewers, or the National Press Club. But a far wider audience is likely to be envisioned.

Both the text and the context will direct the critic's attention to the wider audience. The critic who has investigated the imperatives giving rise to rhetoric should know the political, social, and economic issues that are uppermost in the minds of potential listeners. Specific references to foreign policy, for example, alert the critic to the possibility that the speaker wishes to send a message to the leaders of other countries or to supporters or potential adversaries at home. Knowing the context, setting, and content of the speech, the critic can begin to make informed assumptions about the audience the speaker hoped or needed to reach.[20]

AUDIENCE VARIABLES

What a critic needs to know about an audience can be grouped under three essential variables. These elements are "variable" in that their *impact* and significance varies—they may differ in importance and in relevance depending on the rhetorical characteristics of the situation. These variables are the listeners' *knowledge,* their *group identification,* and their *receptivity* to the speech and the topic.

In order for a critic to begin to understand how an audience may respond to a speech, it is essential to understand what the audience knows about the subject under consideration, about current related events, and about the speaker. In addition to knowledge pertinent to the specific rhetorical event, audiences have general knowledge, which may or may not be relevant, that grows out of their educational background and personal experiences. The critic hopes to understand interactions and make reasonable judgments about how well and in what ways speakers have adapted such elements as language choice, basic arguments, supporting evidence, and the like, to audiences; in order to carry out an operational analysis that can lead to a sound judgment, the critic must know what the audience knows.

Take, for instance, the use of historical analogy. A speaker who compares contemplated American government policy toward El Salvador with American actions in Vietnam could reasonably assume that the Vietnam experience is recent and general enough for most listeners to have personal knowledge of it. As a speaker delves further into the past, however, his or her audience's knowledge of history may be a function of their educational background. Furthermore, particular audiences can be expected to know more about particular subjects because of their cultural identity, their professional activities, or the perceived impact of the topic on their own lives. Some audiences may know more not only about a given subject, but about current events in general because they tend to read newspapers, watch television documentaries and special reports, or discuss issues with other well-informed people. Also, some audiences will know more about the particular speaker than will other audiences. They may have been that speaker's constituents, or have read things that the speaker has written, or have belonged to the same social or religious organizations, and so forth. The ways in which a speaker capitalized on, or failed to take into account, what an audience *knows* is an important critical concern, one that the critic can assess only if he or she is aware of audience knowledge.

What anyone knows is not only a function of that person's educational level and personal intellectual practices; knowledge is shaped partly by the *groups with which one identifies.* This group affiliation, in addition to furthering knowledge, also influences the way people interpret and use knowledge. Members of the Sierra Club, for example, probably know more about conservation than many other people do; they are likely to read publications, attend meetings, and generally gather specific information that will provide them with more detailed facts about such matters as federal land management policy, criteria for designating wilderness areas, or potential industrial uses of public lands. But along with this knowledge there is also a *point of view* that members of a group tend to share. Catholics, Presbyterians, Episcopalians, Pentecostals, and Jehovah's Witnesses may all "know" the Bible; they may all be able to quote passages or relate the essential ingredients of a particular scriptural narrative. They nevertheless hold widely divergent views of what the Bible means not only theologically but in very practical terms relating to

31

day-to-day human relations. Association and identification with particular groups will predispose audience reactions to messages.

Other group identifications derive from less voluntary factors. One may elect to join the Sierra Club or to change one's religious affiliation, but one cannot change his or her age or sex or ethnic background. Also, it is much more difficult to modify one's social status or economic circumstances than it is to join or drop out of a particular interest group or formal organization. The critic must also be aware of how these group identifications may exert influence on audiences. Polish organizations in Chicago have a cultural and emotional relationship to Eastern Europe that is bound to affect their response to a speaker who addresses the problems of American foreign policy in that area; blue-collar workers threatened with unemployment will view speeches on economic policy from that very personal perspective; older Americans' real stake in the Social Security program will shape their reaction to speeches that deal with that issue. Because the speaker's task is to adapt to a variety of groups within audiences, often groups with *conflicting* orientations, the critic's job of sorting out the possible responses of audiences is likewise difficult. The effective critic must understand the problems that arise from the speaker's efforts to persuade heterogeneous elements within audiences in order to describe and evaluate the speaker's solutions to these rhetorical problems.

Just as listeners' knowledge about a given subject derives partly from the groups with which they identify, both the knowledge and group identification have an impact on the *receptivity of an audience* to both subjects and speakers. The receptivity of an audience depends partly on *saliency*.

An issue or topic is salient to a group when that group sees the subject as important to them, as impinging directly on their lives. The basic act of receiving a message takes some effort on the part of the receiver. To choose to listen to a speech or read a pamphlet or attend a meeting is an act based on some initial receptivity. Most open meetings of school boards, for example, will be sparsely attended. But if there is a threat of some schools being closed, or a plan to redistrict areas served by particular schools in order to change busing patterns, large crowds will very likely be present. Parents will attend these meetings, in spite of conflicting demands on their time and energy, because they believe that their children's education, safety, or social adjustment will be significantly affected by the outcomes of the meetings. Some audiences might not be disposed to take a serious or intense interest in foreign policy, but if they are farmers whose livelihood is affected by a grain embargo, or college students whose education could be interrupted by compulsory military service, certain aspects of foreign policy will be salient to them and will compel their receptivity to a discussion of the issue.

Receptivity in this sense concerns the listeners' willingness to engage themselves as a part of the communication process. The critic must realize that a speaker's rhetorical problem often involves the *creation* of saliency. That is, there are times when audiences or potential audiences do not readily perceive the relevance of issues, or do not see the relevance in the way the speaker wishes them to see it. For example, some listeners may see the "cleaning-up-the-environment" issue as remote to their personal experience, but to those who lived through the Love Canal disaster, pollution is a very real and harrowing threat. To those living in small towns or relatively nonindustrialized areas, the problem of pollution might be seen as a "big-city" one that doesn't touch them directly. To some people, environmental controls have relevance because they believe that such controls can affect their health and the health of their children; others see relevance in the issue of government controls that increase manufacturing costs and thus affect them negatively in an economic way. The critic's task is to discern how audiences might answer the question, "Is this issue relevant to me and in what ways?" Then the critic will be better able to analyze the extent to which, and the ways in which, a speaker attempted to solve the saliency problems of the situation.

In conjunction with saliency, receptivity concerns the audience's disposition toward a subject or a speaker; it is important for the critic to understand listeners' attitudes, so that he or she can better uncover rhetorical problems. Certain topics may be received by audiences in a hostile, friendly, or fearful way. (Likewise, audiences can be hostile or indifferent, respectful, or suspicious toward a speaker; this point is developed more fully in the following chapter in the examination of the role of the speaker.) For example, a PTA audience may respond positively toward a speaker dealing with improving the quality of playground equipment; the same audience might approach a speaker dealing with the need to reduce the local school budget with suspicion, or even hostility. A conservative religious group might be negatively disposed to the subject of the church's role in promoting social action. The National Association of Broadcasters might initially be threatened by a discussion of the need for increased government regulation of broadcasting. The National Education Association would be inclined to receive positively a message that dealt with the increased use of national resources to improve the quality of instruction in the public schools.

A painstaking construction of audience variables in a given situation is fundamental to the critical process. In most circumstances, the critic will discover wide variations in the knowledge, group identifications, and receptivity of those who receive messages. But whether the audiences tend to move in the direction of homogeneity or heterogeneity, the message that is designed for them must take into account who they are and where they stand. The speaker will have choices to make and will make them—consciously or unconsciously. The pattern of these choices will contribute to the formation of the speaker's strategy. Understanding precisely what those choices are and judging whether or not they are appropriate—strategically or ethically—is part of the critic's role.

THE CRITICAL USE OF CONTEXT AND AUDIENCE

The critic should realize that the constituents of the rhetorical act discussed in this chapter are those over which the speaker exercises little direct control. A speaker cannot change the past, erase the traditions and values that are part of a culture, escape the technical limitations imposed by television, make an audience of women into men, or convert workers who are fearful of losing their jobs into economically secure people. The context in which a message occurs and the audience or audiences to whom the message is addressed present rhetorical problems or rhetorical opportunities that delineate the boundaries within which a speaker must operate. Rhetoric is the process whereby values may be changed, traditions discarded, class distinctions erased or redefined, and future action shaped. But any given message, at a particular moment in time, is constrained by contextual and audience factors that are then operant. As a painter may be constrained by his or her canvas, a musician by the notes that instruments are capable of producing, and a dramatist by the technical possibilities of stage production, a speaker's possibilities are, in large measure, circumscribed by relevant events and relevant audience variables. The significant challenge for the speaker is to manipulate those factors over which he or she does have more control—for example, the construction of arguments, the selection of evidence, the identification and appeal to values, the language employed, and the manner of delivery—so as to influence real audiences living in real contexts. The critic can only begin to appreciate a speaker's wisdom and skill, or lack of it, when the critic fully comprehends the constraints under which a speaker labors.

Perhaps the best way to epitomize the critic's task in regard to context and audience is to say that the critic must answer the fundamental question: What is there in the rhetorical situation that presents a clear indication of the rhetorical problems that a speaker must solve and the rhetorical opportunities that exist to be used? This chapter has suggested important elements to be dealt with by the critic as he or she goes about answering that overarching question. These elements can be summarized by directing the critic's efforts toward answering the following subsidiary questions:

1. What *political, social, or economic factors,* both historical and immediate, brought the issue into *rhetorical* being?
2. What *cultural values and practices* in the society were relevant to the issue?
3. What *varying perceptions of the issue* existed at the time the message was given?
4. What *rhetorical conventions* shaped audience expectations of how, in what circumstances, and within what limitations the message was to be sent and received?
5. What *prevailing ethical standards* were relevant to the message?
6. What were the particular *circumstances of the setting* for a speech, and in what ways did they determine what a speaker could or could not do?
7. What was the composition of the *immediate audience* to whom a message was addressed?
8. Who was the *larger audience,* or audiences, if any, to whom the message was addressed?
9. In what ways were the *audiences' knowledge, group identifications,* and *receptivity* relevant to the issue being addressed?

As the critic answers these questions, he or she will construct a framework within which analysis, interpretation, and evaluation of the message as it functions rhetorically can take place.

One other constituent of the rhetorical act must be considered before the critic can turn to an intensive investigation of the text of the message itself: the examination of the speaker as a unique constituent in the rhetorical act is the subject of the next chapter.

Notes

1. As C. V. Wedgewood observed, "The historian's choice of significant issues is often different from that of contemporaries." *The King's War: 1641-1647* (London: Collins Fontante, 1958), p.11.
2. The concept of "rhetorical imperatives" is discussed more fully and illustrated in James R. Andrews, "The Passionate Negation: The Chartist Movement in Rhetorical Perspective," *Quarterly Journal of Speech,* 59 (1973), 196-208.
3. See the chapter on "The Unfinished Revolution," in Kurt W. Ritter and James R. Andrews, *The American Ideology: Reflections of the Revolution in American Rhetoric* (Falls Church, Va.: SCA Bicentennial Monograph Series, 1978), pp. 93-117.
4. See, e.g., Gordon Wood, "Rhetoric and Reality in the American Revolution," *William and Mary Quarterly,* 3rd Ser., 23 (1966), 3-32.
5. See examples of two critical studies that deal with this issue: Walter R. Fisher, "Gladstone's Speech at Newcastle-on-Tyne," *Speech Monographs,* 26 (1959), 255-262; James R. Andrews, "Coercive Rhetorical Strategy in Political Conflict: A Case Study of the *Trent* Affair," *Central States Speech Journal,* 24 (1973), 253-261.
6. See, e.g., James R. Andrews, "Piety and Pragmatism: Rhetorical Aspects of the Early British Peace Movement," *Speech Monographs,* 34 (1967), 423-436.
7. See the example of the radical Henry Hunt's attack on the Tory Prime Minister George Cauney in James R. Andrews, "History and Theory in the Study of the Rhetoric of Social Movements," *Central States Speech Journal,* 31 (1980), 276-279.
8. I have developed this point in some detail in "Reflections of the National Character in American Rhetoric," *Quarterly Journal of Speech,* 62 (1971), 316-324, and what follows draws extensively on that study.
9. Erik H. Erikson, *Childhood and Society,* 2d ed. (New York: W. W. Norton, 1963), p. 318.
10. See, e.g., David M. Potter, *People of Plenty: Economic Abundance and the American Character* (Chicago: U. of Chicago Press, 1954), p. 49.
11. Kenneth Keniston, *Young Radicals* (New York: Harcourt, Brace and World, 1968), p. 66.
12. Gabriel A. Almond, *The American People and Foreign Policy* (New York: Harcourt, Brace, 1950), p. 52.
13. In *Speech Criticism: Methods and Materials,* ed. by William A. Linsley (Dubuque, Iowa: Wm. C. Brown, 1968), p. 376.
14. Cited in Robert T. Oliver, *History of Public Speaking in America* (Boston: Allyn & Bacon, 1965), p. 235.
15. Cited in Richard Hofstader, *Great Issues in American History* (New York: Vintage, 1958), I, p. 322.
16. "I Accept Your Nomination," *Voices of Crisis: Vital Speeches on Contemporary Issues,* ed. by Lloyd W. Matson (New York: Odessey Press, 1967), p. 125.
17. See Robert M. Post, "Pathos in Robert Emmet's Speech From the Dock," *Western Journal of Speech Communication,* 30 (1966), 19-25.
18. See Marie Hochmuth Nichols, "Lincoln's First Inaugural Address," *Anti-Slavery and Disunion, 1858-1861: Studies in the Rhetoric of Compromise and Conflict,* ed by J. Jeffery Auer (New York: Harper & Row, 1963), pp. 392-414.

19. Robert T. Oliver, "William H. Seward on the 'Irrepressible Conflict,' October 25, 1858," *Anti-Slavery and Disunion,* pp. 29–50.
20. See Forbes Hill's discussion of "target audience" in "Conventional Wisdom— Traditional Form," esp. p. 375.

3 Constituents of the Rhetorical Act: The Speaker

"Knowing" any person is an extremely difficult task. All of us present different pictures of ourselves to different people in different circumstances. The roles we play, the settings in which we find ourselves, the expectations of others, our own motives—all contribute to the extremely complex whole that makes up the "real" person. People have many sides, and no one can hope to see all those sides; we rarely understand or are even aware of every facet of our own personalities. When we communicate with others, most of us tend to manipulate, consciously or unconsciously, the aspects of ourselves that we wish others to see; and those who communicate with us form impressions, intended or unintended, of what we are.

We know that we ourselves and those around us define us as students, or as friends, daughters, as brothers, lovers, rivals, co-workers, and so forth. At the same time we may think of ourselves and be seen as Christians, or scientists, or Democrats, or vegetarians. And as situations change, what we and others think is most important about us, what is most relevant to the situation, also changes.

If we project these individual human circumstances into the public communication setting, we can see that speakers and audiences interact in such a way as to "define" the person who is sending the message. This "definition" is what is termed the speaker's *ethos* or the composite *perception* an audience has of a speaker. This

37

perception is not a complete, or in all ways accurate, reflection of a "real" person; it is what an audience *thinks* about a person at any given time. It is formed by a variety of factors to which the critic must turn his or her attention. Chief among these considerations are the context out of which the speech arises and into which it intrudes itself; the speaker's prior reputation; the audience's needs, expectations, and priorities; the content and rhetorical characteristics of the message itself; and the manner in which the speech is given.

CONTEXT AND ETHOS

Considerable attention was given in the last chapter to the elements in the context that can influence a rhetorical interaction. These factors can be viewed from the standpoint of their potential to influence an audience's perception of a speaker. Certain events or trends that gave rise to rhetoric in the first place may affect attitudes toward speakers.

Take, for example, what has come to be known as the Watergate scandal. The revelations about the inner workings of government, the generally condemned unethical or even illegal actions of political figures, and the sense of violation of the public trust that arose from news accounts and congressional hearings, created serious issues related to honesty and integrity of government, the powers of the presidency, the balance of powers between the branches of government, and a host of related issues that had to be dealt with rhetorically in subsequent political campaigns.

Part of the fallout from the Watergate experience was a profound suspicion of politicians. Any speaker who was a professional politician faced potential hostility from an audience because he or she could be perceived as a part of the whole system that had produced Watergate. Indeed, one of Jimmy Carter's principal assets when he was elected President might have been that he was not associated with the Washington establishment. In other circumstances, his lack of experience would have been a negative factor; given the context of the mid-1970s such a potentially harmful perspective could be turned to the speaker's advantage. Thus, the dissociation of then-Governor Carter from professional politicians could have been a factor in shaping a positive ethos for many listeners.[1]

Social and cultural elements within a context also can bear on ethos. Even though potential listeners may not know a speaker, they may associate him or her with a group or cause that suggests a network of values. For example, if an audience gathers for a speech in favor of ERA, its members may identify the speaker as a feminist. To some audiences this label will suggest an interwoven fabric of positive values: The speaker is in favor of equality; the speaker believes in the right of women to determine their own destinies and control their own bodies; the speaker believes women should have confidence and respect for themselves. For other listeners, a feminist represents threatening or negative values: The speaker is too aggressive and competitive; the speaker scoffs at the values of home and family; the speaker hates men. Of course, neither set of perceptions is likely to be entirely true in any objective sense. What is important is that the audience's social and cultural set, which grows out of its experiences of the imperatives calling forth the rhetoric, can predispose the members to view any speaker in a particular way, and, accordingly, influence the speaker's *ethos*.

Because of the impact of context on ethos, the critic of public address needs constantly to be reminded that perceptions of speakers *at the time they spoke* are influenced by that time and are not colored, as the critic's perceptions might be, by subsequent historical events. To have been an abolitionist before the Civil War, for example, was to be labeled a fanatic by most audiences and to ensure a negative ethos in most circumstances. Lincoln, whose popular image of "the great emancipator" has come down to later generations, took great pains to dissociate himself from the abolitionists right up to and including the presentation of his First Inaugural Address.[2] Speakers in England in the early nineteenth century who advocated reform of Parliament in order to enlarge the franchise vehemently denied the merest suggestion that they were "democrats."[3] To be against slavery and for democracy may seem to the contemporary student automatically positive virtues; what the critic must realize is that the context helps determine what is virtuous and thus contributes to the speaker's ethos.

THE SPEAKER'S REPUTATION

Our discussion of contextual factors relates to a speaker's reputation. If one is identified in a particular way with a particular issue, one takes on the generalized reputation that audiences associate with like-minded individuals. But many speakers are, or audiences believe them to be, known quantities. Listeners' awareness of anything that has occurred in a speaker's past can affect their prejudgment of the speaker.

One of the first matters about which an audience is likely to have information is the speaker's *issue orientation*. Because of other speeches, political actions, written works, or reports of positions the speaker has taken, the audience can have some awareness of the speaker's stand on the topic under consideration. Sometimes such information will be relatively concrete. The audience may know, for example, that the speaker voted against a constitutional amendment to prohibit school busing. Sometimes what is known is more vague: The speaker is a "conservative." And sometimes what the audience thinks it knows about the speaker is the result of labels attached by the speaker's opponents: He is a "big spender." The critic's task, then, is to assemble all the available data about a speaker's actions or statements about a particular issue and assess the extent to which and the ways in which these positions were made public and were interpreted by others.

The speaker may also bring to the speaking situation a public *character*. His or her past actions, not only those associated with the specific issue being discussed, will contribute to audiences' impressions of the speaker's sincerity, trustworthiness, judgment, and ethical qualities. A good example of the impact of this aspect of ethos is that of General Dwight D. Eisenhower. Eisenhower, a hero of World War II, was generally regarded as an honest, trustworthy man who was used to solving massive problems. His political position on major issues was virtually unknown when he entered politics; indeed, most political leaders did not even know whether he was a Democrat or a Republican.

As the critic attempts to reconstruct the public character of a speaker, much more is relevant than the speaker's identifiable stand on issues. The speaker's entire public life, as well as that part of his or her private life that is known or has been reported, is significant.

A speaker's reputation is also made up, in part, of an audience's beliefs about the speaker's *intelligence* and *experience*. It is apparent that for some listeners a speaker will be seen as someone who "knows what he's talking about." Aspects of the speaker's past will have established him or her as an authority on the question at hand. Simply being identified in an audience's mind as an expert can enhance a speaker's ethos.

A noted medical researcher, for example, may be expected to be regarded favorably by an audience gathered to hear a discussion of ways to prevent heart disease. Coaching clinics throughout the country attract eager young athletes who are willing to listen with great attention to a famous coach who has established authority by producing a string of winning teams. Eisenhower is an example of one of whose favorable image made him trustworthy. During the election campaign of 1952, he was able to strike a responsive chord in the American public with the announcement, "I shall go to Korea." Eisenhower succeeded not because that statement revealed a specific plan for ending the war, but because he was viewed as an authority on military matters who could end a conflict that threatened to drag on endlessly.

An audience's perception of the depth and genuineness of the speaker's interest in them and their problems can also contribute to the speaker's reputation. A speaker's ability, then, is tempered by the audience's conviction of his or her sincerity. Such qualities as consistency, for example, can influence listeners' views of a speaker's sincerity. A speaker who has changed his or her mind on issues can be seen as one who has grown and developed over the years, whose views have matured, or whose experiences have altered earlier convictions or attitudes. On the other hand, such a person may be viewed as an opportunist whose principles are easily adapted to prevailing popular currents of thought. Politicians often belabor one another with statements made in the past. During the 1980 presidential campaign, for example, President Carter tried to make much of Ronald Reagan's statements, made some years previously, advocating radical revisions in the Social Security system. Congressmen from relatively conservative districts are frequently attacked for talking conservatively at home and voting liberally in Washington; such attacks seem clearly designed to call into question the sincerity and integrity of those officeholders.

Experience can relate not only to a speaker's expertise but also to his or her perceived interest in, and identification with, the audience. A speaker and an audience who have shared experiences and common tastes, similar backgrounds or even mutual prejudices, tend to be in sympathy with one another. A speaker who is seen as "one of us" may be viewed in a friendly light in comparison with a speaker about whom the audience is inclined to ask, "What does he know about it's like to be poor?"—or to be black—or to work for a living—or to be lonely—or whatever.

Audiences can be gullible; their yearnings for solutions to their problems can lead them to believe what and whom they want to believe. History abounds with examples of those who successfully courted audiences through appeals to their fears and desires in order to obtain power. But audiences can be suspicious, too. They can question the motivations of speakers who appear to have something to gain by soliciting their support. Certainly what the audience believes it knows about a speaker's motivations forms a part of the reputation that the speaker brings to a communicative situation. The used car salesman—fairly or unfairly—has become something of a symbol of the speaker whose word is to be discounted since he is perceived as one who has everything to gain and very little to lose in getting a car off the lot. "What's in it for him" is a silent question that listeners can be expected to ask as they listen to a speaker.

AUDIENCE PRIORITIES

A speaker's reputation, then, is made up of an audience's various perceptions of the speaker, based on what it knows or believes about the speaker. But in this case, the whole is certainly not equal to the sum of its parts. A critic cannot simply catalogue the speaker's strengths and weaknesses according to the speaker's character or intelligence or sincerity. What is *important* about a speaker's reputation, and how that reputation works for or against a speaker, is a function of the audience's needs, expectations, and priorities.

A speaker's character, for example, may be judged by his or her public actions, but whether those actions are interpreted favorably or unfavorably depends on the standards of the listeners. This point was made in the preceding chapter, but it is important to reemphasize it here. Some groups may judge a person to be of "good character" because he or she does not smoke or drink whereas others would find such information largely irrelevant to whether the speaker was, for example, a trustworthy manager of public funds. Other elements of a speaker's reputation, which are usually thought of as favorable, may not always be so: There are those who like to believe that experts or intellectuals operate in a theoretical vacuum and lack "common sense." Many political incumbents have faced the charge that their experience in solving national problems flatly disqualifies them from leadership since the problems they addressed over their years in office remain unsolved.

Furthermore, what constitutes an authority is a very relative matter. Some listeners would pay close attention to a distinguished geologist or astronomer on the question of the age of the earth. Others would reject out-of-hand such persons as authorities and rely, instead, on the opinions of an evangelist who had no pretensions to scientific training or knowledge. Whether Carl Sagan or Jerry Fallwell is the best authority on how the earth was formed depends on who is listening.

Authority can also be misplaced, and the critic needs to be aware of the fact that audiences are sometimes disposed to generalize widely. A distinguished physicist, who might rightly be regarded as an expert on certain scientific matters, may receive close attention when he is giving his opinion on political and social matters, on which he may have no more expertise than any well-informed, intelligent citizen. Audiences may have "heroes"—be they scientists, businessmen, or sports figures—whose authority, although logically limited to the field in which they have direct experience and in which they excel, is enlarged by listeners to include virtually any area in which such persons choose to express opinions. Such a phenomenon is the basis for much "endorsement" advertising, for example.

Authority can be spread and misplaced; it can also be disregarded by audiences when they perceive the basic issue as one lying outside the relevant area of authority. We have previously discussed the importance of understanding the ways in which issues are defined and focused. Take, for example, the issue of government regulation of the automobile industry. Some listeners may well concede that a scientist working for the Environmental Protection Agency is an authority on air pollution control, but audiences may dismiss the speaker's advocacy of strict regulation of emission control devices. Although audiences might grant that the speaker knows well the dangers to health and scientific means of reducing those dangers, they might view the issue as economic, not scientific. Workers in Flint, Michigan, or Kokomo, Indiana, may be more responsive to a speaker whom they regard as an economic or political authority, whose concern is with increasing automobile production. The critic, as a more dispassionate observer, may look at the welter of conflicting arguments and issues and reach a logical conclusion that our ultimate survival may depend on how well we learn to preserve our environment. But the critic does not have to face stockholders who want more profits or a family whose standard of living depends on the wage earner's regular weekly check. What is crucial to listeners *as they see it* is what determines how an issue is focused, and this definition of an issue influences an audience's definition of an authority.

The crucial point here goes back to the definition of ethos. *The perception an audience has of a speaker* is what finally determines that perception; it ultimately rests not on a catalogue of more or less objective personal qualities possessed by the speaker, but, rather, on what is known about those qualities and how they are interpreted by listeners.

ETHOS AND THE MESSAGE

Much of the discussion thus far has been concerned with what an audience knows (or believes it knows) about the speaker prior to a communication event. Part of the critic's task is to understand as fully as possible the ethos a speaker *brings to* a speaking situation. Yet it is also essential that the critic search for and explicate the ways in which the speaker both uses and creates ethos in his or her speech.

The text of the speech itself can reveal the *use of existing ethos* as a persuasive device. A general, for instance, may use an example from his personal experience that reminds his listeners of his military expertise; a political leader may refer to his or her many years of public service; and a business executive may relate a personal anecdote that reveals his or her managerial skills. When President Lyndon Johnson presented his sweeping proposals for a new civil rights law that would effectively end political discrimination in the South, he reminded his audience that his own "roots go deeply into Southern soil," and, as a consequence, he knew "how agonizing racial feelings are."[4] The President was recommending to Congress a bill whose provisions would call forth the bitterest denunciation from southern political leaders. With this statement, Johnson identified himself not as an outsider who disparaged southern traditions, but as a southerner who could cherish his heritage and still demand serious and deep reform. When Prime Minister Winston Churchill, faced with an election challenge from the Labour party, spoke to the British electorate near the end of World War II, he reminded voters of the situation when he had taken office and how he had led the country from "that memorable grim year when we stood alone against the might of Hitler with Mussolini at his tail. We gave all—and we have given all throughout to the prosecution of this war—and we have reached one of the great victorious halting-posts."[5] Speakers, then, will make efforts to exploit what they consider favorable elements of their ethos, and critics will attempt to discover the persuasive potential of such efforts.

It is also possible for speakers to strive to *create* favorable ethos within the speech itself. We have discussed previously some of the forces at work in the context and the audience that can dispose listeners to respond favorably or unfavorably to persuasive messages. As the speaker deals with such forces, he or she may enhance his or her ethos. A speaker with whom an audience can identify is a speaker for whom a positive ethos may be created.

The critic searches for the speaker's attempts to promote identification by discovering: (1) the ways in which the speaker associates himself or his position with an audience's values and, conversely, pictures the opposition as linked to positions upon which an audience looks unfavorably; (2) the ways in which the speaker refutes or minimizes unfavorable aspects of his or her ethos; (3) the extent to which the speaker capitalizes on the positive ethos of those with whom the audience does identify; (4) the ways in which the speaker shows a grasp of the issues that are most important to the audience and a command of facts, information, and interpretations of those issues; (5) the ways in which the speaker seeks to convince audience members that he or she understands their problems and shares their aspirations and concerns; and (6) the ways in which the speaker reveals his or her motivations in order to counter impressions of self-interest.

A speaker may employ any or all of these tactics to enhance the listeners' image of him or her. In responding to speakers, as in so many aspect of life, we often find ourselves relying ultimately on very personal evaluations. On almost any given matter, there is such a welter of confusing and conflicting information that many feel too overwhelmed to make any sense of it. Others simply can't be bothered or are too busy with other things, or can not begin to understand the meaning of masses of data and varieties of incompatible explanations of what those data mean. So we often resolve such difficulties by fixing on a *person* to save us or enlighten us or simply tell us what is best for us to do. Sometimes the results of such dependence are happy; sometimes they are disastrous. But there can be little doubt that reliance on persons we trust is a very potent force in shaping our behavior. The critic who would understand the persuasive impact implicit in a message must assess carefully and thoroughly the ways in which the speaker tries to promote such reliance by listeners.

ETHOS AND DIVERGENT AUDIENCES

One very obvious problem for the speaker, and certainly for the critic, is that a speaker's ethos, by definition, varies with the audience and over time. That is to say, a speaker may have a very positive ethos with one set of listeners and a negative ethos with another. When speakers hope to address mass audiences, this difficulty is compounded.

Major political speeches, for example, must, of necessity, be addressed to people of different ages from different economic and racial backgrounds in different parts of the country. In the case of a major presidential address, not only are many different Americans listening but people and governments throughout the world—some friendly, some unfriendly, some uncertain—are also potential auditors of the message. This complexity may well cause some speakers to attempt to say nothing that offends anyone and thus end up saying nothing. But what is of concern for the critic is the way in which any speaker balances the potential impact of the message on his or her ethos with different groups. In a later section of this book a case study of the varieties and problems of criticism is presented. A speech by then-President Richard Nixon is reproduced, followed by several critical studies of that speech. One of the major issues that emerges from those studies is the question of how Nixon dealt with this very problem of audiences for whom he had divergent images. One solution to the dilemma of differing audiences is offered by a critic who argues, in effect, that Nixon did the most rhetorically wise thing by simply writing off those people whom he had no chance to persuade and concentrating instead on those who were susceptible to his efforts to convince. Another critic takes sharp issue with this assessment, arguing that it was the President's responsibility to answer his critics.[6] No matter what position the critic takes, the fact remains that he or she must grapple with the complexities of ethos, describing and explaining the many facets of the problem as it is faced—or ignored—by the speaker.

THE SPEAKER IN ACTION: ASSESSING DELIVERY

For all that an audience may know or believe about a speaker, for all that a text might reveal about the speaker's efforts to exploit or create audience perceptions, speeches are, after all, actually delivered to an audience. Much of what has been said thus far in this book relates to rhetorical artifacts in general, be they speeches, pamphlets, editorials, or polemical essays. But one of the most obviously unique qualities of a speech is that it is oral and that the audience receives it directly from its originator.

Many speeches are known through reports—either media accounts or through accounts of other people, and many people will hear a two-minute summary of a major speech by a national figure, and, perhaps, see and hear a forty-five-second excerpt from that speech. Nevertheless, a speaker who is actually giving a speech is intimately bound up with the persuasive message itself, and the potential impact of *how* a speaker says what he or she says is inevitably present. Communication researchers W. Barnett Pearce and Bernard J. Brommel observe, "A written message is not the same as the same words spoken aloud. . . ."[7]

The critic who wishes to come to a complete understanding of oral discourse must take delivery into account. Understanding delivery, like understanding everything else rhetorical, can best be done within a full knowledge of the limitations of the situation and the expectations of the audience.

Audiences can and do form impressions of a speaker that have the potential to influence a speaker's ethos on the basis of that speaker's delivery. Rhetorical critics have long assumed that answers to the three basic questions concerning delivery—

How does the speaker sound? How does the speaker look? How does the speaker move?—will give us insights into the nature of that speaker's effectiveness and clues to the image he or she would project.[8] Experimental evidence also points to the conclusion that nonverbal elements in a message have some influence on the audience's reception of the message, although research findings do not conclusively establish a precise cause–effect relationship between specific nonverbal action and audience responses.[9]

Empirical observations from our own experience further confirm the conclusion that nonverbal messages are considered as, and designed to be, persuasive. Advertisers go to great lengths to ensure that their products are promoted by, or seen to be used by, or even seen in the same picture with persons they believe will suggest the rugged or sexy or classy image they wish to project for those projects. Political hucksters do the same thing, surrounding their candidate with his or her family, showing the candidate engaged in earnest conservation with factory workers, picturing the candidate in a friendly and confidential exchange with the President of the United States (if he's popular). It is only common sense to assume that such efforts seek to create the impression that the candidate holds traditional American family values and that he or she is a friend of the working man and a confidant of the powerful.

What a speaker *does* in front of an audience almost always has some effect on that audience. For example, some listeners tend to respond stereotypically to regional dialects. Depending on where one is from, one may form immediate opinions of the intelligence, energy, and educational level of the speaker whose dialect demonstrates him or her to be from the hills of Kentucky or from Alabama or from Brooklyn. Speakers whose monotonous voices bore audiences seem to have the added disadvantage of being less credible, as well.

Correctly or incorrectly, a speaker's vocal qualities can suggest corresponding personality traits to audiences. The author of a highly publicized study of female sexual behavior came to speak at a large university campus. The speaker startled and dismayed some members of the audience because her breathy, "little girl" voice suggested to many that she could not be taken too seriously. Indeed, audiences tend to associate such vocal quality with immaturity. Though nothing the speaker said either strengthened or diminished the scientific validity of her published findings, some auditors may have felt uneasy about accepting those findings because the credibility of the speaker was tarnished by the immature image her voice helped to project. It seems safe to assume that when audiences judge a speaker's voice to be harsh, or nasal, or deviating in some way from "normal" quality, the speaker's ethos will suffer.

The way that speakers look and how they move also contribute to the formation of audience perceptions. Certainly President Carter's casual cardigans were meant to suggest an informality and directness when he gave his "fireside chats" to the American people. The famous smiles of popular politicians from Franklin Roosevelt to Dwight Eisenhower to Ronald Reagan suggested to some a warmth and sincerity that influenced their perceptions of the speaker's reliability and trustworthiness. We have all observed speakers whose tense, tiny movements seem to indicate tentativeness, or whose exaggerated motions distract us or embarrass us.

In fact, delivery of which we are extremely conscious is likely to be delivery that does not help a speaker's ethos or contribute to the successful communication of that speaker's message. "Distracting" mannerisms do just that—they distract us from the message and irritate listeners. I remember an instructor who had the unique ability to balance a piece of chalk on one finger while he discoursed on the wondrous uses of educational statistics. His behavior riveted my attention on the chalk, and the content of the message—along with my regard for the lecturer as a teacher—was lost.

Of greatest interest to the critic is the relationship between the qualities describing a speaker's delivery and the content of the speaker's message. Audiences tend to be sensitive to whether a speaker's nonverbal behavior seems to contradict or deviate from the intended message. Thus, a speaker whose voice, gestures, and appearance convey the impression of remoteness while the message tries to say that the speaker cares about his or her audience, or a speaker who appears to take lightly a serious topic will have his or her ethos impaired. Elements of delivery thus have the potential to interact with verbal elements. For example, in 1976, the national press seemed to draw attention to President Ford's series of unhappy accidents, portraying him as "bumbling." The President's verbal gaffe in his debate with Jimmy Carter in which he alleged that Eastern European countries were free of Soviet domination worked with the *nonverbal* image that was forming in a way that might seriously have compromised Ford's ethos.

The crucial point is that although delivery does seem to influence audience perceptions, it does not seem to be a critical determinant of audience perception in and of itself. What the critic tries to assess is the potential interactions between content and delivery in an effort to uncover aspects that could contribute to the overall perception formed by an audience and, accordingly, could impact on the speaker's ethos.

In this chapter, the fundamental question raised for the critic's consideration is: *What does the speaker bring to the communication situation, or capitalize on within the situation, that influences the audience's perception of that speaker?* The speaker's ethos can serve to help or hinder his or her persuasiveness, and the critic needs an accurate picture of what that ethos is for any given audience at any given time.

The following series of questions will help to summarize this chapter and will serve as a guide to the critic in reconstructing the ethos of the speaker.

1. What are the *historical/political factors* that can influence the audience's perception of the speaker?
2. What are the *social and cultural elements* within the context that bear upon ethos formation?
3. What is the speaker's *orientation toward the issue* under consideration?
4. How have the speaker's past actions served to form a *public character* perceived by the audience?
5. What is the audience's view of the speaker's *intelligence and experience*?
6. What does the speaker's past suggest to an audience about the speaker's *genuine interest* in its needs and concerns?
7. What factors in the speaker's background are most *salient* to the audience?
8. What devices, techniques, or strategies does the speaker *employ in the message itself* to enhance his ethos?

9. How does the speaker's ethos *vary among potential receivers* of his or her message?
10. What *distinguishing features in the speaker's delivery* can be described, and what is their potential for audience influence?
11. What potential for influencing ethos exists in the *relationship between the content of the speaker's message and his or her delivery*?

Notes

1. See, e.g., J. Louis Campbell, "Jimmy Carter and the Rhetoric of Charisma," *Central States Speech Journal*, 30 (1979), 174–186; Christopher Lyle Johnstone, "Electing Ourselves in 1976: Jimmy Carter and the American Faith," *Western Journal of Speech Communication*, 42 (1978), 241–249; John H. Patton, "A Government as Good as Its People: Jimmy Carter and the Restoration of Transcendence to Politics," *Quarterly Journal of Speech*, 63 (1977), 249–257.
2. See Nichols, "Lincoln's First Inaugural Address," *Anti-Slavery and Disunion*, p. 401, pp. 403–404.
3. See James R. Andrews, "The Rhetoric of Coercion and Persuasion: The Reform Bill of 1832," *Quarterly Journal of Speech*, 56 (1970), 187–195.
4. Lyndon B. Johnson, "We Shall Overcome," in James R. Andrews, *A Choice of Worlds: The Practice and Criticism of Public Discourse* (New York: Harper & Row, 1973), p. 85.
5. Winston S. Churchill, "The Conservative Programme," *British Public Addresses, 1828–1960*, ed. by James H. McBath and Walter R. Fisher (Boston: Houghton Mifflin, 1971), p. 469.
6. See pp. 000
7. W. Barnett Pearce and Bernard J. Brommel, "Vocalic Communication in Persuasion," *Quarterly Journal of Speech,* 58 (1972), 305.
8. See, e.g., Robert G. Gunderson's classic description of Daniel Webster on the stump in "Webster in Linsey-Woolsey," *Quarterly Journal of Speech*, 38 (1951), 23.
9. See, e.g., W. Barnett Pearce and Forrest Conklin, "Nonverbal Vocalic Communication and Perception of a Speaker," *Speech Monographs*, 38, (1971), 235–241; John Waite Bowers, "The Influence of Delivery on Attitudes toward Concepts and Speakers," *Speech Monographs*, 32 (1965), 154–158; David W. Addington, "The Relationship of Selected Vocal Characteristics to Personality Perception," *Speech Monographs*, 35 (1968), 492–503; David W. Addington, "The Effect of Vocal Variations on Ratings of Source Credibility," *Speech Monographs*, 38 (1971), 242–247.

4

Understanding Rhetorical Texts: Analysis, Interpretation, and Judgment

As difficult as it is to understand the many complex forces at work in the rhetorical environment, beginning rhetorical critics often find the analysis of the text itself more baffling. Yet the text is at the heart of the critic's work: Only through the careful analysis of its intricacies can the critic begin to interpret its overall functioning and judge its rhetorical worth.

As was mentioned earlier, a careful and thoughtful reading of the text should precede examination of other elements in the rhetorical act. Some critics will prefer to carry out a more detailed textual analysis initially, turning then to contextual factors to enlarge their understanding of the text and to refine and enrich their interpretation and evaluation. As the critical process has been described here, the culmination is analysis, interpretation, and judgment. But, in either case, the text itself must be of central critical concern.[1]

The text of a speech is an organic whole. It lives because its parts function together. No sensible student of rhetoric assumes that any persuasive message is produced additively—that is, that logic is added to emotion or that style is added to content in order to produce the final result. Nevertheless, in order to understand the physiology—how all the parts function together—it is necessary to study the anatomy—how each of the parts is constructed. To that end, the critic begins by systematically taking apart the text through an orderly analysis.

The critic begins to look for features that are fundamentally under the speaker's control. Though the speaker must take contextual features into account in constructing a message, they cannot be readily modified or influenced. The speaker cannot, for example, change the age or sex of his or her listeners; he or she cannot alter historical events or refashion cultural values. And whereas the speaker may be in part responsible for his or her own ethos and certainly can make efforts to manipulate his or her image, an audience's perception of the speaker is not entirely dependent on the speaker's choices. The text of the speech, however, does represent the speaker's *choices*—out of the range of possible material to be used and ways that the material might be put together, the speaker has selected certain material and certain arrangements to accomplish a purpose. In trying to identify these choices, the critic may be guided by certain categories that direct attention to crucial aspects of the discourse.

Argument

Any speech makes certain assertions about reality. The speech grows out of a situation in which the speaker perceives the need to induce listeners to believe or feel or act in certain ways. The speaker has a conclusion he or she wishes to see accepted or a course of action taken. The principal conclusion of the speech, along with the reasons that sustain that conclusion, is the argument of the speech.

Studying the argument of the speech provides the critic with internal evidence of the speaker's purpose. What is the speaker really getting at? What is the speaker trying to do? These questions are best answered through an examination of the speaker's own ideas. The speaker may not clearly or directly state his or her purpose, but the speech itself will surely reveal the speaker's intention.

Perhaps the most famous speech in which the speaker's *stated* purpose is not the purpose revealed by the argument of the speech is Marc Anthony's fictional funeral oration for Julius Caesar in Shakespeare's tragedy. The explicitly stated purpose of simply providing the requisite forms for a decent burial—"I come to bury Caesar, not to praise him"—is revealed as patently opposite to the implicit purpose that the speech itself reveals: to incite the mob to take vengeful action against Caesar's assassins.

The overall argument of the speech is made up of a number of specific arguments, units that in themselves make assertions or draw conclusions; taken together, arguments are designed to achieve the speaker's purpose. The critic who would understand how a speaker thinks and how that speaker wishes to direct the thinking of the audience must consider these units to illuminate the relationship between the fundamental parts of an argument. An argument is made up of a specific bits of information or motivational material that can be called the *data*, a *conclusion*, and some form of *ideational link* between the two. Another way of describing an argument would be to say that it is the process whereby a speaker presents an idea which he or she wishes to have accepted, offers evidence that will promote acceptance, and demonstrates why/or how the evidence is sufficient to warrant acceptance of the idea.

It is very important for the critic to realize that the parts of an argument do not dictate its organization and that the speaker will not always explicitly state all the parts of an argument. Indeed, one of the critic's tasks is to identify the implicit parts of an argument and to reconstruct the argument in its entirety in order to understand precisely the relationship between its parts. Only then will the critic uncover the hidden assumptions, the sometimes invisible links in the chain that the speaker hopes to forge. And only then will the critic have the precise data necessary to judge the worth of the argument.[2]

To understand an argument more fully, let us take an example. The following is an excerpt from President Lyndon Johnson's speech on behalf of a civil rights bill that he was preparing to send to Congress in 1963:

> The history of this country in large measure is the history of expansion of that right to all of our people. Many of the issues of civil rights are very complex and most difficult. But about this there can and should be no argument: every American citizen must have an equal right to vote.
>
> There is no reason which can excuse the denial of that right. There is no duty which weighs more heavily on us than the duty we have to insure that right. Yet the harsh fact is that in many places in this country men and women are kept from voting simply because they are Negroes.
>
> Every device of which human ingenuity is capable has been used to deny this right. The Negro citizen may go to register only to be told that the day is wrong, or the hour is late, or the official in charge is absent.
>
> And if he persists and, if he manages to present himself to the registrar, he may be disqualified because he did not spell out his middle name, or because he abbreviated a word on the application. And if he manages to fill out an application, he is given a test.
>
> The registrar is the sole judge of whether he passes this test. He may be asked to recite the entire Constitution or explain the most complex provisions of state law.
>
> And even a college degree cannot be used to prove that he can read and write. For the fact is that the only way to pass these barriers is to show a white skin.
>
> Experience has clearly shown that the existing process of law cannot overcome systematic and ingenious discrimination. No law that we now have on the books, and I have helped to put three of them there, can insure the right to vote when local officials are determined to deny it. In such a case, our duty must be clear to all of us.
>
> The Constitution says that no person shall be kept from voting because of his race or his color. We have all sworn an oath before God to support and to defend that Constitution. We must now act in obedience to that oath.[3]

All the parts of an argument can be seen clearly in this passage. The conclusion of the argument is that black Americans are wrongly being denied their constitutional right to vote simply because they are black. The data offered to support this conclusion are a series of specific examples of devices used to thwart blacks in their attempts to register. There are two explicit links between the data and the conclusion: The barriers to voting are based on race since "The only way to pass these barriers is to show a white skin"; and, to establish racial barriers to voting is wrong since "The Constitution says that no person shall be kept from voting because of his race or color." Implicit links between data and conclusion are also to be found.

The argument carries weight when there is a shared assumption that there is no justification for the violation of the Constitution and when there is a shared adherence to the value embodied by the concept of "equality under the law."

In the analysis of arguments, critics often find useful a model that has been adapted from the work of the English philosopher Stephen Toulman.[4] The Toulman model can be useful because it offers a diagrammatic way of looking at the parts of an argument, at how they articulate, and particularly, at how the link between the data and the conclusion may be established—implicitly or explicitly. The parts of the model are as follows:

(D) *Data*. These are the "facts" as the speaker sees them and presents them to the audience.
(C) *Claim*. This is the conclusion that the speaker draws from the facts.
(W) *Warrant*. This is a statement, whether explicit or implied, that justifies moving from the Data to the Claim.
(B) *Backing*. This is specific information, whether implicit or explicit, that supports the Warrant.
(R) *Reservation*. This is a statement that identifies possible areas of exception to the Warrant and Claim. (It need not appear in the speech.)
(Q) *Qualifier*. This is a statement that indicates the degree of certainty with which the Claim may be held.

Put in the form of a diagram, the model would look like this:

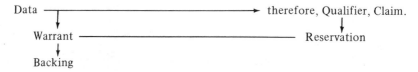

On first encounter, the model may seem somewhat complex to the beginning critic. But the subtleties of an argument are not always apparent on the initial reading, and the model is designed to illuminate complexities. Let us consider the model using the Johnson passage once again. The Johnson argument might be diagrammed as follows:

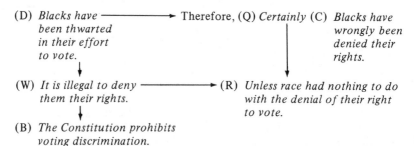

In light of this diagram, the Johnson argument might be restated like this: Blacks have been thwarted in their efforts to vote; *since* it is illegal to do this *because* the

Constitution prohibits discrimination, *therefore* blacks have wrongly been denied their rights *unless* it can be shown that they were not barred from voting because of their color.

Although the critic might initially feel that using the Toulman model to lay out an argument is a somewhat intricate process, it is possible through practice to become more adept at diagramming. This method suggests that a very careful reading of the text, guided by some systematic approach to each argument, can uncover the complex relationship between ideas and evidence.

Systematic analysis of arguments also can illuminate for the critic the ways in which individual arguments form links in the chain of reasoning that supports *the* argument of the speech. One might continue with an examination of the Johnson speech, for example, in which the *Claim* of the argument as diagrammed can be seen to become the *Data* for the argument that follows:

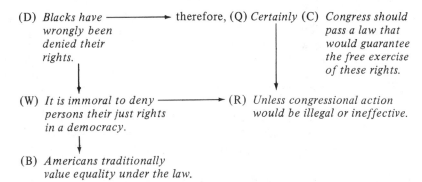

(D) *Blacks have* —————▸ therefore, (Q) *Certainly* (C) *Congress should*
    wrongly been   *pass a law that*
    denied their   *would guarantee*
    rights.   *the free exercise*
                                                      of these rights.

(W) *It is immoral to deny* —————▸ (R) *Unless congressional action*
    persons their just rights   *would be illegal or ineffective.*
    in a democracy.

(B) *Americans traditionally*
    value equality under the law.

The separate arguments, and the way they relate to each other, form the building blocks of *the* argument of the speech. The careful analysis of these arguments will begin to uncover data that form the basis for the critical investigation of other analytical categories.

Supporting Materials

Within any ideational unit of the speech, the speaker will make some effort to make the conclusion understandable and believable to the audience. The critic's task is to identify the forms of support used and to determine the role played by any supporting device in the development of an argument.

The basic forms of supporting material are generally known to students of rhetoric. Most supporting material could be classified as example, definition, analogy, testimony, statistical data, and scientific results. The analysis of the text leads the critic carefully to classify these forms and to note the extent and nature of their use.

It is of prime importance that the critic realize that, whereas identification of forms of support is necessary, *merely* identifying them leads to no significant insights. To say only that a speaker used numerous examples or relied heavily on statistics does not, in itself, provide much illumination of the discourse. What is significant is the *function* that supporting material performs.

53

The critic seeks to uncover both logical and psychological dimensions in support for an idea. *Examples* that are specific and real may serve to demonstrate that actual cases do exist; yet, unless their typicality can also be demonstrated or is accepted, their psychological power is generally more formidable than their logical power. Examples help to make vivid and real generalizations that might otherwise be abstract; thus they promote audience identification. *Definition* serves the logical function of explaining what terms mean. It is also basic to audience adaptation since it recognizes the possibility of audience members' technical or educational limitations. It has the potential to reassure an audience that the speaker does have a psychologically positive concern for them and an awareness of their limitations. On the other hand, it could cause an informed audience to view the speaker as partronizing or pompous. *Analogy* is a means of comparing the known or experienced with the unknown or unexperienced. To the extent to which the two ideas or things juxtaposed really are comparable in essential elements, analogies lead to logical predictions of what the unknown will be like. Analogies relate the familiar with the unfamiliar, providing listeners with an identification point from which to move on to what may be more complex or little known to them; the potentially threatening nature of the unknown may thus be reduced. *Testimony* by a relevant expert enhances the logical quality of the conclusions reached by the speaker. It may also serve to promote audience confidence in the speaker by allying him or her with recognized authority. *Statistical data*, when recent and accurate, may logically support conclusions related to such matters as how widespread a particular problem is or the rate at which a problem is increasing. It can also suggest to an audience that the problem is encompassing enough to be likely to affect them. *Scientific results* provide empirical evidence in support of generalizations. Like testimony, scientific results bring to bear the findings of experts in the field under discussion. Both scientific results and statistical data also possess a positive psychological appeal in a society such as ours, which places value on things that may be called "scientific."

The critic, then, examines the discourse to determine what kinds of supporting material were used and to discover how they were used. One procedure that the critic could employ in examining supporting material would be to use a modified Toulman model to uncover function. That is, the critic could focus on a particular piece of support, determine the conclusion that support seeks to justify, and then speculate on the Warrant or Warrants that would be necessary to justify progress from the Data to the Claim. The two following examples, though not exhaustive or detailed, serve to illustrate the process.

(D) *Example:* John, who ――――――→ (C) The pressures to succeed
wants to go to medi-   are so great as to en-
cal school, needs an   courage cheating.
A– in his English lit
course to maintain his
high academic aver-
age. The final term
paper counted 50 per-
cent of his grade, so
he got his roommate,
an English major, to
write it for him.

(W) John could not have succeeded
without cheating.

(D) *Analogy:* When a bill cutting ――→ (C) The effect of the present
corporate taxes was passed   bill to cut corporate taxes
before, prices remained the   will be to increase profits
same while profits increased.   while prices stay fixed.

(W) Economic circumstances are
similar and the effect of
similar bills on profits and
prices will be the same.

Such an exercise could help the critic describe how supporting materials seem designed to serve the ends of the speaker. It also offers insights into how arguments may be working and will provide the critic with specific data upon which to base observations on the logical soundness and/or psychological appeal of the overall argument of the speech. Such judgments may occur to the critic as he or she proceeds with the analysis of the text. These judgments, however, must be tentative. Only when the analysis of the text is complete and the critic begins to discern patterns and relationships in the discourse itself, and to relate these patterns to the context outside the discourse, can the critic make more definitive judgments.

Structure

As the critic analyzes the arguments that contribute to the goal of furthering the speaker's purpose, the critic will begin to discern the ways in which these arguments are put together in order to suggest relationships between them. Each idea developed by the speaker becomes the backdrop against which the next idea is painted. Thus, the ideas and supporting material of the speech form a pattern that the critic can identify and study to determine how well the speaker appears to be using the form in which the material is presented to move the audience toward acceptance of the persuasive purpose of the speech.

It is probably best for the critic to organize this phase of analysis by constructing a detailed outline of the speech. The critic should seek to identify the main ideas of the speech, arrange supporting material to discover the ways in which it serves to make the ideas believable and understandable to the audience, uncover the transitions and internal summaries that function to tie the ideas together, and isolate the ways in which the speaker sets the context for the speech in the introduction and gives direction to further audience thought and action in the conclusion. Such a reconstruction of the speech should point out for the critic the logical and psychological connections between the parts of the speech.

The critic is then in a position to understand the ways in which the speaker has arranged his or her ideas and material in order to promote such connections for the audience. That is, the critic, understanding how the speaker's ideas relate to each other, can describe the ways in which the speaker patterned those ideas into a meaningful sequence. The sequencing of ideas demonstrates how the speaker perceives, and/or wishes the audience to perceive, the nature of the issues under consideration. For example, if a speaker arranges his or her ideas in a *chronological* pattern, a historical view of the situation is suggested. This form will imply that what has happened in the past leads to the present state of events and provides clues with which to deal with present problems.

Several different patterns of organization are open to the speaker, and different patterns may predominate in different parts of the speech. These patterns are important to understand because they demonstrate the speaker's perspective on the problem and suggest the movement of ideas he or she wishes the audience to follow. A *topical* arrangement of ideas suggests independent ideas, which, taken together, show what the speaker thinks are the most relevant factors in the case. A speaker, for example, may develop economic, military, and political facets of a particular case, implying that moral or social considerations are not germane. A *cause-to-effect* or *effect-to-cause* development emphasizes the consequences of actions and events and can lead to the prediction of outcomes of actions taken by others as contrasted or compared with those advocated by the speaker. A *problem-solution* pattern defines the way the speaker perceives the problem, suggests criteria for the satisfactory solution of the problem, and shows how the speaker's solution meets those criteria. A *climactic* pattern may lead an audience from the most simple ideas to the most complex, or from ideas that are generally accepted and hence likely to be emotionally neutral to those that are more controversial and may generate highly intense emotional responses.

An investigation of the pattern or patterns that can be discerned in the speech points the critic's way to a fuller disclosure of the speaker's point of view with regard to the topic itself and to the speaker's conception of ways to motivate audiences. It should be understood, however, that the speaker may not *present* the speech in such a way that the pattern is immediately apparent. The critic's careful outline of the speech, for example, may show that when the speaker offers an idea that an audience might consider controversial or might react to with some initial antagonism, the speaker is using an indirect approach, carefully reviewing the evidence before fully disclosing the conclusion. In effect, the speaker turns the logical outline upside down, presenting the supporting material before disclosing the main idea that it supports. Another way of looking at this phenomenon might be to say that the critic, in order to see how ideas and evidence relate, prepares a *deductive* outline whereas the speaker may choose to deliver the speech *inductively*.

Style

Style is perhaps the most difficult single constituent of the rhetorical act for the critic. That is because the way in which a speaker uses language—from word choice to sentence construction to figurative devices—is so intimately bound up with the speaker's own personality and perspective, the audience's experiences and expectations, and the demands and constraints of the time that dictate "taste." The analysis of style is also complicated by the fact that it is very difficult to describe in such a way as to identify its unique qualities, and because it is so interwoven with meaning and argument.

Perhaps the overarching question for the critic to attempt to answer when considering style is concerned with the "fitness" of language. Traditionally, the test of good style is that it is clear, correct, appropriate, and exhibits pleasing aesthetic qualities. These criteria all depend on interaction among speaker, audience, and context. What is clear to one audience, to use an obvious example, may not be clear to an audience with less technical expertise or practical experience. Language that is appropriate in a classroom may not be appropriate when used in a formal address. The critic can examine these factors—clarity, correctness, appropriateness, and aesthetic appeal—seeking to discover how the language chosen and put together fits the constraints and expectations of the total situation. But the important thing for the critic to keep in mind in this analysis is that "fit" implies a *relationship*. The style of a speech is the result of the relationship between qualities and their potential to influence audiences.

A significant issue implied in fitness transcends the qualities of good style that have been enumerated. The critic has the additional responsibility to uncover the social, ethical, and logical implications of the use of language.

An argument, for example, may be furthered not only by supporting material. By using a parallel construction, for instance, a speaker may suggest parallel ideas or consequences to his or her audience so that language construction furthers analogy and thus becomes "evidence" in and of itself. As an example, a speaker might allege that "The American determination to insure liberty for all led to us found this nation. To insure liberty we fought each other over the issue of whether or not men and women could be held as property by other men. To insure liberty we twice sent our young men to die on battle grounds of Europe. To insure liberty we must stand ready today to sacrifice our bounty and our blood in whatever part of the world that liberty is threatened." The parallel construction of this segment clearly implies that historical situations are comparable to the present situation; it acts as a "proof" that what was done before must be done again. The critic, in this case, has the right to question whether such a stylistic construction is "fitting" support for the conclusion. The critic's scrutiny of style includes the search for the ways in which style is used to further the argument of the speech.

In his or her effort to understand the operation of style, the critic may focus on a number of specific stylistic elements. Analysis may be directed as discerning the *tone* of the speech suggested by style. Language signals the speaker's attitude—whether serious or light, comic or tragic, sympathetic or hostile, realistic or idealistic—toward the audience and the topic itself. A close study of style can reveal the *level of generality,* ranging from the abstract to the concrete, and the *level of complexity* evident in the choice of mono-or polysyllabic words, the length and configuration of sentences, and the like. The *diction* of the speech is indicated by the way the speaker's language suggests the level of formality with which he or she approaches the audience and the topic. The *texture* of the speech is uncovered by paying close attention to the speaker's stylistic devices; that is, by the way in which the speaker uses such schemes as parallelism or antithesis, figurative language such as similes or metaphors, and imagery.

The critical analysis of style, then, is guided by the careful examination of the *functions* of language in discourse. The critic's goal thus is to describe the ways in which language is *used* to promote the purpose of the speech and the potential influences of this use of language on listeners.

INTERPRETATION

The analysis of a speech provides the critic with a mass of specific detail concerning the way in which the speech has been crafted by the speaker's choices. As the analysis proceeds, the critic will inevitably, if peripherally, begin to assess the meaning of these data and their interrelatedness. But only when the analysis is finished can the critic devote full attention to drawing out and examining the patterns that have begun to emerge from the analysis.

After scrutinizing the argument, supporting material, structure, and style of a speech, the critic knows, if we may return to an earlier analogy, the anatomy of the discourse. Now the critic must make inferences about the physiology of the discourse. This process of inferring *how the discourse works* is interpretation.

Interpretation of a rhetorical work always involves the search for the meaning and function of the various parts of the text as they relate to the context. The critic's task is to explain how the text and context are mutually dependent and mutually effective; only through such an explanation can the critic promote readers' understanding and appreciation for the speech.

Traditionally, critics have sought to interpret a speech by assessing the ways in which the data show that the speaker has identified his or her rhetorical problems and opportunities and has adapted the materials of the speech to meet these circumstances. The audience has assumed a central place in traditional criticism, and the critic has sought to find significance in the speaker's adaptations to a particular audience. This critical focus tends to bear most directly on a speech as a unique event, a situation in which a speaker has a specific purpose to accomplish with a specific group of auditors. A traditional critical interpretation would be addressed to this situation.

Perhaps one of the most potent forces in shaping the thinking approach of modern critics has been the work of Kenneth Burke.[5] Burke's *dramatic criticism* is based on his conception of human beings as symbol-using animals who act out the social drama that is life by inducing action and shaping attitudes in others through language. For Burke, rhetoric is a means of using language to overcome the divisions that exist between people. He sees "the use of language as a symbolic means of inducing cooperation in beings that by nature respond to symbols."[6] *Identification,* a key term in the Burkeian scheme, is promoted when language is used to reduce divisiveness and to bring the speaker and listener closer together in their conceptions and perceptions of the world around them, the ultimate achievement being a psychological fusion that Burke calls *consubstantiality*.

A rhetor's language choices form a pattern that Burke calls a *strategy*, which is not a term employed exclusively by Burkeian critics. Indeed, almost any critic who describes a pattern of choices made by a speaker could be said to be describing a strategy. A traditional critic could look at a speaker's methods of adaptation to an audience and describe the way these methods work together to promote the speaker's purpose as a strategy. Generally, however, critics tend to consider strategy as a representation of a speaker's deliberate design in persuasion; choices have normally been thought of and written of as if they were *conscious* choices. Burke, who contends that identification "can include a partially 'unconscious' factor in appeal,"[7] conceives of strategies as the means of bringing about identification, and therefore admits the possibility that all strategies are not wholly intentional. The critic who would draw on Burke in interpreting a rhetorical act would seek to discover and illuminate the strategies operating through language that promotes the desired end of identification.

Traditionally, speeches have tended to be examined by critics as discrete entities. And, in a sense they are, the way a century or historical period is discrete, the way a painting or a film is descrete, and the way a man's life is discrete. Speeches have a beginning and ending that can be defined—arbitrarily, to be sure, but still logically. Nevertheless, rhetorical events are part of a *process*; they are influenced by and can influence other events. To understand fully the circumstances surrounding a speech act, the critic will need to understand other speech acts that have a bearing on it. Nevertheless, it would be absurd to say that useful criticism cannot result from the intensive investigation of one speech just as it would be ridiculous to assert that a critical analysis of *Hamlet* is not possible without a full analysis of all of Shakespeare's works, of all Elizabethan drama, or of all drama, for that matter. Even so, it surely must be recognized that rhetorical events can be shaped and directed by rhetorical events that have preceded them. Circumstances can circumscribe the limits of rhetorical options, for example, or mold audience expectations.

With this reality of the relatednes of rhetorical acts in mind, some critics have turned their attention to the ways in which situation can exert influence on discourse, that is, that similar contexts can evoke similar rhetorical responses. *Genre* denotes a similar grouping or species, and generic rhetorical criticism is a search for generalities that can be made about discourses in such matters as purpose, style, form, types of proof, and the like. Understanding generic features may lead the critic to a fuller comprehension of what an audience expects in certain situations, and may lead to the formulation of a set of criteria whereby the critic can determine how well any speaker has met those expectations. Mohrmann and Leff in their study of Lincoln, proposed Lincoln's Cooper Union address as an example of the genre of ingratiation,[8] arguing that political speeches are meant to ingratiate the speaker with significant audiences. Such an observation, if it is accepted, has implications for the understanding and evaluation of political speeches.

Acutely aware of the interrelatedness of rhetorical events, other critics have focused on units larger than the single speech and have studied the rhetorical processes involved in debates over important issues, political and other campaigns, and social movements. The obvious difficulty for the critic is in the almost overwhelming amount of rhetorical material that needs to be studied. Movement studies have become a significant area of investigation in rhetoric, but ways of organizing, processing, and interpreting the rhetorical artifacts of these movements are still to be refined.[9] But the critic of movement rhetoric assumes the task of interpreting a significant single rhetorical event in the light of rhetoric that precedes and follows it, seeking to find the meaning of rhetorical strategies in the way discourse progresses over time, the way it influences events, the way it is influenced by events, and how the whole process contributes ultimately to some resolution of the issue that called for movement in the first place.

It is not possible in the limited space available to describe, even as briefly as has been done previously, all the varieties of rhetorical criticism that are yielding useful perceptions of how rhetoric functions. The work of Lloyd Bitzer on situational rhetoric, of Ernest Bormann on fantasy theme analysis, and of Thomas Farrell on social reality are only a few examples of important theoritical work that is breaking new ground and providing imaginative and illuminating ways of interpreting rhetorical events.[10] Careful study of the results of such inquiries can enlarge the novice critic's view of the possibilities of criticism.[11]

Regardless of the method of interpretation that directs the critic's efforts, it should be recognized that a crucial function of interpretation is to isolate the significant. No critique will evenhandedly discuss every aspect of the discourse that is capable of being discussed. The purpose of an exhaustive analysis of a rhetorical act is not to provide material that demands the critic's attention. Indeed, to consider the analytical categories as some kind of checklist of items that must be discussed is to move toward a sterile, formulaic description that submerges interpretation. On the basis of the data, the critic discovers—and can *substantiate* that discovery—what is most meaningful in the discourse under investigation. Interpretation, by examining and explaining the unique and the meaningful in discourse, is then a creative process that leads to insight and not a clerical chore that simply touches all the bases.

JUDGMENT

In the first chapter of this book criticism was defined as "the systematic process of illuminating and evaluating products of human activity." The final step in the process that has been described thus far is evaluation—reaching a reasoned judgment. "Reasoned" is to be emphasized. The rhetorical critic does not judge a speech on the basis of quick impressions; any critic who has gone through the analytical and interpretive stages of investigation has become intimately aware of the workings of the discourse in its context. It remains to reach a defensible conclusion on the quality of the speech.

A judgment may take different forms. Essentially, the judgment made on a rhetorical act or series of acts depends on the standards of judgment—the criteria— that are employed. In reaching a judgment, and in evaluating the judgments reached by other critics, we must look to the criteria advanced explicitly or implicitly suggested.

The criteria may derive from a variety of perspectives, depending on the critic's perception of his or her function, the nature of the evidence that has been uncovered in the examination of the discourse, or the demands—self- or situationally imposed—on the speaker. Basically, judgments are made on the gounds of audience receptiveness and potential audience effects, logical and intellectual validity, and social consequences. Some critics might wish to say that rhetoric can be judged as an art form; that is the *ultimate* judgment. An artistic work, however, one that is unflawed, is one that encompasses *all* the relevant possible criteria: Rhetoric has truly reached the highest artistic pinnacle when it can be said to be effective, intellectually sound, and of benefit to humanity. That is the perfection toward which the best rhetoric strives, but which cannot frequently be reached.

Even though a speech may be flawed in one sense it can still be judged positively with regard to the other elements that are subsumed under the overriding artistic evaluation. Critics, however, no matter how systematic they are and no matter how rigidly they adhere to the demand that their conclusions be based on soundly arguable conclusions, will differ in their values and in their views of both the nature and role of rhetoric. This being so, certain bases for judgment may be more important to some critics that to others.

Judgments based on audience receptiveness will be determined by the potential effect of the discourse. (We have already discussed in some detail the problems of determining effect.) If a speech is judged effective it is, according to this criterion, a "good" speech. Judged by intellectual or logical validity, a speech may be determined to be a "good" if the arguments advanced are sound, based on the best possible evidence available and leading to the conclusions that are warranted by that evidence. Using social consequences as a criterion, a critic would reach a positive judgment about a speech that promoted social welfare and contributed to furthering values that were most conducive to a full realization of the human and humane potential of listeners.

Depending on the critic's point of view, for example, he or she might consider the results of the analysis of a particular argument in different ways. A critic might look at an argument and determine that, since it so closely conformed to the prejudices and beliefs of the audience, it needed little development and was thus a good argument because the conclusion reached would be readily acceptable to the designated listeners. Another critic looking at the same argument might point to the fact that the example used was stereotypical, and even though the audience accepted its stereotypical quality as fact, it was not strong enough to support logically the conclusion drawn from it. A third critic could point out that the examples played on the darker prejudices of the audience and thus reinforced a conception of another group of individuals in such a way as to promote strife and divisiveness.

These perspectives are not mutually exclusive. The same critic might look at material in the speech and evaluate its worth with all three viewpoints in mind. Certain cases might make ethical considerations more relevant than logical ones, and vice versa. The paramount consideration for the critic is that he or she articulate criteria and demonstrate clearly and logically how the rhetorical effort under consideration meets them.

SUMMARY

Analysis, interpretation, and judgment are the principal means whereby the critic pursues his or her art. All these means are part of the process characterized by rigorous and careful examination in which the discourse and its context become the data out of which sound critical conclusions grow.

To summarize these steps and to help the beginning critic organize his or her approach to the rhetorical act, the following set of questions may serve as a guide:

1. What is the principal argument of the speech?
2. What is the implied purpose of the speech? How does it compare with the stated purpose?
3. What are the individual arguments? How are they constructed?
4. What specific forms of support can be identified? How do they function to promote conclusions?
5. What are the main ideas of a speech? How do they relate to the specific materials presented and to each other?
6. What functions do introduction, conclusion, and transitions play in promoting the movement of the speech?
7. Is a predominant pattern of development evident in the speech? Are there subpatterns within the speech?
8. What do the patterns suggest about the speaker's perspective on the issues involved and his or her perception of a desirable audience perspective?
9. How may the speech's tone, level of generality, level of complexity, diction, and texture be described?
10. What function does language appear to play in furthering the argument of the speech?
11. Given the analytical findings, what consistent patterns or strategies emerge in the areas of argument, supporting material, structure, and style?
12. How may these patterns be related to the entire rhetorical situation—context, audience, speaker—in which the rhetorical act took place?
13. What significant rhetorical meaning or meanings can be placed on this act within the rhetorical process of which it forms a part?
14. In what ways and to what extent does the speech engage the audience?
15. In what ways and to what extent does the speech exhibit sound intellectual and reasonable judgment?
16. What are the probable consequences to society of the speech's ideas and information, and the strategic patterns of ideas and information?

Notes

1. This is not to say that the speech itself is always the most important single variable in a context. The critic should not fall into the trap of believing that the speech is always *the* causal factor in whatever follows it. For insights into the impact, of lack of it, of the speech itself, see, e.g., Wayne C. Minnick, "A Case Study in Persuasive Effect: Lyman Beecher on Duelling," *Speech Monographs*, 38 (1971), 262–276; Robert W. Norton, "The Rhetorical Situation is the Message: Muskie's Election Eve Broadcast," *Central States Speech Journal*, 22 (1971), 171–178.
2. The notion of "good" argument, and related questions of judgment, is discussed later in this chapter.
3. *Congressional Record, House of Representatives*, March 15, 1963, 5059–5061.
4. Stephen E. Toulman, *The Uses of Argument* (Cambridge: Cambridge University Press, 1958); see, also, Wayne Brockriede and Douglas Ehninger, "Toulman on Argument: An Interpretation and Application," *Quarterly Journal of Speech*, 46 (1960), 44–53; Charles Arthur Willard, "On the Utility of Descrip-

tive Diagrams for the Analysis and Criticism of Arguments," *Communication Monographs*, 43 (1976), 308–319.

5. See particularly Kenneth Burke, *A Grammar of Motives and a Rhetoric of Motives* (New York: Meridian Books, 1962). An excellent example of Burke's own rhetorical criticism is "The Rhetoric of Hitler's 'Battle,'" in *The Philosophy of Literary Form* (New York: Vintage Books, 1957), pp. 164–189. See, also, Marie Hochmuth Nichol's essay on Burke, "Kenneth Burke and the 'New Rhetoric,'" *Quarterly Journal of Speech*, 38 (1952), 133–144.

6. Burke, *A Grammar of Motives and A Rhetoric of Motives*, p. 567.

7. Kenneth Burke, "Rhetoric—Old and New," *The Journal of General Education*, 5 (1951), 203. For an interesting and perceptive discussion of intentionality, see Robert L. Scott, "Intentionality in the Rhetorical Process," *Rhetoric in Transition: Studies in the Nature and Uses of Rhetoric*, ed. by Eugene E. White (University Park: The Pennsylvania State University Press, 1980), pp. 39–60.

8. Michael C. Leff and G. P. Mohrmann, "Lincoln at Cooper Union: A Rhetorical Analysis of the Text," *Quarterly Journal of Speech,* 60 (1974), 346–358.

9. An entire issue of the *Central States Speech Journal*, 31 (1980), 225–319, was devoted to the rhetorical study of movements. Included in the issue are Leland M. Griffin, "On Studying Movements"; Michael Calvin McGee, "'Social Movement': Phenomenon or Meaning?"; David Zarefsky, "A Skeptical View of Movement Studies"; Stephen E. Lucas, "Coming to Terms with Movement Studies"; Robert S. Cathcart, "Defining Social Movements by Their Rhetorical Form"; James R. Andrews, "History and Theory in the Study of the Rhetoric of Social Movements"; Carol J. Jablonski, "Promoting Radical Change in the Roman Catholic Church: Rhetorical Requirements, Problems and Strategies of the American Bishops"; Ralph R. Smith, "The Historical Criticism of Social Movements"; Charles J. Stewart, "A Functional Approach to the Rhetoric of Social Movements"; Herbert W. Simons, "On Terms, Definitions and Theoretical Distinctiveness: Comments on Papers by McGee and Zarefsky." See also, Suzanne Volmar Riches and Malcolm O. Sillors, "The Status of Movement Criticism," *Western Journal of Speech Communications*, 44 (1980), 275–287.

10. See Lloyd F. Bitzer, "The Rhetorical Situation," *Philosophy and Rhetoric*, 1 (1968), 1–14, and his most recent essay, "Functional Communication: A Situational Perspective," *Rhetoric in Transition*, pp. 21–38; Ernest G. Bormann, "Fantasy and Rhetorical Vision: The Rhetorical Criticism of Social Reality," *Quarterly Journal of Speech*, 58 (1972), 396–407; Thomas B. Farrell, "Knowledge, Consensus, and Rhetorical Theory," *Quarterly Journal of Speech*, 62 (1976), 1–14; James W. Chesebro and Caroline D. Hamsher, "Contemporary Rhetorical Theory and Criticism: Dimensions of the New Rhetoric," *Speech Monographs*, 42 (1975), 311–334.

11. See the Select Bibliography for an extensive list of relevant studies.

Afterword: The Practice of Rhetorical Criticism

Herbert Muller once wrote, ". . . most precious are the works that man has consciously preserved, in defiance of time."[1] Among the most precious works that we have sought to preserve are rhetorical ones, products of human thought and imagination that define the world we live in, make sense of what we have experienced, and influence events that shape our future.

In the crucial civilizing task of preservation, the rhetorical critic plays an important role. For preservation implies not only the physical maintenance of intellectual artifacts but also learning to understand them, to judge their worth, and to apply what is valuable in them to various facets of human activity.

The rhetorical critic's central concern must be with discourse. The introductory principles discussed in this book are designed to focus the beginning critic's attention on rhetorical messages as they exist within social and historical contexts. The complex of interactions that take place between a speaker and his or her audience is never easy to understand fully—indeed, *total* comprehension of any rhetorical exchange is not to be obtained. The critic, nevertheless, strives to come as close to the achievement of that goal as he or she can to contribute his or her mite to the ongoing work of other rhetorical scholars.

Becoming a critic involves the careful practice of a craft. The rhetorical critic "practices" in the sense that any professional does, through the continuous application of specialized knowledge to situations for which he or she is trained. The critic also "practices" in the sense that he or she works at the task in order to enhance proficiency. A rhetorical critic is perpetually a student, learning more about rhetorical theory, reading the great mass of recorded human discourse, studying and assessing the criticism of others, and immersing himself or herself in the social-political-historical milieu in which discourse takes place. Most importantly, however, a practicing rhetorical critic *does* criticism.

The first efforts at criticism will be modest. The critic needs to become familiar with and confident in the use of the data with which he or she habitually works and the tools that will enable the critic to analyze materials with thoroughness, interpret findings with clarity and imagination, and judge discourse with discrimination.

The aim of this book is to provide the beginning critic with a systematic way of undertaking the critical process. Basic to any critical system or methodological approach is the stipulation that the critic be prepared to investigate the texts, the contexts, and their interactions. The critics' proficiency will grow with increased experience and expanding knowledge, and will develop as they apply imaginative and disciplined efforts to understand rhetorical acts. A painter may break exciting new ground with his or her creative use of form, balance, color, or perspective; but form, balance, color, and perspective are fundamental concepts that the artist must understand in order to use them in a novel or arresting manner. The critic as artist must delve deeply into the components of the communication act, understanding the basic processes of inception, construction, presentation, and reception of rhetorical messages; only then may the critic's findings be communicated to others in a clear, reasoned, and insightful manner.

The questions presented as summaries in the preceding chapters offer a starting point from which to begin to do criticism. New questions or new ways of raising old questions will occur to the critic as he or she gains in maturity. The critic will soon realize that a single piece of criticism rarely answers all the questions; indeed, many questions will be irrelevant or of minor importance in certain cases. But, taken as a whole, they suggest a broad set of topics that are worthy of careful consideration.

The goal, of course, is to write good criticism. Good criticism is that which ultimately promotes a richer understanding of the influence and operation of discourse and contributes to the comprehension and refinement of humane values. Such goals are reached through the systematic and thorough investigation of relevant evidence, which leads to reasoned conclusions based on sound argument, and through the formulation of judgments based on clear, defensible criteria.

The best way to reach these goals is to undertake criticism seriously and to apply rigorous standards of scholarship to the undertaking. Practice will never make the critic perfect, but as we develop in our art we will grow in our own perceptiveness and in our appreciation of the ways in which human beings have sought to solve human problems; we may also contribute to the knowledge of the uniquely human process of communication and to the preservation of the highest standards of human conduct. Such a task is well worth undertaking.

Note

1. Herbert J. Muller, *The Uses of the Past* (New York: Mentor Books, 1954), p. 393.

Part II

A Case Study in Criticism

In 1968 Richard Nixon was elected President of the United States following a campaign in which America's involvement in Vietnam was a paramount issue. In the months following his inauguration pressure on President Nixon to solve the Vietnam problem continued to mount, and the protests that characterized the last years of the Johnson administration were unabated. President Nixon had publicly stated that protest would not influence his policy, but a national moratorium on the war held on October 15, 1969, secured intensive media coverage, and a second moratorium was scheduled for November 15. The President's speech on national television on November 3, 1969, was given extensive publicity prior to its delivery and was certainly one of the most important policy addresses of the decade.

This significant speech was studied by several prominent rhetorical critics. What follows is the text of President Nixon's speech and four critical studies of that speech. Also included is an exchange between two of the critics, Campbell and Hill. The speech and the critical responses can be read with great profit by novice or practicing critics. These essays demonstrate how different critics can approach the same speech from varying perspectives, with contrasting methodologies, and can reach differing critical judgments. The Campbell-Hill exchange is an excellent illustration of divergent views on the nature, function, and method of rhetorical criticism held by two distinguished rhetorical scholars.

Address to the Nation on the War in Vietnam, November 3, 1969

Richard M. Nixon

Good evening, my fellow Americans:

Tonight I want to talk to you on a subject of deep concern to all Americans and to many people in all parts of the world—the war in Vietnam.

I believe that one of the reasons for the deep division about Vietnam is that many Americans have lost confidence in what their Government has told them about our policy. The American people cannot and should not be asked to support a policy which involves the overriding issues of war and peace unless they know the truth about that policy.

Tonight, therefore, I would like to answer some of the questions that I know are on the minds of many of you listening to me.

How and why did America get involved in Vietnam in the first place?

How has this administration changed the policy of the previous administration?

What has really happened in the negotiations in Paris and on the battlefront in Vietnam?

What choices do we have if we are to end the war?

What are the prospects for peace?

Now, let me begin by describing the situation I found when I was inaugurated on January 20.

—The war had been going on for 4 years.

—31,000 Americans had been killed in action.

—The training program for the South Vietnamese was behind schedule.

—540,000 Americans were in Vietnam with no plans to reduce the number.

—No progress had been made at the negotiations in Paris and the United States had not put forth a comprehensive peace proposal.

—The war was causing deep division at home and criticism from many of our friends as well as our enemies abroad.

In view of these circumstances there were some who urged that I end the war at once by ordering the immediate withdrawal of all American forces.

From a political standpoint this would have been a popular and easy course to follow. After all, we became involved in the war while my predecessor was in office. I could blame the defeat which would be the result of my action on him and come out as the peacemaker. Some put it to me quite bluntly: This was the only way to avoid allowing Johnson's war to become Nixon's war.

But I had a greater obligation than to think only of the years of my administration and of the next election. I had to think of the effect of my decision on the next generation and on the future peace and freedom in America and in the world.

Let us all understand that the question before us is not whether some Americans are for peace and some Americans are against peace. The question at issue is not whether Johnson's war becomes Nixon's war.

The great question is: How can we win America's peace?

Well, let us turn now to the fundamental issue. Why and how did the United States become involved in Vietnam in the first place?

Fifteen years ago North Vietnam, with the logistical support of Communist China and the Soviet Union, launched a campaign to impose a Communist government on South Vietnam by instigating and supporting a revolution.

In response to the request of the Government of South Vietnam, President Eisenhower sent economic aid and military equipment to assist the people of South Vietnam in their efforts to prevent a Communist takeover. Seven years ago, President Kennedy sent 16,000 military personnel to Vietnam as combat advisers. Four years ago, President Johnson sent American combat forces to South Vietnam.

Now, many believe that President Johnson's decision to send American combat forces to South Vietnam was wrong. And many others—I among them—have been strongly critical of the way the war has been conducted.

But the question facing us today is: Now that we are in the war, what is the best way to end it?

In January I could only conclude that the precipitate withdrawal of American forces from Vietnam would be a disaster not only for South Vietnam but for the United States and for the cause of peace.

For the South Vietnamese, our precipitate withdrawal would inevitably allow the Communists to repeat the massacres which followed their takover in the North 15 years before.

—They then murdered more than 50,000 people and hundreds of thousands more died in slave labor camps.

—We saw a prelude of what would happen in South Vietnam when the Communists entered the city of the Hue last year. During their brief rule there, there was a bloody reign of terror in which 3,000 civilians were clubbed, shot to death, and buried in mass graves.

—With the sudden collapse of our support, these atrocities of Hue would become the nightmare of the entire nation—and particularly for the million and a half Catholic refugees who fled to South Vietnam when the Communists took over in the North.

For the United States, this first defeat in our Nation's history would result in a collapse of confidence in American leadership, not only in Asia but throughout the world.

Three American Presidents have recognized the great stakes involved in Vietnam and understood what had to be done.

In 1963, President Kennedy, with his characteristic eloquence and clarity, said: " . . . we want to see a stable government there, carrying on a struggle to maintain its national independence.

"We believe strongly in that. We are not going to withdraw from that effort. In my opinion, for us to withdraw from that effort would mean a collapse not only of South Vietnam, but Southeast Asia. So we are going to stay there."

President Eisenhower and President Johnson expressed the same conclusion during their terms of office.

For the future of peace, precipitate withdrawal would thus be a disaster of immense magnitude.

—A nation cannot remain great if it betrays its allies and lets down its friends.

—Our defeat and humiliation in South Vietnam without question would promote recklessness in the councils of those great powers who have not yet abandoned their goals of world conquest.

—This would spark violence wherever our commitments help maintain the peace— in the Middle East, in Berlin, eventually even in the Western Hemisphere.

Ultimately, this would cost more lives.

It would not bring peace; it would bring more war.

For these reasons, I rejected the recommendation that I should end the war by immediately withdrawing all of our forces. I chose instead to change American policy on both the negotiating front and battlefront.

In order to end a war fought on many fronts, I initiated a pursuit for peace on many fronts.

In a television speech on May 14, in a speech before the United Nations, and on a number of other occasions I set forth our peace proposals in great detail.

—We have offered the complete withdrawal of all outside forces within 1 year.

—We have proposed a cease-fire under international supervision.

—We have offered free elections under international supervision with the Communists participating in the organization and conduct of the elections as an organized political force. And the Saigon Government has pledged to accept the result of the elections.

We have not put forth our proposals on a take-it-or-leave-it basis. We have indicated that we are willing to discuss the proposals that have been put forth by the other side. We have declared that anything is negotiable except the right of the people of South Vietnam to determine their own future. At the Paris peace conference, Ambassador Lodge has demonstrated our flexibility and good faith in 40 public meetings.

Hanoi has refused even to discuss our proposals. They demand our unconditional acceptance of their terms, which are that we withdraw all American forces immediately and unconditionally and that we overthrow the Government of South Vietnam as we leave.

We have not limited our peace initiatives to public forums and public statements. I recognized, in January, that a long and bitter war like this usually cannot be settled in a public forum. That is why in addition to the public statements and negotiations I have explored every possible private avenue that might lead to a settlement.

Tonight I am taking the unprecedented step of disclosing to you some of our other initiatives for peace—initiatives we undertook privately and secretly because we thought we thereby might open a door which publicly would be closed.

I did not wait for my inauguration to begin my quest for peace.

—Soon after my election, through an individual who is directly in contact on a a personal basis with the leaders of North Vietnam, I made two private offers for a rapid, comprehensive settlement. Hanoi's replies called in effect for our surrender before negotiations.

—Since the Soviet Union furnishes most of the military equipment for North Vietnam, Secretary of State Rogers, my Assistant for National Security Affairs, Dr. Kissinger, Ambassador Lodge, and I, personally, have met on a number of occasions with representatives of the Soviet Government to enlist their assistance in getting meaningful negotiations started. In addition, we have had extended discussions directed toward that same end with representatives of other governments which have diplomatic relations with North Vietnam. None of these initiatives have to date produced results.

—In mid-July, I became convinced that it was necessary to make a major move to break the deadlock in the Paris talks. I spoke directly in this office, where I am now sitting, with an individual who had known Ho Chi Minh [President, Democratic Republic of Vietnam] on a personal basis for 25 years. Through him I sent a letter to Ho Chi Minh.

I did this outside of the usual diplomatic channels with the hope that with the necessity of making statements for propaganda removed, there might be constructive progress toward bringing the war to an end. Let me read from the letter to you now.

"Dear Mr. President:

"I realize that it is difficult to communicate meaningfully across the gulf of four years of war. But precisely because of this gulf, I wanted to take this opportunity to reaffirm in all solemnity my desire to work for a just peace. I deeply believe that the war in Vietnam has gone on too long and delay in bringing it to an end can benefit no one—least of all the people of Vietnam. . . .

"The time has come to move forward at the conference table toward an early resolution of this tragic war. You will find us forthcoming and open-minded in a common effort to bring the blessings of peace to the brave people of Vietnam. Let history record that at this critical juncture, both sides turned their face toward peace rather than toward conflict and war."

I received Ho Chi Minh's reply on August 30, 3 days before his death. It simply reiterated the public position North Vietnam had taken at Paris and flatly rejected my initative.

The full text of both letters is being released to the press.

—In addition to the public meetings that I have referred to, Ambassador Lodge has met with Vietnam's chief negotiator in Paris in 11 private sessions.

—We have taken other significant initiatives which must remain secret to keep open some channels of communication which may still prove to be productive.

But the effect of all the public, private, and secret negotiations which have been undertaken since the bombing halt a year ago and since this administration came into office on January 20, can be summed up in one sentence: No progress whatever has been made except agreement on the shape of the bargaining table.

Well now, who is at fault?

It has become clear that the obstacle in negotiating an end to the war is not the President of the United States. It is not the South Vietnamese Government.

The obstacle is the other side's absolute refusal to show the least willingness to join us in seeking a just peace. And it will not do so while it is convinced that all it has to do is to wait for our next concession, and our next concession after that one, until it gets everything it wants.

There can now be no longer any question that progress in negotiation depends only on Hanoi's deciding to negotiate, to negotiate seriously.

I realize that this report on our efforts on the diplomatic front is discouraging to the American people, but the American people are entitled to know the truth—

the bad news as well as the good news—where the lives of our young men are involved.

Now let me turn, however, to a more encouraging report on another front.

At the time we launched our search for peace I recognized we might not succeed in bringing an end to the war through negotiation. I, therefore, put into effect another plan to bring peace—a plan which will bring the war to an end regardless of what happens on the negotiating front.

It is in line with a major shift in U.S. foreign policy which I described in my press conference at Guam on July 25. Let me briefly explain what has been described as the Nixon Doctrine—a policy which not only will help end the war in Vietnam, but which is an essential element of our program to prevent future Vietnams.

We Americans are a do-it-yourself people. We are an impatient people. Instead of teaching someone else to do a job, we like to do it ourselves. And this trait has been carried over into our foreign policy.

In Korea and again in Vietnam, the United States furnished most of the money, most of the arms, and most of the men to help the people of those countries defend their freedom against Communist aggression.

Before any American troops were committed to Vietnam, a leader of another Asian country expressed this opinion to me when I was traveling in Asia as a private citizen. He said: "When you are trying to assist another nation defend its freedom, U.S. policy should be to help them fight the war but not to fight the war for them."

Well, in accordance with this wise counsel, I laid down in Guam three principles as guidelines for future American policy toward Asia:

—First, the United States will keep all of its treaty commitments.

—Second, we shall provide a shield if a nuclear power threatens the freedom of a nation allied with us or of a nation whose survival we consider vital to our security.

—Third, in cases involving other types of aggression, we shall furnish military and economic assistance when requested in accordance with our treaty commitments. But we shall look to the nation directly threatened to assume the primary responsibility of providing the manpower for its defense.

After I announced this policy, I found that the leaders of the Philippines, Thailand, Vietnam, South Korea, and other nations which might be threatened by Communist aggression, welcomed this new direction in American foreign policy.

The defense of freedom is everybody's business—not just America's business. And it is particularly the responsibility of the people whose freedom is threatened. In the previous administration, we Americanized the war in Vietnam. In this administration, we are Vietnamizing the search for peace.

The policy of the previous administration not only resulted in our assuming the primary responsibility for fighting the war, but even more significantly did not adequately stress the goal of strengthening the South Vietnamese so that they could defend themselves when we left.

The Vietnamization plan was launched following Secretary Laird's visit to Vietnam in March. Under the plan, I order first a substantial increase in the training and equipment of South Vietnamese forces.

In July, on my visit to Vietnam, I changed General Abrams' orders so that they were consistent with the objectives of our new policies. Under the new orders, the primary mission of our troops is to enable the South Vietnamese forces to assume the full responsibility for the security of South Vietnam.

Our air operations have been reduced by over 20 percent.

And now we have begun to see the results of this long overdue change in American policy in Vietnam.

—After 5 years of Americans going into Vietnam, we are finally bringing American men home. By December 15, over 60,000 men will have been withdrawn from South Vietnam—including 20 percent of all our combat forces.

—The South Vietnamese have continued to gain in strength. As a result they have been able to take over combat responsibilities from our American troops.

Two other significant developments have occurred since this administration took office.

—Enemy infiltration, infiltration which is essential if they are to launch a major attack, over the last 3 months is less than 20 percent of what it was over the same period last year.

—Most important—United States casualties have declined during the last 2 months to the lowest point in 3 years.

Let me now turn to our program for the future.

We have adopted a plan which we have worked out in cooperation with the South Vietnamese for the complete withdrawal of all U.S. combat ground forces, and their replacement by South Vietnamese forces on an orderly scheduled timetable. This withdrawal will be made from strength and not from weakness. As South Vietnamese forces become stronger, the rate of American withdrawal can become greater.

I have not and do not intend to announce the timetable for our program. And there are obvious reasons for this decision which I am sure you will understand. As I have indicated on several occasions, the rate of withdrawal will depend on developments on three fronts.

One of these is the progress which can be or might be made in the Paris talks. An anouncement of a fixed timetable for our withdrawal would completely remove any incentive for the enemy to negotiate an argreement. They would simply wait until our forces had withdrawn and then move in.

The other two factors on which we will base our withdrawal decisions are the level of enemy activity and the progress of the training programs of the South Vietnamese forces. And I am glad to be able to report tonight progress on both of these fronts has been greater than we anticipated when we started the program in June for withdrawal. As a result, our timetable for withdrawal is more optimistic now than when we made our first estimates in June. Now, this clearly demonstrates why it is not wise to be frozen in on a fixed timetable.

We must retain the flexibility to base each withdrawal decision on the situation as it is at that time rather than on estimates that are no longer valid.

Along with this optimistic estimate, I must—in all candor—leave one note of caution.

If the level of enemy activity significantly increases we might have to adjust our timetable accordingly.

However, I want the record to be completely clear on one point.

At the time of the bombing halt just a year ago, there was some confusion as to whether there was an understanding on the part of the enemy that if we stopped the bombing of North Vietnam they would stop the shelling of cities in South Vietnam. I want to be sure that there is no misunderstanding on the part of the enemy with regard to our withdrawal program.

We have noted the reduced level of infiltration, the reduction of our casualties, and are basing our withdrawal decisions partially on those factors.

If the level of infiltration or our casualties increase while we are trying to scale down the fighting, it will be the result of a conscious decision by the enemy.

Hanoi could make no greater mistake than to assume that an increase in violence will be to its advantage. If I conclude that increased enemy action jeopardizes our remaining forces in Vietnam, I shall not hestitate to take strong and effective measures to deal with that situation.

This is not a threat. This a statement of policy, which as Commander in Chief of our Armed Forces, I am making in meeting my responsibility for the protection of American fighting men wherever they may be.

My fellow Americans, I am sure you can recognize from what I have said that we really only have two choices open to us if we want to end this war.

—I can order an immediate, precipitate withdrawal of all Americans from Vietnam without regard to the effects of that action.

—Or we can persist in our search for a just peace through a negotiated settlement if possible, or through continued implementation of our plan for Vietnamization if necessary—a plan in which we will withdraw all of our forces from Vietnam on a schedule in accordance with our program, as the South Vietnamese become strong enough to defend their own freedom.

I have chosen this second course.

It is not the easy way.

It is the right way.

It is a plan which will end the war and serve the cause of peace—not just in Vietnam but in the Pacific and in the world.

In speaking of the consequences of a precipitate withdrawal, I mentioned that our allies would lose confidence in America.

Far more dangerous, we would lose confidence in ourselves. Oh, the immediate reaction would be a sense of relief that our men were coming home. But as we saw the consequences of what we had done, inevitable remorse and divisive recrimination would scar our spirit as a people.

We have faced other crises in our history and have become stronger by rejecting the easy way out and taking the right way in meeting our challenges. Our greatness as a nation has been our capacity to do what had to be done when we knew our course was right.

I recognize that some of my fellow citizens disagree with the plan for peace I have chosen. Honest and patriotic Americans have reached different conclusions as to how peace should be achieved.

In San Francisco a few weeks ago, I saw demonstrators carrying signs reading: "Lose in Vietnam, bring the boys home."

Well, one of the strengths of our free society is that any American has a right to reach that conclusion and to advocate that point of view. But as President of the

United States, I would be untrue to my oath of office if I allowed the policy of this Nation to be dictated by the minority who hold that point of view and who try to impose it on the Nation by mounting demonstrations in the street.

For almost 200 years, the policy of this Nation has been made under our Constitution by those leaders in the Congress and the White House elected by all of the people. If a vocal minority, however fervent its cause, prevails over reason and the will of the majority, this Nation has no future as a free society.

And now I would like to address a word, if I may, to the young people of this Nation who are particularly concerned, and I understand why they are concerned, about this war.

I respect your idealism.

I share your concern for peace.

I want peace as much as you do.

There are powerful personal reasons I want to end this war. This week I will have to sign 83 letters to mothers, fathers, wives, and loved ones of men who have given their lives for America in Vietnam. It is very little satisfaction to me that this is only one-third as many letters as I signed the first week in office. There is nothing I want more than to see the day come when I do not have to write any of those letters.

—I want to end the war to save the lives of those brave young men in Vietnam.

—But I want to end it in a way which will increase the chance that their younger brothers and their sons will not have to fight in some future Vietnam someplace in the world.

—And I want to end the war for another reason. I want to end it so that the energy and dedication of you, our young people, now too often directed into bitter hatred against those responsible for the war, can be turned to the great challenges of peace, a better life for all Americans, a better life for all people on this earth.

I have chosen a plan for peace. I believe it will succeed.

If it does succeed, what the critics say now won't matter. If it does not succeed, anything I say then won't matter.

I know it may not be fashionable to speak of patriotism or national destiny these days. But I feel it is appropriate to do so on this occasion.

Two hundred years ago this Nation was weak and poor. But even then, America was the hope of millions in the world. Today we have become the strongest and richest nation in the world. And the wheel of destiny has turned so that any hope the world has for the survival of peace and freedom will be determined by whether the American people have the moral stamina and the courage to meet the challenge of free world leadership.

Let historians not record that when America was the most powerful nation in the world we passed on the other side of the road and allowed the last hopes for peace and freedom of millions of people to be suffocated by the forces of totalitarianism.

And so tonight—to you, the great silent majority of my fellow Americans—I ask for your support.

I pledged in my campaign for the Presidency to end the war in a way that we could win the peace. I have initiated a plan of action which will enable me to keep that pledge.

The more support I can have from the American people, the sooner that pledge can be redeemed; for the more divided we are at home, the less likely the enemy is to negotiate at Paris.

Let us be united for peace. Let us also be united against defeat. Because let us understand: North Vietnam cannot defeat or humiliate the United States. Only Americans can do that.

Fifty years ago, in this room and at this very desk,[1] President Woodrow Wilson spoke words which caught the imagination of a war-weary world. He said: "This is the war to end war." His dream for peace after World War I was shattered on the hard realities of great power politics and Woodrow Wilson died a broken man.

Tonight I do not tell you that the war in Vietnam is the war to end wars. But I do say this: I have initiated a plan which will end this war in a way that will bring us closer to that great goal to which Woodrow Wilson and every American President in our history has been dedicated—the goal of a just and lasting peace.

As President I hold the responsibility for choosing the best path to that goal and then leading the Nation along it.

I pledge to you tonight that I shall meet this responsibility with all of the strength and wisdom I can command in accordance with your hopes, mindful of your concerns, sustained by your prayers.

Thank you and goodnight.

NOTE: The President spoke at 9:32 p.m. in his office at the White House. The address was broadcast on radio and television.

On November 3, 1969, the White House Press Office released an advance text of the address.

[1] Later research indicated that the desk had not been President Woodrow Wilson's as had long been assumed but was used by Vice President Henry Wilson during President Grant's administration.

Under the Veneer: Nixon's Vietnam Speech of November 3, 1969

Robert P. Newman

With the political honeymoon over, with his Congressional critics nipping at his heels and threatening full-scale attacks, and a major outpouring of antiwar sentiment probable on the October 15 Moratorium, Richard M. Nixon announced, on October 13, 1969, that he would make a major address about Vietnam November 3. The advance notice was unusually long for presidential addresses; the stakes in the burgeoning combat were unusually high. Vietnam had broken his predecessor, and Richard Nixon did not care to let himself in for the same treatment.

Part of the tension in October was due to the President's earlier incautious remark that he would not allow his program to be influenced by demonstrations in the streets. This gratuitous irritant to the peace forces guaranteed a massive turnout for the October 15 Moratorium, and it was partially to defuse the Moratorium that the President announced his speech so early. In this effort, the early announcement was perhaps successful; the size of the October 15 turnout remained impressive, but its tone was muted. All but the most violent of the protesters cushioned their stance with an anticipation that on November 3, when the President could speak without appearing to have yielded to pressure, he would announce major steps to end the war.

Even after the Moratorium, announcement of the coming address had its effect on the peace movement. From October 15 until Nixon spoke, plans for the November antiwar events were affected by anticipation of the Presidential speech. Had the prognosis for the November 3 speech been unfavorable, the peace forces would have strained every nerve to mount their greatest effort in mid-November But Presidential aides let it be known that Nixon had attended to the Moratorium, even though he did not approve it, and the Washington gossip mills were rife with predictions that, on November 3, the President would produce good news for peace. For two weeks, the doves relaxed. Perhaps, thought many, Nixon has really got the word, and the November push won't be necessary after all.

Every channel of public intelligence built up the significance of the November 3 effort. The President was known to be "almost totally preoccupied" with drafting the speech during the last two weeks of October.[1] Whether in the White House, at Camp David, or on the road, he was writing, revising, reflecting. The speech had to "convey an authentic note of personal involvement," rather than appear as a run-of-the-mill ghost-written production; and for this reason, all ten drafts were pristine Nixon. Ray Price, one of the President's top writers, had no idea what was in it: "I contributed nothing—not even a flourish."[2] Evans and Novak, executive-watchers of more than usual competence, noted on the day of the speech: "In stark contrast to his last major speech on Vietnam, almost six months ago, Mr. Nixon's talk tonight has been written by one hand alone—the President's hand."[3]

Buildup? On the night of November 3, Caesar himself could not have upstaged Richard Nixon.

In retrospect, expectations were so high that not even the Sermon on the Mount could have fulfilled them. The President had focused the spotlight so long and so carefully that only rhetorical perfection would have been equal to the occasion.

THE BACKGROUND

One of the first questions to be raised about a major address by Nixon, who for years was dogged with the nickname "Tricky Dick," would be "Is he sincere?" Nixon did not survive the political wars by the simple-minded morality of a country parson. He had scuttled Helen Gahagan Douglas, done in Alger Hiss, run interference for Eisenhower, fought Jack Kennedy to a virtual draw, and outlasted Barry Goldwater. He is a politician, which is to say that he has run a gauntlet the pa-

[1] Robert B. Semple, Jr., "Speech Took 10 Drafts, And President Wrote All," *The New York Times*, November 4, 1969, p. 17.

[2] *Ibid.*

[3] Rowland Evans and Robert Novak, "Nixon's Appeal for Unity," (Baltimore) *News-American*, November 3, 1969, p. 7B.

rameters of which are set, not by the Marquis of Queensberry, but by the necessities of survival.[4] From such an old pol, some temporizing might be expected.

When, therefore, he claimed, on November 3, to have a plan for peace, which he must unfortunately keep secret due to the perverseness of the enemy, some scepticism was expressed. Did he mean it? Did he really have a secret plan? Did he intend to close out the war, or was this just another maneuver to justify the same old business?

The reaction of the peace forces was largely predictable. Few were more blunt than Nixon's erstwhile nemesis, Senator Kennedy, as quoted by the *Times*:

> I do not wish to be harsh nor overly critical, but the time has come to say it: as a candidate, Richard Nixon promised us a plan for peace once elected; as chief executive, President Nixon promised us a plan for peace for the last 10 months. Last night he spoke again of a plan—a secret plan for peace sometime. There now must be doubt whether there is in existence any plan to extricate America from this war in the best interest of America—for it is no plan to say that what we do depends upon what Hanoi does.[5]

But when it comes to judging the President's sincerity, by all the canons of truth, Mansfield of Montana and Fulbright of Arkansas are superior judges. After five years of dealing with LBJ, they can be counted on to smell a fraud. Both want rapid withdrawal from Vietnam. Both have registered profound opposition to the course of the war. When, after conferences with the President, and caveats about the pace of withdrawal, they nonetheless acknowledge that the President does intend to get out, one must believe them. Both want withdrawal to be programmed independently of what Hanoi does, but both accept as genuine the President's wish to wind down the war.[6]

Were the testimony of the two leading Democratic Senators not conclusive, the ever-watchful White House press contingent, and the major liberal columnists, might be cited in their support. James Reston, whom I shall quote later on matters less favorable to Nixon's cause, regarded Nixon's sincerity as "almost terrifying."[7] And Richard Harwood and Laurence Stern of *The Washington Post* accept as true "that the President, a veteran of the Korean War Settlement, is intent on liquidating the American involvement in Vietnam under a veneer of tough talk."[8] The veneer is highly visible, for all to see; but under it is the intention of winding down the American part of the war in Vietnam. What he said, he meant.

But what is the shape of his commitment to withdrawal? Has he now, after all

---

[4] For a candid statement of the pressures operating on politicians, and the hard choices they make in the struggle for survival, see John F. Kennedy, *Profiles in Courage* (New York, 1956), ch. I.

[5] November 5, 1969, p. 10.

[6] Mansfield has generally been more sympathetic to the President's position than Fulbright; the Majority Leader joined Minority Leader Hugh Scott in sponsoring a resolution expressing qualified suport of the President on November 7. See UPI dispatch. "40 Senators Back Cease-Fire Plea," *The New York Times*, November 8, 1969, p. 10.

[7] "Nixon's Mystifying Clarifications," *The New York Times*, November 5, 1969, p. 46.

[8] "Polls Show the 'Silent Majority' Also Is Uneasy About War Policy," *The Washington Post*, November 5, 1969, p. A19.

these years of supporting the anticommunist effort in Indochina, decided that it was a mistake and that we *should* withdraw? Or is he merely bowing to political expediency, withdrawing because he can do no other and still retain power? An understanding both of his rhetoric and of his politics depends on answers to these questions.

There are those who maintain that the President is nonideological, a consummate politician and nothing more. This view is concisely expressed by Edwin Newman of NBC News: "But Mr. Nixon is as he is, and it is as well for him, and perhaps for the country, that he is so little ideological. He is neither embarrassed nor bound by having written in 1964 that the war in Vietnam was a life and death struggle in which victory was essential to the survival of freedom, and by having said in Saigon in April, 1967, that the great issue in 1968 would 'not be how to negotiate defeat but how to bring more pressure to bear for victory.' "[9]

There is indeed much evidence in Nixon's recent behavior to indicate that the anticommunist cold war ideology which he so powerfully embraced has now been modified: the SALT talks are underway with apparently serious intent; economic and travel restrictions applied to China for twenty years have been relaxed, and we are talking to the Chinese in Warsaw; germ warfare has been disavowed; and the military budget is, for the first time in years, on the way down. Does all this add up to a new Nixon, one who can willingly disengage from Vietnam?

Nixon's massive, sustained, vigorous hostility to Ho Chi Minh and his movement simply cannot be wiped out overnight. It was, after all, Nixon who as early as 1954 did his best to launch an American expeditionary force against Ho Chi Minh and in support of the French. On April 16, 1954, Nixon appeared for an off-the-record session before the American Society of Newspaper Editors, meeting in Washington, and said that "if France stopped fighting in Indo-China and the situation demanded it the United States would have to send troops to fight the Communists in that area."[10] This 1954 speech was the first sign that the battle to maintain a noncommunist government in Saigon, whether of French colonials or of French-trained Vietnamese generals, was precisely Richard Nixon's battle. And consistently since, with no exception until the campaign of 1968, he has supported that battle.

One must approach the Nixon rhetoric, then, entertaining the hypothesis that he is disengaging reluctantly, that his heart is not in it, that only the pressure of public opinion has caused him to embrace what he for fifteen years rejected. And one of the strong reasons for believing that the President does have a plan to phase out this war rapidly is the possibility that by late 1970 even the American Legion will be tired of fighting.

A second approach to understanding the President's speech lies in reflection on the various audiences to whom he was speaking.

There were at least three domestic audiences of consequence. First, his friends: the conservative Republicans who voted him into office and the Wallaceites he is now courting, largely a hawkish group, for whom he had the message, "Do not despair. I'm not heeding the demonstrators. We have to withdraw, but we don't

[9] "One Man Alone," *The New York Times Book Review*, November 23, 1969, p. 10.

[10] Luther A. Huston, "Asian Peril Cited; High Aide Says Troops May Be Sent if the French Withdraw," *The New York Times*, April 17, 1954, p. 1. Someone in Paris is alleged to have blown his cover, and Nixon was identified as the "High Aide" the next day. See also Bernard Fall, *Hell in a Very Small Place: The Siege of Dien Bien Phu* (New York, 1966), ch. IX.

have to give away a thing to the Viet Cong." Second, the "silent majority," some of whom had voted for him and some of whom had voted for Humphrey, many of them fence-straddlers on the war, all of them open, as Nixon saw it, to the plea, "I am winding down this war, but in a methodical and reasonable way which you ought to support." Third, the convinced doves, to whom he said, "Knock it off, I am the President, and disengaging from Vietnam is my bag. I respect your right to dissent, but don't carry it too far." In this latter group the youth, to whom he addressed a specific appeal, probably fit.

Abroad, he was concerned first with the South Vietnamese and other American client states: "We'll keep the faith, we won't desert you, and if the VC get tough again, we'll match them." There was also a clear word for Hanoi and other communist states: "You are going to have to come to terms with Thieu, or we will hang on forever; and if you escalate, the whole ball game is off."

One vital task of criticism is to decide which audience, and which message, was paramount. One is aided in making this decision by the recent publication of a startling book by a Nixon staffer, Kevin Phillips, an assistant to the Attorney General. In *The Emerging Republican Majority*,[11] Philips analyzes socioeconomic data to conclude that the white working-class voters who produced 9,906,473 votes for George Wallace in the last election can be turned into permanent Republicans. This can be done, says Phillips, by taking over the Wallace message (which rejects peacenik and Black demands) and peddling it with enough sophistication to retain the present registered Republican clientele. Since the consevative, middle-class sun belt cities are growing at the expense of the Democratic cities in the East, this combination will give the Republicians a permanent majority.

The President has not, obviously, endorsed the book; but it fairly represents the strategy with which he fought the last election, and no repudiation of Phillips has been forthcoming: he assisted Attorney General Mitchell until February 1970. And it was to precisely this group, the Wallaceites, that the "veneer of tough talk" was directed. Nixon's rhetorical strategy was thus influenced by a political strategy: placate the doves not at all, appeal to the patriotism of the silent majority, but above all, show the "lower-middle-class clerks in Queens, steelworkers in Youngstown, and retired police lieutenants in San Diego"[12] *that you are their champion.* This is the rhetoric of confrontation.

It is a rhetoric which the Nixon administration, up to now, has largely delegated to the Vice-President. Careful scrutiny of Nixon's text will provide support for the thesis that he sought confrontation. He made numerous references to humiliation, disaster, and defeat, all of which outcomes he projects on to his opponents; these are fighting words. They were incorporated in the speech against the better judgment of Henry Kissinger,[13] and, according to columnists Evans and Novak, against the advice of Republican leaders in Congress to "give the doves something": "Mr. Nixon rejected that advice because he consciously wanted to split off what he regards as a small minority of antiwar activists from his 'great silent majority' of

[11] (New Rochelle, 1969).
[12] The categories of Wallace supporters are those of Andrew Hacker in his sympathetic review of Phillips, "Is There a New Republican Majority?" *Commentary,* XLVIII (November 1969), 65–70.
[13] Robert B. Semple Jr., "Nixon's November 3 Speech: Why He Took the Gamble Alone," *The New York Times,* January 19, 1970, p. 23.

Americans. He was striving for a polarization of opinion isolating the dissenters and thereby dooming the extremist-led Nov. 15 march on Washington."[14]

This divide-and-isolate strategy was not dictated by the circumstances. The substance of President's plan could have been made palatable to many of his opponents. There were three crucial action programs: (1) avoid precipitate withdrawal; (2) keep the timetable secret; and (3) maintain a noncommunist government in Saigon. Given the division within the peace forces, who ranged from Friends to anarchists, he could easily have explained why the whole timetable could not be announced while announcing the next phase of withdrawal, which he did within six weeks anyway; he could have acknowledged the desirability of broadening the base of the Saigon government; and he could have put a higher priority on a cease fire. Had he done these things, he could have substantially alleviated the fears of many doves.

He not only failed to make these gestures of conciliation, he went far to agitate his opponents. He need not have injected the abrasive discussion of how the war started and how we got involved. He need not have talked as if all his opponents favored precipitate withdrawal. He need not have paraded before us again the controversial domino theory. He need not have done these things, that is, unless he had already decided to write off the dissenters and to start building his "emerging Republican majority" with Wallaceite support. But the decision was his. Anthony Lewis, Pulitzer Prize Winner of *The New York Times*, put it this way: "The puzzle is why he chose to speak as he did. He could so easily have expounded the same policy in less doom-laden rhetoric."[15]

THE ARGUMENT

There were, according to the President, five questions on the minds of his listeners.

"How and why did America get involved in Vietnam in the first place?

"How has this Administration changed the policy of the previous Administration?

"What has really happened in the negotiations in Paris and the battlefront in Vietnam?

"What choices do we have if we are to end the war?

"What are the prospects for peace?"[16]

After a brief description of the "situation I found when I was inaugurated on Jan. 20th," he turns to what he claims is the "fundamental issue," why and how did we become involved in the first place. This is a surprising candidate for priority in any discussion today. One might have thought that the burning question was how to get out. The President's chief foreign policy advisors, his allies on Capitol Hill, and the memorandum he got from the Cabinet bureaucracy all urged him to

---

[14] Rowland Evans and Robert Novak, "Nixon's Speech Wedded GOP Doves to Mass of Americans," *The Washington Post*, November 6, 1969, p. A23.

[15] Anthony Lewis, "The Test of American Greatness in Vietnam," *The New York Times*, November 8, 1969, p. 32.

[16] All quotations from the speech are from *The New York Times* text, carried November 4, 1969, p. 16.

skip discussions of the causes and manner of our involvement. Yet the history comes out with top billing. How and to what extent it is distorted is an interesting subject, but not our major concern here. This was a deliberative speech, and the President is arguing for a specific policy.

The substance of his policy argument, scattered throughout the speech, deals with four alternative plans for achieving disengagement. (The possibility of escalation is reserved as a club with which to scare the North Vietnamese into cooperating with Nixon's preferred plan for disengagement, but it is not offered as a full-fledged course of action in its own right).

First, the Presdient could "end the war at once by ordering the immediate withdrawal of all American forces. From a political standpoint, this would have been a popular and easy course to follow." But it is not Nixon's course; it is craven advice, and it draws his most concentrated fire.

It would, for one thing, constitute a defeat. Given Mr. Nixon's historic commitment to a noncommunist South Vietnam, and his visceral reaction to being bested by communists any time on any issue (as revealed in his autobiographical *Six Crises*)[17] it is not surprising that he makes much of this argument. Even though, as he claims, he could blame the defeat on his predecessor, this would not be an honorable course.

Whether acknowledging defeat in Vietnam would be a wise course is another matter. Mr Nixon's mentor, Eisenhower, recognized that, in the much more defensible war in Korea, we sustained a substantial defeat of MacArthur's objectives of rolling back the communists to the Yalu River. Most Americans seemed to approve a less-than-satisfactory settlement; avoidance of defeat did not then commend itself as the greatest good.

Similarly, in the abortive Bay of Pigs invasion, American-trained troops and American strategy suffered great humiliation. But, as Theodore Draper says of John F. Kennedy, "the President know how to end the misery, without deception or whimpering, in a way that made him seem to grow in defeat."[18] The trauma of defeat varies with the character of the captain, as de Gaulle proved once again in Algeria. But then Nixon is no Kennedy or de Gualle.

When one asks, "How can the anguish and terror of a loss in Vietnam be mitigated?" the answer has to be something other than the repeated stress on the necessity of avoiding defeat which we heard from President Nixon November 3. There is a case to be made for the honesty and therapeutic value of admitting that we were in over our heads, that we cannot police the whole world, that we really should not, as the military once told us, become involved in a ground war on the Asian continent.

Nixon does not reject immediate withdrawal solely on the basis of its intrinsic evil as a symbol of defeat. It would also lead to a train of undesirable consequences, all of which he ticks off as reasons for repudiating such a policy. It would damage the credibility of other American commitments; encourage communist aggressiveness everywhere; lead not only to the collapse of South Vietnam but all of Southeast Asia; result in horrendous massacres when the Viet Cong take over;

[17](Garden City, N.Y., 1962).
[18]*The Dominican Revolt* (New York, 1968).

and cause us to lose confidence in ourselves, with "inevitable remorse and divisive recrimination."

It might, indeed, do all of these things. These are consequences which need to be considered, *but they need to be considered only if immediate withdrawal is a serious alternative plan which the President needs to refute.* It is hard to see that it had such status. The sharpest challenge to his policy came from Senator Goodell and those who favored phased but definite withdrawal, with a specific deadline by which all American troops, or at least all combat troops, would be out. The call for immediate and total withdrawal came from a minority faction of the peace movement; and in rebutting it as if it were the most serious challenge to his preferred course, Nixon was drawing a red herring across the trail of his opponents, attacking a straw man whose demolition he could portray as destruction of the dissenters generally. This argumentative strategy seems to have succeeded with the silent majority; it festers and repels when one attends to his rhetoric carefully.

The second alternative plan for disengagement is negotiation. Mr Nixon holds open some slight hope that this might still be the road out; but after a long and frustrating year of meeting with the enemy in Paris, he does not put much faith in it. In this he is undoubtedly correct. North Vietnam has not now, and is not likely to acquire, any faith in negotiated agreements. For those who can remove the distorting lenses of national self-righteousness, which of course always reveal the other party as culprit in scuttling international agreements, the evidence points overwhelmingly to a justification of Hanoi's attitude.[19] But this need not concern us here. Aside from the debater's points Mr. Nixon makes by detailing the substance of U.S. negotiating proposals, and his claim that "Hanoi has refused even to discuss our proposals," this is a blind alley.

The third possible way to get out of Vietnam has the weightiest support behind it, both in the Senate and elsewhere; it is to withdraw steadily with a fixed terminal date. Here is the option upon which attention should have been focused. Here is the real challenge to presidential decision making. If the President were to reason with the most reasonable of his critics, he should have spent the bulk of his energies showing why this plan is disadvantageous compared to his; yet the emphasis it receives is minor.

The few swipes he takes at fixed-schedule withdrawal are instructive. "An announcement of a fixed timetable for our withdrawal would completely remove any incentive for the enemy to negotiate an agreement. They would simply wait until our forces had withdrawn and then move in." This attack is curious indeed. Have we not already written off the prospects for negotiation? Under what possible logic would the enemy be more likely to "wait until our forces had withdrawn and then move in" if they have a terminal point for that wait than if they do not? Is this not likely to happen whether the timetable is secret or public? Here is the core of the dispute between the President and his detractors, and he attends to it with a casual and obfuscating logic that defies belief.

The only other attack on the idea of a *terminus ad quem* for withdrawal is based on its alleged inflexibility; Mr. Nixon does not want to be "frozen in on a fixed timetable." One can accept that some flexibility in such an operation might

---

[19] Probably the best source on American violations of the Geneva Agreement on Vietnam is George M. Kabin and John W. Lewis, *The United States in Vietnam,* rev. ed. (New York, 1969).

be in order. This seems not to have deterred our officials from setting up, if not a rigid schedule, at least a terminal date for the accomplishment of other objectives. One must strain one's imagination somewhat to conceive Mr. Nixon incapable of extending a deadline for withdrawal in the face of Vietcong attacks which he defined as serious.

Here is the sum total of the President's refutation of the most serious challenge his program faces. It is hardly worth the candle.

So, finally, we come to alternative number four, the plan adopted and defended by the President. This scenario was worked up by Herman Kahn of the Hudson Institute. The July, 1968 *Foreign Affairs* carried an article by Kahn setting forth his plan for deescalation: build up Arvin, withdraw most American combat units, leave behind a reservoir of between 200,000 and 300,000 men to "deter a resumption of major hostilities."[20] This is now Nixon's plan, with the additional proviso that no long-range schedule be announced.

One needs, at this stage, to view the plan as a whole, inspecting the justifications for it, the reasons for preferring it to alternatives, the rhetoric in which it is clothed. A number of salient points need close scrutiny. As with any policy proposal, the payoff stage is the prediction of future consequences: how will the plan work?

Specifically, one needs to know whether it is probable that (1) the Vietcong and Hanoi will tolerate the presence of 450,000, 400,000, or 350,000 foreign troops while the hated Thieu regime attempts to develop combat effectiveness; (2) the Vietcong and Hanoi will beyond that tolerate the indefinite presence in the country of 250,000 or more occupation troops; (3) the shaky regime in Saigon will really develop political support and military muscle sufficient to keep the communists at bay; (4) the American public, including the great silent majority, the Emerging Republican Majority, and all the rest of us, will tolerate this kind of semipermanent occupation even if combat casualties drop to zero; and (5) there will be less right-wing recrimination should this plan fail than if there is a fast, clean withdrawal.

The President's defense on all these points deserves the closest inspection. We need, in a situation where Mr. Nixon admits "that many Americans have lost confidence in what their Government has told them about our policy," some indication of the evidence on which these assumed consequences are based, whether it be from the CIA, the military, the State Department, Sir Robert Thompson, or wherever. We need some assurance that the President is capable of what social psychologists call "tough-minded empathy," or the ability to see this plan as Hanoi sees it, and not just from the compulsively optimistic viewpoint of the Department of Defense.

There is nothing. The plan is there, take it or leave it. There is a warning to Hanoi to go along or else. There is a recognition that "some of my fellow citizens disagree" with the plan he has chosen. There is a rejection of demonstrations in the street, an appeal to the young people of the nation to turn their energies to constructive ends, a call for patriotism, a reference to Woodrow Wilson (at whose desk he spoke). In defense of his plan, there is only a contemptible rhetorical device, "My fellow Americans, I am sure you can recognize from what I have said that we really have only two choices open to us if we want to end this war. I can order an

[20] "If Negotiations Fail," XLVI, 627-641.

immediate precipitate withdrawal of all Americans from Vietnam without regard to the effects of that action. Or we can persist in our search for a just peace through . . . our plan for Vietnamization." Here it is, all over again, the false dilemma, the black or white position, the collapse of all alternative strategies into the one most offensive and easiest to ridicule. Only two choices: my plan, or the cut-and-run cowardice of the rioters in the streets.

It is, perhaps, a consummation to be expected of the politician who perfected the technique of "The Illusion of Proof."[21]

For the attentive public to accept the Nixon program of open-ended, no-deadline withdrawal, we have got to have answers which he does not provide. Literally dozens of his opponents have protested that he is giving Saigon the best excuse in the world for not broadening its base, for not coming to terms with the Buddhists and General Khanh, for not cracking down on corruption, for not accommodating to the demands of peasants in the countryside. As Reston put it, "For if his policy is to stick with the South Vietnamese until they demonstrate that they are secure, all they have to do is prolong their inefficiency in order to guarantee that we will stay in the battle indefinitely."[22] No defense of the President's plan could ignore the logic of this argument; yet ignore it is precisely what Mr. Nixon did.

CONSEQUENCES

The announcement that the President would speak about the war on November 3 had consequences in itself. The October Moratorium was weakened; an attitude of "let's wait and see" may have deterred many would-be doves from participating. But the significant consequences were of course after the speech.

The stock market, that sensitive barometer of America's morale and business health, dropped. At 10:30 on the morning of the 4th, prices were down 7.72 on the Dow-Jones industrial average. Stocks largely recovered later in the day, and closed mixed; but the people who handle the money clearly didn't think the President had pulled a coup.

One consequence of the speech, given Nixon's past debilitating relationship with the journalistic fraternity, was a serious lowering of his credibility. Reston put it this way: "The result is that the really important men reporting on the Presidency—not the columnists but the reporters and White House correspondents—are now wondering about the President after his Vietnam speech and his partisan reaction to the elections. He invited them to believe that he would not be like President Johnson, that he would be open and candid. But his approach and reaction to the elections have not been open and candid but personal and partisan. Like Johnson he has dealt with the politics of his problem but not with the problem of Vietnam."[23]

[21] See Barnet Baskerville, "The Illusion of Proof," *Western Speech*, XXV (Fall 1961), 236–242.
[22] James Reston, "Washington: The Unanswered Vietnam Questions," *The New York Times*, December 10, 1969, p. 54.
[23] James Reston, "Washington: The Elections and the War," *The New York Times*, November 7, 1969, p. 46.

The effects in Saigon were electric. As the *Times* headline read on November 10, "Nixon's Impact: Thieu is Helped Through a Tight Spot."[24] The National Assembly had been raising hell, a motion of no confidence was being discussed in the lower house, and a petition calling for a nationwide referendum was being circulated. Nixon stopped all this. His reaffirmed commitment to stay until there was no more challenge to "freedom" strengthened Thieu's hand immeasurably. Not being one to bite the hand that upholds him, Thieu recorded his gratitude for the press: this was "one of the most important and greatest" speeches made by an American President.[25]

The three domestic audiences identified at the beginning of this essay reacted predictably. Nixon's supporters, the hawks and the Emerging Republican Majority, were delighted. Columnist Joseph Alsop rejoiced hugely: "Whether you agree or disagree with its content, this remarkable speech was one of the most successful technical feats of political leadership in many, many years."[26]

The silent majority was impressed. Gallup, who clocked them in by telephone immediately after the speech, found 77% approving. And in his regular survey of presidential performance, taken November 14-16, approval of the President generally rose 12% over the previous month, to a high of 68%.[27] Although as Gallup noted, there was some question as to the durability of this result, the speech did sell; the "terrifying sincerity" was just what the public wanted to see. But the long pull is yet ahead.

The doves were horror-struck. There had been much reason to believe that the speech would be conciliatory, that the rhetoric would be encouraging. One consequence of the toughness of the speech was that registrations for buses to Washington for the November 13-15 events flooded in;[28] and the ultimate crowd in Washington could be said to be a direct result of Nixon's challenge to the dissidents. The effete ones were not going to take it lying down.

The candid conclusion must be that the President cheered his friends and disheartened his enemies. The peace movement is in disarray, planning no more massive marches, resigned to campus and campaign activities—until the President slips, or Hanoi trips him. As of the end of December, Richard Starnes of Scripps-Howard put it succinctly: "Peace Marchers Give Round to Nixon."[29]

EPILOGUE

The Nixon style in this speech has been characterized as "tough talk." But this is not the same as saying it was rough; Nixon did preserve the amenities. As Reston put it, "He put Spiro Agnew's confrontation language into the binding of a hymn

[24] Terence Smith, *The New York Times,* November 10, 1969, p. 2.

[25] Terence Smith, "Thieu Hails the Speech: 'One of the Most Important,'" *The New York Times,* November 5, 1969, p. 10.

[26] Joseph Alsop, "Nixon Leadership is Underestimated," *The Washington Post,* December 29, 1969, p. A13.

[27] George Gallup, "Nixon Support Soars to 68%," *The Washington Post*, November 24, 1969, p. A1.

[28] David E. Rosenbaum, "Thousands Due in Capital In War Protest This Week," *The New York Times,* November 9, 1969, pp. 1, 56.

[29] *The Pittsburgh Press*, December 26, 1969, p. 15.

book."[30] But hymn books are not the only score from which the Administration sings. The cruder, more abrasive tunes are coming steadily from the Vice-President; and it is worth inquiring as to whether the Nixon tune must be heard against the accompaniment of his second in command.

The arguments that have raged in Washington as to whether the Vice-President plays the role of hatchet man to Nixon's above-the-battle dignity just as Nixon was once the hatchet man for Eisenhower, has now largely been resolved. Agnew comes up with his own script. His purple-passioned prose is indigenous, and with the exception of his November 13 blast against the television networks, which according to Clark Mollenhoff "was developed in the White House,"[31] the ideas as well as the language are his.

But even when he is doing his own thing, Mr. Agnew represents the President's true gut feelings.[32] The relationship is one of willing supporter, not ventriloquist's dummy. If Agnew were not around to ventilate the President's pique, someone else would have to be commandeered to put out the purple-passioned prose. The President himself, of course, could do it very well; the summer of 1969 he reverted to a former style with his colorful speeches at General Beadle State College and the Air Force Academy; but the reaction to these by the President's staff was less than enthusiastic, and he has since then turned over the rough talk to the Vice-President.

What we have, then, in the President's speech, is the substance of toughness without the rough style. And the President's text is indeed sanitized. What he might have said, what his style would have been were he not consciously trying to retain the old Republican genteel clientele, one can discover by reading Agnew. The visceral language, the blunt insults, the uncompromising hostilities are missing.[33]

But a presidential address must meet higher standards than campaign oratory or the speeches of lesser figures. Nixon's speech did not meet them. Neither his rhetorical strategies nor his substantive argument were sound. Yet the most likely time for healing and realistic rhetoric has passed. The President's personal involvement in Government decisions will grow, his commitment to what we are doing now will increase, his access to noncongruent intelligence will decrease, the youth will become more alienated. Nixon is not LBJ, and the total closing of filters that occurred in the last days of the Johnson Administration probably will not happen again; but the prospect for improvement is slight. One can always hope that another Clark Clifford is waiting in the wings to restore sanity, or another Eugene McCarthy will appear in the hustings to startle a self-deluded establishment.

A fitting summary of the whole business is provided by Anthony Lewis:

> The preeminent task of Richard Nixon's Presidency is to heal a nation torn apart by Vietnam. The President knew that when he took the oath of office, and it is no less urgently true today. Part of the process must be to

---

[30] James Reston, November 5, 1969.

[31] E. W. Kenworthy, "Nixon Aide Says Agnew Stand Reflects White House TV View," *The New York Times,* November 16, 1969, p. 78.

[32] Robert B. Semple, Jr., "Agnew: The Evidence is That He's Speaking for Nixon," *The New York Times,* November 2, 1969, Sec. 4, p. 3.

[33] But the old debator's syndrome is very much present. A good capsule description of what this means is in Earl Mazo and Stephen Hess, *Nixon: A Political Portrait* (New York, 1968), p. 7.

help the American people know, and accept, the unpleasant truths about the war: that we got into it by stealth and for reasons at best uncertain; that the Government we defend in South Vietnam is corrupt and unrepresentative; that in the course of fighting we have killed people and ravaged a country to an extent utterly out of proportion to our cause, and that, in the old sense of dictating to the enemy, we cannot "win." In those terms, Mr. Nixon's speech to the nation last Monday evening was a political tragedy.[34]

It was not just the speech that was a political tragedy; the speech merely made visible tragic policy decisions—to maintain the goals and propaganda of the cold war, to seek confrontation with those who want change, to go with a power base confined to white, nonurban, uptight voters. Given such decisions, the shoddy rhetoric, the tough talk, the false dilemmas are inevitable. Instant criticism, via the networks, while desirable, cannot begin to do justice to such policies and such rhetoric. They require more searching exploration. As the saying goes, presidential rhetoric is much too important to be left to presidents.

[34] *The New York Times*, November 8, 1969. p. 32.

The Quest Story and Nixon's November 3, 1969 Address

—————————————————————— *Hermann G. Stelzner*

The Quest story is a literary genre in which the subjective experiences of life are central. The themes in such stories vary, but the genre is one of the oldest, hardiest, and most popular. Perhaps its persistent appeal is due to "its validity as a symbolic description of our subjective personal experience of existence as historical."[1] The Quest story describes a search for "something" the truth or falsity of which is known only upon the conclusion of the search.

Although the themes and the details change, the form or "the fixity" of Quest stories is fairly stable,[2] one reason why the Quest story is archetypal. When the essential elements of the story interact with the subjective experiences of individuals verbal transactions occur. Occasionally universal human reactions are elicited.

The practical world of political affairs shares many themes with the imaginative world of fiction. When a leader of a body politic and his people seek to resolve a problem, they may be engaged in a Quest. A leader speaks and orders a

[1] W. H. Auden, "The Quest Hero," *Texas Quarterly,* IV (Winter 1961), 82. This analysis borrows much from Auden. The essential elements of the Quest story are Auden's, slightly modified. General accounts of the Quest story and archetypal patterns can be found in numerous works. Maud Bodkin's *Archetypal Patterns in Poetry* (London, 1934) and Northrop Frye's *Anatomy of Criticism* (Princeton, 1957) and *Fables of Identity* (New York, 1963) are indispensable to a study of the method.

[2] Wayne Shumaker, *Literature and the Irrational* (Englewood Cliffs, N.J., 1960), p. 135.

reality, a form; he offers an *objective* experience of the social, political, or moral life. However, to become viable it must interact with the *subjective* experiences of his listeners. If a given problem, war and peace, for example, occurs frequently enough, perhaps a close examination of all such speeches might yield an archetypal pattern. Thus far, however, the rhetorical criticism of speeches has not proceeded from this perspective. This exploratory effort centers on a single speech.

When President Richard M. Nixon spoke to the nation on November 3, 1969 about the war in Vietnam he indicated how central it was to him, his Administration, and his people: "I did not wait for my inauguration to begin my quest for peace."[3] The connotations of "quest" and Nixon's strong, personal identification with it—"my," not *our* or *the,* convey an orientation and a potential pattern of behavior that suggest that this speech and the archetypal Quest story share similarities.[4] To place the speech within the genre of the Quest story is merely to classify it. But the essential elements of the Quest story may then provide a way into the speech, and they may yield insights that other critical approaches do not obtain. The critical prism refracts light differently as a function of the way it is turned. The light refracted from this angle may be a different "color" from that obtained from some other facet of the prism.[5] Finally, the objective political experience of Vietnam structured by President Nixon and the listeners' subjective experiences of life should interact. What in the chosen and arranged language of the speech increases the probability of a verbal transaction? What goes on in the speech?

The five essential elements of a Quest story are stated here and developed below. These elements also function as a rhetorical partition, providing terms for the analysis and forcing the parts of the analysis to comment on one another. The essential elements are (1) a precious Object and/or Person to be found and possessed or married; (2) a long journey to find the Object, because its whereabouts are not originally known to the seekers; (3) a Hero; (4) the Guardians of the Object who must be overcome before it can be won; and (5) the Helpers who with their knowledge and/or magical powers assist the Hero and but for whom he would never succeed.

1. *A precious Object and/or Person to be found and possessed or married.* Because the conflict in Vietnam was central in the political scene Nixon inherited on his inauguration, he sketches its background in swift, broad strokes; it serves as a refresher for listeners and as a point of departure. He advances five questions that preview the direction his remarks will take: (1) "How and why did America get involved in Vietnam in the first place?" He terms it the "fundamental issue." (2) "How has this Administration changed the policy of the previous Administra-

---

[3] The text for this analysis is found in *Vital Speeches,* XXXVI (November 15, 1969), 66–70. Each paragraph of the text was numbered, 1–125. Thus this statement appears in paragraph 41 of the text.

[4] This speech is the product of Nixon's mind and hand. He "solicited ideas from his large corps of speechwriters but did not order drafts from them . . . or otherwise use their literary talents." The speech went "through 10 drafts, all written by the President himself." Nixon felt the address "must convey an authentic note of personal involvement. He clearly felt that the speech would not carry such a message if someone else wrote it." These descriptions suggest other dimensions of a "quest." Robert B. Semple, Jr., "Speech Took 10 Drafts, and President Wrote All," *The New York Times,* November 4, 1969, p. 17.

[5] For example, see Robert P. Newman, "Under the Veneer: Nixon's Vietnam Speech of November 3, 1969," *QJS,* LVI (April 1970), 168–178.

tion?" Centering on this question allows Nixon to capitalize on the public frustration with the Johnson approach and to avoid any serious consideration of the "fundamental issue." (3) "What has really happened in the negotiations in Paris and the battlefront in Vietnam?" Nixon's reports are scattered throughout the speech. (4) "What choices do we have if we are to end the war?" This is a central question but Nixon examines only two choices. (5) "What are the prospects for peace?"

Nixon does not make the precious Object immediately clear, withholding its precise nature and character. Instead he alludes to the October 15, 1969 Moratorium and comments briskly and adversely on a peace proposal endorsed by its leaders. Intending to unveil a new view, he weakens the old before announcing it, thus avoiding a direct conflict.

Nixon early makes clear that whatever the policy, it will be influenced by the long view of the national and international scene. He refers obliquely to the young, telling the Now and In generation they must yield to his "greater obligation" to think of the "next generation" and of the "future of peace and freedom in America and in the world." The view is global. Nixon's treatment of time and the next generation suggests that stability and settledness will emerge from the as yet undisclosed precious Object.

But Nixon's statements are not altogether consistent. He appears troubled as he searches for a view that will be acceptable to an anxious audience at home and to the international audience as well:[6] "I had to think of the effect of my decision on the next generation, and on the future of peace and freedom in America and in the world." Three sentences later he offers a view that restricts, if it does not altogether compromise, the breadth of his concern: "The great question is: How can we win America's peace?" If this is indeed the *great question*, what has happened to the world? Has there been a shift in perspective? A possible explanation for these contradictory emphases must be hazarded.

The first statement is not only global; it also emphasizes future time. The second statement is restricted and time is not specifically mentioned. Measured against the first statement the second suggests being accomplished in a shorter time. The second statement springs out of Nixon's need to recognize early emotional stresses and divisiveness at home. It suggests that they can be resolved sooner than later. The long war has often been justified as an international obligation. The national patience has worn thin. Nixon offers something to quiet the impatience. He centers on and satisfies self.

The prized Object is finally announced. It is a "just peace," a "just and lasting peace." Nixon makes clear that the peace his opponents seek cannot be prized. Their method of achieving it and the effects of it tarnish the Object. A just peace is more valuable than a pragmatic peace because it lies beyond men and the moment; it transcends both. Here, of course, is the higher peace of an Upper World and such an Object is potentially persuasive when the opponents in South Vietnam, the Communist North Vietnamese supported by Communist China and the Soviet Union, represent the demonic powers of a Lower World.

---

[6]General Ky of South Vietnam is reported to have said before the speech was delivered that it would be addressed to the American audience. See James Reston, "Nixon's Mystifying Clarifications," *The New York Times,* November 5, 1969, p. 46.

Further, if America achieves only an immediate peace, which Nixon defines as the "popular and easy course," she will not have set a goal worthy enough to meet the requirements of a "lasting peace," which concerns "many people in all parts of the world." Peace in Vietnam is not enough; peace in Vietnam must serve the "cause of peace . . . in the Pacific and the world." The prized Object has been located and defined.

2. *A long journey to find the Object, because its whereabouts are not originally known to the seekers.* The journey takes place in both time and space. For the United States it began "fifteen years ago" when North Vietnam "launched a campaign to impose a Communist government on South Vietnam." Nixon quickly summarizes the actions taken by Presidents Eisenhower, Kennedy, and Johnson who sent men and materials into the conflict.

Time is central in Nixon's analysis. It is partially because the war has been "long and bitter" that he rejects the policy of immediate withdrawal. His many references to its proponents are his open acknowledgment of their strength, but he is certain that a lengthy, bitter military and psychological effort cannot simply stop.

The fifteen long years also condition the peace he will accept. His opposition seeks a pragmatic peace. But the time already spent and still to be spent in the search will further dignify the Object. Nixon makes a "just peace" and an "immediate peace" via withdrawal into antithetical images, a timeless value versus a momentary value; the former has weight, the latter is weightless and ephemeral.

The search for a weightless ephemeral Object cannot be rewarding; it is a journey into Nowhere, a journey "to the end of the night," and the effect would be chaos, Nixon claims. He acknowledges his journey is into a "dangerous" Unknown. But in contrast to the gesture or policy of despair his opponents offer (Nixon resists calling it suicide), his policy has *significant form.* A policy of despair always lacks a reliable and objective narrator. Nixon stresses that the young are idealistic; idealism is antithetical to objectivity and reliability.

However valuable a "just peace" may be, Nixon understands that it must not appear to be beyond reach. Time is both a physical measure and a psychological state, and he senses that to satisfy his listeners he must make the timeless future somehow concrete and reasonably immediate. He announces some of the gains his approach has achieved: "Now we have begun to see the results of this long-overdue change in American policy in Vietnam." The results indicate that both the war and the battle with time can be won.

3. *A Hero.* The precious Object cannot be won by anybody, but only by the one person who possesses the right qualifications of breeding and character. Further, the Quest story presents a Test or a series of Tests by which the unworthy are screened out, and the Hero revealed.

There are two types of Quest Hero. The first has a superior arete manifest to all. No one doubts that he can win the Golden Fleece if anyone can. The second has a concealed arete. He turns out to be the Hero when his manifest betters have failed. His zeal is plodding and pedestrian. He enlists help because unlike his betters he is humble enough to take advice and kind enough to give assistance to people who, like himself, appear to be nobody in particular.

Hero images often appear in public addresses, and they are symbolic. In Nixon's speech both types of Hero appear and his portrayals of them build support for himself and his policy. The Heroes are structured in polar terms, but because they faced a common problem, Vietnam, the polarities are not in direct moral or ethical conflict. The portrayal is not developed as good-bad, strong-weak, right-wrong, but as practical-impractical, workable-unworkable, or feasible-unfeasible. For example, Nixon acknowledges that "many believe that President Johnson's decision to send American combat forces to South Vietnam was wrong." Nixon supports the decision, but observes: "And many others, I among them, have been strongly critical of the way the war has been conducted." His criticism of Woodrow Wilson also centers on practicality, workability, and feasibility.

Early in the speech Nixon reports on the efforts of Presidents Eisenhower, Kennedy, and Johnson to achieve success in Vietnam. Immediately following the factual citations, Nixon employs Kennedy for support and refers to him in a special way. About one aspect of American policy, Kennedy spoke, Nixon states, with "characteristic eloquence and clarity," and these are attributes of men of superior arete.

If Kennedy, a Hero of superior arete, appears early in the speech, not until it is almost concluded does Nixon place another figure who is similarly described. Woodrow Wilson, says Nixon, had a "dream for peace." And he "spoke words which caught the imagination of a war-weary world . . . : 'This is the war to end wars'." Heroes of superior arete can express the affairs of state in apocalyptic terms. They have an imaginative conception of the whole of nature.

These two Heroes are much alike in another way. Kennedy died a tragic death while in office. Listeners need not be reminded. Wilson did not die in office, but Nixon says that he "died a broken man," and he stresses that Wilson's "dream" was "shattered on the hard reality of great power politics." These two examples remind listeners that the leadership offered by visionary Heroes may result in a "tragic fall" if an idealized goal cannot be achieved.

About his policy and himself, Nixon is emphatic; he does not offer a vision beyond his ability to produce: "I do not tell you that the war in Vietnam is the war to end wars." He hopes only to "increase the chance that . . . younger brothers and . . . sons" of the men in Vietnam "will not have to fight in some future Vietnam some place in the world."

Nixon knows that he is not a Kennedy or a Wilson, but he does not disassociate himself completely from them. He reports that he, too, is a statesman, aspiring to the title of peacemaker in the world. How? He tells listeners he speaks from the room, "in this room" where Wilson spoke about the "war to end wars." He tells them about Wilson's desk, "at this very desk" Wilson spoke. The desk is in the room and via television in the presence of listeners. Nixon has kept it and apparently works at it. A moral value is not only expressed; it is also displayed.

Nixon also emphasizes the kind of Hero he is by not taking advantage of a fallen Hero, his predecessor. If he supported immediate withdrawal, it would bring defeat, but he could "blame" it on Johnson and "come out as the peacemaker." To achieve peace at another's expense is a low form of honor. Nixon knows that many citizens mistrust Johnson, whose fall is partially explained in moral terms. More than a few citizens believe Johnson capable of the very action Nixon rejects as unworthy of a man of stature. He puts distance between himself and Johnson.

Nixon also equates many of the dissenting young people with the first type of

Hero. He delivered this speech two weeks after the first Moratorium (October 15, 1969).[7] Another demonstration was planned for November. Nixon announced his speech far in advance (on October 13, 1969), strategically placing it between the two convocations. That the Moratorium was an eloquent and dramatic statement-act is a value judgment. That it was largely an expression by the young is fact.

That Nixon equates the young with the first type of Hero is clear from evidence in the address. He states that "some" people urged him to order "the immediate withdrawal of all American forces." In Quest stories Heroes of superior arete often ride straight up the golden path to win the prized Object. Nixon alludes to such activity; immediate withdrawal means "without regard to the effects of that action." Further, to ride straight up the path wins the applause of the multitude; it would have been a "popular . . . course to follow." Nixon acknowledges that the young have "energy and dedication." He also respects their "idealism," a term he specifically reserves for the young.

Nixon and his supporters are the second type of Hero. In 1960 he had jousted with a Hero of the first type, was defeated, and hovered near political death. Patiently and industriously he brought himself back to political health. He and his policy for Vietnam are counterbalances to the first type of Hero. Whatever is done must not risk death—political or any other kind. Withdrawal from Vietnam means "collapse" in all "Southeast Asia." Immediate withdrawal, equated with "defeat," would result in a "collapse of confidence" in America's leadership "not only in Asia but throughout the world." Our collapse would "promote recklessness" and "spark violence" which ultimately would "cost more lives"—more death. An idealistic policy, Nixon suggests, might create a Hell on Earth.

It is interesting to compare Nixon's personal political fortunes with those he has described for the state if the wrong course is chosen. Defeat in 1960 did not mean total collapse for him. Defeat again in California in 1962 did not mean total collapse. Affairs in the world of individual men are reversible. In affairs of state they are not. Or is it that the Hero who has suffered, and understands what to suffer means, wishes to protect his people from the agonies he has personally experienced? He must also know full well that if the nation emerges from Vietnam suffering as he has personally suffered, his place in the history books (the annals of the time) will be dimmed.

Nixon's policy for Vietnam is disciplined, cautious, and pragmatic. He will not go straight up the path. He has provided for options. Realizing that peace might not be achieved "through negotiation" he had ready "another plan." He will work earnestly; even before his inauguration he began his quest. For Nixon peace is not a vision. It is a "concern" and a "goal." Consistent with the type of Hero he is, he asks to be judged by the cumulative effects of his labors, not by the moral intensity of his strivings.

If Nixon's policy is disciplined, cautious, and pragmatic, the language that

[7]Unnamed associates of Nixon offer a different interpretation for the timing of the speech. They say that the President had decided as early as August 1969 to give the country an accounting of the war and that he wanted to key "such an accounting . . . to the first anniversary of the bombing halt in early November." Further, in "the words of one high source," early announcement was necessary to "give Hanoi fair warning and a chance to turn around in Paris." Robert B. Semple, Jr., "Nixon's Nov. 3 Speech: Why He Took the Gamble Alone," *The New York Times,* January 19, 1970, p. 23.

displays it is hard, rigid, and barren. Word choices are both familiar and unpretentious. Images are absent; the texture is flat.

Noticeably lacking are Biblical images. Yet the speech is directed largely to a silent majority, the generations nurtured on war and Biblical imagery. However, this is a secular war and God does not explicitly support our policy; nor is He explicitly on our side. Three rhetorical considerations explain the absence of such imagery. First, this speech is not so much a war message as it is a message about a war. Second, Vietnam is a small war that Presidents Eisenhower, Kennedy, and Johnson sought to localize and restrain. Nixon, too, aims to deflate it. Biblical images have magnitude, scope, and thrust. Thus, on both logical and aesthetic grounds they are simply "too large" for the problem. Third, Biblical images connote ethical and moral values. Keeping the war secular, and justifying it with political, military, and economic values, deprives the opposition of a potential issue. Further, Nixon does not give the silent majority an opportunity to consciously consider if the Biblical imagery and the Vietnam war are consistent. He avoids constructing for them a potentially disturbing dilemma.

Either type of Hero-president can use the power of the Office to further policies. Nixon reports on many of his efforts. He sent emissaries across the water (another part of the long journey) to the symbolic capital of the civilized—and thus safe—world, Paris, to meet with the North Vietnamese. He himself crossed the water to inspect the unsafe world and to receive firsthand reports about our efforts to stabilize it, a dimension of civilization. Then from Guam, that piece of secure United States territory nearest the conflict, he intoned from afar a shift in foreign policy. The policy is given a potentially potent name, Vietnamization. The phonetic similarities between Vietnamization and Americanization suggest our continued influence and concern. He also announces that other "significant initiatives which must remain secret to keep open some channels of communications" are in progress. Further, he sends a letter to Ho Chi Minh through an unnamed representative who had known Minh personally for 25 years; a dimension of intrigue is added to the effort. In some reports there are signs of hope. Nixon refers to the "deadlock" in negotiations, but perhaps new energies will come from this tired metaphor. He refers to the letter he received from Ho Chi Minh, "three days before his death." The letter says nothing new, but may not its writer's death be read as a hopeful harbinger of some new movement? Of what significance is the report of Minh's death, if not that? In deadlock and in death itself is the potential for rebirth.

Nixon's policy, language, and behavior reveal him as a Hero whose omnipotence and omniscience are limited.

4. *The Guardians of the Object who must be overcome before it can be won.* They may simply be a further test of the Hero's arete, or they may be malignant in themselves.

That the government of North Vietnam is both different from and in opposition to the United States is understood. In the popular mind, North Vietnam is malignant simply because it is communist; external motives are neither necessary to its behavior nor can they ever fully explain its behavior. Nixon does nothing to soften that view. Rather he emphasizes and develops it. An evil government will instigate and support revolutions: in the time past, in the present time, and in the future. Nixon's language is extremely severe: "murdered," "thousands . . . died in slave labor camps," "civilians were clubbed, shot, . . . and buried in mass graves," "a bloody reign of terror," and a "nightmare" in South Vietnam describe the North Vietnamese activities; the government is presented as being much worse than an undeveloped version of ourselves. Surely in an address about a war the image of the dual experience, a contest between two sides, friends and enemies, is expected. Nixon emphasizes animality and bestiality.

But the North Vietnamese also present further tests to the Hero and the American people. Nixon details the proposals the United States has advanced. We will work in common and will be openminded. Except for the right of the people of South Vietnam to determine their own future "anything is negotiable." Again and again Nixon remarks on the responses to such proposals. Hanoi has "refused even to discuss our proposals." In Paris a "deadlock" developed. Further negotiation "depends only on Hanoi's deciding to negotiate." The silent, uninvolved, non-participating North Vietnamese made success difficult. Nixon's tone is objective. But to stress his personal exasperation, he concludes with a folksy idiom consistent with his common-sense observation: "Well, now, who's at fault?"

A war message and the Quest story share the presupposition that one side is good, the other bad. But our *objective experience* of social and political life informs us otherwise. The moral ambiguities of political conflicts do not adhere to the proposition. But in war, men stereotype, reserving the good for their side and the bad for their opponents. And any virtues an enemy may possess are ignored.[8]

5. *The Helpers who with their knowledge and/or magical powers assist the Hero and but for whom he would never succeed.* Ideally, all citizens in a democracy will be Helpers, but in a "free society" dissent is recognized and tolerated. However, if dissenters take to the streets they might bind a president and circumscribe his options. In such a situation, what may be of greater danger than a dissenting Chorus is a confused, perplexed, and silent Chorus. To a Hero in need of support a formless and mute Chorus presents problems. How does a Hero-president "divine" what a silent majority will hear? Although Nixon can neither see it nor hear it, he has personal resources. His private vision furnishes him direction.

The rhetorical strategy emerges slowly and develops late. The approach to silent America is through young America, or for purposes of a rhetorical antithesis "shrill America." The young have been described. They are fervent, vocal, idealistic, energetic, and dedicated. These are positive virtues. Nixon counters them with a single negative particular that explains how the young have gone wrong. The positive virtues have been turned "into bitter hatred." Bitter hatred is irrational. It is, Nixon suggests, the tragic flaw in the character of the young.

If a democracy tolerates dissent and if men of station and experience have something to say to those (the young) who have achieved less, it is reasonable to assume that the young will attend to the President. It is also reasonable to assume that the President may speak directly to any audience. Yet when Nixon addresses the young, he casts doubt on these assumptions. He asks permission: "I would like to address a

---

[8]Nixon's descriptions of the North Vietnamese are consistent with this observation. He does express emotion apart from intellect and there is a certain automatism in the analysis. However, it is inaccurate to use the metaphor of intoxication, which often designates the complete breakdown of rhetorical control. There is little doubt that what listeners are asked to embrace is in part a projection from Nixon's own emotional life. Insofar as the public scene is concerned, an obsessive repetition of verbal formulas may not stand up in objective discussions of public policy, and the audience may not become as cohesive as the speaker may like.

word, if I may, to the young people of this nation." The deliberately artificial idiom creates a cool and distant relationship. A superior depicts himself begging favors of an inferior and in the inversion Nixon discards the rhetorical mask of sociability. He comes close to portraying himself as a "silent American" or still better for his purposes a "silenced American." If the president approaches the young in this fashion, he suggests to others that the young people are a serious problem.

Nixon, however, had stated a policy. He had forcefully declared that he would not be "dictated" to "by the minority." Should other adults adopt his stance? If the connotations of the word "dictate" central to our involvement in Vietnam are extended, the answer is positive. If we are helping South Vietnam to avoid being dictated to by a belligerent minority, surely the people at home can also resist being dictated to.

The stance provides Nixon with an opportunity to give added force to nostalgic values: "I know it may not be fashionable to speak of patriotism or national destiny these days." The negative emphasizes the positive. These values are the beacon lights that confirm the reality of democratic form. They indicate that democracy is not yet, at least, invisible and unrecognizable. A citizenry and a nation unaware of their form live a death.

Together the discussion of the young and of values prepares that audience Nixon has yet to address directly: "So tonight, to you, the great silent majority of my fellow Americans, I ask for your support."[9] Silent America has been invited to speak; it need not ask permission. A formal fashion is preserved. Further, Nixon's private vision rhetorically developed before a public, creates a new form or audience, the "silent majority." The Helpers in the citizen Chorus who were confused and perplexed are made cohesive and real. They are no longer invisible and unrecognizable to themselves. They are also made visible and recognizable to others.

Nixon gives added meaning to patriotism and destiny by commenting on their history and heritage. "Two hundred years ago" America "was the hope of millions" and the "wheel of destiny" has now placed "any hope the world has for the survival of peace and freedom" squarely upon her. Survival suggests life; its absence, death. To his silent majority Nixon says: He who rejects his heritage rejects humanity, and thus himself. Rejection of self is a form of suicide that affects others. A conscious rejection of heritage, humanity, and self by Americans will cause the hopes of others (Vietnamese primarily, but other millions as well) "to be suffocated," still another form of death, perhaps even murder in the first degree.

If history and heritage are rejected, then further tragedy may be expected. Sooner or later we would have "more wars," which "would cost more lives." But Nixon carefully avoids an ultimate conclusion. He does not say that the United States would be overcome. If we desert Asia, we would "lose confidence in ourselves." As we "saw the consequences . . . inevitable remorse and divisive recrimination would scar our spirit as a people." Here, too, he avoids a final conclusion, but he describes a country peopled by "nameless strangers." The conclusions drawn from Nixon's objective statements are easily cast into images of self-extinction.

[9]Associates report that Nixon had difficulty developing a satisfactory conclusion for the speech. He had jotted down numerous phrases he wanted to use but could not find room for. One read: "I don't want demonstrations, I want your quiet support." The line in the text seems to have emerged from such jottings. Semple, "Nixon's Nov. 3 Speech . . . ," p. 23.

When the silent majority speaks, it participates. Constructive action may then occur at home and abroad. But the silent majority speaks not only because it has been asked to. Unless it speaks and participates, it will act much like the North Vietnamese who earlier had been portrayed as nonspeakers and uninvolved participants. The silent majority cannot or will not speak and act like the young; yet neither can it not speak and not act as the North Vietnamese have done. Where then should it place itself? The silent majority will take a middle position, out of choice perhaps, but not until choice has been suggested by the polarities of Nixon's rhetorical structure. For his policy Nixon has a public. He has Helpers.

The resolution of the Vietnam war Nixon terms a quest, a "big" word suggesting magnitude, great risks, and tremendous moments. A true quest has moments so large that they lack definite boundaries and risks of such magnitude that they cannot easily be faced or exactly described by those who must endure them. To look for a paper clip is not a true quest.

Nixon positions the word in the right place—early in the speech. But the word itself is wrong. His policy does differ from those of his predecessors. But it remains one of cautious, subtle modifications. He offers no new imaginative whole; indeed he blunts such considerations. Immediate withdrawal has magnitude, and potentially great risks and moments. Nixon rejects it. Those who call for a serious discussion of war as an important instrument of foreign policy ask fundamental questions of value. They are nearer to Wilson than to Nixon. To the call, Nixon is silent.

Nixon's political narrative also fails as a quest because he does not structure a direct confrontation between himself and the leader of the Guardians of the Object. It is Nixon who prophesies that immediate withdrawal means the loss of Asia and the loss of respect throughout the world. But has Ho Chi Minh or his successor claimed that great a victory growing out of the war? If yes, why doesn't Nixon confront them or him? Let him meet and overthrow the claims of his opponents and show that they are braggadocios. Nixon's prophecy may be correct. But he may also claim more for the Guardians than they claim for themselves. To that extent his political analysis is braggadocian.

Nixon's confrontation with the young is direct. And his listeners have both seen and heard the young. Many believe social unrest at home is an urgent matter. They have again been asked to be patient about Vietnam. Many seem willing, but their frustrations remain intense. Nixon directs them to satisfy them by meeting, testing, and overthrowing the claims of young, loud, windy, braggadocios. The strategy adds little nobility or grandeur to his Quest.

Within the development of his Quest, Nixon illustrates how a Hero as one historical personage may move to larger Heroic groups.[10] There was the Great but Woolly Woodrow, Paternal Ike, Dashing John, and finally Black Lyndon. All had opportunities and moments. Now Somber Richard, a different Hero, appears to establish a new Heroic group, the silent majority.

The relationship between Nixon and the silent majority parallels in general outline a standard myth pattern. Nixon fought political battles, lost, and disappeared. He had fallen, becoming a part of the silent minority. During his absence various events caused his followers and others to wonder whether they and their

[10] I am indebted to Professor Ernest Bormann, University of Minnesota, who read a draft of this essay and suggested this insightful interpretation.

world had fallen. Nixon's risen political body now speaks with a strong voice, uniting and reuniting others with him.

Listeners who sensed the Devil in all around them were assured, if not exhilarated. Traditional values such as the confident love of country, of personal and public honor, of pride in soldiership and citizenship were affirmed. This Hero does not believe that these values are sins. He will confront those who do.

Evaluated in literary terms Nixon's political narrative is obviously not a good Quest story. It is not altogether convincing. There are too many loose ends and too many unanswered questions. It is peopled by flat characters and its language is dull and unimaginative.

This speech was not offered to the public as a literary work. It deals with practical political problems and if evaluated accordingly it accomplishes some objectives. Although divisiveness in the political community remains, Nixon gains an audience and time. He finds listeners who will respond to his words and images. He gains a firmer possession of the policy he lays out before them and makes himself ready for the next series of events he must deal with in Vietnam.

An Exercise in the Rhetoric Of Mythical America

Karlyn Kohrs Campbell

This major policy address on the Vietnam War was, in part, a response to the October moratorium demonstration, despite Nixon's assertion that he would, under no circumstances, be affected by it.[1] The address was followed by an even larger moratorium demonstration in November and by Spiro Agnew's harsh attacks on the news media for their analyses and evaluations of the President's speech.[2] This criticism is an attempt to appraise this discourse primarily in terms of criteria suggested within the address by the President himself.

At the outset the President tells us that there is deep division in the nation partly because many Americans have lost confidence in what the government has told them about the war. In the President's opinion the people of the nation should be told the truth. The three criteria the President explicitly suggests are truth, credibility, and unity, and he later implies a fourth criterion based on responsibility and ethical principles. In other words Nixon tells us that the address is intended to relate the truth, increase the credibility of Administrative statements about the war, unify the nation, and remind us of our duties as Americans.

Two serious misrepresentations cast doubt on the truthfulness of the President. First, he misrepresents his opposition by treating them as a homogeneous group who seek immediate, precipitate withdrawal epitomized by the slogan "Lose in Vietnam; bring the boys home." Hence he also misrepresents the policy options

[1] Cited in "Beyond the Moratorium," *New Republic,* Vol. 161 (October 25, 1969), p. 7.
[2] See Chapter 6 in Campbell, *Critiques of Contemporary Rhetoric.*

available to him. As the President recognizes, somewhat indirectly, there are four alternatives to the policy of Vietnamization: escalation, immediate and precipitate withdrawal, disengagement through negotiation, and a scheduled withdrawal with a fixed date of termination. He mentions the possibility of escalation only as a threat to Hanoi, should increased enemy activity jeopardize the process of Vietnamization. The primary focus of the President's refutation is immediate, precipitate withdrawal—a justifiable argumentative stance only if the bulk of his opposition supported this policy. Instead most of his critics supported the fourth option—a scheduled withdrawal with a fixed date of termination, such as former Senator Charles Goodell's proposed disengagement plan, which called for total withdrawal of all American troops in a year's time but continued economic and military aid to South Vietnam at the discretion of Congress and the President.[3] A few critics, such as Eugene McCarthy, advocated a negotiated settlement. But only a small minority of the peace movement supported immediate, total withdrawal. The President's characterization of his opposition is designed to make the alternatives to Vietnamization appear as extreme as possible so that the voices urging them will not be heeded. The misrepresentation of the opposition and the consequent focus on immediate, total withdrawal as the most important alternative allow the President to transform a complex policy question into a simple either-or decision:

> I am sure that you can recognize from what I have said that we have only two choices open to us if we want to end the war. I can order an immediate precipitate withdrawal of all Americans from Vietnam without regard to the effects of that action. Or we can persist in our search for a just peace through . . . Vietnamization. . .

The misrepresentation of his opposition makes the only apparent alternative to his policy as unattractive and radical as possible. This strategy may gull the audience, and it may make his speech more persuasive for some listeners, but the technique violates his earlier promise to tell the truth.

The second misrepresentation occurs in relation to what the President calls the "fundamental issue. Why and how did the United States become involved in Vietnam in the first place?" He answers this question with a dubious description of the beginning of the war:

> Fifteen years ago North Vietnam, with the logistical support of Communist China and the Soviet Union, launched a campaign to impose a Communist government on South Vietnam by instigating and supporting a revolution.

Now "fifteen years ago" was 1954, the year of the Geneva Agreements that were to unify Vietnam through elections to be held in 1956. Those elections never occurred because the United States supported Diem, who refused elections and attempted to destroy all internal political opposition, Communist and otherwise. The Vietcong

---

[3]Charles E. Goodell, "Set a Deadline for Withdrawal," *New Republic,* Vol. 161 (November 22, 1969), p. 13.

did not persuade Hanoi or Peking or Moscow to aid them against Diem until about 1959. By 1965 South Vietnam was clearly losing, the point at which President Johnson decided to send in United States combat forces.[4]

The surprising decision to give top priority to the historical question, in a policy address that perforce must concern itself with the best means of disengagement, merits consideration. The President's attempt to perpetuate the now largely discredited justifications for United States intervention serves at least two functions. First, it allows Nixon to appeal to history and historical values, to the prior decisions of Presidents Eisenhower, Kennedy, and Johnson and to Woodrow Wilson and his dream of a just peace. Nixon's policy becomes the logical outcome of the decisions and values of his predecessors, and Nixon's way becomes the American way. Second, emphasis on the origins of the war structures the argument so that the primary justifications for the policy can be ethical rather than pragmatic. The speech contains no information about how the plan will work, no evidence for the consequences predicted, and no analysis of how the Vietcong or Hanoi will view it. Instead almost all the justifications are ethical; Vietnamization is "the right way." Although the misrepresentation of the beginning of the war may be believed because of the authority of the speaker, the evasion of the hard questions of feasibility and costs is not consistent with the President's promise to tell the truth.

Two major contradictions damage the President's status as a truthteller. Early in the speech he tells the audience that immediate withdrawal would be the popular and easy course, enhancing the prestige of the Administration and increasing its chances of reelection. Yet at the end of the speech it is clear that the President believes his opposition is a "vocal minority" and that his policy represents the will of the "great, silent majority." If so, isn't his policy the popular and easy one with the best chance of returning him to the White House?

Similarly early in the speech Nixon explains that immediate and total withdrawal would be a disaster for the South Vietnamese because it would inevitably allow the Communists to repeat the massacres that followed their takeover of the North.[5] In response former Senator Goodell remarked that this argument rests on the assumption that the South Vietnamese army would be powerless to prevent a complete takeover of the South. Yet at the time of the address the South Vietnamese had over a million men under arms, while the Vietcong had about 100,000, and the North Vietnamese had about 110,000 in the South.[6] If these smaller armies could take over and massacre, then the president's proposed policy of Vietnamization is surely doomed because it assumes that the South Vietnamese army, with American equipment and training, can successfully take over the fighting of the war

---

[4] "Nixon's Non-Plan," *New Republic,* Vol. 161 (November 15, 1969), p. 10; Tom Wicker, "In the Nation: Mr. Nixon Twists and Turns," *New York Times,* 9 November 1969, p. E15.

For a detailed summary of the history of United States involvement in Vietnam, see "Historical Report on U.S. Aggression in Vietnam 1964 to 1967, Testimony by Charles Fourniau" and "Juridical Report on Aggression in Vietnam, Testimony by the Japanese Legal Committee," in John Duffett ed., *Against the Crime of Silence* (New York: O'Hare Books, 1968), pp. 79-90, 105-118.

[5] For an analysis of the massacre issue, see Tran Van Dinh, "Fear of a Bloodbath," *New Republic,* Vol. 161 (December 6, 1969), pp. 11-14.

[6] Goodell, "Set a Deadline for Withdrawal," p. 13.

and defeat both the Vietcong and the North Vietnamese. The two notions seem somewhat contradictory.

The overwhelming questions concerning credibility are, of course, whether the President really had a secret plan for withdrawal and whether he really intended to end the war? The events that followed this address answered these questions for most Americans. Shortly after the address a Gallup poll reported that the Nixon Administration is facing the same crisis in public confidence on the war that confronted the Johnson administration: 69 percent of the Americans feel that the Administration is not telling the American people all they should know about the war, and 46 percent disapprove of the President's way of handling the Vietnam situation.[7] One critic, after careful analysis of the credibility issue, concludes that Nixon had a plan and sincerely intended to end the war. However, even this critic says "that his heart was not in it, that only the pressure of public opinion had caused him to embrace what he for fifteen years rejected,"[8] and that the address seriously lowered his credibility with newsmen.[9]

In an immediate sense the speech may be called highly credible but, at the same time, extremely divisive. Gallup reported that 77 percent of those who heard it gave the President a vote of confidence;[10] still the divisions over the war were not healed. In fact the address played an important part in exacerbating the bitter conflict between what the President termed the "silent majority" and a "vocal minority" fervently seeking to prevail "over reason and the will of the majority." He characterized dissenters as a small group trying to impose their views and dictate policy "by mounting demonstrations in the streets," terms that place them outside acceptable processes for change in a democratic society. He implied that the opposition was a partial cause for the continuation of the war when he said that "the more divided we are at home, the less likely the enemy is to negotiate." Finally he says that "only Americans," presumably only *dissenting* Americans, "can humiliate and defeat the United States." These statements belie the theme of unity and contradict his earlier assertion that "honest and patriotic Americans have reached different conclusions as to how peace should be achieved." In fact one critic has argued that the address was deliberately designed to isolate dissenters from the majority of opinion.[11] If this address is to unify Americans and fulfill the President's Inaugural promise to "bring us together," it will do so only to the degree that the speaker has silenced his opposition or shamed them into acquiescence.

The President also suggests a fourth criterion. The notion of responsibility or obligation appears frequently, and the President emphasizes that his policy is not the easy, but the right, way. An ethical principle seems implicit. However, despite his numerous protestations, the address does not call on Americans to assume responsibility. First, the President never holds the United States responsible in any way for its part in the war despite the role of the United States in undermining the Geneva Agreements. Instead he places all blame for the initiation and escalation of the war on North Vietnam, China, and Russia. Similarly he places all blame for the

[7]*Los Angeles Times,* 7 March 1971, p. 11.
[8]Robert P. Newman, "Under the Veneer: Nixon's Vietnam Speech of November 3, 1969," *Quarterly Journal of Speech,* Vol. 56 (April 1970), pp. 170-171.
[9]*Ibid.,* p. 176.
[10]*Los Angeles Times,* 5 November 1969, p. I25.
[11]Newman, "Under the Veneer," p. 172.

failure to negotiate a settlement on Hanoi. Praise and blame on such controversial and complicated questions can be assigned so simply and clearly only if the intent is to avoid all responsibility. Second, the President's repeated assertion of *his* responsibility, including his responsibility to choose the best path and lead the nation along it, becomes the individual citizen's *ir*responsibility: The President will decide, the President will lead, and the President will be responsible; while the "silent majority" of "forgotten Americans" will follow, patriotic and undissenting, in the sure knowledge that quiet acquiescence to his considered judgment is the path to victory, peace, and honor.

The powerlessness and frustration felt by dissenters and demonstrators in the face of this rhetoric should be mirrored to some extent in all of us. The President tells us, in effect, there is nothing we can do. By definition, if we are vocal and dissenting, we are the minority whose will must not prevail and to whom no heed will be paid. The only alternative is to join "the great, silent majority" in support of his policy.

In addition as many commentators have pointed out, the policy of Vietnamization, viewed at its worst, is war by proxy in which the Vietnamese supply the bodies while we supply guns, money, and advice.[12] In this sense the policy is a means to avoid the responsibility for making moral judgments about the war. Whether it is viewed as war by proxy or as a long, slow, costly process for ending American involvement, the policy of Vietnamization makes the pace of American withdrawal dependent on decisions made in Hanoi and Saigon and on factors almost wholly beyond United States control. Vietnamization may be "the right way," but it is also a way that limits United States' responsibility severely by placing the burden of decision on others. If the enemy is irresponsible, the threat, although disclaimed, is clear: Troop withdrawals will stop and military action will escalate; and it will be *their* responsibility. As a consequence Americans clearly are not asked to assume moral obligations.

From the point of view of the critic, the most intriguing statements in the speech are these:

I have chosen a path for peace. I believe it will succeed. If it does succeed, what the critics say now won't matter. If it does not succeed, anything I say then won't matter.

The two statements about criticism are cryptic and more than a little mystifying. What does the President mean when he says, "If it does succeed, what the critics say now won't matter"? Presumably he expects the critics to be negative and dissatisfied as they have often been. If they point out weaknesses in the policy, in the arguments, in the truth of what he says, if they point out contradictions and inconsistencies, and if the policy does not succeed, then what? Is the criticism of no matter? Such criticism should provide a partial explanation of why the policy did not work and what was faulty in the decision-making process. The same is true of the criticism of a rhetorical discourse. If the rhetorical act fails, the critics' comments are important because criticism should give some reasons for the failure of

[12] "Nixon's Non-Plan," p. 10.

the rhetoric. Clearly, however, the President is giving notice that under no circumstances will he be affected by what the critics say, and such warning is precisely the tragedy, for criticism is the mechanism by which to improve the quality of rhetoric and of decision making. But Nixon has been quite bitter about criticism, as was evident in his concession speech of the 1962 gubernatorial campaign in California.[13]

What does the President intend when he says, "If it does succeed, what the critics say now won't matter"? In such a case the President would have proved the critics wrong, vindicating himself and calling the critics' methods and assumptions into serious question. In all likelihood such a moment would be gratifying for the President. However, if we take the rhetorical act as an analogy, can we consider the critical comments inconsequential simply because the address was successful (at least in terms of the Gallup poll)? I think not. It may be futile to warn against the rhetorician who misrepresents, who is self-contradictory, who is divisive while asserting his desire for unity, or who disclaims responsibility while praising the idea of fulfilling moral obligations. But unless we become careful, discriminating critics, questioning and evaluating, we shall be constrained to make poor decisions and supporting policies destructive of ourselves, our society, and the world. In this respect Agnew's attacks on the concept of immediate critical analysis and evaluation are particularly ironic because his protest suggests that the policy and the address are both extremely fragile. The decision worth making and the policy deserving support, as well as the rhetorical act of quality, will withstand, even be strengthened by, critical scrutiny, and such criticism is the essence of democratic decision making.

Finally this address is an example of the perpetuation of American mythology. The President describes a mythical America whose business is the defense of freedom, whose strength has resulted from facing crises and rejecting the easy way, whose greatness has been the capacity to do what had to be done when it was known to be right. This mythical America is the last hope for the survival of peace and freedom in the world; this most powerful nation will not allow the forces of totalitarianism to suffocate the hopes of the peoples of the earth. This is a nation of destiny.

Nonmythical America presents quite a different picture. Nonmythical America supports totalitarian governments all over the world. Nonmythical America is engaged in a war in South Vietnam in which it is systematically destroying the civilian population and agricultural capacity of the country it is ostensibly defending. Nonmythical America practices a racism that makes a mockery of its mythic principles. The examples could go on and on. Concentrating so on the details of this address—whether this point or that is true or distorted—the critic can so easily forget that all these considerations rest on the speaker's assumption of a mythical America, which always seeks justice, freedom, and right despite difficulty and cost. These considerations become irrelevant and fragmented outside this mythic context. One commentator has made the point that "the only salutary aspect of Vietnam [is] the fact that it is forcing us to examine the misconceptions about ourselves and the world on which postwar American foreign policy has been based."[14]

[13] Richard Bergholz, "Nixon Admits Defeat, Indicates Intention to Give Up Politics," Los Angeles Times, 8 November 1962, p. 1.
[14] Fred Warner Neal, "Government by Myth," The Center Magazine, Vol. 2 (November 1969), p. 2.

Although this speech fails to meet the President's criteria of truth, credibility, unity, and responsibility, the most significant criticism is that this rhetorical act perpetuates the myths about America, which must be debunked and shattered if we are to find solutions to the problems that threaten imminently to destroy us. The "silent majority" may want to get out of Vietnam and to save face; it cannot have both—at least not quickly.

To avoid Vietnams of the future we must make a concerted effort to discover and scrutinize *non*mythical America. If in that scrutiny we pay particular attention to the rhetorical discourses that thresh out and formulate ideas of ourselves and our society, we may begin to solve the problems of the *real* America and of this shrinking world. That President Nixon in unwilling or unable to face the *real* problems is precisely the reason why this address is doomed to be so disappointing. It is, as almost every commentator has recognized, just "more of the same."[15]

[15] See, for example, Robert J. Donovan, "Verdict on President's Speech Up to 'Great Silent Majority,' " *Los Angeles Times,* 4 November 1969, p. 1; "The Legitimacy of Protest," *New York Times,* 9 November 1969, p. E14; John W. Finney, "The Critics: It is Not a Plan to End U.S. Involvement," *New York Times,* 9 November 1969, p. E1.

Conventional Wisdom—Traditional Form —The President's Message of November 3, 1969

Forbes Hill

More than one critique of President Nixon's address to the nation on November 3, 1969 has appeared,[1] which is not remarkable, since it was the most obvious feature of the public relations machine that appears to have dammed back the flood of sentiment for quick withdrawal of American forces from Southeast Asia. To be sure, the dike built by this machine hardly endured forever, but some time was gained—an important achievement. It seems natural, then, that we should want to examine this obvious feature from more than one angle.

Preceding critiques have looked at Nixon's message from notably non-traditional perspectives. Stelzner magnified it in the lens of archetypal criticism, which reveals a non-literary version of the quest story archetype, but he concluded that the President's is an incomplete telling of the story that does not adequately interact with the listeners' subjective experiences. Newman condemned the message as "shoddy rhetoric" because its tough stance and false dilemmas are directed to white, urban, uptight voters. Campbell condemned it on the basis of intrinsic criticism because though its stated purposes are to tell the truth, increase credibility, promote unity,

[1] Robert P. Newman, "Under the Veneer: Nixon's Vietnam Speech of November 3, 1969," *QJS,* 56 (Apr. 1970), 168–178; Hermann G. Stelzner, "The Quest Story and Nixon's November 3, 1969 Address," *QJS,* 57 (Apr. 1971), 163–172; Karlyn Kohrs Campbell, "An Exercise in the Rhetoric of Mythical America," in *Critiques of Contemporary Rhetoric* (Belmont, Calif.: Wadsworth, 1972), pp. 50–58.

and affirm moral responsibility, its rhetoric conceals truth, decreases credibility, promotes division, and dodges moral responsibility. Then, stepping outside the intrinsic framework, she makes her most significant criticism: the message perpetuates myths about American values instead of scrutinizing the real values of America.

I propose to juxtapose these examinations with a strict neo-Aristotelian analysis. If it differs slightly from analyses that follow Wichelns[2] and Hochmuth-Nichols,[3] that is because it attempts a critique that re-interprets neo-Aristotelianism slightly—a critique guided by the spirit and usually the letter of the Aristotelian text as I understand it. What the neo-Aristotelian method can and should do will be demonstrated, I hope, by this juxtaposition.

Neo-Aristotelian criticism compares the means of persuasion used by a speaker with a comprehensive inventory given in Aristotle's *Rhetoric*. Its end is to discover whether the speaker makes the best choices from the inventory to get a favorable decision from a specified group of auditors in a specific situation. It does not, of course, aim to discover whether or not the speaker actually gets his favorable decision; decisions in practice are often upset by chance factors.[4] First the neo-Aristotelian critic must outline the situation, then specify the group of auditors and define the kind of decision they are to make. Finally he must reveal the choice and disposition of three intertwined persuasive factors—logical, psychological, and characterological—and evaluate this choice and disposition against the standard of the *Rhetoric*.

THE SITUATION

The state of affairs for the Nixon Administration in the fall of 1969 is well known. The United States had been fighting a stalemated war for several years. The cost in lives and money was immense. The goal of the war was not clear; presumably the United States wanted South Viet Nam as a stable non-Communist buffer state between Communist areas and the rest of Southeast Asia. To the extent that this goal was understood, it seemed as far from being realized in 1969 as it had been in 1964. In the meantime, a large and vocal movement had grown up, particularly among the young, of people who held that there should have been no intervention in Viet Nam in the first place and that it would never be possible to realize any conceivable goal of intervention. The movement was especially dangerous to

[2] Herbert A. Wichelns, "The Literary Criticism of Oratory," in Donald C. Bryant, ed., *The Rhetorical Idiom: Essays in Rhetoric, Oratory, Language, and Drama* (1925; rpt. Ithaca: Cornell Univ. Press, 1958), pp. 5–42.

[3] Marie Hochmuth [Nichols], "The Criticism of Rhetoric," in *A History and Criticism of American Public Address* (New York: Longmans, Green, 1955) III, 1–23.

[4] Aristotle, *Rhetoric* I. 1. 1355b 10–14. "To persuade is not the function of rhetoric but to investigate the persuasive factors inherent in the particular case. It is just the same as in all other arts; for example, it is not the function of medicine to bring health, rather to bring the patient as near to health as is possible in his case. Indeed, there are some patients who cannot be changed to healthfulness; nevertheless, they can be given the right therapy." (Translation mine.) I understand the medical analogy to mean that even if auditors chance to be proof against any of the means of persuasion, the persuader has functioned adequately as a rhetorician if he has investigated these means so that he has in effect "given the right therapy."

the Administration because it numbered among its supporters many of the elements of the population who were most interested in foreign policy and best informed about it. There were variations of position within the peace movement, but on one point all its members were agreed: the United States should commit itself immediately to withdraw its forces from Viet Nam.

The policy of the Nixon Administration, like that of the Johnson Administration before it, was limited war to gain a position of strength from which to negotiate. By fall 1969 the Administration was willing to make any concessions that did not jeopardize a fifty-fifty chance of achieving the goal, but it was not willing to make concessions that amounted to sure abandonment of the goal. A premature withdrawal amounted to public abandonment and was to be avoided at all costs. When the major organizations of the peace movement announced the first Moratorium Day for October 15 and organized school and work stoppages, demonstrations, and a great "March on Washington" to dramatize the demand for immediate withdrawal from Viet Nam, the Administration launched a counterattack. The President announced that he would make a major address on Viet Nam November 3. This announcement seems to have moderated the force of the October moratorium, but plans were soon laid for a second moratorium on November 15. Nixon's counterattack aimed at rallying the mass of the people to disregard the vocal minority and oppose immediate withdrawal; it aimed to get support for a modified version of the old strategy: limited war followed by negotiated peace. The address was broadcast the evening of November 3 over the national radio and television networks.

THE AUDITORS AND THE KIND OF DECISION

An American President having a monopoly of the media at prime time potentially reaches an audience of upwards of a hundred million adults of heterogeneous backgrounds and opinions. Obviously it is impossible to design a message to move every segment of this audience, let alone the international audience. The speaker must choose his targets. An examination of the texts shows us which groups were eliminated as targets, which were made secondary targets, and which were primary. The speaker did not address himself to certain fanatical opponents of the war: the ones who hoped that the Viet Cong would gain a signal victory over the Americans and their South Vietnamese allies, or those who denied that Communist advances were threats to non-Communist countries, or those against any war for any reason. These were the groups the President sought to isolate and stigmatize. On the other hand, there was a large group of Americans who would be willing to give their all to fight any kind of Communist expansion anywhere at any time. These people also were not a target group: their support could be counted on in any case.

The speaker did show himself aware that the Viet Cong and other Communist decision-makers were listening in. He represented himself to them as willing and anxious to negotiate and warned them that escalation of the war would be followed by effective retaliation. The Communists constituted a secondary target audience, but the analysis that follows will make plain that the message was not primarily intended for them.

The primary target was those Americans not driven by a clearly defined ideological commitment to oppose or support the war at any cost. Resentment of the sacrifice in money and lives, bewilderment at the stalemate, longing for some movement in a clearly marked direction—these were the principal aspects of their state of mind assumed by Nixon. He solicited them saying "tonight—to you, the great silent majority of my fellow Americans—I ask your support."[5]

His address asks the target group of auditors to make a decision to support a policy to be continued in the future. In traditional terms, then, it is primarily a deliberative speech. Those who receive the message are decision-makers, and they are concerned with the past only as it serves as analogy to future decisions. The subjects treated are usual ones for deliberation: war and peace.[6]

DISPOSITION AND SYNOPSIS

The address begins with an enthymeme that attacks the credibility gap.[7] Those who decide on war and peace must know the truth about these policies, and the conclusion is implied that the President is going to tell the truth. The rest of the *proem* is taken up by a series of questions constructing a formal partition of the subjects to be covered. The partition stops short of revealing the nature of the modification in policy that constitues the Nixon plan. The message fits almost perfectly into the Aristotelian pattern of *proem,* narrative, proofs both constructive and refutative, and epilogue. Just as *proem* has served as a general heading for a synoptic statement of what was done in the first few sentences, so the other four parts will serve us as analytical headings for a synopsis of the rest.

The narrative commences with Nixon's statement of the situation as he saw it on taking office. He could have ordered immediate withdrawal of American forces, but he decided to fulfill "a greater obligation . . . to think of the effect" of his decision "on the next generation, and on the future of peace and freedom in America, and in the world." Applicable here is the precept: the better the moral end that the speaker can in his narrative be seen consciously choosing, the better the *ethos* he reveals.[8] An end can hardly be better than "the future of peace and freedom in America, and in the world." The narrative goes on to explain why and how the United States became involved in Viet Nam in the first place. This explanation masquerades as a simple chronological statement—"Fifteen years ago . . ." but thinly disguised in the chronology lie two propositions: first, that the leaders of America were right in intervening on behalf of the government of South Viet Nam; second, that the great mistake in their conduct of the war was over-reliance on American combat forces. Some doubt has been cast on the wisdom of Nixon's choice among the means of persuasion here. The history, writes one critic, "is a surprising candidate for priority in any discussion today. . . . The President's chief foreign policy advisors, his allies on Capitol Hill, and the memorandum he got from

[5] Text as printed in *Vital Speeches,* 36 (15 Nov. 1969), 69.
[6] Aristotle *Rhetoric* I. 4. 1359b 33–1360a 5.
[7] Aristotle *Rhetoric* III. 14. 1415a 29–33. Here Nixon functions like a defendant in a forensic speech. "When defending he will first deal with any prejudicial insinuation against him . . . it is necessary that the defendant when he steps forward first reduce the obstacles, so he must immediately dissolve prejudice."
[8] See Aristotle *Rhetoric* III. 16. 1417a 16–36.

the Cabinet bureaucracy all urged him to skip discussions of the causes and manner of our involvement. Yet history comes out with top billing"[9] This criticism fails to conceive the rhetorical function of the narrative: in the two propositions the whole content of the proofs that follow is foreshadowed, and foreshadowed in the guise of a non-controversial statement about the historical facts. Among traditional orators this use of the narrative to foreshadow proofs is common, but it has seldom been handled with more artistry than here.

Constructive proofs are not opened with an analytical partition but with a general question: what is the best way to end the war? The answer is structured as a long argument from logical division: there are four plans to end American involvement; three should be rejected so that the listener is left with no alternative within the structure but to accept the fourth.[10] The four plans are: immediate withdrawal, the consequences of which are shown at some length to be bad; negotiated settlement, shown to be impossible in the near future because the enemy will not negotiate in earnest; shifting the burden of the war to the Vietnamese with American withdrawal on a fixed timetable, also argued to have bad consequences; and shifting the burden of the war to the Vietnamese with American withdrawal on a flexible schedule, said to have good consequences, since it will eventually bring "the complete withdrawal of all United States *combat ground* forces," whether earnest negotiations become possible or not. Constructive proofs close with one last evil consequence of immediate withdrawal: that it would lead eventually to Americans' loss of confidence in themselves and divisive recrimination that "would scar our spirit as a people."

As refutative proof is introduced, opponents of the Administration are characterized by a demonstrator carrying a sign, "Lose in Viet Nam"; they are an irrational minority who want to decide policy in the streets, as opposed to the elected officials—Congress and the President—who will decide policy by Constitutional and orderly means. This attack on his presumed opponents leads to a passage which reassures the majority of young people that the President really wants peace as much as they do. Reassuring ends with the statement of Nixon's personal belief that his plan will succeed; this statement may be taken as transitional to the epilogue.

The epilogue reiterates the bad consequences of immediate withdrawal—loss of confidence and loss of other nations to totalitarianism—it exhorts the silent majority to support the plan, predicting its success; it evokes the memory of Woodrow Wilson; then it closes with the President's pledge to meet his responsibilities to lead the nation with strength and wisdom. Recapitulation, building of *ethos,* and reinforcing the right climate of feeling—these are what a traditional rhetorician would advise that the epilogue do,[11] and these are what Nixon's epilogue does.

Indeed, this was our jumping-off place for the synopsis of the message: it falls into the traditional paradigm; each frame of the paradigm contains the lines of argument conventional for that frame. The two unconventional elements in the paradigm —the unusual placement of the last evil consequence of immediate withdrawal and the use of the frame by logical division for the constructive proofs—are there for

---

[9] Newman, p. 173.
[10] See Aristotle *Rhetoric* II. 23. 1398a 30–31. This basic structure is called method of residues in most modern argumentation textbooks.
[11] Aristotle *Rhetoric* III. 19. 1419b 10–1420a 8.

good rhetorical reasons. That last consequence, loss of confidence and divisive recrimination, serves to lead into the refutation which opens with the demonstrator and his sign. It is as if the demonstrator were being made an example in advance of just this evil consequence. The auditor is brought into precisely the right set for a refutation section that does not so much argue with opponents as it pushes them into an isolated, unpopular position.

Because of the residues-like structure, the message creates the illusion of proving that Vietnamization and flexible withdrawal constitute the best policy. By process of elimination it is the only policy available, and even a somewhat skeptical listener is less likely to question the only policy available. Approaching the proposal with skepticism dulled, he perhaps does not so much miss a development of the plan. In particular, he might not ask the crucial question: does the plan actually provide for complete American withdrawal? The answer to this question is contained in the single phrase, "complete withdrawal of all United States *combat ground* forces." It is fairly clear, in retrospect, that this phrase concealed the intention to keep in Viet Nam for several years a large contingent of air and support forces. Nixon treats the difference between plan three, Vietnamization and withdrawal on a fixed schedule, and plan four, Vietnamization and withdrawal on a flexible schedule, as a matter of whether or not the schedule is announced in advance. But the crucial difference is really that plan three was understood by its advocates as a plan for quick, complete withdrawal; plan four was a plan for partial withdrawal. The strategic reason for not announcing a fixed schedule was that the announcement would give away this fact. The residues structure concealed the lack of development of the plan; the lack of development of the plan suppressed the critical fact that Nixon did not propose complete withdrawal. Although Nixon's message shows traditionally conventional structure, these variations from the traditional show a remarkable ability at designing the best adaptations to the specific rhetorical situation.

LOGICAL AND PSYCHOLOGICAL PERSUASIVE FACTORS

Central to an Aristotelian assessment of the means of persuasion is an account of two interdependent factors: (1) the choice of major premises on which enthymemes[12] that form "the body of the proof" are based, and (2) the means whereby auditors are brought into states of feeling favorable to accepting these premises and the conclusions following from them. Premises important here are of two kinds: predictions and values. Both kinds as they relate to good and evil consequences of the four plans to end American involvement, will be assessed. The first enthymeme involving prediction is that immediate withdrawal followed by a Communist takeover would lead to murder and imprisonment of innocent civilians. This conclusion

[12]For the purpose of this paper the term enthymeme is taken to mean any deductive argument. Aristotle gives a more technical definition of enthymeme that fits into the total design of his organon; in my opinion it is not useful for neo-Aristotelian criticism.

[13]Remarkably enough Aristotle does not state this general rule, though it clearly underlies his treatment of the historical example, *Rhetoric* II. 20.

110

follows from the general predictive rule: the future will resemble the past.[13] Since the Communists murdered and imprisoned opponents on taking over North Viet Nam in 1954 and murdered opponents in the city of Hue in 1968, they will do the same when they take over South Viet Nam. Implied also is an enthymeme based on the value premise that security of life and freedom from bondage are primary goods for men;[14] a Communist takeover would destroy life and freedom and therefore destroy primary goods for men.

Presumably no one would try to refute this complex of enthymemes by saying that life and freedom are not primary goods, though he might argue from more and less;[15] more life is lost by continuing the war than would be lost by a Communist takeover, or American-South Vietnamese political structures allow for even less political freedom than the Communist alternatives. Nixon buries these questions far enough beneath the surface of the message that probably auditors in the target group are not encouraged to raise them. One could also attack the predictive premise: after all, the future is not always the past writ over again. But this kind of refutation is merely irritating; we know that the premise is not universally true, yet everyone finds it necessary to operate in ordinary life as if it were. People on the left of the target group, of course, reject the evidence—North Viet Nam and Hue.

A related prediction is that immediate withdrawal would result in a collapse of confidence in American leadership. It rests on the premise that allies only have confidence in those who both have power and will act in their support.[16] If the United States shows it lacks power and will in Viet Nam, there will be a collapse of confidence, which entails further consequences: it would "promote recklessness" on the part of enemies everywhere else the country has commitments, i.e., as a general premise, when one party to a power struggle loses the confidence of its allies, its enemies grow bolder.[17] The conclusion is bolstered by citations from former presidents Eisenhower, Johnson, and Kennedy: the statement of the "liberal saint," Kennedy, is featured.

It is difficult to attack the related premises of these tandem arguments. They rest on what experience from the sandbox up shows to be probable. The target group consists of people with the usual American upbringing and experience. Someone will question the premises only if he questions the world-view out of which they develop. That view structures the world into Communist powers—actual or potential enemies—and non-Communist powers—allies. America is the leader of the allies, referred to elsewhere as the forces of "peace and freedom" opposed by "the forces of totalitarianism." Because of its association with freedom, American leadership is indisputably good, and whatever weakens confidence in it helps the enemies. Only a few people on the far left would categorically reject this structure.

The foregoing premises and the world-view fundamental to them are even more

---

[14]See Aristotle *Rhetoric* I. 6. 1362b 26–27 for life as a good; I. 8. 1366a for freedom as the object of choice for the citizens of a democracy.

[15]The subject of *Rhetoric* I. 7. Chaim Perelman and L. Olbrechts-Tyteca, commenting on this chapter, indicate that there is usually a consensus on such statements as 'life is good'; the dispute is over whether life is a greater good than honor in this particular situation. See *The New Rhetoric: A Treatise on Argumentation,* trans. John Wilkinson and Purcell Weaver (Notre Dame, Ind.: Univ. of Notre Dame Press, 1969), pp. 81–82.

[16]See Aristotle *Rhetoric* II. 19. 1393a 1–3.

[17]This principle follows from *Rhetoric* II. 5. 1383a 24–25.

likely to be accepted if the auditors are in a state of fear. Fear may be defined as distress caused by a vision of impending evil of the destructive or painful kind.[18] This message promotes a state of fear by the nature of the evil consequences developed—murder and imprisonment of innocents, collapse of leadership in the free world, and reckless aggressiveness of implacable enemies. America is the prototype of a nation that is fearful; her enemies are watching their opportunities all over the globe, from Berlin to the Middle East, yes even in the Western Hemisphere itself. The enemies are cruel and opposed to American ideals. They are strong on the battlefield and intransigent in negotiations. Conditions are such that America's allies may lose confidence in her and leave her to fight these enemies alone. But these circumstances are not too much amplified: only enough to create a state of feeling favorable to rejecting immediate withdrawal, not so much as to create the disposition for escalation.

Nixon claims to have tried hard to make a negotiated settlement, but he could not make one because the Communists refused to compromise. The evidence that they would not compromise is developed at length: public initiatives through the peace conference in Paris are cited, terms for participation of the Communist forces in internationally supervised elections offered, and promises made to negotiate on any of these terms. Then there were private initiatives through the Soviet Union and directly by letter to the leaders of North Viet Nam, as well as private efforts by the United States ambassador to the Paris talks. These efforts brought only demands for the equivalent of unconditional surrender. The citation of evidence is impressive and destroys the credibility of the position that negotiations can bring a quick end to the war.

Nixon does not explicitly predict that the plan for negotiated settlement will not work ever; on the contrary, he says that he will keep trying. But if the auditor believes the evidence, he finds it difficult to avoid making his own enthymeme with the conclusion that negotiated settlement will never work; the major premise is the same old rule, the future will be like the past. Nixon gives another reason, too: it will not work while the opposite side "is convinced that all it has to do is wait for our next concession, and our next concession after that one, until it gets everything it wants." The major premise—no power convinced that victory is probable by forcing repeated concessions will ever compromise—constitutes a commonplace of bargaining for virtually everyone.

Peace is seen in these arguments as almost an unqualified good. Although compromise through bargaining is the fastest way to peace, the other side must make concessions to assure compromise. Reasons for continuing the war, such as an ideological commitment, are evil. There is no glory in war and prolonging it is not justified by political gains made but only by a commitment to higher values like saving lives and preserving freedom. Prolonging the war is also justified as avoiding future wars by not losing Southeast Asia altogether and not promoting the spirit

[18] Aristotle *Rhetoric* II. 5. 1382ᵃ 21–22. Aristotle treated the *pathe* as states of feeling that a man enters into because he draws certain inferences from the situation around him: he sees, for example, that he is the type of man who experiences pity when faced with this type of victim in these circumstances. The means of getting a man to draw inferences are themselves logical proofs; hence *pathos* does not work apart from the logical proofs in a message but through them. See Aristotle *Rhetoric* II. 1. 1378ᵃ 19–28 and my explication in James J. Murphy, ed. *A Synoptic History of Classical Rhetoric* (New York: Random House, 1972).

of recklessness in the enemies. "I want," states Nixon, "to end it [the war] in a way which will increase the chance that their [the soldiers'] younger brothers and their sons will not have to fight in some future Vietnam. . . ."

A listener is prone to reject the likelihood of a negotiated peace if he is angry with his opponents. Anger is a painful desire for revenge and arises from an evident, unjustified slight to a person or his friends.[19] People visualizing revenge ordinarily refuse compromise except as a temporary tactic. Nixon presents the American people as having been slighted: they value peace, and their leaders have with humility taken every peace initiative possible: public, private, and secret. The Communist powers wish to gain politically from the war; they have rebuffed with spite all initiatives and frustrated our good intentions by demanding the equivalent of unconditional surrender. Frustration is, of course, a necessary condition of anger.[20] Again, Nixon does not go too far—not far enought to create a psychological climate out of which a demand for escalation would grow.

Nixon announces that his plan for Vietnamization and American withdrawal on a flexible timetable is in effect already. Its consequences: American men coming home, South Vietnamese forces gaining in strength, enemy infiltration measurably reduced, and United States' casualties also reduced. He predicts: policies that have had such consequences in the past will have them in the future, i.e., the future will be like the past. Again, the undisputed value that saving lives is good is assumed. But in this case the argument, while resting on an acceptable premise, was, at the time of this speech, somewhat more doubtful of acceptance by the target group. The evidence constitutes the problem: obviously the sample of the past since the policy of Vietnamization commenced was so short that no one could really judge the alleged consequences to be correlated with the change in policy, let alone caused by it. There is, then, little reason why that audience should have believed the minor premise—that the consequences of Vietnamization were good.

A temporizing and moderate policy is best presented to auditors who while temporarily fearful are basically confident. Nothing saps the will to accept such a proposal as does the opposite state, basically fearful and only temporarily confident. Confidence is the other side of the coin from fear: it is pleasure because destructive and painful evils seem far away and sources of aid near at hand.[21] The sources of aid here are the forces of the Republic of South Viet Nam. They have continued to gain in strength and as a result have been able to take over combat responsibilities from American forces. In contrast, danger from the enemy is receding—"enemy infiltration . . . over the last three months is less than 20 per cent of what it was over the same period last year." Nixon assures his auditors that he has confidence the plan will succeed. America is the "strongest and richest nation in the world"; it can afford the level of aid that needs to be continued in Viet Nam. It will show the moral stamina to meet the challenge of free world leadership.

For some time rumors about gradual American withdrawal from Viet Nam had been discounted by the peace movement. The only acceptable proof of American intentions would be a timetable showing withdrawal to be accomplished soon. Thus the third plan: withdrawal on a fixed timetable. Nixon predicts that announcing of

[19] Aristotle *Rhetoric* II. 2. 1378a 30–32.
[20] Aristotle *Rhetoric* II. 2. 1379a 10–18.
[21] Aristotle *Rhetoric* II. 5. 1383a 16–19.

a timetable would remove the incentive to negotiate and reduce flexibility of response. The general premise behind the first is a commonplace of bargaining: negotiations never take place without a *quid pro quo;* a promise to remove American forces by a certain date gives away the *quid pro quo.* For most Americans, who are used to getting things by bargaining, this premise is unquestionable. Only those few who think that the country can gain no vestige of the objective of the war are willing to throw away the incentive. The premises behind the notion of flexibility—that any workable plan is adaptable to changes in the situation—is a commonplace of legislation and not likely to be questioned by anyone. Nixon adds to this generally acceptable premise a specific incentive. Since withdrawal will occur more rapidly if enemy military activity decreases and the South Vietnamese forces become stronger, there is a possibility that forces can be withdrawn even sooner than would be predicted by a timetable. This specific incentive is illusory, since it is obvious that one can always withdraw sooner than the timetable says, even if he has one; it is hard to see how a timetable actually reduces flexibility. Everyone makes timetables, of course, and having to re-make them when conditions change is a familiar experience. But the average man who works from nine to five probably thinks that the government should be different: when it announces a timetable it must stick to it; otherwise nothing is secure. This argument may seem weak to the critic, but it is probably well directed to the target group. The real reason for not announcing a timetable has already been noted.[22]

One final prediction is founded on the preceding predictions—whenever a policy leads to such evil consequences as movement of Southeast Asia into alliance with the enemy and a new recklessness on the part of enemies everywhere, it will eventually result in remorse and divisive recrimination which will, in turn, result in a loss of self-confidence. Guiltlessness and internal unity, the opposites of remorse and recrimination, are here assumed as secondary goods leading to self-confidence, a primary good. The enthymeme predicting loss of self-confidence consequent on immediate withdrawal is summary in position: it seems to tie together all previous arguments. It comes right after a particularly effective effort at *ethos* building—the series of statements developed in parallel construction about not having chosen the easy way (immediate withdrawal) but the right way. However, it rests on the assumption that the long term mood of confidence in the country depends on the future of Southeast Asia and the recklessness of our enemies. Since these two factors are only an aspect of a larger picture in which many other events play their parts, it is surely not true that they alone will produce a loss of confidence. The enthymeme based on this assumption, placed where it is, however, does not invite questioning by the target group. Doubtful though it may look under searching scrutiny, it has an important function for the structure of psychological proof in this message. It reinforces the vague image of the danger of facing a stronger enemy in a weakened condition: America itself would be less united, less confident, and less able to fight in the future if this consequence of immediate withdrawal were realized.

[22]Since he gave this speech Nixon has made a general timetable for American withdrawal, thus, presumably, showing that he was not utterly convinced by his own argument. But he has never quite fixed a date for complete withdrawal of all American support forces from Viet Nam; he has been consistent in maintaining that withdrawal as a bargaining point for negotiation with the Viet Cong and North Vietnamese.

Other things being equal, the more commonplace and universally accepted the premises of prediction in a deliberative speech, the more effective the speech. This is especially true if they are set in a frame that prepares the auditor psychologically for their acceptance. There is almost no doubt that given the policy of the Nixon Administration—Vietnamization and partial withdrawal on a flexible schedule not announced in advance—the message shows a potentially effective choice of premises. In some cases it is almost the only possible choice. Likewise the value structure of the message is wisely chosen from materials familiar to any observer of the American scene: it could be duplicated in hundreds of other messages from recent American history.

Several additional value assumptions are equally commonplace. Betraying allies and letting down friends is assumed to be an evil, and its opposite, loyalty to friends and allies the virtue of a great nation. This premise equates personal loyalty, like that a man feels for his friend, with what the people of the whole nation should feel for an allied nation. Many people think this way about international relations, and the good citizens of the target group can be presumed to be among them.

Policies endorsed by the people they are supposed to help are said to be better policies than those not endorsed by them. This statement undoubtedly makes a good political rule if one expects participation in the execution of policy of those to be helped. Policies that result from the operation of representative government are good, whereas those made on the streets are bad. This value is, of course, an essential of republican government: only the most radical, even of those outside the target group, would question it. Finally, Nixon assumes that the right thing is usually the opposite of the easy thing, and, of course, *he* chooses to do the right thing. Such a value premise does not occur in rhetorics by Aristotle or even George Campbell; it is probably a peculiar product of Protestant-American-on-the-frontier thinking. Its drawing power for twentieth-century urban youngsters is negligible, but the bulk of the target group probably is made up of suburbanites in the 35–50 category who still have some affinity for this kind of thinking.

Some shift from the traditional values of American culture can be seen in the tone of Nixon's dealing with the war: the lack of indication that it is glorious, the muted appeal to patriotism (only one brief reference to the first defeat in America's history), the lack of complete victory as a goal. But nowhere else does the culture of the post-atomic age show through; by and large the speech would have been applauded if delivered in the nineteenth century. That there has been a radical revolution of values among the young does not affect the message, and one might predict that Nixon is right in deciding that the revolution in values has not yet significantly infected the target group.

CHARACTEROLOGICAL AND STYLISTIC FACTORS

Nixon's choice of value premises is, of course, closely related to his *ethos* as conveyed by the speech. He promises to tell the truth before he asks the American people to support a policy which involves the overriding issues of war and peace—phraseology that echoes previous Nixonian messages. He refrains from harsh criticism of the previous administration; he is more interested in the future America than in political gains; such an avowal of disinterestedness is the commonest topic for self-character building.

Nixon is against political murders and imprisonments and active pushing initiatives for peace. He is flexible and compromising, unlike the negotiators for the enemy. He chooses the right way and not the easy way. He is the champion of policy made by constitutional processes; his opponents conduct unruly demonstrations in the streets. But he has healthy respect for the idealism and commitment of the young; he pledges himself in the tradition of Woodrow Wilson to win a peace that will avoid future wars. He has the courage to make a tasteful appeal to patriotism even when it's unpopular. Such is the character portrait drawn for us by Richard Nixon: restrained not hawkish, hardworking and active, flexible, yet firm where he needs to be. He seems an American style democrat, a moral but also a practical and sensitive man. The message is crowded with these overt clues from which we infer the good *ethos* of political figures in situations like this. Any more intensive development of the means of persuasion derived from the character of the speaker would surely have been counter-productive.

The language of Nixon's message helps to reinforce his *ethos*. His tone is unbrokenly serious. The first two-thirds of the message is in a self-consciously plain style —the effort is clearly made to give the impression of bluntness and forthrightness. This bluntness of tone correlates with the style of deliberative argumentation:[23] few epideictic elements are present in the first part of the speech. Everything seems to be adjusted to making the structure of residues exceedingly clear.

About two-thirds of the way through, the message shifts to a more impassioned tone. The alternative plans are collapsed into two, thus polarizing the situation: either immediate withdrawal or Nixon's plan for Vietnamization and unscheduled withdrawal. From here on parallel repetitions are persistent, and they serve no obvious logical function, but rather function to deepen the serious tone. There is, in short, an attempt to rise to a peroration of real eloquence. The qualities aimed at in the last third of the message seem to be gravity and impressiveness more than clarity and forthrightness. The effort seems to tax the speechwriter's literary skill to the limit, and the only new phrases he comes up with are the "silent majority" and the description of the energies of the young as "too often directed to bitter hatred against those they think are responsible for the war." All else is a moderately skillful pastiche of familiar phrases.

GENERAL ASSESSMENT

A summary answer can now be given to the question, how well did Nixon and his advisors choose among the available means of persuasion for this situation? The message was designed for those not ideologically overcommitted either to victory over Communism or to peace in any case while frustrated by the prolonged war. It operates from the most universally accepted premises of value and prediction; it buries deep in its texture most premises not likely to be immediately accepted. Enough of the means for bringing auditors into states of fear, anger, and confidence are used to create a psychological climate unfavorable to immediate withdrawal and favorable to Vietnamization. The goals—life, political freedom, peace, and self-

---

[23] See Aristotle *Rhetoric* III. 12. 1414a 8–19.

confidence—are those shared by nearly all Americans, and connections of policies to them are tactfully handled for the target group. The structure is largely according to tradition: it can best be seen as falling into the four parts, and the right elements are contained in each of the parts. Two minor variations from the traditional are artfully designed to realize evident psychological ends. Conventional wisdom and conventional value judgments come dressed in conventional structure. The style of the narrative and proofs reflects adequately Nixon's reliance on clearly developed arguments from accepted premises; the style of the latter part of the message shows a moderately successful attempt at grandeur. In choice and arrangement of the means of persuasion for this situation this message is by and large a considerable success.

Neo-Aristotelian criticism tells a great deal about Nixon's message. It reveals the speech writer as a superior technician. It permits us to predict that given this target group the message should be successful in leading to a decision to support the Administration's policies. It brings into sharp focus the speechwriter's greatest technical successes: the choice of the right premises to make a version of the domino theory plausible for these auditors and the creation of a controlled atmosphere of fear in which the theory is more likely to be accepted. Likewise, the choice of the right means of making success for peace negotiations seems impossible and the building of a controlled state of anger in which a pessimistic estimate of the chances for success seems plausible. Also the finely crafted structure that conceals exactly what needs to be concealed while revealing the favored plan in a context most favorable to its being chosen.

What neo-Aristotelianism does not attempt to account for are some basic and long-run questions. For instance, it does not assess the wisdom of the speaker's choice of target audience as does Newman, who wanted the President to alleviate the fears of the doves. All critics observe that Nixon excludes the radical opponent of the war from his audience. Not only is this opponent excluded by his choice of policy but even by the choice of premises from which he argues: premises such as that the Government of South Viet Nam is freer than that of North Viet Nam, or that the right course is the opposite of the easy one. Radical opponents of the war were mostly young—often college students. The obvious cliché, "they are the political leadership of tomorrow," should have applied. Was it in the long run a wise choice to exclude them from the target? An important question, but a neo-Aristotelian approach does not warrant us to ask it. There is a gain, though, from this limitation. If the critic questions the President's choice of policy and premises, he is forced to examine systematically all the political factors involved in this choice. Neither Newman nor Campbell do this in the objective and systematic fashion required by the magnitude of the subject. Indeed, would they not be better off with a kind of criticism that does not require them to do it?

Nor does the neo-Aristotelian approach predict whether a policy will remain rhetorically viable. If the critic assumes as given the Nixon Administration's choice of policy from among the options available, he will no doubt judge this choice of value and predictive premises likely to effect the decision wanted. To put it another way, Nixon's policy was *then* most defensible by arguing from the kinds of premises Nixon used. It seems less defensible at this writing, and in time may come to seem indefensible even to people like those in the target group. Why the same arguments for the same policy should be predictably less effective to people so little removed in time is a special case of the question, why do some policies remain rhetorically viable for decades while others do not. This question might in part be answered by pointing, as was done before, to the maturing of the students into political leadership. But however the question might be answered, neo-Aristotelianism does not encourage us to ask it. As Black truly said, the neo-Aristotelian comprehends "the rhetorical discourse as tactically designed to achieve certain results with a specific audience on a specific occasion"[24] in this case that audience Nixon aimed at on the night of November 3, 1969.

Finally, neo-Aristotelian criticism does not warrant us to estimate the truth of Nixon's statements or the reality of the values he assumes as aspects of American life. When Nixon finds the origin of the war in a North Vietnamese "campaign to impose a Communist government on South Vietnam by instigating and supporting a revolution," Campbell takes him to task for not telling the truth. This criticism raises a serious question: are we sure that Nixon is not telling the truth? We know, of course, that Nixon oversimplifies a complex series of events—any speaker in his situation necessarily does that. But will the scholar of tomorrow with the perspective of history judge his account totally false? Campbell endorses the view that basically this is a civil war resulting from the failure of the Diem government backed by the United States to hold elections under the Geneva Agreements of 1954. But her view and Nixon's are not mutually exclusive: it seems evident to me that both the United States and the Communist powers involved themselves from the first to the extent they thought necessary to force an outcome in their favor in Viet Nam. If a scientific historian of the future had to pick one view of the conflict or the other, he would probably pick Nixon's because it more clearly recognizes the power politics behind the struggle. But I am not really intending to press the point that Campbell commits herself to a wrong view, or even a superficially partial one. The point is that she espouses here a theory of criticism that requires her to commit herself at all. If anyone writing in a scholarly journal seeks to assess the truth of Nixon's statements, he must be willing to assume the burden of proving them evidently false. This cannot be done by appealing to the wisdom of the liberal intellectuals of today.[25] If the essential task were accomplished, would the result be called a *rhetorical* critique? By Aristotle's standards it would not, and for my part I think we will write more significant criticism if we follow Aristotle in this case. To generalize, I submit that the limitations of neo-Aristotelian criticism are like the metrical conventions of the poet—limitations that make true significance possible.

[24] Edwin B. Black, *Rhetorical Criticism: A Study in Method* (New York: Macmillan, 1965), p. 33.

[25] Richard H. Kendall, writing a reply to Newman, "The Forum," *QJS,* 56 (Dec. 1970), 432, makes this same point, particularly in connection with Newman's implication that ex-President Johnson was a fraud. "If so, let us have some evidence of his fraudulent actions. If there is no evidence, or if there is evidence, but an essay on the rhetoric of President Nixon does not provide proper scope for a presentation of such evidence, then it seems to me inclusion of such a charge (or judgment) may fall into the category of gratuitous." Newman in rejoinder asks, "Should such summary judgments be left out of an article in a scholarly journal because space prohibits extensively supporting them? Omission might contribute to a sterile academic purity, but it would improve neither cogency nor understanding." I would certainly answer Newman's rhetorical question, yes, and I would go on to judge that view of criticism which encourages such summary judgments not to be a useful one.

The Forum: "Conventional Wisdom—Traditional Form": A Rejoinder

Karlyn Kohrs Campbell

Professor Hill's analysis of Nixon's Vietnamization address in this issue of *QJS*, has added a neo-Aristotelian critique to the roster of criticisms of that speech already published. However, Professor Hill has invited controversy by attacking the methodologies of the other critics, chiefly Professor Robert Newman and myself. I have taken advantage of the opportunity to respond because I think the conflict highlights certain important issues in rhetorical criticism.

Professor Hill legitimates his methodology by appealing to the authority of Aristotle, but in the tradition of heretics, I must demur at several points from his interpretation of the "true faith." I am chiefly concerned with his exclusion of considerations of truth and ethical assessments and with his treatment of the "target audience."

In responding to the exclusion of the truth criterion, I am inclined to appeal to "conventional wisdom" and "traditional form" in interpreting Aristotelian methodology. Thonssen and Baird, for example, treat the evaluation of logical content as one of determining "how fully a given speech enforces an idea; how closely that enforcement conforms to the general rules of argumentative development; and how nearly the totality of the reasoning approaches a measure of truth adequate for purposes of action" (*Speech Criticism*, 1948, p. 334) and specifically call for the rigorous testing of evidence and argument (p. 341). Aristotle himself wrote that rhetoric is valuable "because truth and justice are by nature more powerful than their opposites; so that, when decisions are not made as they should be, the speakers with the right on their side have only themselves to thank for the outcome. . . . [A proper knowledge and exercise of Rhetoric would prevent the triumph of fraud and injustice.]" (*Rhetorica*, trans. Lane Cooper, 1. I. 1355a 21-24). These statements are at odds with Hill's assertion that "neo-Aristotelian criticism does not warrant us to estimate the truth of Nixon's statements or the reality of the values he assumes . . ." (p. 385). In fact, there is a puzzling inconsistency in Professor Hill's essay. On the one hand, Newman and I are chided for questioning the President's choice of policy and premises, on the other, Hill himself takes pains to justify the choice of premises, stating that an assessment of the choice of major premises is central to an Aristotelian account. He discusses the truth of the premises used, e.g., "we know that the premise is not universally true, yet everyone finds it necessary to operate in ordinary life as if it were," "they rest on what experience from the sandbox up shows to be probable," and so forth (pp. 378, 379). Similarly, there are numerous comments indicating Hill's recognition of the highly deceptive nature of this speech in which Nixon said we were to be told the truth, e.g., "this explanation masquerades as . . . ," "but thinly disguised in the chronology . . . ," "this phrase concealed the intention . . . ," and finally, "the finely crafted structure that conceals exactly what needs to be concealed . . ." (pp. 376, 377, 384). As I see it, Hill is arguing for the truth and acceptability of the major premises while recognizing the deception central to the *logos* of this address. The final statement I have cited makes the point of his critique explicit in regard to questions of truth: what we are to applaud as critics is highly skillful deception and concealment. As a critic, that is a bitter pill I cannot swallow.

The issue I have raised not only involves considerations of truth but ethical assessments, and I propose that an amoral reading of Aristotle is open to question. In the section on deliberative rhetoric to which Hill directs us, Aristotle reiterates that rhetoric "combines the science of logical analysis with the ethical branch of political science . . ." (1. 4. 1359b 9-11). Similarly, immediately following the analogy to health care cited by Hill comes the statement that "sophistic dialectic, or sophistical speaking, is made so, not by the faculty, but by the moral purpose" (1. 1. 1355b 16-18). These statements are coherent parts of a teleology defining man as rational and an ethic stating that moral good consists in acting in obedience to reason (*Ethica Nicomachea*, trans. W. D. Ross, 1. 13 1102b 13-28). It seems to me that Aristotle enables the critic to recognize the skillful use of the faculty, i.e., the best (most effective) choices from the inventory, and to condemn the moral purpose and the rhetorical act as sophistic, perhaps even "shoddy." And Aristotle's description of the nature of deliberative rhetoric provides an additional warrant for combining concerns for truth and ethics. He says that the aim of deliberation is determination of advantage and injury with primary emphasis on expediency (1. 3. 1358b 22-24), suggesting that questions of practicality and feasibility are essential to rational decision-making in deliberative addresses. Consequently, I take it that even an Aristotelian critic, confronting a deliberative speech that seeks to avoid questions of expediency and conceals the true nature of the policy being advocated (which Hill admits), might be justified in making a negative assessment.

Finally, Aristotle says that the deliberative speaker must "know how many types of government there are; what conditions are favorable to each type; and what things . . . naturally tend to destroy it" (1. 4. 1360a 20-23), elements relevant to deliberative rhetoric which lead me to object to Hill's assessment of the speech in terms of a "target audience." As he recognizes, political factors and the political context are germane to criticism. There is no dispute that this was a major policy address by the President to the nation. But contrary to Hill's assertion that Aristotelian methodology does not warrant questioning whether or not Nixon should have chosen to ignore parts of his constituency, I submit that Aristotle encourages the critic to recognize that this was not simply a speech by Richard Nixon, but a deliberative address from the Presidency—as institution, symbol, and role—*to all citizens in this republic-democracy.* I am not satisfied that the kind of divisiveness created through this rhetorical act in this political context can be excused by delineating a "target audience." In my critique, I argued that the President eliminated the concept of a "loyal opposition" by creating a dichotomy between the "great silent majority" that supports administrative policy and a "vocal minority" seeking to prevail "over reason and the will of the majority." Aristotle said that the end of democracy is liberty, and if that ambiguous term is to mean anything, it has to include the liberty to dissent from policy without being labeled in terms that suggest that dissent is subversive, if not traitorous. I recognized that Nixon paid lip service to the idea of a loyal opposition ("Honest and patriotic Americans have reached different conclusions as to how peace should be achieved."), but the remainder of the address contradicts this strongly, e.g., "the more divided we are at home, the less likely the enemy is to negotiate" and "only Americans [presumably only *dissenting* Americans] can humiliate and defeat the United States." To assess the speech in terms of a "target audience" is to ignore the special kind of disunity created by the speech which, I believe, is a threat to the political processes of our system of government, particularly when propounded by its chief executive.

As I read Professor Hill's criticism of the analyses of Professor Newman and myself, it seems to me that he believes a major shortcoming of both is a lack of "objectivity." He implies that neo-Aristotelian methodology is "objective," genuinely rhetorical (rather than political or ideological), and, in fact, is the only legitimate methodology—it makes "true significance possible" (p. 386). However, as I understand it, Hill's conception of objectivity requires the critic to remain entirely within the closed universe of the discourse and the ideology or point of view it presents. No testing of premises or data is permitted except that determining the degree of *acceptability* to the immediate audience or, more narrowly, to that part of it that is the speaker's target. This is, of course, commendably consistent with his exclusions of considerations of truth and ethics, but it hardly qualifies as objectivity. It is, in fact, to choose the most favorable and partisan account a critic can render. For example, it is to accept the perspective of the advertiser and applaud the skill with which, say, Anacin commercials create the false belief that their product is a more effective pain reliever than ordinary aspirin. As a consequence, the methodology produces analyses that are at least covert advocacy of the point of view taken in the rhetorical act—under the guise of objectivity. Recognizing that anyone reading my critique of this address will know that I am politically liberal (the same, I think, is true of Professor Newman), my simple rejoinder is that anyone reading Hill's critique will know that he is politically conservative.

The particular point on which he takes me to task, my objections to Nixon's view of the origins of the war, is highly illustrative. Professor Hill writes, "When Nixon finds the origin of the war in a North Vietnamese 'campaign to impose a Communist government on South Vietnam by instigating and supporting a revolution,' Campbell takes him to task for not telling the truth" (p. 385). But Nixon said, "Fifteen years ago North Vietnam, *with the logistical support of Communist China and the Soviet Union,* launched a campaign . . ." (emphasis added). What I said was:

> Now "fifteen years ago" was 1954, the year of the Geneva Agreements that were to unify Vietnam through elections to be held in 1956. Those elections never occurred because the United States supported Diem, who refused elections and attempted to destroy all internal political opposition, Communist and otherwise. The Vietcong did not persuade Hanoi or Peking or Moscow to aid them against Diem until about 1959. By 1965 South Vietnam was clearly losing, the point at which President Johnson decided to send in United States combat forces (*Critiques of Contemporary Rhetoric,* 1972, p. 52).

Professor Hill has condensed both Nixon's and my own comments about the North Vietnamese campaign *with* alleged aid from China and Russia into the simpler notion of a North Vietnamese campaign to instigate revolution and impose a Communist regime on the South. This condensation, although understandably desirable from a conservative point of view and understandably unacceptable from a liberal viewpoint, hardly qualifies as an objective appraisal of Nixon's characterization of the origins of the war or of my response to it. My point was and is that Nixon wished to disclaim all U.S. responsibility for the events with which we now wrestle in Indochina and place all blame on a monolithic Communist conspiracy. I think it highly doubtful that the "scientific historian" to whom Hill refers would support that characterization.

It should also be evident that I do not agree with Professor Hill that neo-Aristotelianism is the only, or even the best, methodology for rhetorical criticism. As Hill's essay illustrates, such an approach has explanatory power for revealing how a speaker produced the effects that he did on one part of the audience, what Hill calls the "target audience," but it ignores effects on the rest of the audience, and it excludes all *evaluations* other than the speech's potential for evoking intended response from an immediate, specified audience. Because I do not believe that the sole purpose of criticism is an assessment of a discourse's capacity to achieve intended effects, I cannot accept Hill's monistic view of critical methodology. I am strongly committed to pluralistic modes of criticism, considering that the questions the critic asks have such a significant effect on the answers generated. I think we know more about Nixon's rhetorical act because a variety of critical approaches have been brought to it than if Professor Hill's critique stood alone.

The objections I have made so far to Professor Hill's views of criticism and of critical methodology have been, I believe, important ones, but my final objection is, for me, the most important. In describing and defending the uses of rhetoric, Aristotle says that we should be knowledgeable about both sides of a question so that "if our opponent makes unfair use of the arguments, we may be able in turn to refute them," and he continues, to remark that although rhetoric and dialectic, abstractly considered, "may indifferently prove opposite statements. Still, their basis, in the facts, is not a matter of indifference . . ." (1. 1. 1355a 30-37). If rhetoric is to be justified, then rhetorical criticism must also be justifiable. For criticism, too, is rhetoric. Its impulse is epideictic—to praise and blame; its method is forensic—reason-giving. But ultimately it enters into the deliberative realm in which choices must be made, and it plays a crucial role in the processes of testing, questioning, and analyzing by which discourses advocating truth and justice may, in fact, become more powerful than their opposites.

The analogy that Professor Hill draws between neo-Aristotelian methodology and metrical conventions as "limitations that make true significance possible" (p. 386) is an interesting one, particularly for an Aristotelian. After all, it was Aristotle who recognized that poetry could not be defined metrically: "though it is the way with people to tack on 'poet' to the name of a metre . . . thinking that they call them poets not by reason of the imitative nature of their work, but indiscriminately by reason of the metre they write in" (*De Poetica,* trans. Ingram Bywater, 1. 1447b 12-16). Perhaps a more apt analogy is that the strict application of a rhetorical inventory may make the critic a versifier, but not a poet.

The Forum: "Reply to Professor Campbell"

Forbes Hill

Professor Campbell's rejoinder states clearly the positions opposed to mine on certain important issues in criticism. I mean the model neo-Aristotelian critique, embodying an ideal form of neo-Aristotelian methodology based on a closer reading of the *Rhetoric* than common to many following Thonssen and Baird, to raise just such issues. They may be grouped in the following three questions: 1) Does neo-Aristotelianism warrant a critic to praise a leader for addressing a target audience and pushing the citizens who are off-target into an isolated and helpless position? 2) Does Aristotle's text authorize excluding considerations of truth from rhetorical critiques, and should such considerations be excluded? 3) Does the text authorize excluding considerations of morality from rhetorical critiques, and should such considerations be excluded? To all parts of these questions I answer yes—though in some particulars it must be a qualified yes. I understand Professor Campbell to answer no in every particular.

Aristotle nowhere uses the concept of target audience. This adaptation of Aristotelian theory to modern conditions is necessary because Aristotle put together his lectures on rhetoric with a group of Athenian students in mind. For them, auditors of a deliberative speech suggested three to five thousand decision-makers gathered in the Pnyx within the sound of the orator's voice. All these decision-makers were male citizens born on that rocky coastland; none were very rich by any standard; few were well-traveled; few had allegiances abroad. In short, they were a highly homogeneous group. That is what Aristotle assumed when he made a demographic analysis into categories of young, old, rich, poor, well-born and powerful. He did not use categories like Greek-descent and non-Greek descent, educated and uneducated, or urban and rural. And he seemed to assume that a speaker will be able to get all sub-groups of auditors to shout assent as did the Achaeans in the epic.

Obviously an American president communicating through the electronic media makes no assumption about getting assent from all his auditors; the audience is not homogeneous enough to permit it. He must start the preparation of his message by trying to decide who his potential supporters are, that is by making a construct of a target audience. Such procedure is entirely in line with Aristotle's. which starts with the question: who is expected to make a decision for or against what? The group expected to make a decision in this case can be only part of that auditing the discourse. When we thus extend Aristotle's method to deal with the greater national audience of a modern country, we are working along Aristotelian lines, not following his *Rhetoric* like a slavish copyist.

Aristotle aside, is it reasonable to demand, as Professor Campbell does, that the President not declare certain groups off-target but promote unity in the nation? It is—up to a point. But if the critic demands that he win over everyone in a policy address to the nation—not a discourse in praise of freedom but a policy address— an unreasonable standard is being maintained. Not Truman, nor even Eisenhower ever met that standard; it was not met save perhaps when Roosevelt asked Congress to declare war after Pearl Harbor. But Roosevelt also derided the money-changers in the temple; was he not acting on the sound precept that someone has to be off-target, that every drama needs an antagonist? Only if the critic wants an American president to fail scrutiny, will he hold up such a standard.

What did Aristotle decree was the role of truth in rhetorical criticism? Professor Campbell interprets the passage about rhetoric being useful since when true and just causes do not win out that must be because of the inadequacy of their advocates' use of rhetoric[1] to mean that Aristotle demands us to determine the truth of an advocate's statements as part of a critique of his rhetoric. That interpretation is in my opinion incorrect. The passage itself assumes that the same rhetoric used to advocate true and just causes is also used by the advocates of untrue and unjust ones. A little further on Aristotle says that though rhetoric persuades impartially to contrary conclusions, we (i.e., good people like us) should not use it to advocate bad causes (*Rhet.* I. 1. 1355a 29-33). A distinction is presupposed here between rhetoric—used to argue either to true conclusions or false—and how a good person uses it—only to argue conclusions he believes to be true. The means of persuasion themselves (enthymemes, examples, and the like) are considered free of truth value, but we who use them should be committed to truth. Rhetoric is the study of our use of the means, not our commitments to ends.

This notion that the means of persuasion are in themselves truth-indifferent fits with other Aristotelian doctrines. Take the well-known distinction between demonstrations and dialectical arguments. The former proceed from premises that are true, primary, immediate, better known than and prior to their conclusions (*Post An.* I. 1 71b 20-25; *Top* I. 1. 100a 25-30) elsewhere called first principles. The latter assume as starting points premises chosen by the respondent from among those generally accepted (*Top.* I. 1. 100b 23-24). Now rhetoric is the counterpart not of demonstrative reasoning but of dialectic. Instead of assuming as premises statements accepted by a single respondent, it assumes those believed by the type of people who are in attendance as decision-makers. In a few cases these premises may be first principles, but they seldom are. That is because men debate about human affairs, which are in the realm of the contingent (*Rhet.* I. 2. 1357a 22-23). Indeed, the more accurately a rhetorician examines his premises, the more likely he is to light on the first principles of some substantive field, and then he will have left the field of rhetoric altogether (*Rhet.* I. 2. 1358a 23-26). Another way of putting the distinction between dialectic or rhetoric and the study of demonstrative reasonings is to say that the former argue from probable premises to probable conclusions

---

[1] Aristotle, Rhetoric I. 1. 1355a 21-24. This paraphrase, like Lane Cooper's translation (used by Campbell), construes a text that is here utterly ambiguous. Literal translation: "Rhetoric is useful because true and just causes are by nature more powerful than their contraries, so that when decisions do not turn out according to what is fitting, necessarily [they] have been defeated through themselves." What does 'themselves' refer to in this passage? True and just causes? Their contraries? Or must we from our own minds supply 'advocates of true and just causes' as subject of 'have been defeated' and antecedent of 'themselves'? 'Their contraries' has had defenders, e.g., Victorius and Spengel, cited by Edward Meredith Cope, *The Rhetoric of Aristotle with a Commentary,* rev. and ed. by John Edwin Sandys (Cambridge: at the University Press, 1877), Vol. I, p. 23. But Mr. Cope rightly asks why, if true and just causes are naturally superior, would they be defeated by their contraries? Making 'advocates of true and just causes' the subject brings sense to the argument, but these words certainly have to be supplied out of thin air. I mention this ambiguity because one who would maintain that Aristotle believed determining truth necessary to rhetorical criticism probably needs to give what I consider an incorrect reading of this passage, but he also needs to think the text as we have it here meaningful enough to bear a definitive interpretation. This is probably not the case.

(*Rhet.* I. 2. 1357ª 27-28). What does probability mean in this statement? A common Aristotelian synonym is *ta endoxa* (what are today called subjective probabilities), defined in the *Topics* as propositions accepted by all, or by the majority, or by the most distinguished people (*Top.* I. 1. 100b 22-24).

It is easy to see from this review of Aristotelian doctrine that Aristotle positively commands the critic of demonstrative arguments to inquire whether or not premises are true, but he says that if a rhetorician examines accurately into this question he leaves the field, ceasing to be a rhetorician and beoming some other kind of scholar. Dialecticians are commanded to examine whether the premises are accepted by all or by the majority, or by the most distinguished people; rhetoricians, by implication, must examine whether the premises will be accepted by the type of people who are decision-makers in this particular case.[2]

A careful look at my critique shows that this is precisely the activity I engaged in. The generalization I worked from is that other things being equal, the more commonplace and universally accepted the premises of prediction and value in a deliberative discourse, the more effective the discourse will be. Applying this principle to Nixon's address, I remarked that "we [the reader, myself, and all other potential members of Nixon's target audience] know that the premise [the future will be like the past] is not universally true, yet everyone finds it necessary to operate in ordinary life as if it were." Professor Campbell accuses me of being inconsistent with my interpretation of what Aristotle demands of a critic by making a judgment about the truth of the premises Nixon used. My remark, taken in context, however, can clearly be seen as a prediction about the acceptability of the premise to potential decision-makers. So can all other comments that taken alone seem to be about the truth of premises or the reality of values.

Only once did I depart from this methodological limitation: when I wrote that Nixon's account of the origins of the war would be preferred by the historian of the future to Campbell's. I was indeed in violation of my own principles. This is, perhaps, as happy an example as could be found of the peril of entering into controversy over the truth of a contemporary speaker's statements.

What is at work in her analysis compelling the conclusion that the United States is responsible for what has happened in Viet Nam is the revisionist theory of the cold war, so popular now in New Left circles. The theory isolates America's militant support of the *status quo ante* as the key element disrupting world peace, in contrast to Communist reaction, which is largely defensive. It informs the whole of Professor Campbell's critique. Naturally Richard Nixon does not analyze the situation this way, and of course, that must mean he is guilty of gross misrepresentation.

If a critic will write of Nixon's address from any such point of view, he has the choice of two ways to treat his theme. He can carefully sift the evidence for the revisionist view as it relates to the war in Viet Nam, or he can simply assume statements reflecting this view—like "the truth is that America supports totalitarian governments all over the world"—are to be accepted by his reader. In either case he is not writing rhetorical criticism.

In the broadest sense rhetorical criticism of any kind primarily assesses how a message relates to some group of auditors. In doing this it may, and usually must,

[2]See Lloyd F. Bitzer, "Aristotle's Enthymeme Revisted," *QJS,* 45 (Dec. 1959), 407.

secondarily consider some questions about how the message relates to what is known about the external world. Whenever this secondary consideration becomes the greater part of a critique it ceases to be a rhetorical critique—unless, of course, rhetoric is defined to include the universe.

Criticism of any kind, however, rests on established principles of one sort or another. A discourse where many starting-points must be taken on trust is an epideictic speech, or to put it another way, a tract for the faithful. Readers not among the faithful are blocked off from whatever insights about structure and strategies the critique may present. To assess the truth of a contemporary speaker's claims is to take either the scholarly way or the partisan way out of the area of rhetorical criticism. Of course, a critic is just as certainly led out of the area if he judges Nixon accurate in his account of the origins of the war. I hereby apologize for my inconsistency in characterizing Nixon's statement of these origins as more adequate than Campbell's.

It is not always plain whether Professor Campbell thinks that President Nixon fails to tell the truth because he is mistaken or because he deliberately tries to give a false impression. Her rejoinder, though, charges me with applauding deception, which she finds central to the *logos* of the address. I said the finely crafted structure concealed what needs to be concealed, but I avoided using the word deception because it implies a wrongful intention to suppress what the suppressor knows to be true. It demands a judgment on Nixon's intentions, his knowledge of the truth in this case, and the wrongfulness in this case of suppressing the truth. When speaking to my neighbors for George McGovern (as I often have lately; Professor Campbell's inference to the contrary I am a liberal) I easily make these judgments, but when writing rhetorical criticism I avoid them. Both Aristotle and sound critical practice sanction avoidance.

I appeal first to the passage cited by Campbell. Aristotle develops his categorization of rhetoric as the counterpart of dialectic by saying

[rhetoric's] function is to examine both proof and counterfeit proof, just as dialectic's is [to examine] both real and counterfeit syllogism. For the sophistry is not in the art [*dynamis* in this context = *techne*], but in the moral purpose [*proairesis*]. Except here a man will be a *rhetor* whether in relation to his art or to his moral purpose, but there [in the case of dialectic] he will be classified as a sophist in relation to his moral purpose, but a dialectician not in relation to the moral purpose, but in relation to his art (*Rhet*. I. 1. 1355b 15–21).

Professor Campbell interprets Aristotle as enabling "the critic to recognize the skillful use of the faculty and to condemn the moral purpose and the rhetorical act as sophistic." True, but this interpretation misses the important distinction here drawn: the distinction between artistic judgment and ethical judgment. Built into the language is the proper distinction about dialectic: viewed artistically someone is a dialectician if he understands dialectical method; viewed ethically he is a sophist if he uses this method to bad ends. Employing a non-Aristotelian technique, we might distinguish between $rhetor_1$, who understands the art of rhetoric, and $rhetor_2$, who uses it purely for self-serving ends. Judgments about $rhetor_1$ are rhetorical criticism; those about $rhetor_2$ are in the field of ethics.

What the text shows us here follows from an important Aristotelian preoccupation. Whereas Plato wished to bring all arts and sciences (*technai kai epistemai*) under a single deductive system unified by the idea of the good, Aristotle conceived of the arts and sciences as separate and distinct areas of study, each with its own first principles (or probable premises that serve the function of first principles). His great endeavor was to separate all human knowledge into these studies and outline for each the basic principles.[3] He also created hierarchies—political science is for him the architectonic study which coordinate subfields like ethics, the rationale of personal moral choice, and dialectic-rhetoric, the study of methods for arguing about political and ethical subjects (*Nic. Eth.* I. 1. 1094a 27-30).

What I have just said about the Aristotelian doctrine of the moral neutrality of rhetoric as art and the consequent separation of ethical judgments and rhetorical judgments is not the whole truth; a large section of the *Rhetoric*, (I. 4 to I. 9) is devoted to the value premises from which a speaker may argue. In this section we find a hierarchy of goods—admitted and disputed. We might see the section as an objective description of what people believe—of the value consensus of Aristotle's time. But it clearly is not that; it consists of an adaptation to rhetoric of the rationalized value system of the *Nicomachean Ethics.* Aristotle here commits himself to his own value system. How can he, then, maintain the moral neutrality of rhetoric? Perhaps Campbell is right saying that "an amoral reading of Aristotle is open to question."

Professor Olian in an admirable article, which thoroughly establishes that the dominant thrust of the *Rhetoric* is amoral, maintains that we can see these sections as descriptive and not Aristotle's own value system just so long as we understand that he is describing the values of persons of breeding, wealth, and education (*hoi aristoi*) and not the values of the masses (*hoi polloi*)[4] I will not here attempt a complete examination of this sophisticated view. I only hazard the opinion that if one understands the full context of Aristotle's remarks about the best citizens he will judge that sound ethical principles are discovered by finding they held by such citizens. But they are verified as being the true principles by an argument from the parts: alternative principles are demonstrably inferior so these must be the right principles. I think that Aristotle establishes by reasoning and not empirically that his value system is the right one.

Aristotle attempts to have matters both ways in the *Rhetoric.* His prologue makes rhetoric the counterpart of dialectic, i.e. amoral. But he introduces the section on value premises by calling it an offshoot (*paraphues*) of the ethical branch of politics. An even better translation might be "a graft onto the ethical branch of politics." He does not say that rhetoric is the mirror-image of ethics; its connection to ethics is not that intimate. But even this way of verbalizing the matter does not quite get him out of contradicting himself.

Friedrich Solmsen, in my opinion the greatest of the twentieth century interpreters of the *Rhetoric,* explained that the first draft of Aristotle's lectures maintained the moral neutrality of the art with consistency. Later drafts, however, introduced the value system precisely because it was needed in any treatment of the art that would be competitive with the completeness of rival sophistic rhetorics all

---

[3] I have drawn here, on a good popular treatment, John Herman Randall, Jr., *Aristotle* (New York: Columbia Univ. Press, 1960), pp. 32-58.

[4] J. Robert Olian, "The Intended Uses of Aristotle's *Rhetoric,*" *SM,* 35 (June 1968), 137.

of which laid claim to having ethical foundations.[5] The evidence for this explanation is skimpy, but it has some inherent probability.

As a practical matter it makes for better neo-Aristotelian criticism to interpret the *Rhetoric* as if it were consistently amoral. There are two reasons why. First, no critic can realistically commit himself to Aristotle's value system as a basic inventory of American values and their hierarchy. Aristotle omits thrift, hardworkingness, chastity, piety, honesty, and humility from the list of virtues. (As Lawrence Rosenfield once remarked to me, he does not know about the Protestant ethic.) He omits progress and efficiency from the list of goods. It is by no means plain that happiness in the Aristotelian sense of the term is or should be the ultimate goal for the rational mid-century American. If, then, we are forced to abandon the value system to which Aristotle was committed, what should we do when judging a discourse—commit ourselves to a value system of our own? Or should we try objectively to describe what we think are the value commitments of the target group—the decision-makers in this case?

The second reason why in practice a neo-Aristotelian critic should give an amoral reading to the *Rhetoric* is that if he judges a speaker's values not to match reality, he is inevitably driven to decide the truth on questions that are best avoided: e.g., "who is really responsible for the cold war?" It has already been argued that attempting to answer such questions leads us to take an indefinite leave of absence from rhetorical criticism.

One more minor point: I never advocated critical monism. The several critical methods applied to this address have each produced essays with considerable virtues. Stelzner, in particular, revealed facets of its artistry I had not dreamed of before. Nevertheless, I think neo-Aristotelianism can do more to render a comprehensive assessment on it than other methods. This has something to do with Nixon and his *logographers* being products of highly traditional training. Their tendency is ever to produce another brand of the conventional wisdom structured in traditional forms.

The same is emphatically not true of other discourses. In *Critiques of Contemporary Rhetoric* Campbell prints an essay of Eldridge Cleaver's. By neo-Aristotelian standards that essay must be judged childishly ineffective: the society at large constitutes the body of decision-makers in this case, and these decision-makers will predictably not respond favorably to this selection of means of persuasion from the available inventory. But experience with hundreds of discussions warns me that in some sense Cleaver's essay is a considerable work of art. If neo-Aristotelianism compels a quick negative judgment on it, that is probably because Cleaver plays another kind of ball game from a different game plan. A method that has more explanatory power for Cleaver's game can certainly be found, as Professor Campbell's critique of the essay well shows.

FORBES I. HILL
Queens College, CUNY

[5] Friedrich Solmsen, *Die Entwicklung der Aristotelischen Logik und Rhetorik,* IV, *Neue Philologische Untersuchungen* (Berlin: Weidmann, 1929). For English presentations of material from this book see Forbes I. Hill, "The Genetic Method in Recent Criticism on the Rhetoric of Aristotle," Diss. Cornell 1963, and George Kennedy, *The Art of Persuasion in Greece* (Princeton, N.J.: Princeton Univ. Press, 1963), pp. 82–85.

Part III Critical Examples

The following studies are examples of rhetorical criticism written by perceptive, mature critics who approach their tasks from different theoretical perspectives, employing varying methodologies. As the bibliography at the end of this book indicates, the studies represented here are only a small sample of rhetorical criticism. Nevertheless, they do tend to illustrate the variety of critical approaches.

In reading these studies, the student of criticism will find it helpful to structure his or her response to them by reconsidering the basic principles discussed in this book. A suggested pattern for the close and careful reading of these studies is as follows:

1. Read the study carefully. Identify other studies cited in the footnotes that could increase the understanding of the critical work, then read the appropriate cited studies.
2. Summarize the content of the study.
3. Discern the ways in which and the extent to which the study exemplifies particular critical functions, discusses the problems of context and audience, and describes and analyzes the role of the speaker or speakers.
4. Attempt to describe as precisely as possible the method of analysis used, the nature and soundness of interpretations based on that analysis, and the evaluation made along with the implicit or explicit criteria for such evaluations.
5. Enumerate and describe the strengths and weaknesses of the study as a piece of criticism.
6. Consider the implications of the study for the practice of criticism.

The Second Persona

Edwin Black

The moral evaluation of rhetorical discourse is a subject that receives and merits attention. It is not necessary to dwell on why rhetorical critics tend to evade moral judgments in their criticism, or on why the whole subject has the forbiddingly suspicious quality of a half-hidden scandal. Suffice it to note that the motives for doubting the enterprise are not frivolous ones. Most of us understand that the moral judgment of a text is a portentous act in the process of criticism, and that the terminal character of such a judgment works to close critical discussion rather than open or encourage it.

Moral judgments, however balanced, however elaborately qualified, are nonetheless categorical. Once rendered, they shape decisively one's relationship to the object judged. They compel, as forcefully as the mind can be compelled, a manner of apprehending an object. Moral judgments coerce one's perceptions of things. It is perhaps for these reasons that critics are on the whole diffident about pronouncing moral appraisals of the discourses they criticize. They prefer keeping their options open; they prefer allowing free play to their own perceptual instruments; they prefer investigating to issuing dicta. These are preferences that strongly commend themselves, for they are no less than the scruples of liberal scholarship.

Nevertheless there is something acutely unsatisfying about criticism that stops short of appraisal. It is not so much that we crave magistracy as that we require order, and the judicial phase of criticism is a way of bringing order to our history.

History is a long, long time. Its raw material is an awesome garbage heap of facts, and even the man who aspires to be nothing more than a simple chronicler still must make decisions about perspective. It is through moral judgments that we sort out our past, that we coax the networks and the continuities out of what has come before, that we disclose the precursive patterns that may in turn present themselves to us as potentialities, and thus extend our very freedom. Even so limited a quest as conceiving a history of public address requires the sort of ordering and apportioning that must inevitably be infected with moral values. The hand that would shape a "usable past" can grasp only fragments of the world, and the principles by which it makes its selections are bound to have moral significance.

The technical difficulty of making moral judgments of rhetorical discourses is that we are accustomed to thinking of discourses as objects, and we are not equipped to render moral judgments of objects. Ever since Prometheus taught us hubris, we in the West have regarded objects as our own instruments, latent or actual, and we have insisted that an instrument is a perfectly neutral thing, that it is solely the use to which the instrument is put that can enlist our moral interest. And it was, of course, the ubiquitous Aristotle who firmly placed rhetoric into the instrumental category.[1] Thanks in part to that influence, we are to this day disposed to regard discourses as objects, and to evaluate them, if at all, according to what is done with them. If the demagogue inflames his audience to rancor, or the prophet

[1] Aristotle, _Rhetoric_, 1355a–b.

exalts their consciousness, in either case we allow ourselves a judgment, but the judgment is of consequences, real or supposed. We do not appraise the discourse in itself except in a technical or prudential way. Our moral judgments are reserved for men and their deeds, and appropriately the literature of moral philosophy is bent toward those subjects. My purpose here is by no means to challenge this arrangement. Instead, I propose exploring the hypothesis that if students of communication could more proficiently explicate the saliently human dimensions of a discourse—if we could, in a sense, discover for a complex linguistic formulation a corresponding form of character—we should then be able to subsume that discourse under a moral order and thus satisfy our obligation to history.

This aspiration may seem excessively grand until we remember that we have been at least playing about its fringes for a long time in criticism. The persistent and recurrently fashionable interest among rhetorical and literary critics in the relationship between a text and its author is a specific expression of the sort of general interest embodied in the hypothesis. Despite our disputes over whether the Intentional Fallacy is really a fallacy, despite our perplexities over the uses of psychoanalysis in criticism and the evidentiary problems they present, despite even the difficulties posed the critic by the phenomenon of ghost writing, where the very identity of the author may be elusive, we still are inclined to recognize, as our predecessors have for many centuries, that language has a symptomatic function. Discourses contain tokens of their authors. Discourses are, directly or in a transmuted form, the external signs of internal states. In short, we accept it as true that a discourse implies an author, and we mean by that more than the tautology that an act entails an agent. We mean, more specifically, that certain features of a linguistic act entail certain characteristics of the language user.

The classic formulation of this position is, of course, in the *Rhetoric* and the *Poetics.* There we find the claim developed that a speech or set of speeches, constituting either the literal discourse of a public man or the lines associated with a role in a play, reveal two dimensions of character: the moral and the intellectual. It is common knowledge that the discussion of moral character—ethos—in the *Rhetoric* is for many reasons an intriguing account, that the discussion of intellectual character—dianoia—which appears mainly in the *Poetics* is cryptic and evidently incomplete in the form in which we have it, and that there are ample textual hints that we are to take ethos and dianoia as distinguishable but complementary constituents of the same thing. They are aspects of the psyche. In a play their tokens suggest to the audience the psyche of a character. In a speech they suggest the speaker.

It is also common knowledge that today we are not inclined to talk about the discursive symptoms of character in quite the way men did in Aristotle's time. We are more skeptical about the veracity of the representation; we are more conscious that there may be a disparity between the man and his image; we have, in a sense, less trust. Wayne Booth, among others, has illuminated the distinction between the real author of a work and the author implied by the work, noting that there may be few similarities between the two, and this distinction better comports than does the classical account with our modern sense of how discourses work.[2] We have learned

[2] Wayne C. Booth, *The Rhetoric of Fiction* (Chicago, 1961), esp. Part II, "The Author's Voice in Fiction."

to keep continuously before us the possibility, and in some cases the probability, that the author implied by the discourse is an artificial creation: a persona, but not necessarily a person. A fine illustration of this kind of sensibility appears in a report on the 1968 Republican convention by Gore Vidal:

> Ronald Reagan is a well-preserved not young man. Close-to, the painted face is webbed with delicate lines while the dyed hair, eyebrows, and the eyelashes contrast oddly with the sagging muscle beneath the as yet unlifted chin, soft earnest of wattle soon-to-be. The effect, in repose, suggests the work of a skillful embalmer. Animated, the face is quite attractive and at a distance youthful, particularly engaging is the crooked smile full of large porcelain-capped teeth. The eyes are the only interesting feature: small, narrow, apparently dark, they glitter in the hot light . . . .[3]

Note that last twist of the knife: the eyes are *"apparently* dark." Not even the windows of the soul can quite be trusted, thanks to optometry.

The Vidal description is more nearly a kind of journalism than a kind of criticism, but its thrust is clearly illustrative of the distinction we have become accustomed to making—the distinction between the man and the image, between reality and illusion. And we have to acknowledge that in an age when seventy percent of the population of this country lives in a preprocessed environment, when our main connection with a larger world consists of shadows on a pane of glass, when our politics seems at times a public nightmare privately dreamed, we have, to say the least, some adjustments to make in the ancient doctrine of ethical proof. But however revised, we know that the concept amounts to something, that the implied author of a discourse is a persona that figures importantly in rhetorical transactions.

What equally well solicits our attention is that there is a second persona also implied by a discourse, and that persona is its implied auditor. This notion is not a novel one, but its uses to criticism deserve more attention.

In the classical theories of rhetoric the implied auditor—this second persona— is but cursorily treated. We are told that he is sometimes sitting in judgment of the past, sometimes of the present, and sometimes of the future, depending on whether the discourse is forensic, epideictic, or deliberative.[4] We are informed too that a discourse may imply an elderly auditor or a youthful one.[5] More recently we have learned that the second persona may be favorably or unfavorably disposed toward the thesis of the discourse, or he may have a neutral attitude toward it.[6]

These typologies have been presented as a way of classifying real audiences. They are what has been yielded when theorists focused on the relationship between a discourse and some specific group responding to it. And we, of course, convert these typologies to another use when we think of them as applying to implied auditors. That application does not focus on a relationship between a discourse and an actual auditor. It focuses instead on the discourse alone, and extracts from it the

---

[3]"The Late Show," *The New York Review of Books,* XI (September 12, 1968), 5.
[4]Aristotle, Book I, Ch. 3.
[5]Aristotle, Book II, Chs. 12–13.
[6]See for example Irving L. Janis, Carl I. Hovland, *et al., Personality and Persuasibility* (New Haven, 1959), esp. pp. 29–54.

audience it implies. The commonest manifestation of this orientation is that we adopt when we examine a discourse and say of it, for example, "This is designed for a hostile audience." We would be claiming nothing about those who attended the discourse. Indeed, perhaps our statement concerns a closet speech, known to no one except ourselves as critics and its author. But we are able nonetheless to observe the sort of audience that would be appropriate to it. We would have derived from the discourse a hypothetical construct that is the implied auditor.

One more observation must be made about these traditional audience typologies before we leave them. It is that one must be struck by their poverty. No doubt they are leads into sometimes useful observations, but even after one has noted of a discourse that it implies an auditor who is old, uncommitted, and sitting in judgment of the past, one has left to say—well, everything.

Especially must we note what is important in characterizing personae. It is not age or temperament or even discrete attitude. It is ideology—ideology in the sense that Marx used the term: the network of interconnected convictions that functions in a man epistemically and that shapes his identity by determining how he views the world.

Quite clearly we have had raging in the West at least since the Reformation a febrile combat of ideologies, each tending to generate its own idiom of discourse, each tending to have decisive effects on the psychological character of its adherents. While in ages past men living in the tribal warmth of the *polis* had the essential nature of the world determined for them in their communal heritage of mythopoesis, and they were able then to assess the probity of utterance by reference to its mimetic relationship to the stable reality that undergirded their consciousness, there is now but the rending of change and the clamor of competing fictions. The elegant trope of Heraclitus has become the delirium of politics. Thus is philosophy democratized.

It is this perspective on ideology that may inform our attention to the auditor implied by the discourse. It seems a useful methodological assumption to hold that rhetorical discourses, either singly or cumulatively in a persuasive movement, will imply an auditor, and that in most cases the implication will be sufficiently suggestive as to enable the critic to link this implied auditor to an ideology. The best evidence in the discourse for this implication will be the substantive claims that are made, but the most likely evidence available will be in the form of stylistic tokens. For example, if the thesis of a discourse is that the communists have infiltrated the Supreme Court and the universities, its ideological bent would be obvious. However even if a discourse made neutral and innocuous claims, but contained the term "bleeding hearts" to refer to proponents of welfare legislation, one would be justified in suspecting that a general attitude—more, a whole set of general attitudes were being summoned, for the term is only used tendentiously and it can no more blend with a noncommittal context than a spirochete can be domesticated.

The expectation that a verbal token of ideology can be taken as implying an auditor who shares that ideology is something more than a hypothesis about a relationship. It rather should be viewed as expressing a vector of influence. These sometimes modest tokens indeed tend to fulfill themselves in that way. Actual auditors look to the discourse they are attending for cues that tell them how they are to view the world, even beyond the expressed concerns, the overt propositional sense, of the discourse. Let the rhetor, for example, who is talking about school integration use a pejorative term to refer to black people, and the auditor is confronted with more than a decision about school integration. He is confronted with a plexus of attitudes that may not at all be discussed in the discourse or even implied in any way other than the use of the single term. The discourse will exert on him the pull of an ideology. It will move, unless he rejects it, to structure his experience on many subjects besides school integration. And more, if the auditor himself begins using the pejorative term, it will be a fallible sign that he has adopted not just a position on school integration, but an ideology.

Each one of us, after all, defines himself by what he believes and does. Few of us are born to grow into an identity that was incipiently structured before our births. That was, centuries ago, the way with men, but it certainly is not with us. The quest for identity is the modern pilgrimage. And we look to one another for hints as to whom we should become. Perhaps these reflections do not apply to everyone, but they do apply to the persuasible, and that makes them germane to rhetoric.

The critic can see in the auditor implied by a discourse a model of what the rhetor would have his real auditor become. What the critic can find projected by the discourse is the image of a man, and though that man may never find actual embodiment, it is still a man that the image is of. This condition makes moral judgment possible, and it is at this point in the process of criticism that it can illuminatingly be rendered. We know how to make appraisals of men. We know how to evaluate potentialities of character. We are compelled to do so for ourselves constantly. And this sort of judgment, when fully ramified, constitutes a definitive act of judicial criticism.

A PARADIGM

Since a scruple of rationality mandates that claims be warranted, and since the most convincing sanction of a critical position is its efficacy, we turn now to a test. That test will be an essay in the original sense of the word: a trial, an attempt, an exploration. The subject of the essay is a small but recurrent characteristic of discourses associated with the Radical Right in contemporary American politics. That characteristic is the metaphor, "the cancer of communism."

The phrase, "the cancer of communism," is a familiar one. Indeed, it may be so familiar as to approach the condition of a dead metaphor, a cliché. What is less familiar is that this metaphor seems to have become the exclusive property of spokesmen for the Radical Right. Although speakers and writers who clearly are unsympathetic to the Right do sometimes use "cancer" as the vehicle of metaphors, the whole communism-as-cancer metaphor simply is not present in "liberal" or Leftist discourses.[7] Yet it seems to crop up constantly among Rightists—Rightists who

[7]Norman Mailer, for example, has lately been making "cancer" and "malignancy" the vehicles of frequent metaphors, but the tenor of these metaphors, usually implied, seems to be something like "the dehumanization that results from technological society." It clearly is not "communism," although Soviet society is not exempt from Mailer's condemnations. One can also find occasional references to the "cancer of racism" among left-of-center spokesmen, but these references seem to be no more than occasional. Where, as in Mailer, cancer is a frequently recurring metaphorical vehicle, the analysis that follows may, with appropriate substitution of tenors, be applied. In Mailer's case, at least, it works.

sometimes have little else in common besides a political position and the metaphor itself. Perhaps the best source of illustration of the metaphor is the Holy Writ of the John Birch Society, *The Blue Book* by Robert Welch. More than most of his compatriots, Welch really relishes the metaphor. He does not simply sprinkle his pages with it, as for example does Billy James Hargis. Welch amplifies the figure; he expands it; he returns to it again and again. For example:

". . . every thinking and informed man senses that, even as cunning, as ruthless, and as determined as are the activists whom we call Communists with a capital 'C', the conspiracy could never have reached its present extensiveness, and the gangsters at the head of it could never have reached their present power, unless there were tremendous weaknesses to make the advance of such a disease so rapid and its ravages so disastrous."[8] And again: "An individual human being may die of any number of causes. But if he escapes the fortuitous diseases, does not meet with any fatal accident, does not starve to death, does not have his heart give out, but lives in normal health to his three score years and ten and then keeps on living—if he escapes or survives everything else and keeps on doing so, he will eventually succumb to the degenerative disease of cancer. For death must come, and cancer is merely death coming by stages, instead of all at once. And exactly the same thing seems to be true of those organic aggregations of human beings, which we called cultures or civilizations."[9] And again: '. . . collectivism destroys the value to the organism of the individual cells—that is, the individual human beings—without replacing them with new ones with new strength. The Roman Empire of the West, for instance, started dying from the cancer of collectivism from the time Diocletian imposed on it his New Deal."[10] And again: "Until now, there is a tremendous question whether, even if we did not have the Communist conspirators deliberately helping to spread the virus for their own purposes, we could recover from just the natural demagogue-fed spread of that virus when it is already so far advanced."[11] And again: "We have got to stop the Communists, for many reasons. One reason is to keep them from agitating our cancerous tissues, reimplanting the virus, and working to spread it, so that we never have a chance of recovery."[12] And finally: "Push the Communists back, get out of the bed of a Europe that is dying with this cancer of collectivism, and breathe our own healthy air of opportunity, enterprise, and freedom; then the cancer we already have, even though it is of considerable growth can be cut out."[13]

There are other examples to be taken from Welch's book, but we have a sample sufficient for our biopsy. Welch, of course, is an extreme case even for the Radical Right. He cultivates the metaphor with the fixity of a true connoisseur. But though the metaphor is not present in the discourses of all Rightists, it seems almost never to appear in the discourses of non-Rightists. It is the idiomatic token of an ideology, the fallible sign of a frame of reference, and it is what we essay to explore.

This metaphor is not the only idiomatic token of American rightwing ideology. There is, to name another, the inventory of perished civilizations that crops up in

[8] Robert Welch, *The Blue Book of the John Birch Society* (Belmont, Mass., 1961), p. 41.
[9] *Ibid.,* p. 45.
[10] *Ibid.,* p. 46.
[11] *Ibid.,* pp. 53–54.
[12] *Ibid.,* p. 55.
[13] *Ibid.*

discourses that are right of center. It is a topos that goes a long way back into our history, and that has evidently been associated with a Rightist orientation for more than a century. Perry Miller, writing of the political conservatism of nineteenth-century revivalism, notes of a sermon delivered in 1841 that it "called the roll . . . of the great kingdoms which had perished—Chaldea, Egypt, Greece, Rome—but gave America the chance, unique in history, of escaping the treadmill to oblivion if it would only adhere to the conserving Christianity. In the same year, George Cheever, yielding himself to what had in literature and painting become . . . a strangely popular theme in the midst of American progress, told how he had stood beneath the walls of the Colosseum, of the Parthenon, of Karnak, and 'read the proofs of God's veracity in the vestiges at once of such stupendous glory and such a stupendous overthrow.' "[14] Miller goes on to observe, "William Williams delivered in 1843 a discourse entitled 'The Conservative Principle,' and Charles White one in 1852 more specifically named 'The Conservative Element in Christianity.' These are merely examples of hundreds in the same vein, all calling attention to how previous empires had perished because they had relied entirely upon the intellect, upon 'Political Economy,' and upon 'false liberalism.' "[15]

That topos is with us yet, and it is almost as much a recurrent feature of Rightist discourse as the communism-as-cancer figure. Both the topos and the metaphor are examples of an idiomatic token of ideology.

Regarding the communism-as-cancer metaphor, it could make considerable difference to critical analysis whether a preoccupation with or morbid fear of cancer had any psychopathological significance, whether such a fear had been identified by psychiatrists as a symptom of sufficient frequency as to have been systematically investigated and associated with any particular psychological condition. If that were the case—if psychiatry had a "line" of any kind on this symptom—such clinical information could be applicable in some way to those people who are affected by the communism-as-cancer metaphor. Moreover, if an obsessive fear of cancer were the symptom of an acknowledged and recognizable psychological condition, the tendency of Rightist discourse to cultivate this fear may work to induce in its auditors some form of that psychological condition. Such would be the enticing prospects of a marriage between science and criticism, but unfortunately both psychiatry and clinical psychology are frigid inamoratas, for the literature of neither recognizes such a symptom. It remains, then, for the critic alone to make what sense he can of the metaphor:

1) Cancer is a kind of horrible pregnancy. It is not an invasion of the body by alien organisms, which is itself a metaphor of war, and therefore suitable to the purposes of the Radical Right. Nor is it the malfunction of one of the body's organs—a mechanical metaphor. The actual affliction may, of course, be related to either or both of these; that is, some kinds of cancer may in fact be produced by a virus (invasion), or they may be the result of the body's failure to produce cancer-rejecting chemicals (malfunction), but these are only the hypotheses of some medical researchers, and not associated with the popular conception of cancer. Cancer is conceived as a growth of some group of the body's own cells. The cancer is a part of oneself, a sinister and homicidal extension of one's own body. And one's attitude

[14] *The Life of the Mind in America* (New York, 1965), pp. 70–71.
[15] *Ibid.*, p. 71.

toward one's body is bound up with one's attitude toward cancer; more so than in the case of invasions or malfunctions, for neither of these is an extension of oneself. It is a living and unconscious malignancy that the body itself has created, in indifference to, even defiance of, the conscious will. And because one's attitude toward one's body is bound up with one's attitude toward cancer, we may suspect that a metaphor that employed cancer as its vehicle would have a particular resonance for an auditor who was ambivalent about his own body. We may suspect, in fact, that the metaphor would strike a special fire with a congeries of more generally puritanical attitudes.

2) In the popular imagination, cancer is thought to be incurable. Now this is a curious aspect of the metaphor. If the metaphor serves to convey the gravity, agony, and malignancy of communism, why would it not convey also its inexorability, and thus promote in the auditor a terror that robs him of the will to resist? That consequence would seem to be contrary to the Rightist's objectives. Why, then, is the metaphor not excessive?

Some auditors possibly are affected by the metaphor or understand it in this way—that is, as a metaphor conveying not just the horror of communism but also the inevitability of its triumph. Hence, Rightists seem less inhibited by the fear of nuclear war than others. Perhaps there is associated with this metaphor not a different estimate of the probable effects of nuclear war, but rather a conviction that the body-politic is already doomed, so that its preservation—the preservation of an organism already ravaged and fast expiring—is not really important.

We must understand the *Weltansicht* with which the metaphor is associated. The world is not a place where one lives in an enclave of political well-being with a relatively remote enemy approaching. No, the enemy is here and his conquests surround one. To the Rightist, communism is not just in Russia or China or North Vietnam. It is also in the local newspaper; it is in the magazines on the newsstand; it is in television and the movies; it has permeated the government at all levels; it may even be in the house next door. We understand well enough that when the Rightist speaks of communism he refers to virtually all social welfare and civil rights legislation. What we understand less well is that when he refers to America, he refers to a polity already in the advanced stages of an inexorable disease whose suppurating sores are everywhere manifest and whose voice is a death rattle.

And what organs of this afflicted body need be spared amputation? The country is deathly ill. Its policies are cowardly; its spokesmen are treasonous; its cities are anarchical; its discipline is flaccid; its poor are arrogant; its rich are greedy; its courts are unjust; its universities are mendacious. True there is a chance of salvation—of cure, but the chance is a slight one, and every moment diminishes it. The patient is *in extremis*. It is in this light that risks must be calculated, and in this light the prospect of nuclear war becomes thinkable. Why not chance it, after all? What alternative is there? The patient is dying; is it not time for the ultimate surgery? What is there to lose? In such a context, an unalarmed attitude toward the use of atomic weapons is not just reasonable; it is obvious.

3) The metaphor seems related to an organismic view of the state. The polity is a living creature, susceptible to disease; a creature with a will, with a consciousness of itself, with a metabolism and a personality, with a life. The polity is a great beast: a beast that first must be cured, and then must be tamed. The question arises, what is the nature of other organisms if the state itself is one? What is the

individual if he is a cell in the body-politic? Contrary to what one might expect, we know that the Rightist places great emphasis on individualism, at least verbally. Recall, for example, Goldwater's often used phrase, "the whole man," from the 1964 campaign.[16] It is true, the Rightist is suspicious of beards, of unconventional dress, of colorful styles of living. He has antipathy for deviance from a fairly narrow norm of art, politics, sex, or religion, so that his endorsement of individualism has about it the aura of a self-indulgent hypocrisy. Nonetheless, there is something of great value to him that he calls individualism, and if we would understand him, we must understand what he means by individualism. He probably acts consistent with his own use of the term.

It appears that when the Rightist refers to individualism, he is referring to the acquisition and possession of property. Individualism is the right to get and to spend without interference, and this is an important right because a man asserts himself in his possessions. What he owns is what he has to say. So conceived, individualism is perfectly compatible with an organismic conception of the polity. And moreover, the polity's own hideous possession—its tumor—is an expression of its corruption.

4) At first glance the metaphor seems to place communism in the category of natural phenomena. If one does not create a cancer, then one cannot be responsible for it, and if communism is a kind of cancer, then it would seem that one cannot develop a moral attitude toward its agents. This would constitute a difficulty with the metaphor only if people behaved rationally. Fortunately for the metaphor—and unfortunately for us—there is a demonstrable pervasive and utterly irrational attitude toward cancer that saves the metaphor from difficulty. Morton Bard, a psychologist who investigated the psychological reactions of a hundred patients at Memorial Sloan-Kettering Cancer Center, found that forty-eight of them spontaneously expressed beliefs about the cause of their illness that assigned culpability either to themselves or to others or to some supernatural agent.[17] His study suggests, in other words, that an extraordinarily high proportion of people who have cancer—or for our purposes it may be better to say *who become convinced* that they have cancer—are disposed to blame the cancer on a morally responsible agent. Surely it is no great leap from this study to the suspicion that an auditor who is responsive to the metaphor would likely be just the sort of person who would seek culpability. The link between responsiveness to the metaphor and the disposition to seek culpability lies, perhaps, in religious fundamentalism. Various studies indicate that the members of Radical Right organizations tend also to be affiliated with fundamentalist religious sects.[18] Surely it is possible that a life-time of reverent attention to sermons that seek a purpose behind the universe can end by developing a telic cast of mind, can end by inducing some people to seek purpose and plan behind everything, so that they must explain political misfortunes and illnesses alike by hypothesizing conspiracies.

5) Cancer is probably the most terrifying affliction that is popularly known. So

---

[16] For example, roughly the last third of Goldwater's speech accepting the Republican nomination in 1964 was a panegyric to individuality and nonconformity.

[17] "The Price of Survival for Cancer Victims," *Trans-action,* III (March/April 1966), 11.

[18] See, for example *The Radical Right,* ed. Daniel Bell (Garden City, N.Y., 1964), esp. Seymour Martin Lipset, "Three Decades of the Radical Right: Coughlinites, McCarthyites, and Birchers (1962)," pp. 373–446.

terrible is it, in fact, that medical authorities have reported difficulty in inducing people to submit to physical examinations designed to detect cancer. For many, it seems, cancer has become unthinkable—so horrifying to contemplate that one cannot even admit the possibility of having it. The concept of cancer is intimately connected with the concept of death itself. Thus, to equate communism with cancer is to take an ultimately implacable position. One would not quit the struggle against death except in two circumstances: either one acknowledged its futility and surrendered in despair, or one transmuted the death-concept into a life-concept through an act of religious faith.

Given the equation, communism = cancer = death, we may expect that those enamored of the metaphor would, in the face of really proximate "communism," tend either to despairing acts of suicide or to the fervent embrace of communism as an avenue to grace. The former, suicidal tendency is already discernible in some Rightist political programs, for example, the casual attitude toward nuclear warfare that has already been remarked in another connection. If it were possible for a communist agency to increase its pressure on the United States, we could expect to see the latter tendency increasing, with some of our most impassioned Rightists moving with equal passion to the Left. John Burnham, Elizabeth Bentley, Whitaker Chambers, and others famous from the decade of the fifties for having abandoned the Communist Party have already traveled that road in the opposite direction. The path clearly is there to be trod.

6) Finally, we may note the impressive measure of guilt that seems to be associated with the metaphor. The organism of which one is a cell is afflicted with a culpable illness. Can the whole be infected and the part entirely well?

As the Archbishop in the second part of *Henry IV* says in the midst of political upheaval:

> . . . we are all diseas'd;
> And with our surfeiting and wanton hours
> Have brought ourselves into a burning fever,
> And we must bleed for it . . .

The guilt is there. Coherence demands it, and the discourse confirms it. It finds expression in all the classic patterns: the zealous righteousness, the suspiciousness, the morbidity, the feverish expiations. The condition suits the metaphor; the metaphor, the condition.[19]

What moral judgment may we make of this metaphor and of discourse that importantly contains it? The judgment seems superfluous, not because it is elusive, but because it is so clearly implied. The form of consciousness to which the metaphor is attached is not one that commends itself. It is not one that a reasonable man would freely choose, and he would not choose it because it does not compensate him with either prudential efficacy or spiritual solace for the anguished exactions it demands.

In discourse of the Radical Right, as in all rhetorical discourse, we can find en-

---

[19] Some illuminating comments on the component of guilt in Rightist style and ideology can be found in Richard Hofstadter, "The Paranoid Style in American Politics," *The Paranoid Style in American Politics and Other Essays* (New York, 1967), esp. pp. 30–32.

ticements not simply to believe something, but to *be* something. We are solicited by the discourse to fulfill its blandishments with our very selves. And it is this dimension of rhetorical discourse that leads us finally to moral judgment, and in this specific case, to adverse judgment.

If our exploration has revealed anything, it is how exceedingly well the metaphor of communism-as-cancer fits the Rightist ideology. The two are not merely compatible; they are complementary at every curve and angle. They serve one another at a variety of levels; they meet in a seamless jointure. This relationship, if it holds for all or even many such stylistic tokens, suggests that the association between an idiom and an ideology is much more than a matter of arbitrary convention or inexplicable accident. It suggests that there are strong and multifarious links between a style and an outlook, and that the critic may, with legitimate confidence, move from the manifest evidence of style to the human personality that this evidence projects as a beckoning archetype.

The Eagleton Affair: A Fantasy Theme Analysis

Ernest G. Bormann

The 1972 presidential campaign was an exciting one for the rhetorical critic who wished to concentrate on the emotions and motives inherent in the symbolic action which was creating, no matter how momentary, a social reality for the American electorate. In a recent issue of the *Quarterly Journal of Speech* I described a fantasy theme approach to the discovery and analysis of rhetorical visions in the persuasion of campaigns and movements.[1] Examining the campaign of 1972 from that critical viewpoint reveals that the rhetoric provides an intriguing case study in the ways in which political unknowns become widely known persona.[2]

---

[1] Ernest G. Bormann, "Fantasy and Rhetorical Vision: The Rhetorical Criticism of Social Reality," *QJS*, 58 (Dec. 1972). 396–407.

[2] I am using the term *persona* in a relatively traditional way as the characters in a dramatic work, the speaker or voice of a poem or other literary work (although not necessarily the author), and the public personality or mask that an individual uses to meet a public situation. Since a fantasy theme analysis emphasizes the dramatizing aspects of rhetoric a critic needs a term to distinguish the public mask or personality of individuals from other aspects of their personality. The commonly used term *image* is unsatisfactory because it has been used for so many different concepts that it no longer communicates much of anything. Not only do professional persuaders tend to use the term *image* for such diverse purposes as to describe the overall general impression of a public figure, of institutions and of products, but scholarly commentators have also used the term to indicate a wide range of symbolic events. See for example, Daniel Boorstin, *The Image: A Guide to Pseudo-Events in America* (1961; rpt. New York: Harper and Row, 1964). See also Kenneth Boulding, *The Image* (Ann Arbor: Univ. of Michigan Press, 1956). *Persona,* as I use the term, is restricted to the character a public person plays in a given dramatization. When the same persona acts in a series of fantasy themes that chain through the public, the cumulative dramatizations create a more generalized character or persona as part of the rhetorical visions of the various rhetorical communities. The concept of *image* also tends to be static whereas fantasy theme analysis requires a term which conveys the dynamic notion of action and also connotes the potential for change.

In addition, the emotional evocation of dismay and frustration and the motivation commonly called *apathy* which characterized the chaining fantasies of those who earlier had been excited and impelled by the dramas of the New Politics rhetorical vision are illuminated and clarified by a fantasy theme of the campaign rhetoric of late summer and early fall. Finally, a critical analysis of the major fantasies that chained through the American electorate reveals the awesome power of the electronic media to provide, in the form of breaking news, the dramatizations that cause fantasies to chain through large sections of the American electorate and that thus provide the attitude reinforcement or change that results in voting behavior which elects a president and a vice president.[3]

No political campaign begins with a blank slate. Each party in a campaign has a well defined rhetorical vision which gives its members a sense of identity and which provides the basic assumptions upon which the party campaigns. On occasion a campaign will see the rise of a rhetorical vision that is either based upon elements from the older visions reshaped into a new pattern or one which rejects the older visions entirely. Often the emergence of a rhetorical vision is indexed by the term *new*. Such labels as the "New South," the "New Deal," and the "New Left" are shorthand ways of referring to rhetorical visions which have emerged clearly enough so people can refer to them and understand the basic elements of the vision when they are so characterized. As a new vision takes shape interested observers will often discuss and debate the meaning of a label. The rhetoric surrounding a new label when a vision is emerging is often couched in definitional terms but the real question at issue is essentially the character of the rhetorical vision indicated by the terms. A critic can often locate the period in history when a new rhetorical vision is emerging by searching for commentary relating to the meaning of labels such as "Black Power" and "New Left." Once the vision has clearly emerged and is well understood the discussion of definitions tends to die out. The campaign of 1972 is of particular interest because it saw the rise of and the demise of a rhetorical vision in the form of the "New Politics."

What I propose to do in the brief confines of this essay is to concentrate on only one side of the campaign of 1972. I will begin with a capsule summary of the New Politics rhetorical vision of George McGovern and then move to a description and evaluation of one major fantasy that chained through the American electorate. My current estimate is that there were four major news events which provided the dramatization needed to start fantasies chaining through the communication system associated with the campaign of 1972. They were the Watergate Affair, the Eagleton Affair, the McGovern plan to give people 1000 dollars, and the peace negotiations of late October and early November. I will examine only the Eagleton Affair.

---

[3]There is a whole literature of "voting studies" which can be interpreted to prove that the electronic media do not influence voting behavior. The survey studies of voting behavior are apparently at odds with another large body of research literature which indicates that relatively short persuasive messages can change scores on attitude scales. For a summary of some of the conflicting studies see Carl I. Hovland, "Reconciling Conflicting Results Derived from Experimental and Survey Studies of Attitude Change," in Richard V. Wagner and John J. Sherwood, eds., *The Study of Attitude Change* (Belmont, California: Wadsworth Publishing, 1969), pp. 184-199. The problem with the voting studies is that the research designs tend to encourage the collection of data so gross that they miss the impact of television messages on the symbolic reality of the American electorate.

The Eagleton fantasy theme was largely ignited and fueled by the mass media, particularly by television, and was an important factor in the dying out of the New Politics rhetorical vision.

Prior to the primary in California the McGovern character was a shadowy one in the fantasy themes of the general public. He was identified, if at all, as a dove, a stock antiwar persona. The pro-McGovern people, however, were deep into a rich rhetorical vision which contained powerful emotional evocations and compelling motives to action. The McGovern rhetorical vision had much in common with the over-reaching traditional Democratic Party rhetoric, particularly in its view of the Republicans as the party of the rich and the privileged oriented toward big business. Like the traditional Democratic vision, the New Politics rhetoric saw the persona of Richard Mihous Nixon as essentially that of Tricky Dick. The slogan that catches the persona in both visions is: would you buy a used car from him? Despite the similarities, the McGovern vision has some crucial differences with the traditional Democratic Party rhetoric.

The rhetorical strategy which undergirded the McGovern vision was an emphasis upon the drama of character. The style and tone of the vision was that of high drama verging from melodrama to tragedy. The New Politics was more than politics according to its rhetoric; it was a movement that encompassed all of life from aesthetics to social style. Or, put another way, politics was elevated in the vision of the McGovernites into the fundamental and all important drama of life. The fantasy themes contained little humor, little irony, little satire. Potentially the scenario was one of tragedy or of glorious redemption in the mode of the mythic drama of the Christian religion. The rhetoric spoke of a turning point in history, of a "last chance," of no hope should the movement fail.[4]

The fantasy themes of the New Politics tended to be character sketches which stressed the moral superiority of the heroes and the evil nature of the villains. The vision had its roots back to the persona of clean Gene McCarthy and the 1968 campaign. The motives embedded in the rhetoric included a personal attachment to a persona of high ethical character for whom a participant would work and strong impulses to strive for such goals as ending the war, aiding the poor, the women, and the minorities. The emotional evocations of the vision were powerful and included admiration for a persona almost saintly in motivation and a hatred of the villainous devil figures. The McGovern rhetoric created a social reality which saw such villainous characters as Lyndon Johnson, Richard Daly, and Hubert Humphrey as the enemy. The vision saw both major parties as essentially corrupted by the war, both as racist and closed. The dream was of a purging of the Democratic party which would oust the bosses, the minions of the military industrial complex, and the racist elements from all of society but particularly from the South.

As the McGovern campaign grew more and more successful until its final triumph at the Miami convention, the vision solidified and the emphasis on villains became sharp and clear in the fantasy themes of the movement. The arch-enemy was Tricky Dick and his laughable hatchetman Spiro Agnew but these persona

[4]For a study of the New Politics rhetorical vision see Linda Putnam, "The Rhetorical Vision and Fantasy Themes of McGovern Campaign Planners," *Moments in Contemporary Rhetoric and Communication*, 2 (Fall 1972), 13–20. The entire issue of *Moments* is devoted to the campaign.

hovered in the background. The more tangible villains, the ones that were the main characters in the fantasy themes, were those symbolized by the Chicago convention of 1968 and these included the devil figures of Lyndon Johnson, Richard Daly, and Hubert Humphrey, all of whom stood for a closed convention, barricaded behind barbed wire, protected by police, a convention which barred the young, the poor, the blacks, the Chicanos, the Indians, and the women. Now the leadership of McGovern backed by the army of the formerly disenfranchised would defeat the old politicians.

The participants in the New Politics rhetorical vision saw themselves as a coalition of various liberation movements that would open the party and give power to the people. The style of the New Politics was openness, participation, community, and cooperation while the style of the old politics was closed, barricaded, unresponsive. The persona of McGovern in the vision of his followers before and during the Miami convention was that of St. George on a crusade. He was not really a politician. He was an honest, sincere, decent man who just happened to be in politics. The fantasy themes presented McGovern patiently working for party reform, opening it up to the people, standing courageously against the Vietnam war, and forging a dedicated and mighty army of hard-working volunteers who finally were to get their chance within the system. One salient scenario presented those who had been outside the walls in Chicago as on the floor in Miami.[5]

After Senator McGovern received the nomination the usual reconciliation of factions within the party in preparation for a campaign was made more difficult because of the collision of key elements of the old rhetorical vision of the Democratic Party with the rhetorical vision of the New Politics. The old vision saw labor at the core of the party; in the new vision, labor bosses such as George Meany were among the villians of the old politics. The labor movement was racist, conservative, and closed off from the poor and the minorities. In the old vision party regularity was a virtue. After all, the party was a coalition and the New Deal fantasy themes dramatized keeping the ethnic groups, the blacks, labor, and the South all under one umbrella. The new vision saw party regulars such as Mayor Daly of Chicago as the enemy. The new vision would sacrifice the racist South (symbolized in the persona of George Wallace) for the sake of the minorities. If the party was not purged the participants in the new vision were ready to leave the ranks.

Clearly, however, success at the polls required a new rhetoric which would transcend the two competing visions within the party. Unless the rhetoricians within both visions could find a strategy to fashion a coherent drama on the basis of the common materials within the two visions, one undergirded by the old mythic assumptions of the traditional rhetoric, the party had little possibility of winning the election in November.

The McGovern leadership group began the rhetorical effort at the convention itself. Fantasy themes began to chain through the McGovern delegations around the theme of *pragmatism*. Invoking the ultimate legitimizer of most political party visions, that is, winning an election, a move was made by the McGovern forces to create a unifying rhetoric.

[5]*Time* reported this version: "Ted Pillow, 20, Iowa, vividly recalls the 1968 Democratic Convention in Chicago. He was one of the protesters outside the hall, taunting police, throwing rocks, breaking windows and fleeing down side streets. Last week in Miami Beach he was sitting inside the convention hall as a member of the Iowa delegation." (24 July 1972), p. 27.

How could a new vision be fashioned to transcend the competing visions within the party? The McGovern campaign strategy was to continue to emphasize *persona*. In an article entitled, "St. George Prepares to Face the Dragon," *Time* magazine noted, "The McGovern Campaign will be similar to the personality-oriented, almost evangelical appeal for faith in a candidate that was unsuccessful for Edmund Muskie."[6] Why did the rhetoricians of the New Politics decide to emphasize fantasy themes based on persona? Certainly they knew that the Muskie candidacy had foundered and that the reports of Muskie's lashing out at a newspaper publisher and breaking down in tears had dramatized a fantasy theme which chained through the American electorate and severely damaged the Muskie persona. Emphasis on persona is a risky strategy unless the heroes can remain, in the words of presidential candidate Eisenhower when Richard Nixon was accused of double dealing in 1952, as "clean as a hound's tooth." What alternatives were open to the planners of the McGovern persuasion? They could have chosen to emphasize *scene*. The refrain of McGovern's acceptance speech was, after all, "Come home America." They could have emphasized *action* which was the strategy adopted by official Republican campaign rhetoricians.

In many respects the emphasis on persona is understandable. The rhetorical strategy had worked in the primaries and brought success at Miami. The nature of the opposition indicated that an emphasis on persona was a strong rhetorical ground. If the challenger selected action as a strategy he would be at a distinct disadvantage since the president is, by the nature of the office, where the action is. Then, too, the breaking news surrounding the Nixon persona during the 1970s presented the president in action scenarios. The Nixon persona had withdrawn troops from Vietnam, signed an arms limitation agreement with Russia, agreed to seating Red China in the United Nations, traveled to China, and traveled to Russia. In the campaign, many fantasy themes were available to dramatize the president as persona in action.[7] In addition, the scenarios in which the president was the leading actor were not all that unattractive. The persona of Nixon, on the other hand, seemed a good target for attack. Certainly those who participated in the New Politics vision and hated the persona would be tempted to frame rhetorical dramas in which Richard Milhous Nixon was the center of attack.

The unifying rhetoric at the Miami convention began first with the emphasis on a villainous persona. Bad as Mayor Daly might be, and bad as Hurbert Humphrey might be, still, those deep in the New Politics vision ought to join forces with their old enemies within the party in order to defeat Nixon. As much as the old politicians disliked the new, would it be worth four more years of Nixon to carry on the internal battle. Senator McGovern developed the theme in his acceptance speech. "Now to anyone in this hall or beyond who doubts the ability of Democrats to join together in common cause I say never underestimate the power of Richard Nixon to bring harmony to Democratic ranks."[8]

The second rhetorical strategy which began at the convention was to find a new

[6](24 July 1972), p. 9.
[7]Which is precisely what many of the paid political announcements produced by the Committee to Reelect the President did do. Their persuasion on television tended to show montages of the President at work in the White House, walking along a beach with his wife, walking on the Great Wall of China, meeting with the Russian leaders, and so forth.
[8]CBS Network Coverage of the Convention, 14 July 1972.

symbolic persona who could bridge the competing visions. Traditionally the nomination of a vice president serves as a symbolic welding of the disparate visions within in a party. The McGovern team began its search with Edward Kennedy who would have been ideal except the Kennedy persona was so potent it might have overshadowed the candidate himself. When Kennedy would not accept, the McGovern forces turned to an attractive young senator with strong ties to the competing Democratic rhetorical vision, strong with labor, strong with the regulars but also young and attractive, much in the mold of the Kennedy persona. Senator Thomas Eagleton seemed to provide a personality which could be fashioned into a transcending figure.

With the decision in Miami to select Senator McGovern the campaign for the votes of the electorate got under way in all seriousness. Now the fantasy themes that would chain out through the American public would carry with them the motives to go or not to go to the polls and, just as importantly, to vote for either the Nixon persona or the McGovern. For many the McGovern public figure was vague and shadowy at this stage; even the professionals of the media had not formed a clear rhetorical vision of that portion of the campaign dominated by McGovern. The traditional rhetorical vision of the professional news person and political commentator was that of politicians as essentially ambitious people out to get elected, scrambling about for political advantage, generally hypocritical. Wise inside-dopesters such as professionals never were taken in by appearances and never took a politician's words for anything more than smokescreen.[9]

The Miami convention provided the first big chance for newsmen to chain out on the dramatic action of events. One of the first fantasies to spread through the media was that of the McGovern machine. Some media reports dramatized the New Politics as just the Old Politics honed to a sharper than usual edge.[10] Larry Hart and Frank Mankiewicz emerged as characters in the drama; for some reporters, they were the able people who had harnessed the high idealism of a lot of students and new lefists and poor people to a volunteer organization that had outmachined Richard Daly himself.

---

[9]The concept of inside-dopster is explained in detail in David Reisman, Nathan Glazer, and Reuel Denney, *The Lonely Crowd: A Study of the Changing American Character* (1950; rpt. Garden City, N.Y.: Doubleday Anchor Books, 1953), pp. 210–217.

Riesman, Glazer, and Denney note, "There are political newsmen and broadcasters who, after long training, have succeeded in eliminating all emotional responses to politics and who pride themselves on achieving the inside-dopesters' goal: never to be taken in by any person, cause, or event." (p. 211) For further discussion of the media professionals' vision and its motive which causes them to seek out the dramatic, see David Berg, "Rhetoric, Reality, and Mass Media," *QJS*, 58 (Oct. 1972), 255–263. Richard Dougherty, McGovern's press secretary during the 1972 campaign, bitterly castigated the press because they gave McGovern "a hell of a beating." He was referring to the Eagleton Affair. He concluded, "The man they offered up for the people to judge was a caricature of the real man, and most reporters knew it. I would guess that 90 percent of the news people who covered McGovern voted for him. Why, if that was their ultimate personal judgment of him, could they not pass that judgment on to the public? Hard news wouldn't let them. It wouldn't have been objective reporting. You can write about a candidate who is being sneaky and bumbling: that's objective reporting. But you can't write about a candidate who is being kind and forgiving: that's editorializing." "The Sneaky Bumbler," *Newsweek*, 8 Jan. 1973, p. 7.

[10]*Time* magazine, for example, headlined its convention cover story: "Introducing . . . the McGovern Machine" (24 July 1972), p. 18.

In a sense the fantasy fit in well with the media vision where no politician is as virtuous as he or she maintains and the ultimate legitimatization for politics is winning. They had miscalculated McGovern's chances for many months. Now he had won. Now he was legitimatized. The fantasy accounted for their miscalculation and also put St. George the self-righteous in his place. They had miscalculated because they had not realized that the McGovern machine had such a thorough and effective grass roots organization. As the McGovern forces crushed all attempts to seat the contested delegates from the opposition and as it began to play down issues like women's liberation, abortion reform, and amnesty, the fantasy began to chain through the media that McGovern had worked a miracle and that he just might be ruthless enough and his machine might be well organized and disciplined enough to pull off a second miracle and unseat the President.

McGovern and the television cameras went to Sylvan Lake in the Black Hills of South Dakota to rest and plan for the campaign. The American public had every reason to pay more attention to the McGovern persona as it was portrayed by the media for he was now a potential president. The confident nominee had barely time to be seen on the television screens enjoying a well-earned rest in the serene mountains when a dramatic news story broke.

On Tuesday, July 25, 1972, Senators McGovern and Eagleton called a press conference in the Black Hills. That evening, Roger Mudd, sitting in for Walter Cronkite, asserted that an obviously "nervous" Eagleton had told the press of his mental health problems. The producers cut to a film clip of McGovern and Eagleton walking with a parade of supporters, workers, and newsmen to a building where the press conference was to be held. The film cut to Eagleton's statement which included the crucial phrase, "on three occasions in my life I have voluntarily gone into hospitals as a result of nervous exhaustion." As the press conference continued, the network producers cut to shots of Mrs. Eagleton and Mrs. McGovern, to Senator McGovern watching Senator Eagleton, and to the questions and answers of both senators. In answer to a question, Senator McGovern said, "I don't have the slightest doubt about the wisdom of my judgment in selecting him as my running mate nor would I have any hesitancy at all in trusting the United States Government in his hands." The producers cut back to Roger Mudd who said that the decision to hold a press conference "obviously followed a major crisis in the McGovern camp and apparently was precipitated by persistent rumors that Senator Eagleton had a possible drinking problem."[11]

The story of Senator Eagleton's nervous exhaustion was top priority news on all three major television networks. Key excerpts from the press conference were shown to the huge audiences that watch the dinner time and late evening news. David Brinkley on his journal on NBC mentioned electric shock therapy and noted that "it has been a long time since the office of the vice president got so much attention."

The story had the human interest required to chain out in all directions through the American electorate. Millions of people who had little impression of the McGovern persona and less of the Eagleton presence were suddenly attending to both. How far would the fantasy chaining process go? How compelling would the drama

[11] My reconstruction of the network newscasts is based upon videotape recordings of the broadcasts. I will identify the date and the network in the text.

become for the majority of the American people? The answer to such questions depended partly upon new developments or, in dramatic terms, new complications and partly upon the rhetorical art with which the drama was presented.

Senator McGovern had expressed support of Senator Eagleton in the first press conference. In long film clips on all networks reporters questioned McGovern again and again about the nature and extent of his support for Senator Eagleton. ABC News on July 26th featured in interview between Harry Reasoner and George McGovern. They were pictured seated at a picnic table beside Sylvan Lake. Reasoner asked, "Can you flatly say that if you had known this before you selected him your decision would have been the same?" McGovern, "Absolutely. There would have been no difference." A bit later in the interview Reasoner asked, "Suppose Senator Eagleton in the face of whatever reaction there is to this announcement wanted to leave the ticket, what would your attitude be, sir?" McGovern answered, "I would . . . I would discourage that. I don't want him to leave the ticket. I think . . . uh . . . I think we're going to win the election. I think he's going to be a great vice president. If anything were to happen to me I think he would make a great president. I will do everything I can to discourage any move on his part to leave the ticket. He's not considering that, though, by the way." Later in the same newscast, Howard K. Smith asserted, "In the chat with reporters today McGovern escalated numerically his support of Eagleton. He was, he said '1000 percent resolved to keep Eagleton as a running mate.'"

Where is the rhetorical dimension of the Eagleton Affair? Assuming, as I do, that rhetoric is an art, where is the artistry? Both the strategists for McGovern and for Nixon made rhetorical choices affecting the dramatizations that were presented to the American people. The media professionals also made rhetorical choices. Thus the dramatizations that appeared on the television network news programs on July 25, 26, 1972, were joint artistic efforts of the Nixon, McGovern, and media rhetoricians. (The same process was, of course, operating in radio, newspapers, and magazines.)

The age of mass communication has seen the rise of a unique mass rhetoric fashioned by groups of artists of strangely mixed objectives and approaches. Both McGovern and Nixon publicists had a clear persuasive objective and a general notion of how they would have liked to have their position presented on network television news. The two antagonistic groups had to make their rhetorical choices with an eye both to the symbolic responses of the other and to those of the "objective" media professionals. In one sense, if the Nixon forces gained, the McGovern forces would lose, and vice versa, but the essentially zero-sum game of the two campaigns was mediated by the electronic journalists with their own intent and the success or failure of each candidate's rhetoric was to some extent dependent upon the cooperation of the media professionals. The fact that the network news seldom dramatizes events as advocates wish they would accounts for some of the anger and disillusionment with the media.

McGovern's people made some of the more important early rhetorical choices. They decided to hold a press conference. Since their man was a newly nominated presidential candidate they could, if they were skillful in the way they planned and conducted the news briefing, assure themselves of free television time and of a very large audience.

The McGovern strategists certainly could select the scene for the drama. They might select, as they did, Sylvan Lake in the Black Hills of South Dakota; they could have chosen Washington, D.C., or Barnes Hospital in St. Louis. The strategists could also select the persona of the drama. Should, for instance, the McGovern persona take center stage with the Eagleton persona standing silently by? Should the McGovern persona be separated in space, for example, Senator Eagleton holding a press conference in Washington, D.C., with McGovern simply answering reporters' questions in the Black Hills? Should other persona be present? To indicate the extent of the rhetorical choices, one possible alternative for the McGovern rhetoricians could have been to have Senator Eagleton make his announcement from Barnes Hospital with a battery of doctors who would testify as to his medical record and to the present state of his mental health. The McGovern persona might then have stayed in South Dakota and expressed noncommital concern.

The contemporary strategist for mass audiences needs to be skilled at estimating the response of the mediating professionals and should draft messages, select time, scene, and persona with a view to getting the fantasy themes most likely to chain dramas persuasive to his position on prime-time evening television. In estimating the responses of the professionals and in their decisions as to persona, scene, and dialogue, the McGovern forces made some rhetorical errors of the first magnitude. They selected as the scene the Black Hills vacation retreat of Senator McGovern and they had the McGovern persona at the Eagleton press conference. Not only that, but McGovern made a strong statement supporting Senator Eagleton.

Everything about the setting, the persona, and the lines they spoke reinforced the support of McGovern for the Eagleton persona and his identification with it. In addition, no other major persona of the Democratic Party was on the scene to lend symbolic unity and support to the decisions.

On television the media reporters appeared delighted if a bit incredulous about the McGovern support and kept prodding for clear and unequivocal expressions of such commitment. Clear expressions of positions in risky situations are rare in political campaigns but they are good news just because of that fact.

Having gotten the McGovern persona, epitome of the New Politics, to express unequivocal support, the rhetoricians of the media went to work to create a good news story. The media professionals evaluate a good story as one having the ability to hold the interest of the audience. Human interest stories dramatizing fantasies that chain out through the public raise television ratings.

When the McGovern forces called the news conference and staged the opening scenes of the Eagleton Affair they, of course, lost control of the story. They could affect future symbolic events but they could not completely control them as they could with the dramatizations they presented during the television time they purchased.

The stage was now set for dramatic action from the Nixon persona. In line with the overall Nixon rhetoric of playing down persona and emphasizing action, the Nixon decision came quickly and was delivered by the surrogate persona of MacGregor. On July 26th, film clips of MacGregor appeared on several network newscasts. On CBS MacGregor claimed that the Republicans knew about Eagleton's health record but, even before the announcement, had received "a mandate and directive from the President that no one connected with him in any way governmentally or politically would have any comment whatever to make."

The Nixon rhetoricians would keep the persona of the President out of the drama. By doing so they gained little but they also risked little. In a situation where the public opinion polls indicated that Nixon was ahead, the temptation to take a conservative position and not gamble was strong. The Nixon forces had, however, taken the same rhetorical stance in the much closer campaign of 1960 in regard to the religion of his opponent, John F. Kennedy. On that occasion the rhetoricians for Kennedy had set a scene in Houston, Texas and provided the Kennedy persona with dramatic antagonists in the form of a group of protestant ministers. Kennedy made a strong direct defense of his religion and its role in his functioning as a president should he be elected. The fantasy theme of the Kennedy confrontation apparently chained out to the advantage of the Senator. His campaign organization subsequently bought time to show an artistic dramatization of the scene in the form of a documentary film on television stations throughout the country. In 1960 the low-risk decision nonetheless cost the campaign of Richard Nixon votes because of the artistry with which the skillful Kennedy rhetoricians presented the media and the public with further dramatizations.[12]

After the news conference announcing Eagleton's medical history the media rhetoricians had their turn. They operated under stringent time limitations. Their dramatic format was that of an "anchor man" with star status, the Walter Cronkite, Roger Mudd, David Brinkley, John Chancellor, Harry Reasoner, Howard K. Smith persona, playing the leading role and the lesser reporters serving as narrative voices, a mass media chorus, speaking from the scene of action. The narrator convention serves to tie the events that are dramatized into some sequence and fit them into an interpretative frame. The convention of narrator generally requires that the persona of the reporter be an "objective" voice.

The illusion of objectivity is created by the device of having the narrator attribute all editorial comments, unverified statements of fact, and opinion statements to others. Thus when the narrator chorus began to assert that pressure was building up on McGovern to dump Eagleton, the narrators always attributed the information to others. For instance, NBC reporter Bob Clark mentioned from South Dakota (July 26th) that the Democrats were keeping a calm public face but "off the record, a number of Democrats agree with most Republicans that the Eagleton disclosures have hurt the McGovern ticket." NBC reporter John Dancy asserted (July 27th) that "one of McGovern's top aides privately calls the disclosure a blow to their chances." ABC reporter Sam Donaldson maintained (July 28th) that the "Senator's top staff men are deeply worried about the Eagleton affair." Reporter Stephen Geer of ABC added, "McGovern's advisors are concerned because he has been on the defensive." Since the narrators present an objective voice they seem removed from partisanship and thus, in a political campaign, are often more credible sources than most of the partisan campaigners.

The dramatic structure of the network news in presenting an event such as the Eagleton developments consists of a lead-in by the star persona, a narrative commentary with short film clips of dramatic action presented either by the star or one of the lesser reporters, and transitional material usually provided by the anchor man. The media rhetoricians' artistry in selecting from the materials presented by the campaign rhetoricians and their skill in weaving new materials of their own

---

[12]See for example Harold Barrett, "John F. Kennedy Before the Greater Houston Ministerial Association," *Central States Speech Journal*, 15 (Nov. 1964), 259–266.

manufacture into an interpretative frame has much to do with the way the story catches on and chains through the public (or fails to do so) and with the persuasive impact of the chaining fantasy. Whether the drama as it chains through the general public contains motives to vote for Nixon or for McGovern or for neither is of less importance to the media rhetoricians than that it does chain widely. The charge that the media are liberal or conservative or systematically biased in their dramatizations is too simple, in my estimation. The media rhetoricians are hard-headed dramatists more interested in success at the box office than in partisan political persuasion.

A drama to be compelling requires plausibility, action, suspense, and sympathetic characters. Developing audience interest in a drama which emphasizes character takes time and time is in short supply on the evening news (as contrasted, say, with daytime television dramas where time is in long supply and where the dramas tend to emphasize character at the expense of action). Because of the shortage of time on the evening news the skillful media professional tends to go for conflict and suspense. The McGovern rhetoricians thus were operating under a handicap because of their decision to emphasize character when it came to utilizing one of the most credible outlets of television, that of the network sponsored newscasts.

Now the professional news people began the artistic interpretation of the events. The day after the original press conference several networks interviewed a former alcoholic, Senator Hughes of Iowa, identified as Senator Muskie's vice presidential choice had the Maine Senator received the nomination. Hughes was supportive of Eagleton's staying on the ticket and asserted that the American people had "outgrown this immaturity" in regard to mental health. The Hughes persona was one of the few characters selected by the media rhetoricians which fit the fantasy that Eagleton's mental health problems were no drawback for the ticket and that, indeed, the American people would be sympathetic to him. Early in the breaking news the fantasy theme that Eagleton should stay on the ticket and demonstrate the maturity of the electorate appeared to be a viable one. For the most part, however, the professional journalists sought to dramatize the conflict.

CBS News on July 27th did an able and artistic job of finding and presenting the controversy. Roger Mudd began by listing all of the major newspapers which had come out for Eagleton's withdrawal. Reporter Duke interviewed Mankiewicz and Hart and both reiterated that the decision to keep Eagleton had been made and that it was irrevocable. Next CBS cut to an interview with Howard Metzenbaum, identified as a Cleveland attorney and millionaire fund raiser for McGovern. Metzenbaum was sought out to dramatize the story that the Eagleton disclosures were hurting fund-raising for the McGovern campaign. Metzenbaum was of the opinion that Eagleton would do the right thing and resign. He said, "unfortunately the American people don't comprehend the nature of psychiatric treatment." If Eagleton would resign, he felt, the election might still be won because, fortunately, "in time people do forget." Henry Kimmelman, identified as finance chairman, also appeared briefly, but took no firm stand.

Next the CBS News cut to a long interview with an articulate and attractive persona identified as Matthew Troy, Democratic leader in Queens, New York, and strong McGovern supporter. Troy asserted that people "are really scared that you're giving the power possibly to a man to ... to ... to destroy this world with a nuclear

151

holocaust if he buckles under the pressure of the presidency." Troy had urged McGovern to drop Eagleton. What did McGovern reply? "He told me he was standing by Senator Eagleton and he would not walk away from him."

When a fantasy begins to catch on with a large group of people the evidence of public interest tends to draw outsiders into the social reality for self-serving reasons. Thus an unexpected outside complication is often a component of a major fantasy drama.

On July 27th an unexpected and dramatic complication entered the Eagleton affair when the crusading reporter persona, Jack Anderson, charged that Senator Eagleton had a record of arrests for drunken driving. Another press conference was arranged for Senator Eagleton and again he received extensive coverage on the three major networks. On ABC News Eagleton testified that he had no record of arrests for drunken driving. Eagleton said, "Mr. Anderson's statement to that effect is, in blunt but direct English, a damnable lie." The camera cut to a tight face shot catching the Senator from the hairline to just below the chin. He passed the test of the close-up lens. Clear-eyed, with jutting jaw, he reaffirmed his innocence and his firm resolve to stay in the race and vindicate himself and his record. "I have never been more determined in my life about any issue than I am today about remaining on this ticket. I'm not going to bow to Mr. Anderson. I'm not going to let a lie drive me from this ticket."

The Eagleton rhetoricians had responded brilliantly to the Anderson complication. The Senator's denial, his demeanor during the newscasts, his statements of resolve were appealing. The problem, of course, was the possibility that the crusading reporter was right. For the McGovern rhetoricians the new complication was probably extremely traumatic.

The media peoples' decisions to interview certain individuals (and not others) and then feature these interviews as part of the dramatizations gave them considerable control over the cast of the drama. Picking the cast gave the electronic journalists some control over the action line and the conflict and suspense that resulted and, thus, over the potential of the story to be a big one—that is, to catch the attention of many people and remain in featured position on the evening news for a number of days. The media production people cast such as individuals as Hart, Mankiewicz, Metzenbaum, and Troy into the fantasy as it unfolded. Some of the breaking news was, of course, beyond the control of media production crews. They were restricted by the nature of the material presented by the McGovern and Nixon persuaders. They were also restricted by such intrusions as Jack Anderson's charges. Nonetheless, the room for artistry and the options available are very large and much larger than a rhetorically naive viewer watching the hard news unfold at dinner time is likely to realize. They chose to feature the Troy persona which emerged on television as an attractive, articulate, and dramatic antagonist to keeping Eagleton on the ticket. The Metzenbaum persona was less articulate and less attractive but presented the more "pragmatic" and cynical political position most effectively.

Clearly the fantasies chaining through the media professionals, given their rhetorical vision of politics, influenced their selection of persona. Although I do not have copies of all segments of all networks' newscasts covering the Eagleton Affair, I do have the bulk of them. In none of the segments that I have studied do the networks present a medical authority on Senator Eagleton's health. His doctor never appeared on network news. In many other dramatizations regarding the health of a president, vice president, or candidate for those offices, the reporters often go to the medical men. When President Eisenhower had his heart attack medical material was a prominent part of the news. When Lyndon Johnson was a national leader his health was often discussed. In the instance of the Eagleton candidacy, however, the networks featured the drama of pressure from within the Democratic Party for his resignation.

On July 28th the ABC News showed Eagleton saying, "I'm not quitting. I'm not getting out . . . No, you're not going to get me out of this race . . . never . . . " Howard K. Smith reported that Eagleton was considering taking his case to the people on television as Richard Nixon had in 1952. On NBC News an excerpt from Eagleton's press conference showed Eagleton alluding to the fact that John Kennedy had taken the case of his Catholicism to the people and won and that maybe Eagleton would do something to lay to rest the mental health issue.

By the 28th, fantasy themes which would be supportive and contain sympathetic emotional evocations were beginning to chain out in the media in regard to Eagleton's candidacy. Like Richard Nixon in 1952, he might take his case directly to the people. Like John Kennedy in 1960 he might lay to rest another bigoted political prejudice. On his evening commentary, Howard K. Smith urged McGovern to keep Eagleton since he had expressed 1000 percent support for his running mate and "a switch now would give a wishy-washy impression that would be bad for a presidential candidate." Smith noted that Abraham Lincoln and Winston Churchill had suffered from spells of melancholia which probably should have been treated professionally and yet one had been the greatest president ever and the other had been the greatest prime minister. Eagleton's colleagues in Washington found him to be, "outstandingly vigorous and easy to work with. Moreover, a couple more undocumented charges like Jack Anderson's yesterday and there is going to be a big backlash of sympathy for Eagleton. McGovern would look pretty bad disowning him just as the public may be about to turn for him."

Clearly, some media professionals were beginning to interpret the drama in ways which presented McGovern-Eagleton as heroic figures striking a blow for public understanding of mental problems. The blunder of the McGovern rhetoricians was one of timing in that they temporized and allowed the drama to unfold for too long in this age of electronic media. Here the symbolic role of money in a political campaign in the United States played an important part in the developing rhetoric. In the vision of many citizens, partisans, media professionals, and independents, the drama of politics is rife with monetary implications. In some visions elections can be bought but in most, campaigns require money. The election of 1972 saw a great preoccupation with campaign contributions and financing. The media decision to dramatize the impact of the Eagleton medical record on campaign contributions is indicative of the interpretive frames of the visions. Money symbolizes both the potential for success and for corruption; it symbolizes both the potential for the selling of a president and the selling out of a presidential candidate.

Now the McGovern rhetoricians had to accommodate to the fantasies chaining out from the media dramatization to the effect that their campaign was doomed because, already behind, they would find the sources of campaign funding drying up. At this juncture, I have no evidence of the extent to which the fantasy chained through those groups with the greatest likelihood of contributing to the campaign. Should the fantasy have chained out through those groups, however, it contained motives that would, indeed, shut off contributions. Thus fantasy theme analysis provides a clue to the mechanism by which the oft-noted phenomenon of the self-fulfilling prophecy comes about. The media, by dramatizing the possible impact of the Eagleton Affair on contributions, could trigger fantasy chains among potential contributors which would cause opinion leaders among potential contributors (such as Metzenbaum) to report to the McGovern headquarters that contributions would dry up.

Having allowed the drama to unfold to the point where the fantasies about monetary support were moving through the public, the potential loss of funds became a factor that the McGovern rhetoricians had to deal with on several levels. They had to estimate what, indeed, would happen to the flow of money if they decided to keep the Eagleton persona, which had by now been invested with great symbolic power, power to work either for or against their drive to persuade the American electorate to vote for McGovern. They also had to anticipate what would happen to American public opinion if they severed the powerful Eagleton persona from the ticket. Finally, if they removed Eagleton, could they find a suitable persona to replace him? Could they find a persona with the potential to repair the damage to their rhetoric of character? (Notice that I am phrasing all issues and options in rhetorical terms and such important questions as the ability of the candidate as administrator are bypassed. My analysis focuses on symbolic action. If rhetorical decisions clash with other considerations then a campaign organization might, of course, make a poor rhetorical decision in order to achieve other goals. For instance, if McGovern's forces had had evidence that Senator Eagleton's health was such that he could not assume the duties of president, they might decide to remove him from the ticket even if the Eagleton persona had become so attractive that the decision would have deleterious rhetorical effects.)[13]

The suspense continued to build up over the weekend. On July 30th, Jean Westwood said that she thought Eagleton should resign. Eagleton continued to assert his decision to stay in the race. The news reporters intensified their reports of inside information and rumors of pressures and counterpressures.

On July 31st, CBS News reported that Senator McGovern would announce a final decision soon and that he would meet with Senator Eagleton. Bruce Morton of CBS asserted that Eagleton would argue to stay and McGovern would urge him to leave. The dramatization of CBS News on July 31st, however, clearly was based upon the theme that Eagleton would leave the ticket. CBS carried a feature on how the new vice presidential candidate would be chosen and reported rumors of who the new candidate might be. The commentator, Barry Serafin, narrated films of Eagleton in shirtsleeves on the telephone. Serafin reported that Eagleton was receiving many supportive letters. Eagleton said he had a good case to present, but, according to Serafin, in McGovern he would have a difficult jury.

ABC News reported a poll of Democratic state chairmen and vice chairmen in which eighteen voted to keep Eagleton, seventeen voted to have him step down, and ten refused to comment. NBC News featured a three-way discussion with Chancellor asking questions of Fred Briggs who had been with Eagleton, and John

---

[13]This is a purely hypothetical possibility; I have no information indicating this to be the case.

Dancy who had been with McGovern. Chancellor asked Dancy why did not Mc-Govern ask Eagleton to step down immediately? Why has it gone on this long? (Actually the first report came on the 25th so the Eagleton Affair had been before the public less than a week. Yet when one views the recordings of the television news shows for the week, the saturation coverage does give the impression that the drama has gone on for a long time.) Dancy answered that at first they were going to try to "tough it out" and, of course, that had not worked.

Howard K. Smith's commentary assumes that Eagleton will be dropped and Smith dramatizes a fantasy theme most damaging to McGovern's persona. Eagleton had hardened his resolve to stay. "McGovern, 1000 percent resolved to keep Eagleton, in his phrase, turned to marshmallow and let his national chairwoman tell the public Eagleton had to go," Smith said. He further asserted that McGovern's reputation for leadership had been "sullied by too much yielding to pressure. His 1000 dollar welfare plan went the way his 1000 percent support of Eagleton did."

Tuesday, August 1st, 1972, just a week after it had opened, the drama of the Eagleton Affair came to a close. John Chancellor opened the NBC Evening News with, "Good evening on a day that will make at least an important footnote in American history; for the first time ever, a vice presidential candidate has resigned." The CBS Morning News that day had featured an interview between Barry Serafin and Senator Eagleton. Eagleton said, "I've come out of it stronger that I went in . . . I'm at peace with myself. . . . This may be the most important week of my life. I did the job. I took the heat and I endured."

Tuesday was highlighted by a dramatic irony. CBS featured a news conference with Eagleton and Jack Anderson. The crusading reporter had checked and found his charges were unsubstantiated. He had done the Senator an injustice. "I owe him a great and humble apology." Eagleton made no comment on the film clip but the narrator asserted that Eagleton had said the books were closed on the matter.

Senator McGovern cancelled a talk he had scheduled to give the American people on television in regard to the matter of his decision to drop Eagleton.

David Brinkley, in his journal feature, delivered a bitter attack on politicians without mentioning any candidates by name. But straight out of the inside-dopester vision of the media professional, Brinkley asserted that most people do not believe politicians, that the public had turned sour on politics and politicians.

Eric Sevareid editorialized on CBS to the effect that Eagleton's career at the political summit had been one of the shortest on record but in the course of it he had become a household word and created thousands of friendly sympathizers. Sevareid used the term "Eagleton Affair" in his commentary. He asserted that Eagleton was burned by a fire started by the press and that a fire started by the press could be very hot indeed but that in the long run it was cleansing. Certainly, Sevareid concluded, the affair indicated that the press was not biased in a liberal direction as some had charged.

Sevareid was right. Much of the dramatization (the fire) was an artistic creation of the media. The impact of the media selection of characters and action lines upon the fantasy themes was considerable. When the announcement came of Eagleton's departure from the ticket the dramatic suggestion that McGovern had bowed to pressure for the crassest of political reasons, namely, loss of campaign financing from big contributors, was very strong. Certainly the emphasis on characters relating to financing and allusions to financing on NBC were most important.

155

The most sympathetic character in the drama turned out to be Tom Eagleton.[14] He came through the network news as an open, cleancut, if intense, young man. He recounted his medical problems in some detail. When he decided to stay in the race he was forthright and forceful in his statement about the American people being intelligent and sophisticated about mental health and ready to be understanding about his problem.

The Anderson charges which Eagleton denied put the characterization of Eagleton to the test. If Anderson had proved his charges then the Eagleton persona would have received a damaging blow to its credibility; then all of Eagleton's other testimony, no matter how convincingly portrayed on television, might be wrong also. With a discredited Eagleton persona in the drama, McGovern might not have appeared as the "heavy." When Anderson publicly admitted the charges were untrue, however, the Eagleton character increased its credibility and the halo effect of a man falsely accused increased the sympathy one felt about his earlier statements regarding his mental health.

Finally, as the pressure mounted, Eagleton remained adamant that the would stand firm and fight the charges through to ultimately win the election and thus justify his faith in the American people. A dramatic protagonist who has a clear and sympathetic goal and is willing to stand firm and fight for it, even at a personal sacrifice, is sympathetic. When the Eagleton persona was finally cut down, it was by the one force in the drama he could not fight, the presidential candidate himself.

The persona of Jack Anderson as presented in the Eagleton drama is important not only because it emerged as the antagonist but also because it was a key character in other fantasies relating to the campaign and to the drama of corruption within the Nixon Administration. Jack Anderson had been playing the role of the fearless investigative reporter discovering hidden deals and secret papers. The Anderson character was thus a kind of hero in the rhetorical vision of the New Politics. Now, he was playing the part of an antagonist. As the breaking news presented Anderson as an unethical opportunist trying to gain personal advantage by making unsupported charges, his persona was tarnished. Certainly, within the vision of the New Politics with its emphasis on high ethical standards for persona, the revelations were damaging to Anderson. The tension within the vision came from the role that Anderson was already playing in the fantasy themes related to other matters such as the I.T.T. Affair. If Anderson was lacking in credibility in the Eagleton Affair, could he be a hero in the I.T.T. Affair? How much the loss of credibility of the Anderson persona had to do with the apparent difficulty of the media and the McGovern campaign to make the Watergate Affair chain through the general public in a way that damaged Nixon is an interesting question beyond the scope of this essay. Certainly, however, the Watergate Affair deserves extended criticism from a fantasy theme frame of analysis.

The greatest damage of all the persona came, of course, to that of George McGovern. First there was his rather offhand response. The matter, he said, was really not very important but the decision was made to stop rumors. The persona asserted strong and unequivocal support for his vice president. The persona reiter-

---

[14]On July 28, 1972, Howard K. Smith on ABC reported results of a poll showing 60% sympathetic to Eagleton although there was a 30% negative response to McGovern for being caught unaware of Eagleton's past medical history.

ated that support. The question, however, was never closed. The possibility apparently lingered. The continued rumors of possible "dumping" and then the indirect story that McGovern had signalled Eagleton that he would like a resignation persisted. Eagleton stood firm. Finally, after what seemed like pressure from his more unsavory supporters, the persona made his decision to remove Eagleton for apparently base political motivations.

What motives were embedded in the scenario for those who chained into it? For the New Politics vision the fantasy of Eagleton was more than the rhetoric could absorb in plausible fashion. The leading character in a rhetorical vision which had emphasized persona was revealed as a politician acting in expedient fashion. The motivational pivot went out of the vision. The only remaining spur to action was hatred for the villainous personae such as Nixon and Agnew, but that was much less impelling by itself than when coupled to admiration for a persona of high ethical power. Some continued to work for the candidacy of George McGovern, but for many with less inertia and momentum, the motivation was replaced with *apathy*. Thus the rising tide of apathy can partially be accounted for by the disillusionment of those who participated in the New Politics, responding after the Eagleton Affair. For those who had little impression of George McGovern before the Eagleton Affair became staple fare on television, the fantasy brought reactions of distrust and lack of confidence in the persona.[15]

The viewer who came to sympathize with Eagleton would have every reason to distrust the McGovern character. Eagleton had placed trust in McGovern in a situation of considerable personal risk. The McGovern persona had promised support in Eagleton's time of trial and then when the situation came to a dramatic climax, had "dumped" him. Inconsistency was a highlight of the dramatic action.

The one major piece of prepared campaign persuasion which tapped into the legacy of the Eagleton Affair was produced by the Democrats for Nixon and is, I believe, possibly the most skillful piece of persuasion produced during the campaign. Although the short spot announcement does not mention Eagleton by name, the suggestion connects very strongly with the residue of the Eagleton fantasy. McGovern's picture is presented on a weather vane-like stand. McGovern's position on a question is mentioned, the picture swings to face in the opposite direction and the narrator asserts that McGovern has shifted his position. Several shifts of the picture from left to right ensue until at the end of the announcement the picture is twirling in circles. The power of the announcement comes from its skillfully tapping into the rhetorical visions created by chaining fantasies such as the Eagleton Affair.

Coming at a strategic time in the campaign, capturing prime-time television for long film clips of the characters of the dramas, the fantasy chained throughout the electorate and the role that the McGovern persona played in the fantasy as it was

[15] Columnists Evans and Novak reported a late October poll by interviews in three San Fernando Valley, California precincts selected by elections analyst Richard Scammon. They interviewed 118 voters and found twenty-four registered Democrats decidedly for Nixon. The basic reasons given were the perception that McGovern was ideologically extreme and "habitual complaints about McGovern's inconsistency." *The Minneapolis Star*, 1 Nov. 1972, editorial page. The Harris Survey reported in early November to the effect that McGovern's credibility problem still plagued him. By 61 to 29 percent, a majority agreed with the statement that "he does not inspire confidence as a president should." *The Minneapolis Star*, 6 Nov. 1972, p. 1A.

participated in by large segments of the American public was one of an inconsistent, inept, untrustworthy and politically expedient politician. Since the original dramatization was played out on the network evening news, on radio, and in the supposedly objective columns of the print media, the credibility of the presentation was high. The damage done to a rhetoric based on persona was considerable. Other breaking news events were subsequently interpreted along the same lines and the New Politics rhetorical vision lost its power to generate commitment and action and to attract new converts.

The Eagleton Phenomenon in the 1972 Presidential Campaign: A Case Study in the Rhetoric of Paradox

John H. Patton

Since the breaking of the Watergate affair in recent months, the issue of integrity has been emphasized in retrospect as a crucial question in the 1972 presidential campaign. Watergate notwithstanding, integrity occupied a central position in the campaign all along, especially in relation to the Democratic presidential ticket. It was primarily through what I term "the Eagleton phenomenon" that a decisive paradox on the theme of integrity was enacted. Indeed, among all the aspects of the 1972 presidential campaign the phenomenon of Senator Thomas F. Eagleton provides one of the clearest opportunities for insight into the attitudes and values which played a decisive role in the election. Eagleton came to be associated with integrity in such a paradoxical manner that Senator McGovern's emphasis on substantial issues went largely unperceived. It was a paradox of dramatic proportions illustrated by the remark of historian James MacGregor Burns at the time of McGovern's nomination. When asked to assess McGovern's chances for improving on strategies for long-term American reform Burns noted "the feeling that I have that he (McGovern) really means what he says." Burns went on to claim that "everyone seems to grant Senator McGovern's political honesty."[1] Primarily as a result of the Eagleton phenomenon McGovern became vulnerable on the very issue of political honesty, so that shortly after his campaign began few Americans believed that McGovern meant what he said. By the end of the campaign the same "aura of rock-like integrity" which Shana Alexander has called McGovern's clearest advantage had shattered into pieces of cynical manipulation and personal disloyalty.[2] A remarkable transformation in the ways in which intended meanings were ultimately perceived had occurred.

Ernest Bormann has recently referred to "the Eagleton Affair" as a central

---

[1] "Size-Up of McGovern by a Student of the Presidency," interview with James MacGregor Burns reported in *U.S. News and World Report,* LXXIII, No. 5, July 31, 1972, p. 52.

[2] Shana Alexander, "Eagleton's Saintly Revenge," *Newsweek,* LXXX, No. 20, November 13, 1972, p. 41.

aspect of the 1972 campaign, observing that "the rhetoric provides an interesting case-study in the ways in which political unknowns become widely known persona." His approach centers on "a critical analysis of the major fantasies that chained through the American electorate"[3] and what those fantasies revealed. I share the view that the campaign rhetoric is important because of what it reveals, but here I am not primarily interested in Eagleton as an emergent "persona." Rather, I am concerned with the Eagleton phenomenon as a complex of constituents comprising a rhetorical situation best described by the term paradox. On this view, the substance and strategies of the rhetoric of the major participants in that situation, Eagleton, McGovern, and R. Sargent Shriver, must be considered in relation to each other for the purpose of arriving at as comprehensive an understanding of the paradox as possible.

This paradox is of rhetorical interest precisely because the discourse of the Democratic candidates, Eagleton, McGovern, and Shriver, reveals the influence of disparate values and assumptions which functioned to shape the resulting strategy and action. The paradox emphasizes the importance of assessing the relationships between underlying values, opinions, and beliefs and the nature of the discourse within an existential context. This paper raises the central question: Is it possible to account for this paradox from a rhetorical perspective? I maintain that the Eagleton phenomenon can best be understood by examining the nature of the exigences and perceptions, the impact of the complex variety of values, and the orientation toward disparate audiences revealed by the rhetoric of the major participants in that phenomenon. I am arguing that the rhetoric of paradox presents a unique challenge to the rhetorical critic, a challenge which summons the employment of a methodology of dialectical transformation[4] and situational constituents.[5] Such an approach offers an important alternative to a methodology based upon the traditional standard of effect for dealing with the rhetoric of paradox.

The role of Senator Eagleton is central to the paradox which engulfed the Democratic campaign in 1972 because it was through him that the issue of con-

[3] Ernest G. Bormann, "The Eagleton Affair: A Fantasy Theme Analysis," *Quarterly Journal of Speech,* LIX, No. 2, (April 1973), 143.

[4] By "dialectical transformation" I refer to the notion of dialectic developed by Kenneth Burke primarily in the *Rhetoric* and *Grammar of Motives* and the *Philosophy of Literary Form,* namely that the study of linguistic transformations for the purpose of assessing the motives underlying human activity is essentially a dialectic process. By means of dialectical analysis one is able to arrive at a deeper, more fundamental type of perception, surpassing perception which is exclusively from within or exclusively from without a given phenomenon. Instead, in Burke's words, "there is a third way, the fullest kind of understanding, wherein one gets the immediacy of participation in a local act, yet sees in and through this act as an over-all design, sees and *feels* the local act itself as but the partial expression of the total development." (*A Rhetoric of Motives,* Berkeley and Los Angeles: University of California Press, 1969), p. 195.

[5] By "situational constituents" I refer to the components of a rhetorical situation as described by Lloyd F. Bitzer in his essay, "The Rhetorical Situation," *Philosophy and Rhetoric,* I, No. 1 (Winter 1968). My purpose is not to impose the concepts of "exigence," "audience," and "constraints" as artificial categories for classifying the discourse involved in the Eagleton phenomenon since it seems to me that such an approach abuses Bitzer's construct by reducing it to a mechanistic device. Rather, by adopting a situational perspective and concentrating on the starting-points of the discourse under examination it will be possible to recognize and assess the world-views, value structures, and predominant attitudes and opinions which significantly influenced the substance and strategy of the rhetoric of the Eagleton phenomenon.

science was focused in a decisive way. The Eagleton phenomenon is not simply a series of speeches or an account of historical events. It is best described as a particular rhetorical situation which exposed the influence of rhetoric on cultural values and the power of prevailing world views in shaping the rhetorical process. The critical perspective is primarily one of evaluating the relationship between rhetoric and cultural values, not one of determining the political significance of Senator Eagleton or of judging the rhetorical effectiveness of Eagleton in a strictly Neo-Aristotelian sense. These questions assume primary importance: What were the initial and subsequent exigences involved in the Eagleton phenomenon? What sorts of factors influenced the development of Eagleton's rhetorical strategy? What relationships emerged between the values revealed by Eagleton's initial selection and later removal from the ticket and rhetorical goals and strategies? What implications does the rhetoric of paradox provide for the work of the rhetorical critic?

THE INITIAL EXIGENCE: UNITY AND PARTY HARMONY

The reasons which prompted Eagleton's selection as the Vice-Presidential candidate supply the foundation for much of the subsequent paradox. Lloyd Bitzer's concept of rhetorical exigence, "an imperfection marked by urgency . . . a thing which is other than it should be," offers a useful way of viewing those reasons.[6] To those whose goal was the reform of the rules of the Democratic Party or the nomination of their chosen candidate, the notion of exigence might have sounded out of place since things seemed much more "as they should be" than in many previous years. Yet, in the larger context within and beyond the convention itself there were a number of things which were other than they should be. Regardless of their worth or justification, the McGovern reforms intensified serious divisions within the party. McGovern held little support from traditional Democratic power groups such as labor and white ethnic blocks. When the question shifted from nomination to election, the imperfections of a divided party and a presidential image which lacked appeal to traditional groups created a significant obstacle. This exigence summoned the selection of Thomas Eagleton of Missouri as the Vice-Presidential candidate.

Eagleton was initially perceived as a "noncontroversial figure" who adequately fulfilled the criteria of being "an experienced politician, either Catholic or Jewish, who could appeal to elements of the party that . . . are tending to slip their Democratic moorings."[7] He appealed to those who were dissatisfied with the reformist image conveyed by McGovern. The substance of that appeal was largely a matter of style and approach. Hence, from the beginning Eagleton's candidacy was grounded upon the basis of perception. He would be able to appeal to traditional values in a

---

[6] Lloyd F. Bitzer, "The Rhetorical Situation," 6.

[7] "Why Eagleton Was Picked," *U.S. News and World Report,* LXXIII, No. 4, July 24, 1972, p. 25.

way that McGovern could not, thereby establishing the balance which the ticket required to be viable at a national level. At that time such was McGovern's own account of why Eagleton was chosen, namely that "he seemed to be a person who has widespread confidence from a variety of groups in the Democratic Party."[8]

That his perception as a more moderate spokesman constituted the central purpose for Eagleton's selection is emphasized when his position on a number of issues is compared with McGovern's. Eagleton's voice had been as strong as McGovern's in urging an end to the Vietnam War. In June 1968, his first year in the Senate, he argued that "the first matter of business must be to seek a cease-fire." Thereafter, Eagleton joined with McGovern and Senator Hatfield in an effort to halt war appropriations, observing that ". . . it is power—mainly American power— and not legitimately derived from the consent of the governed that makes public policy in South Vietnam." He was involved in leading Senate fights to trim the defense budget and to finance the welfare program entirely from Federal funds. In fact, the only substantive policy difference between Eagleton and McGovern concerned the issue of the draft. Unlike McGovern, Eagleton strongly supported the draft arguing that "an all volunteer army would be a poor-boys army. I believe that America is not only the land of opportunity but also the land of obligation. One of these obligations is to bear arms in time of war—even a foolish one."[9] The basic difference between the two men thus became not their position on issues, but how they were perceived. No matter what he said, McGovern was to be perceived as "radical" in some form. While Eagleton could not, indeed should not, remove the "radical" image from McGovern, he could provide a positive perspective which would furnish acceptability to the overall perception of the ticket.

The initial exigence thus resulted in a rhetorical strategy of balance, very delicate balance rooted not so much in substance as in perception. McGovern would appeal to those who are ripe for change; Eagleton would appeal to those who wish to temper the pace of change by retaining a sizable portion of the past. The paradox began at this point for while McGovern later shifted his appeal in order to broaden his political base, Eagleton remained entirely consistent with his original appeal and became increasingly popular because of it.

[8] "How McGovern Sees the Issues," *U.S. News and World Report,* LXXIII, No. 6, August 7, 1972, p. 18. The idea that Eagleton was initially selected in response to the exigence of party unity is given further support in a recent article by Joe McGinniss, "Second Thoughts of George McGovern," *New York Times Magazine,* May 6, 1973, 31ff. McGinniss quotes McGovern as saying that "the one guy everybody had on their list was Eagleton. Labor was crazy about him, he was a Catholic from a border state, the blacks thought he was terrific for the work he had done on the District of Columbia Committee. Women said he had enormous appeal to the female voter." (p. 98) McGovern makes a significant qualification, however, observing that "the only list he wasn't on was my own" (p. 98) and indicates that he considered Eagleton "superficial" and lacking in dignity and reserve from the beginning (p. 98), thereby adding a deeply personal element to the nature of the paradox. The paradoxical nature of the Eagleton phenomenon is succinctly captured in McGovern's retrospective remark that "The whole campaign was a tragic case of mistaken identity" (p. 88).
It should also be noted that since the appearance of the McGinniss article, McGovern has publicly repudiated it, calling it a "disreputable and shoddy piece of journalism," as reported in *Time Magazine,* CI, No. 20, May 14, 1973, p. 56.
[9] Christopher Lydon, *New York Times,* July 14, 1972, p. 10.

THE EXIGENCE ALTERED: FOCUS ON INTEGRITY

Having placed so much emphasis on perception as the basis for acceptability, the Democratic ticket was highly vulnerable to any defect which was primarily ethical in nature. No one could imagine McGovern losing influence due to a lack of integrity, yet it was precisely on the issue of personal integrity that his campaign began to collapse. The shift to integrity as the crucial exigence occurred almost as soon as Eagleton was recommended to the convention for nomination. Max Frankel writes that Eagleton was "accepted by the convention but only grudgingly in many delegations." The negative aspects of Eagleton's selection were perceived as a reflection on McGovern rather than Eagleton. Frankel further comments that "many delegates resented the summons to blind acceptance of the Presidential solitary choice."[10] It appeared somewhat inconsistent for McGovern as the champion of reform to follow the old-style procedure of naming his choice for running mate instead of leaving that choice to the newly reformed convention. Taken by itself this incident could be accounted for in terms of practical necessity. However, when viewed within the context of the entire Eagleton phenomenon, this action marks the beginning of a significant pattern. Instead of being praised for selecting a man of Eagleton's calibre, McGovern was perceived as contradicting the values of integrity and loyalty for which he had vigorously fought. Even before his name was officially placed in nomination, Senator Eagleton became the person through whom the integrity of George McGovern would be measured.

Eagleton's acceptance speech to the convention on July 13 demonstrated that the exigence of party unity became superseded by the exigence of integrity. His address considerably heightened the atmosphere for paradox by expressing the values which played a central role in the remainder of the campaign. Eagleton commented that 1972 had been "a year of surprises" which "have shown us something important about ourselves." This implies that the campaign to follow will directly involve the self-perception of Americans. He elaborated by stressing that although some of those surprises have been difficult, "we are learning to find opportunity in them . . . not just uncertainty and fear." The appeal is to values which are positive and uplifting, providing chances where none existed previously.

Finally, Eagleton noted an optimistic quality in diversity asserting that "we are discovering in the threads of our diversity, the fabric of a strong united party."[11] He could not have chosen language which would prove ultimately to be more paradoxical for at the time he was unaware of the biggest surprise which was yet to come. In shortly more than two weeks he would no longer be the Democratic candidate for Vice President. Instead, the exact values which he challenged, values represented by uncertainty and fear, would be indelibly associated with his Presidential running mate. By the time of the election in November, the fabric of the strong united party which Eagleton envisioned would be shredded into an unwearable garment.

[10] "McGovern Names Eagleton Running Mate," *New York Times,* July 14, 1972, p. 11.
[11] Acceptance speech by Senator Eagleton, July 13, 1972, before the Democratic National Convention, Miami Beach, Florida, *Vital Speeches of the Day,* XXXVIII, No. 21, August 15, 1972, p. 642.

In retrospect the conclusion of Eagleton's speech contains an especially important reference in light of what followed. After making the customary pledge to campaign in every state, he departed from political jargon to say: "And let us so conduct ourselves and our campaign and our lives that in later years men may say— 1972 was the year, not when America lost its way, but the year when America found its conscience."[12] Conscience became, as soon as Eagleton spoke the word, the primary value by which the Democratic ticket in 1972 was to be judged and perceived.

FACTORS IN THE DEVELOPMENT OF EAGLETON'S RHETORICAL STRATEGY

On July 25 Senator Eagleton announced that on three occasions he had "voluntarily gone into hospitals as a result of nervous exhaustion and fatigue," that he had received "counseling from a psychiatrist, including electric shock." Eagleton's "week that was" thus began with a strategy which McGovern called a demonstration of "candor and openness."[13] What followed for Eagleton was an excruciating trial by fire which he faced with intense determination, believing that his performance during that week could solidify his place on the ticket. He adopted a strategy of resistance under pressure. In that sense his approach signified a situation without parallel for a political candidate, magnifying the Eagleton phenomenon to such an extent that it dominated the political horizon. As Stephen Darst has observed: "All Nixon had to do (in 1952) was go on television, make his explanation in full view of the millions, and then take no further contributions to his special fund. Eagleton had to appear for a week in crowds, on podiums, beaches, television, at labor meetings, press conferences, everywhere, knowing that even the normal symptoms of decent self-consciousness, an eye-twitch, sweating, any vital life sign, would be weighed, interpreted, and analyzed."[14] If it is true that pressure brings out the essence of a person, then Eagleton was essentially open, straightforward and intensely sincere to such an extent that his being dropped from the ticket translated into an act of cruelty and near inhumanity.

Eagleton's background and personal experience, the character of his ambition, and most importantly, the world view to which he responded all contributed to his performance during the week of trial. Politics and pressure were not new to Eagleton. At the age of sixteen his father took him to hear Churchill's Iron Curtain Speech at Fulton, Missouri. This was followed by tutoring on national and international affairs, as well as speech lessons from a high-ranking St. Louis school official. Moreover, almost all his life Eagleton had been considered an extraordinary person. According to one of his contemporaries Eagleton possessed facial features, voice, and personality "designed to soothe, inspire, and lull some segment of the voting public." Add to this the fact that "he was surrounded not by slick, new-breed media experts but by gnarled, ring-wise, outrageously colorful Kerry Patch

[12]*Ibid.,* p. 643.
[13] "Eagleton's Own Story of His Health Problems," *U.S. News and World Report,* LXXIII, No. 6, August 7, 1972, pp. 16, 17.
[14] Stephen Darst, "Eagleton's Wake," *Harper's Magazine,* CCXLIV, No. 1471, December 1972, p. 80.

politicians," plus the assessment that "from the first Eagleton was considered to be in a class by himself, the finest political horse his trainers had ever seen,"[15] and Eagleton's decision to fight for his place on the ticket instead of resigning in the face of sudden controversy is given considerable illumination. He grew up in an atmosphere of political toughness and received intensely favorable political feed-back, evidenced by his never having lost an election. With this type of personal experience Eagleton could not have adopted a strategy of willing resignation from the ticket without denying the affirmative experiences of his past.

Eagleton's strategy of resistance was further influenced by the nature of his ambition, which was not so much for advancement up the political ladder as it was for the ability to work earnestly and thoroughly. A significant tinge of Puritan work-ethic underlies Eagleton's account of his ambition to his older brother Mark in 1968: "I want to be a great United States Senator. I'd like to be reelected three terms, acquire some seniority and get some good committees and hear James Reston and David Brinkley say someday, 'He's a pretty good Senator. He works hard at it.' "[16] This description establishes a situation which prescribes what the fitting response for Eagleton should be, namely to work harder than ever to main-tain his position. Eagleton's determined effort in his own behalf is clearly explained as an attempt to meet the requirements established by the situation. Regardless of its detrimental effects upon McGovern's candidacy, Eagleton's strategy was entirely fitting given the nature of his ambition. Concerning the idea of fitting response Bitzer has observed that there is a metaphorical sense in which "every situation prescribes its fitting response; the rhetor may or may not read the prescription accurately."[17] This observation indicates that Eagleton's response cannot be under-stood unless we know as exactly as possible to which aspects of the situation he is responding. That he was responding primarily on the basis of past experience and a specific type of ambition assists in clarifying at least some of the layers of the paradox. Given the priority of his assumption that anything may be achieved if you work hard enough it is quite predictable that Eagleton would not have foreseen the consequences of his position for George McGovern. Considerable irony remains be-cause the emphasis on hard work which prompted Eagleton to resist his removal from the ticket was the identical factor which originally caused him to be hospital-ized: "I pushed myself terribly hard—long hours, day and night."[18]

More than anything else, however, Eagleton was responding to a definite world-view which found expression in a concern for simple, personal values much more than for questions of national and international policy. It was a world-view which asked 'Can this man be trusted?,' not 'What are the moral consequences of the War?' Epitomized by the cultural milieu of the Midwest, this way of seeing the world was at the time infinitely more sensitive to the withdrawal of a pledge of "1000 per cent support" than, for example, to the miasma of the Watergate affair. After all, politicians, including Presidents, can be expected to engage in underhanded ploys, but it is something qualitatively different when a man seems to publicly betray one to whom he has publicly pledged loyalty. As Edwin Black has observed the impact

---

[15] Stephen Darst, p. 77.
[16] Christopher Lydon, *New York Times,* July 14, 1972, p. 10.
[17] Bitzer, p. 11.
[18] *U.S. News and World Report,* August 7, 1972, p. 16.

of Eagleton's removal was especially significant on "the ardently committed young" who viewed the event as representing the "ultimate taint" of insincerity by McGovern.[19]

Calvin Trillin reveals the dimensions of this Midwestern world-view in writing about his travels with Eagleton through Missouri in 1970. Trillin observes that Eagleton asked for questions all over the state at Kiwanis luncheons, at colleges and at covered-dish suppers in small towns without much appreciable response. Indeed, with the exception of St. Louis, no questioners sounded angry or excited. He comments that "in some places, a subject like crime or inflation wasn't even brought up. During the entire trip, nobody asked about the bombings that have occurred in cities as close as the Heart of America (Kansas City); nobody asked about campus unrest. In three or four places, someone asked about the country's being more divided or troubled than in the past, but in the atmosphere of the occasion the question sounded as if it might be about some other country."[20]

From the questions that were not asked, the absence of concern about large issues, much is indicated about the real values reflected in that culture. Individual honesty, uncomplicated life styles, energetic and efficient labor, interest in holding on to the accomplished and tangible products of living combined with an acute suspicion about politics in general to create an audience far different than the activist audience conceptualized by McGovern strategists. But Thomas Eagleton was a product of that audience. He heard its voice calling for initiative and determination in a crisis situation. Moreover, the members of that audience, which was soon discovered to extend much beyond Missouri and the Midwest, heard Eagleton with a degree of clarity and sensitivity never accorded to George McGovern. Viewed in this manner, Eagleton's rhetorical strategy can be understood as a phenomenological process, a case in which discourse functioned over a period of time as "both a reaction to and an influence upon those existent societal images which comprise a major portion of the climate of opinion of the times."[21]

THE PARADOX COMPLETED: THE PERCEPTION OF INTEGRITY ABANDONED

Exigences have a way of becoming ultimate. One critic has written that "within the limits specified by each exigence the ultimate or perceived nature of the exigence depends upon the constraints of the receiver. Thus, the ultimate character of an exigence is a conclusion in the mind of its perceiver."[22] Significantly different conclusions were reached by the various participants in the Eagleton phenomenon. Senator McGovern concluded that Eagleton should "step aside" because public debate about his past medical history "continues to divert attention from the great national issues that need to be discussed." McGovern clearly failed to perceive the

[19] Edwin Black, "Electing Time," *Quarterly Journal of Speech,* LIX, No. 2 (April 1973), 128.
[20] Calvin Trillin, "U.S. Journal: Missouri," *The New Yorker,* XLVI, No. 13, May 16, 1970, p. 111.
[21] Richard B. Gregg, "A Phenomenologically Oriented Approach to Rhetorical Criticism," *Central States Speech Journal,* XVII, No. 2 (May 1966), 89.
[22] Arthur B. Miller, "Rhetorical Exigence," *Philosophy and Rhetoric,* V, No. 2 (Spring 1972), 111-112.

import of the Mid-western world-view which became personified in the Eagleton phenomenon. His conclusion thus confronted him with one of the most difficult of all rhetorical problems, how to convince persons to discuss what is "needed" when they themselves sense not that, but other, significantly different needs.

Senator Eagleton concluded that he must abide, however reluctantly, by the wishes of McGovern, saying that his personal feelings were not as vital as the necessity to unify the Democratic party and to elect George McGovern. Neither of those objectives was achieved, yet what held all the outward characteristics of a finale became for Eagleton a fresh beginning because he was perceived as the innocent victim, the man of integrity. This happened in spite of the fact that Eagleton failed to reveal his medical record to McGovern in advance, a fact explained both by the negative implication of the question he was asked, 'Any skeletons rattling around in your closet?,' and by one of the goals of psychiatric counseling itself, namely to remove the stigma frequently associated with mental illness.[23] In any case, as Alexander maintains, "Eagleton's lack of candor at a crucial moment . . . went largely unperceived by the American people."[24]

The public reaction to Eagleton is almost legend by now. At the end of July he had received 90,000 letters, all but 200 favorable, thousands of speaking engagements and numerous offers to write books. John Pierson writes that "he gets standing ovations before, during and after the most ordinary of speeches. People cheer and cheer and cheer." He was introduced at a dinner for Democrats in Jefferson County, Missouri, as a man "whose personal and political courage have rewritten the definition of the word 'courage' " and at the centennial celebration of Maryville College in St. Louis as a man who "won the heart of the entire nation."[25] With such popular support it seemed logical that Eagleton would increase McGovern's acceptability by continuing to campaign for him. Yet, no matter how much Eagleton affirmed his faith and belief in McGovern, his campaign appearances served primarily to remind the public that he was no longer on the ticket, thereby damaging McGovern's credibility with each gesture of intended support. It is probably an overstatement to call it a "classic martyr's revenge" as Alexander does. Nonetheless, her conclusion that "every speech was a new reminder of the cruel rejection he had suffered"[26] is an apt description of the paradoxical consequence of the Eagleton appeal.

The capstone of this paradox came neither from Eagleton nor from McGovern, but from Eagleton's successor as Vice Presidential candidate, R. Sargent Shriver. In his acceptance speech before the Democratic National Committee on August 8 Shriver expressed admiration for the way Senator Eagleton "took his case to the people and the grace with which he bore himself." Having presumably ended reference to Eagleton with this gesture, Shriver moved to a discussion of those national issues which McGovern was so eager to have debated. After listing various "declines"

[23] For an excellent discussion of the notion that mental illness is no different than other forms of illness see Karl Menninger's address "Healthier Than Healthy" found in *Contemporary American Speeches,* ed. Linkugel, Allen, and Johannesen (Belmont, California: Wadsworth Publishing Company, (1969), 54–63.
[24] Shana Alexander, *ibid.*
[25] John Pierson, "Poor Tom Eagleton Is So Popular He Needs an Unlisted Telephone," *Wall Street Journal,* October 24, 1972, pp. 1 and 37.
[26] Shana Alexander, *ibid.*

in the economy, the cities, the war, Shriver observed that "the worst decline is in the people's spirit . . . We have a sense of something lost, something missing." Shriver was absolutely correct. He had read the attitude of America accurately, yet his words confirmed rather than alerted that attitude. Shriver did not specify what he meant by "something missing," but the public mind had already filled in that gap by their belief and perception that what was missing was Tom Eagleton.

For two more paragraphs Shriver elaborated the theme of current American discontent. At one point he declared that "Americans are people of transcendent goals, a people of highest moral purpose," an image which contrasted sharply with the perception that McGovern had abandoned moral purpose when he removed Eagleton. Finally, the new Vice Presidential candidate claimed that above all Americans "are not moved by men concerned with power and manipulation."[27] That perception spoke louder to the hearts of America than any subsequent arguments by McGovern, Shriver, or Eagleton. The quality of integrity remained constant, but now in place of offering hope and potential for the McGovern campaign, it became the symbol of an abandoned virtue. The paradox was complete.

_____ IMPLICATIONS FOR RHETORICAL CRITICISM

The Eagleton phenomenon dramatizes the rhetorical significance of paradox. Called into being as a response to party divisions and misunderstood images, it offered the possibility of positive modifications on both of these fronts. In the process of development, however, the central exigence of the campaign shifted to the issue of integrity, prompting rhetorical strategies which resulted in modifications of a different sort than originally envisioned.

If the critic is to provide an adequate explanation of this phenomenon, he must be concerned about more than the end result of the rhetoric. The major effects of the rhetoric here examined, namely that Eagleton was dropped from the ticket while his public popularity increased and that McGovern's aura of integrity was mangled beyond repair, do not by themselves account for either the substance or the strategy of that rhetoric. For example, the effects may indicate consequences of Eagleton's "work ethic" rhetoric in relationship to McGovern's withdrawal of "1000 per cent" support, but they fail to explain the motivation for what is said or the perception of the disparate audiences to whom it is said by Eagleton and McGovern. On the other hand, a dialectical-situational methodology does account for Eagleton's motivation as stemming from personal ethical values prominent in his past experience and culture, as well as McGovern's strategy as derived from the urgency of broader, substantive issues. Such motivation and perception is of prime rhetorical concern because it forms the basis for the evaluation of rhetoric in relationship to reality. By knowing more precisely what attitudes, values, and beliefs prompt a person to engage in discourse and what attitudes, values, and beliefs influence the perception of his symbolic activity, we are able to assess the nature and impact of the rhetoric in a more comprehensive manner.

[27]Acceptance speech as a candidate for Vice President by R. Sargent Shriver before the Democratic National Committee, August 8, 1972, _Vital Speeches of the Day_, August 15, p. 646.

Both the substance and strategy of the rhetoric of the Eagleton phenomenon was a function of the constraints which influenced the perception of crucial exigences by Eagleton and McGovern, and the complex structure of values underlying the audiences to whom the candidates spoke. This understanding suggests that the rhetoric of paradox involves consideration of what Kenneth Burke calls the sorts of mergers, divisions, and transformations which occur, frequently beneath the surface, in all symbolic actions.[28] Hence, implications for the critic are: 1) the critic should understand the starting points of rhetoric as the basis for the development of rhetorical substance and strategy, whatever the end point may happen to be; 2) the critic should view rhetoric as an on-going process of symbolic transformations in which discourse is an essential element, but not necessarily the primary element; and 3) the critic should be concerned with evaluation in the sense of assessing the significance of relationships between rhetoric and the perceptions, exigences, audiences, constraints, and values operative within the entire context of the communication phenomenon.

[28] Kenneth Burke, *A Grammar of Motives* (Berkeley and Los Angeles: University of California Press, 1969), p. 402ff.

Lincoln at Cooper Union:
A Rationale for Neo-Classical Criticism
G. P. Mohrmann and Michael C. Leff

The last issue of this journal included our critique of Lincoln's Cooper Union Address, and we assume that the neo-classical origins of the analysis were apparent, even though methodological concerns were slighted. A more elaborate statement on methodology appeared in an earlier version, but the editors cautioned that the single article did not offer sufficient scope for both an explication of the rationale and its application. Accepting their advice, we deleted most of the theoretical material, but having offered the critique, we want to explore further its theoretical bases.

Our approach is neo-classical. That is, it is rooted in the rhetorical theory of antiquity. This is the same source that produced neo-Aristotelianism, "the dominant mode of rhetorical criticism of the present century in the United States."[1] Our critique shares most of the presuppositions that inform this traditional mode, but there is one essential difference. Treating "rhetorical discourses as discrete communications in specific contexts,"[2] neo-Aristotelianism is preoccupied with the particular. This orientation implies a rejection of formal criteria and almost forces the critic to rely on the criterion of empirical effect. On the other hand, we treat Lincoln's speech within the framework of the classical conception of oratorical genres. As opposed to the nominalism implicit in neo-Aristotelianism, genre theory

[1] Edwin Black, *Rhetorical Criticism* (New York: Macmillan, 1965), p. 27.
[2] Black, p. 35.

168

permits an abstract conception of audience and of rhetorical situations. It, therefore, enables the critic to seek formal ends for critical judgment.

Our purpose, here, is to explore the potential of genre theory as a corrective to some defects in the neo-Aristotelian mode. We shall begin with reference to the development of neo-Aristotelianism, comment on its rejection of generic distinctions and note the limitations that this rejection imposes. We shall then suggest that the conception of genre can help invigorate critical inquiry based on classical models. We would emphasize, however, the provisional nature of our formulation; we do not consider it to be definitive, and we recognize that our version of neo-classicism has its own limitations.

NEO-ARISTOTELIAN CRITICISM

Although the neo-Aristotelian position is most fully delineated when one moves from "The Literary Criticism of Oratory"[3] to *A History and Criticism of American Public Address*[4] to *Speech Criticism,*[5] Wichelns remains the commanding presence. His essay "set the pattern and determined the direction"[6] of this approach, and the direction in which he moved took "certain Aristotelian conceptions as safe points of departure."[7] The most crucial of these was the centrality of audience. Of course, Aristotle and other classical theorists do not spell out a critical system, but "they do imply one. If a literary work may be said to have three references—to the universe, to the writer, and to the audience—Greek rhetorical theory, like the Renaissance criticism which descends from it, thinks the audience-reference by far the most important."[8] Seeking to revive the dormant rhetorical perspective, Wichelns makes this same reference the basis for the rhetorical analysis of oratory. The importance of this principle can scarcely be exaggerated; without it, modern speech criticism would not have been possible. Nevertheless, Wichelns' determination to separate rhetoric from literature leads to a restricted conception of audience.

As the very title of his essay suggests, he thinks it important to distinguish between literary and rhetorical activity. The literary artist, he asserts, "is free to fulfill" (p. 56) his own law because literature is concerned "with permanent values" (p. 57). The rhetor, however, is "perpetually in bondage to the occasion and the audience" (p. 56). Consequently, criticism of oratory must regard "a speech as a communication to a specific audience" and must be "concerned with effect" (p. 54). Permanence and universality are reserved for the literary critic, because "the result can only be confusion" when a speaker is "made to address a universal

[3] Herbert A. Wichelns, "The Literary Criticism of Oratory," in *Methods of Rhetorical Criticism,* Robert L. Scott and Bernard L. Brock (New York: Harper and Row, 1972), pp. 27–60. Further references to the essay will be to this source.

[4] William Norwood Brigance, ed., I & II (New York: McGraw-Hill, 1943); and Marie Kathryn Hochmuth, ed., III, *A History and Criticism of American Public Address* (New York: McGraw-Hill, 1955).

[5] Lester Thonssen and A. Craig Baird, *Speech Criticism* (New York: Ronald Press, 1948).

[6] Donald C. Bryant, ed., *The Rhetorical Idiom* (Ithaca, New York: Cornell Univ. Press, 1958), p. 5.

[7] Thonssen and Baird, p. 15.

[8] D. A. Russell, "Rhetoric and Criticism," *Greece and Rome,* 2nd Ser., 14 (Oct. 1967), 141-142.

audience" (p. 57). Rhetorical criticism, then, finds its *raison d'etre* in the specifics of the particular situation, and it is in these terms that the critic must interpret the function of "personality," "proof," "arrangement," "delivery," or any other of Wichelns' topics (pp. 56-57), all of which originate in classical theory.

If Wichelns succeeds in establishing rhetorical criticism as an independent activity, his program also obscures formalistic aspects of the classical inheritance. Despite his many borrowings from Aristotle, Whchelns says nothing about oratorical genres. This is hardly accidental, for genre theory is notoriously abstract; it rejects time and place as bases for classification and groups historical situations into general categories. As a result, it raises questions about "the relation of the class and the individuals composing it, the one and the many, the nature of universals."[9] Such questions cannot be a part of Wichelns' program because they smack of literary judgment. It is only in literature that one hears "the voice of the human spirit addressing itself to men of all ages and times" (p. 57), a voice transcending particular situations.

Neo-Aristotelians attempt to modify and escape this particularism. For example, one reads that the consummate critic "appraises the entire event by assigning it comparative rank in the total enterprise of speaking"[10] and that a speech may be criticized "as a finished product having certain rhetorical features which conform agreeably to fixed principles or rules."[11] One reads also of touchstones. But to assign comparative rank or to note agreeable conformity to fixed principles demands some notion of permanence, and such standards simply are not available in a system oriented completely to the specific situation. Here, the appropriate standard is that of immediate effect, and this single criterion makes it difficult, if not impossible, to develop intrinsic artistic standards. The system supplies no logical mechanism for connecting apparently disparate events.

Since Aristotle speaks of oratorical genres, this would seem a likely source for neo-Aristotelian formalism, but neo-Aristotelians, caught up in Wichelns' severe nominalism, cannot exploit this possibility. They may refer to genres, but the distinctions do not become instrumental; limiting or dividing analyses, they do not control them.[12] Ironically, neo-Aristotelians slight the genres even as they embrace the taxonomic categories to which the genres gave purpose, with the result that critics tend to classify "certain grosser properties cast under the heads of the traditional modes and canons," to produce "a mechanical accounting or summing up of how well the speech fits an *a priori* mold."[13] Any critical system will exhibit certain *a priori* features, but it appears that the mold of traditional criticism has become mechanically taxonomic. Stripped of generic distinctions, the neo-classical taxonomy does not encourage interaction between the critical apparatus and the broader purposes of rhetorical discourse, and the critic glances off the relationship that has been accepted as the very excuse for his being—the relationship between speaker and audience. Seeking refuge, critics turn to biography or history, but

---

[9] René Wellek and Austin Warren, *Theory of Literature* (New York: Harcourt, Brace and World, 1956), p. 237.

[10] Thonssen and Baird, p. 18.

[11] Thonssen and Baird, p. 457.

[12] Even a casual reading in *A History and Criticism of American Public Address* reveals that genres are not examined systematically.

[13] Douglas Ehninger, "Rhetoric and the Critic," *Western Speech,* 29 (Fall 1965), 230.

neither is an adequate resolution. That the adducing of historical details offers no escape is reinforced if we turn to an essay representing "the neo-Aristotelian tradition at its best,"[14] Marie Hochmuth Nichols' "Lincoln's First Inaugural."[15]

The most noteworthy feature of this essay is its accumulation of historical detail. Avoiding generalization, Nichols invites the reader to participate in the ambiance of the situation by recounting the particulars that surround it. Disregard the reprinted text of the address, and two-thirds of the article is devoted to a "scrupulous documentation"[16] of the events immediately preceding and following the speech. Such documentation can be an important ancilla, but the final test is whether the critic uses the accumulated detail in ways that add to an understanding and appreciation of the rhetorical transaction. Nichols faces this responsibility in the final third of her essay, but she is unable to overcome the inherent limitations of Wichelns' program.

Adhering to his tenets, she evaluates the speech "as a speech, a medium distinct from other media, and with methods peculiarly its own" (p. 88). The special topics appropriate to this task are "Lincoln's selection of materials, his arrangement, his style, and his manner" (p. 90). What is to unify these lines of inquiry? It is the speaker's purpose. But Nichols warns against the casual assumption that "Lincoln's purpose is easily discernible in the occasion itself" (p. 89), and she implicitly rejects generic considerations when she turns away from the fact that "this was an inaugural ceremony, with a ritual fairly well established" (p. 89). Genre is beside the point because Lincoln's purposes arise from the experiences "of the nation between his election as President and the day of his inauguration" (p. 89). These experiences focus on party, nation, and man, and they lead to this conclusion: "Clearly, he intended to take the occasion of the inauguration to declare the position of the Republican party in regard to the South, to announce his considered judgment in regard to the practical questions raised by the movement of secession, and, in all, to give what assurance he could of his personal integrity" (p. 90).

Compared to the specificity of the earlier historical documentation, the analysis following this statement of purpose is vague. For the most part, the critique is a summary. Including numerous quotations from the text and comparisons with earlier drafts, it certainly reproduces the flow of Lincoln's argument. Yet, it leaves the reader to his own devices in attempting to fathom the forms and topics of argument, the nature of evidence, the interaction among parts of the discourse, and the character of appeals to the audience. Summary simply does not explain how Lincoln "became the affectionate father, the benevolent and hopeful counselor" (p. 95). Moreover, the analysis of style does not probe deeply into the text itself; commentary becomes rigorous and specific only in terms of an external reference— in relation to the wording of earlier drafts. It is interesting to view the style through a consideration of the language Lincoln did not use, but a closer examination of that which he did use is needed to support the claim that his style produced "an image of great-heartedness, great humility and great faith" (p. 99).

To avoid misunderstanding, we want to underline that our purpose here is not

[14] Scott and Brock, p. 21.
[15] Marie Hochmuth Nichols. "Lincoln's First Inaugural," in Scott and Brock, pp. 60–100. Further references to this essay will be to this source.
[16] Black, p. 41.

to belittle this important essay. We merely want to emphasize that the critique exhibits a complete commitment to the unique context of the discourse. This commitment, in turn, produces an analysis that concentrates on external circumstances rather than on the internal development of the speech. The resulting limitations become strikingly apparent when Nichols attempts a general evaluation of the discourse.

Her position is unmistakably clear; the Inaugural Address is a rhetorical masterpiece. But what is the basis for this judgment? It cannot be found in either literary value or cultural force; these criteria are explicitly reserved for literary critics and historians (p. 88). Thus, everything comes down to effect, to the question of whether the discourse did what it was supposed to do. And this particular speech was supposed to enunciate party policy, allay the fears of the secessionists, and establish the orator's personal integrity. The reaction of the South, therefore, becomes the salient index. Yet, by this standard, the speech was the most abject of failures. It did not mollify the secessionists. In fact, Nichols argues convincingly that, after examining the Inaugural, "the South saw little hope from Lincoln" (p. 85). But she flees the inexorable conclusion. Ignoring immediate effect, she contends that "any fair-minded critic, removed from the passions of the times, must find himself much more in agreement with those observers of the day who believed the Inaugural met the 'requirements of good rhetoric' " (p. 95). This will not do. It is patently inconsistent to focus exclusively on the unique and specific situation and then to ask that final evaluation be "removed from the passions of the times."

The problem we have just outlined seems insoluble within the terms of the neo-Aristotelian tradition. Certainly there is but cold comfort in Parrish's observation that "not failure, but low aim, is crime" in speechmaking (p. 100).[17] That only papers over the gap that necessarily yawns between a philosophical dedication to the particular and a desire for a more permanent frame of reference. Parrish correctly recognizes a need for abstract standards, but he does not offer an ultimate grounding for the formalism he proposes. That grounding, we believe, exists in the theory of genres. To explain our position, we must return to the ancients.

GENRE THEORY

As opposed to Wichelns, the dominant position in ancient rhetoric is not that situations are unique and particular, but that they fall into general categories, into "types" or "kinds." The influence of Aristotle is decisive. He describes the three familiar genres of deliberative, forensic and epideictic, maintaining that "rhetoric falls into three divisions [genē], determined by the three classes of listeners to speeches."[18] Since it is the listener who "determines the speech's end and object,"[19] the audience is the central element in the system. Consequently, Aristotle

[17]Wayland Maxfield Parrish, "The Study of Speeches," in *American Speeches,* ed. Wayland Maxfield Parrish and Marie K. Hochmuth (New York: David McKay, 1954), p. 12. See Black, pp. 61–75.
[18]*Rhetoric* (trans. W. Rhys Roberts), I. 3. 1358ª, 36. For comment on a general formalism in Attic oratory see R. C. Jebb, *The Attic Orators* (1876; rpt. New York: Russell and Russell, 1962), I, xcii-civ.
[19]*Rhetoric* I. 3. 1358b, 1.

paves the way for general acceptance of the proposition that "the important aspect of the speech situation is the speaker-audience relationship."[20] At the same time, however, Aristotle marks and emphasizes the similarities among certain kinds of audiences and certain speaking situations; his entire theory ultimately responds to an abstract classification of oratorical requirements.

Later classical rhetoricians thoroughly endorse this theory of genre, and we find Cicero, Quintilian, and other writers consistently treating inventional theory in terms of the three types of speaking. More importantly, the genres give meaning to the whole of the complex taxonomy in classical rhetoric. The five *officia* and their elaborate sub-structures are significant only insofar as they assist the speaker in achieving his goal. That goal, of course, is conditioned by the nature of the audience; the speaker, however, locates his audience with reference to the genre in which he must function. Without the genres, classical rhetorical theory loses contact with the audience, and the elaborate taxonomy becomes meaningless, a system bereft of any rhetorical purpose. For this reason, we believe that any critical program based on classical models must give serious consideration to the genre theory.

The immediate advantage of generic criticism is that it permits the creation of intrinsic standards for rhetorical discourse without losing sight of the audience. Predicated upon the "expectations of the audience and the demands of the situation,"[21] the concept of genre assumes that certain types of situations provoke similar needs and expectations among audiences. Identifying and categorizing these situations are basic to inquiry, and the critic must uncover patterns of need and expectation that bind audiences together, even though they may be far removed in time and place. An adequate description of a genre, then, produces a general index of audience demands; it, therefore, locates the abstract rhetorical problems confronting the speaker and points to intrinsic standards for judging a particular kind of discourse.

To illustrate, we can expand upon the generic underpinning of our approach to the Cooper Union Address. This is a campaign speech, an oratorical form well-known to American audiences and easily distinguished from other types of public address. Nevertheless, this type does not fall within the tripartite Aristotelian division. The anomaly becomes evident when we consider the campaign speech in relation to audience and purpose, the basic components of the Aristotelian distinction. One who listens to a campaign speech is a judge of a future event, and he is urged to do something (i.e. to vote for a particular candidate). This corresponds to the function of the audience in deliberative oratory. The object of judgment, however, is not a policy, as it is in deliberative speaking, but a person, as it is in epideictic. Ends also are blurred; the deliberative orator examines the "expediency or the harmfulness of a proposed course of action"; and the epideictic orator must "praise or attack a man" in order to prove "him worthy of honour or the reverse."[22] Now, the end of campaign oratory is to make the candidate appear worthy and honorable. Nevertheless it makes no sense to argue that the campaign oration is a form of epideictic, since the speaker's goal is to effect a decision, and listeners are asked to judge, not merely to sit as spectators. Evidently, no one of the traditional genres is

[20]Thonssen and Baird, p. 15.
[21]Kathleen M. Hall Jamieson, "Generic Constraints and the Rhetorical Situation," *Philosophy and Rhetoric*, 6 (Summer 1973), 163.
[22]*Rhetoric* I. 3. 1358b, 22–28.

entirely satisfactory, and it follows that intelligent application of the neo-classical approach entails the description of a separate genre for campaign oratory.

In this instance, the problem in the traditional system appears to be an omission rather than an inherent defect, and we found it relatively easy to define the genre and remain consistent with Aristotelian principles. Finding Rosenthal's analysis of ethos suggestive, we approached the campaign oration as an instance of "personal persuasion," as discourse in which the central concern is the audience's attitude toward the candidate.[23] Given this condition, the campaign orator's first responsibility is, by definition, to promote himself as an individual. Both policies and character are in question, but policy is subsidiary to the purpose of creating an identification of thought and feeling between speaker and audience—a demand inherent in the situation. The ultimate objective is ingratiation. Translating all this into neo-classical terminology, we could describe the genre of campaign oratory as speaking in which listeners act as judges of a future event, an election: the end is to effect a judgment of the candidate, a judgment based on character and upon the treatment of issues.

This consideration of generic requirements helped to focus our analysis of the Cooper Union Address. In this case our description of the genre followed Aristotle rather closely. Other situations may demand more radical adjustments of the traditional system. Surely it is unreasonable to expect the tripartite division of antiquity to encompass all subsequent forms of public address. Genres are like institutions.[24] They exhibit a degree of stability over time, but they also grow, change, and decay in response to the conditions of society. Hence they "should not be viewed as static forms but as evolving phenomena."[25] The critic must retain the flexibility needed to adjust to changing circumstances. He must remember that generic distinctions should not force every item into a preconceived category; instead, their proper function is to uncover genuine points of similarity and difference among forms of discourse.

The discovery of these similarities and differences results in the establishment of generic constraints, and the use of these constraints appears to solve the most troublesome problem in neo-Aristotelian criticism—the antithetical tension between the commitment to a particular situation and the need for formal standards of evaluation. Theoretically, the dissipating of this tension can make neo-classicism again available to the rhetorical critic. We intended that our critique of the Cooper Union Address specify some of the potential. The critique itself must stand as the sole witness to our success or failure, but the genesis deserves comment because it helps explain the rationale and points up both strengths and limitations.

THE USES OF NEO-CLASSICISM

The position we have taken in this essay and elsewhere clearly is at one with Black's call for "an alternative to neo-Aristotelianism,"[26] and the literature indicates that the search has been profitable. Nevertheless, it seemed that the common

[23] Paul I. Rosenthal, "The Concept of Ethos and the Structure of Persuasion," *Speech Monographs,* 33 (June 1966), 114–126.
[24] Wellek and Warren, p. 226.
[25] Jamieson, p. 168.
[26] Black, p. 132.

acceptance had become "any alternative to neo-Aristotelianism," and if neo-classicism had become mechanical, arbitrary rejection seemed a short-sighted reaction. To forsake traditional theory completely appeared a dubious course, and an examination of the original sources convinced us that a return to generic distinctions was the key to another useful alternative. And to a large extent genre theory anticipates the contention that the neo-classical taxonomy commits the critic to a static set of categories and deflects the true purpose of criticism. It specifically anchors a discourse in the context of other discourses and the demands of the audience, and it blunts the charge that the neo-classical orientation forces the critic to overlook "the effects of audience, situation and other contemporary discourses on the speaker's behavior."[27]

The system retains schematic features, but that seems an advantage rather than a disadvantage. If criticism is not totally whimsical and subjective, some schema must control the analysis. The critic may concentrate on archetypal metaphors, dramatistic elements, analogues from anthropology and mythology, but there must be standards for sifting and sorting the materials. In this light, the neo-classical taxonomy is but one of many schemata available, and it has the particularly appealing feature of attempting to deal with the entire rhetorical transaction on its own terms. Recently, the most important and instructive analyses have had a non-traditional bias, but many tend to isolate and emphasize a single element or concept. A complete neo-classical approach, however, centers directly on the rhetorical process and divides it into a simple but comprehensive set of constituents. Out of context, the categories can be domineering, but any other schema can become equally oppressive, and genre theory helps prevent a neo-classical tyranny. Keeping the taxonomy within proper bounds, it centers attention where it ought to be, on the speaker-audience relationship, and the system produced seems an excellent filter for the analysis for a particular speech. Examining the Cooper Union Address, for example, we did not feel prisoner to a crabbed and stultifying orthodoxy, nor find ourselves trapped in tangential concerns. We found, instead, that the system forced us to come to grips with the speech as a speech, and we found that it forced us to make choices.[28] Whether we made the proper ones is not as important as the fact that we were not enclosed within arbitrary and debilitating confines.

The system, of course, does have confines. Genre theory presumes types, and a critic ordinarily will use the type to explore the single example. Comparisons are possible, or criticism might center on a series from one genre, but the character of neo-classicism is most appropriate to the analysis of a single speech. If the system cannot address "picketing, sloganeering, chanting, singing, marching, gesturing,"

[27] Joe A. Munshaw, "The Structures of History: Dividing Phenomena for Rhetorical Understanding." *Central States Speech Journal*, 24 (Spr. 1973), 30.

[28] In our critique, we deliberately suppressed details of the analysis. For example, we slighted intricacies in the argument of the first section because the reporting would have been tedious for the reader and would have made the speech appear more formalistic than it really is. We slighted other matters as well. Except by implication, we did not explore Lincoln's use of the rhetorical question or the "our fathers" refrain. We could have extended the latter into each segment of the putative debate with the South, and we might have considered its echoic religious values for an audience all too familiar with the *Lord's Prayer*. We do not mean to imply that these facets of the speech would not be available to a critic of a different persuasion. We do insist, however, that genre and taxonomy brought them to our attention. That we did not report them indicates choices we made rather than any shortcoming in the approach.

and similar communicative phenomena,[29] this limitation does no more than describe the scope of neo-classicism. A more serious problem attends the charge that the neo-classic critic suffers from a rationalistic bias.[30]

From the generic perspective, this bias is an institutional one. Rhetorical genres are grounded in established practices, and genre theory must assume the existence of stable conventions that govern public communication. Capitalizing upon this area of public agreement, genre theory can present a coherent and therefore "rational" account of rhetorical argument. This is advantageous under normal circumstances, but it is quite another matter when circumstances are not normal, in times of rapid change. Here is the most significant limitation to the critical program we are advocating.

This program necessarily works best in situations where the range of disagreement is limited, where there is a broad consensus about what can be argued and how it should be argued. Thus, even an observer as sympathetic as Booth must acknowledge that "the Aristotelian tradition is suited best to analyzing the cogency of . . . rhetoric, from the point of view of someone who is at least in some sense on the inside."[31] Our proposal, then, deals with an insider's rhetoric. Yet, everyone is aware of the outsider's, "the rhetoric of 'conversion,' of transformation—the rhetoric with the effect whether designed or not, of overturning personal ties and changing total allegiances."[32] This radical rhetoric may explicitly attack the stable conventions and institutions of a society; furthermore, it is likely to appear in a form that challenges the established norms of discourse, for attempts to subvert the establishment almost always involve an attempt to subvert its language.

In such situations, genre theory falters. Based on the presumption of stability, the system has no mechanism for explaining idiosyncratic and dramatic changes in ideology or style. The critic may adjust over time, but long-term flexibility is beside the point when one seeks to explain radical rhetoric *in situ*. Worse yet, adherence to a conventional typology can make the critic a captive of the institutional system that nascent rhetorical forms seek to destroy. The resultant analysis will condemn advocates of change because their rhetoric does not conform to conventional expectations, and the nature of that rhetoric may well go misunderstood. Nevertheless, even this limitation may prove to be of some value, if properly appreciated.

A time of rapid and drastic change is one, above all others, that may require stable points of reference. Surely it is hazardous always to evaluate new kinds of discourse in terms of the old, but there is no reason why old genres cannot be touchstones for understanding new developments. In other words, rhetorical criticism might "act on the premise that the study of historical change could greatly profit from a clearer view than we now have of what is changing."[33] We have yet to devise a critical rationale adequate to account for sudden shifts of ideology.

---

[29] Lloyd F. Bitzer and Edwin Black, eds., *The Prospect of Rhetoric* (Englewood Cliffs, New Jersey: Prentice-Hall, 1971), p. 225.

[30] See Black, pp. 91–131, and Karlyn K. Campbell, "The Ontological Foundations of Rhetorical Theory," *Philosophy and Rhetoric,* 3 (Spr. 1970), 97–108.

[31] Wayne C. Booth, "The Scope of Rhetoric Today: A Polemical Excursion," in Bitzer and Black, p. 97.

[32] Booth, p. 102.

[33] Paul Hernadi, *Beyond Genre* (Ithaca, New York: Cornell Univ. Press, 1972), p. 8.

CONCLUSION

In concluding, we can do little more than repeat what we already have said. We simply propose the addition of genre theory as a means of introducing formalism into neo-classical criticism. Squarely within the tradition, this theory does not ask that critics abandon the centrality of the audience. In fact, genre theory acts as a corrective precisely because it allows for a broader conception of audience than is permitted in neo-Aristotelian criticism. If critics can identify situations that create generally similar audience demands, then they can abstract principles that will apply to a wide variety of discourses. Although these principles rest on audience analysis, the audience is conceived in generic terms, and the generalizations produced may offer formal grounds for evaluating speeches of a particular kind. These standards lack the more purely formal characteristics of certain literary genres, but they provide a point of entry into a discourse and focus the critical reaction.

Much remains to be done, of course. Our analysis of the campaign genre remains limited and tentative. To focus the neo-classical taxonomy, we established an *a priori* definition of the end for campaign oratory, and we were then able to construct very broad standards for rhetorical evaluation in a particular instance. Additional instances have to be accumulated before the genre can be described properly and more specific generic constraints developed. More generally, we have not examined genre theory in detail, nor have we attempted a systematic classification of modern rhetorical genres.

Fortunately, the evidence indicates a probing in those directions.[34] Much of the effort has been piecemeal, but this, after all, may prove the most satisfactory route. Modern rhetorical critics usually start with a settled theoretical position and then make an application, but in writing the two essays, we found ourselves attacking the problem form the opposite perspective. The experience was instructive, and perhaps it can be generalized. The progress of rhetorical criticism may depend more on the ability of critics to induce principles from actual critiques than on a concern with abstract issues.

---

[34] See Black, pp. 132-177; Forbes I. Hill, "Conventional Wisdom—Traditional Form: The President's Message of November 3, 1969," *QJS,* 58 (Dec. 1972), 373-386; B. L. Ware and Wil A. Linkugel, "They Spoke in Defense of Themselves: On the Generic Criticism of Apologia," *QJS,* 59 (Oct. 1973), 273-283; and Jamieson. The last two articles include references to a number of related discussions.

Lincoln At Cooper Union:
A Rhetorical Analysis of the Text
Michael C. Leff and Gerald P. Mohrmann

When Abraham Lincoln spoke at the Cooper Union on the evening of February 27, 1860, his audience responded enthusiastically, and the speech has continued to elicit praise throughout the intervening years. Biographers, historians, and

The Practice of Rhetorical Criticism

literary scholars agree that it was "one of his most significant speeches,"[1] one that illustrated "his abilities as a reasoner,"[2] and one to which posterity has ascribed his "subsequent nomination and election to the presidency."[3] Ironically, however, this model of "logical analysis and construction"[4] has failed to generate a critical response in kind. Most of what has been written treats of the background, and, too often, the man as myth has intruded; caught up in the drama of the performance, writers find no bit of information too trivial to report, whether it be the price of tickets or the fit of Lincoln's new shoes.[5] Such details can deepen our appreciation of the event, but they do not illuminate the speech as a speech.

Unhappily, little light is shed by those who do comment on the speech text. Nicolay and Hay assert, for example, that Lincoln's conclusions "were irresistibly convincing,"[6] but their sole piece of supporting evidence is a four-hundred word excerpt. And if they happen to be "firmly in the hero-worshipping tradition,"[7] those of sterner stuff fare no better. Basler makes the curious claim that the rhetorical "high-water mark" occurs toward the end of the first section;[8] Nevins mistakenly argues that the speech "fell into two halves";[9] reputable scholars equate summary and quotation with explication;[10] and it is generally accepted that Lincoln demonstrated a conciliatory attitude toward the South.[11]

Certainly all is not dross in previous studies, but wherever one turns in the literature, no satisfying account of the speech is to be found.[12] We are convinced that a systematic rhetorical analysis can help rectify the situation, and what follows

[1] J. G. Randall, *Lincoln the President* (New York: Dodd, Mead, 1945), I, 135.
[2] Howard Mumford Jones and Ernest E. Leisy, eds., *Major American Writers* (New York: Harcourt, Brace, 1945), p. 681.
[3] Benjamin Barondess, *Three Lincoln Masterpieces* (Charleston: Education Foundation of West Virginia, 1954), p. 3.
[4] R. Franklin Smith, "A Night at Cooper Union," *Central States Speech Journal* 13 (Autumn 1962), 272.
[5] The most influential account of this sort is Carl Sandburg, *The Prairie Years* (New York: Harcourt, Brace, 1927), II, 200–216, but the most complete is Andrew A. Freeman, *Abraham Lincoln Goes to New York* (New York: Coward-McCann, 1960).
[6] John G. Nicolay and John Hay, *Abraham Lincoln: A History* (New York: Century, 1917), II, 219–220.
[7] Richard Hofstadter, *The American Political Tradition* (New York: Alfred A. Knopf, 1948), p. 364.
[8] *Abraham Lincoln: His Speeches and Writings,* ed. Roy P. Basler (Cleveland: World, 1946), p. 32.
[9] Allan Nevins, *The Emergence of Lincoln* (New York: Charles Scribner's Sons, 1950), II, 186.
[10] Randall, pp. 136–137; Basler, pp. 32–33; Nevins, pp. 186–187; Reinhard H. Luthin, *The Real Abraham Lincoln* (Englewood Cliffs, New Jersey: Prentice-Hall, 1960), p. 210.
[11] Randall, p. 136; Barondess, p. 18; Nicolay and Hay, p. 220, Nevins, p. 186; Luthin, pp. 243–244.
[12] Freeman treats of the text briefly, pp. 84–88, and although Barondess ranges from preparation to audience reaction, pp. 3–30, Hofstadter's observation applies, n. 7 above, Earl W. Wiley discusses the address in *Four Speeches by Lincoln* (Columbus: Ohio State Univ. Press, 1927), pp. 15–27, but he limits analysis to the first section of the speech, a limitation also applied in his "Abraham Lincoln: His Emergence as the Voice of the People," in *A History and Criticism of American Public Address,* ed. William N. Brigance (New York: McGraw-Hill, 1943), II, 859–877. In the same volume, the speech is the basis for comments on delivery in Mildred Freburg Berry, "Abraham Lincoln: His Development in the Skills of the Platform," pp. 828–858.

is our attempt to accomplish such an analysis. In that attempt, we center on the text of the speech, but our purpose demands some preliminary remarks about the rhetorical context.

Although it was not until after the speech that Lincoln frankly admitted his presidential aspirations, saying, "The taste *is* in my mouth a little,"[13] he had been savoring the possibility for months. The preceding November, he had written that the next canvass would find him laboring "faithfully in the ranks" unless "the judgment of the party shall assign me a different position,"[14] but even as he wrote, Lincoln was grasping for a different assignment, "busy using the knife on his rivals . . . and doing all he could to enhance his reputation as an outstanding Republican leader."[15] Small wonder that he decided early to "make a political speech of it" in New York.[16] Here was the opportunity to make himself more available to Republicans in the East. The appearance alone would make for greater recognition, but political availability required more; Lincoln had to be an acceptable Republican, and he had to be an attractive alternative to the Democratic candidate.

William A. Seward and Stephen A. Douglas were the presumptive nominees, and they, patently, were Lincoln's antagonists. Moreover, their views on slavery created an intertwining threat that menaced his conception of the party and his personal ambitions. When Seward spoke about a "higher law" and an "irrepressible conflict," he strained Lincoln's sense of moral and political conservatism; these pronouncements smacked too much of radicalism.[17] Douglas, meanwhile, exacerbated the situation with his doctrine of popular sovereignty. Lincoln feared that this siren song would cause wholesale apostasy in Republican ranks, an eventuality all the more likely if the party nominee was tinctured with radicalism. He knew, however, that a middle ground existed, and he long had occupied it with his insistence that slavery should be protected but not extended. Consequently, when Lincoln addressed the Eastern Republicans, both principle and expediency permitted, even dictated, that he speak for party and for self and that he maintain party and self in a position between those taken by Seward and Douglas.

That he took such a course is revealed by an examination of the speech text, but all the external evidence shows a man running hard, if humbly, for political office, and while Lincoln spoke for his party, he spoke first for his own nomination. In fact, the Cooper Union Address is best characterized as a campaign oration, a speech designed to win nomination for the speaker. This identification of genre is basic to our analysis, and the nature of the genre is suggested by Rosenthal's distinction between non-personal and personal persuasion;[18] in the former, the speaker attempts to influence audience attitudes about a particular issue, and ethos

---

[13] Letter to Lyman Trumbull, April 29, 1860. *The Collected Works of Abraham Lincoln,* ed. Roy P. Basler (New Brunswick, New Jersey: Rutgers Univ. Press, 1955), IV, 45.

[14] Letter to William E. Frazer, November 1, 1859, *Collected Works,* III, 491.

[15] Richard N. Current, *The Lincoln Nobody Knows* (New York: McGraw-Hill, 1958), p. 199. For an indication of Lincoln's activities see *Collected Works,* III, 384–521.

[16] Letter to James A. Briggs, *Collected Works,* III, 494.

[17] See Letter to Salmon P. Chase, June 9, 1859, *Collected Works,* III, 384; Letter to Nathan Sargent, June 23, 1859, *Collected Works,* III, 387–388; Letter to Richard M. Corwine, April 6, 1860, *Collected Works,* IV, 36.

[18] Paul I. Rosenthal, "The Concept of Ethos and the Structure of Persuasion," *Speech Monographs* 33 (June 1966), 114–126.

is important insofar as it lends credence to the substance of the argument. In the latter the process is reversed. The focal point is the speaker, and the message becomes a vehicle for enhancing ethos. Campaign orations, on this basis, tend to be examples of personal persuasion, for while "the ostensible purpose of a given speech may be to gain acceptance of a particular policy. . . . the actual purpose is to gain votes for the candidate."[19] In other words, the ultimate goal of the campaign orator is to promote himself as a candidate. Both policies and character are in question, but the treatment of issues is subsidiary to the purpose of creating a general identification between the speaker and the audience. The objective, then, in a campaign oration is ingratiation.

With genre and purpose in mind, we can approach the speech through familiar topics. Addressing himself first to the people of New York, then to the South and finally to the Republican Party, Lincoln divides his speech into three sections, and this pattern of organization invites seriatim analysis of the major dispositional units. Furthermore, argument and style immediately loom as important elements, since they disclose essential characteristics in and significant interrelationships among the main units of the discourse. Consequently, our critique will follow Lincoln's pattern of organization and will have special reference to matters of argument and style. This approach, however, is not without its hazards. The convenience of tracing the natural sequence of the argument may foster fragmentary analysis and obscure the dominant rhetorical motive. Yet to be mindful of the genre is to find a corrective. The central concern is ingratiation, and recognition of this purpose unifies the elements of analysis by giving them a more precise focus; awareness of the ultimate goal becomes shuttle to the threads of structure, argument, and style.

In the address, Lincoln deals exclusively with slavery, and although this inflammatory issue might seem a shaky bridge to ingratiation, the choice is a fitting response to the rhetorical problem. What better point of departure than the paramount issue of the day, the issue with which he was most closely identified, and the issue that had spawned the Republican Party?[20] And Lincoln starts with the very motivation that had driven men to Ripon only a few years before, the question of slavery in the territories. Capitalizing on these initial associations, he counters the emotionalism inherent in the topic by assuming a severely rational posture and enunciating a moderate but firm set of principles. The approach distinguishes him from his chief rivals and solicits an intensified association from Eastern Republicans. These objectives govern the matter and manner of the opening argument, and this argument lays a foundation for subsequent developments in the speech. In the opening section and throughout, Lincoln associates himself and Republicans with the founding fathers and Constitutional principle, and he dissociates rival candidates and factions from those fathers and that principle.

Acknowledging his "fellow citizens of New York," Lincoln begins by adopting

[19] Rosenthal, p. 120.

[20] In 1854, "northern whigs persuaded that their old party was moribund, Democrats weary of planting dominance, and free-soilers eager to exclude slavery from the territories began to draw together to resist the advance of the planting power": Charles A. Beard and Mary R. Beard, *The Rise of American Civilization* (New York: Macmillan, 1937), II, 22. Cf. Don E. Fehrenbacher, "Lincoln and the Formation of the Republican Party" in *Prelude to Greatness* (Stanford: Stanford Univ. Press, 1962), pp. 19-47.

a "text for this discourse."[21] The text is a statement in which Stephen A. Douglas had asserted, "Our fathers, when they framed the government under which we live, understood this question just as well and even better than we do now." Defining terms in catechistic sequence, Lincoln maintains that "the frame of government under which we live" consists of the Constitution and the "twelve subsequently framed amendments" and that "our fathers" are "the 'thirty-nine' who signed the original instrument." He then asks, what is the question "those fathers understood 'just as well and even better, than we do now'?" The answer "is this: Does the proper division of local from Federal authority, or anything else in the Constitution, forbid our Federal Government to control as to slavery in our Federal Territories?" The question joins the issue because it is a matter upon which "Senator Douglas holds the affirmative, and the Republicans the negative."

That Douglas should play the foil is most fitting. National newspaper coverage of the 1858 senatorial campaign had linked the two men together, and the debates were to be published in March.[22] Moreover, Lincoln had continued the argument during 1859, worrying whether the Republican Party would "maintain it's [sic] identity, or be broken up to form the tail of Douglas' new kite."[23] Nevertheless, Lincoln knew that Douglas was vulnerable. The Freeport Doctrine had convinced many in the North that the man was only too "willing to subordinate moral considerations to political expediency."[24] Douglas, then, was an established rival, one whom Lincoln perceived as a threat to party unity, and one whose strategic position was open to attack from principle.

On a tactical level, the "text" quoted from Douglas affords Lincoln an ideal starting point. The allusion to the fathers is a symbolic reference with the potential for universal respect, and Douglas' implicit attack upon the principles that had generated the Republican Party creates an antithesis binding speaker and audience together in opposition to a common enemy. This antithesis is a channel for ingratiation: Lincoln makes Republicanism the voice of rational analysis, and

[21] We follow the text in *Complete Works,* ed. John G. Nicolay and John Hay (New York: Francis D. Tandy, 1905), V, 293–328; we include no footnotes because aside from unimportant exceptions, citations are sequential. This text is more conservative in typography than that edited and published as a campaign document by Charles C. Nott and Cephas Brainerd. The latter appears in *Collected Works,* III, 522–550; 1860, p. 1. Lincoln ignored suggested alterations in the original (Sandburg, II, 210 and 215–216): he proofread the newspaper copy (Freeman, pp. 92–93): pamphlet copies were available by the first of April (*Collected Works,* IV, 38–39); and Lincoln adamantly resisted editorial changes by Nott (*Collected Works,* IV, 58–59). This evidence emphasizes the care with which he contructed the speech, but it also suggests that he anticipated a wider audience from the outset. Publication practices and his own experience told Lincoln that he would reach many who would not hear him speak.

[22] General interest in the debates is underlined by the favorable editorial notice appearing in the Brooklyn *Daily Times,* August 26, 1858, an editorial written by one Walt Whitman; Walt Whitman, *I Sit and Look Out,* ed. Emory Holloway and Vernolian Schwartz (New York: Columbia Univ. Press, 1932), p. 96. For letters referring to publication of the debates, see *Collected Works,* III. 341, 343, 372–374, 515, and 516.

[23] Letter to Lyman Trumbull, Dec. 11, 1858, *Collected Works,* III, 345.

[24] Harry J. Carman and Harold C. Syrett, *A History of the American People* (New York: Alfred A. Knopf, 1952), I, 588. Cf. Fehrenbacher, "The Famous 'Freeport Question,'" in *Prelude to Greatness,* pp. 121–142.

the precise terms of Douglas' assertion form the premises of logical inquiry. Moving into the inquiry, Lincoln pursues a vigorous *ad hominem* attack.[25] He accepts Douglas' logic and then turns it against him.

The argument of the first section develops out of a single hypothetical proposition: if the better understanding evinced by our fathers shows that they believed nothing forbade federal control of slavery in the territories, then such regulatory power is inherent in the governmental frame. Lincoln affirms the antecedent with an elaborate chain of inductive evidence. Instances in the induction consist of actions by the fathers before and after they signed the Constitution because the question "seems not to have been directly before the convention."[26] From the Northwest Ordinance of 1784 to the Missouri Compromise of 1820, Lincoln enumerates seven statutes regulating slavery in the territories, and he accounts for votes by twenty-three of the fathers.[27] Twenty-one voted in favor of such regulation. Since these men were bound by "official responsibility and their corporal oaths" to uphold the Constitution, the implication of their affirmative votes is beyond question. To conclude that the twenty-one would have condoned federal regulation if they thought it unconstitutional would be to accuse these fathers of "gross political impropriety and willful perjury," and "as actions speak louder than words, so actions under such responsibility speak still louder."

Emphasizing deeds and "adhering rigidly to the text," Lincoln cannot offer in evidence "whatever understanding may have been manifested by any person" other than the thirty-nine, nor can he cite the sixteen who left no voting records. But the latter include the likes of Franklin, Hamilton, and Morris, and he believes that this group "would probably have acted just as the twenty-three did." In any event, "a clear majority of the whole" understood that nothing "forbade the Federal Government to control slavery in the Federal Territories," and with the remaining fathers probably agreeing, there can be little doubt about "the understanding of our fathers who framed the original Constitution; and the text affirms that they understood the question 'better than we.' "

Lincoln now uses this understanding to discredit arguments based on the fifth and tenth amendments; he says it is "a little presumptuous" to suggest that the fathers embraced one principle when writing the Constitution and another when writing the amendments. And does not this suggestion "become impudently absurd when coupled with the other affirmation, from the same mouth, that those who did

---

[25] Logicians often define *ad hominem* as a fallacy resulting from an attack upon the character of a man rather than the quality of argument. In this essay, however, we use the term as Schopenhauer does in distinguishing between *ad hominem* and *ad rem* as the two basic modes of refutation. He differentiates in this manner: "We may show either that the proposition is not in accordance with the nature of things, *i.e.,* with absolute, objective truth [*ad rem*]; or that it is inconsistent with other statements or admissions of our opponent, *i.e.,* with truth as it appears to him [*ad hominem*]"; Arthur Schopenhauer, "The Art of Controversy," in *The Will to Live: Selected Writings of Arthur Schopenhauer,* ed. Richard Taylor (New York: Anchor Books, 1962), p. 341. See Henry W. Johnstone, Jr., "Philosophy and *Argumentum ad Hominem,*" *Journal of Philosophy* 49 (July 1952), 489–498.

[26] Lincoln undoubtedly knew that James Wilson, Patrick Henry and Edmund Randolph had discussed the topic (See *Collected Works,* III, 526–527, n. 9.), but he is accurate in asserting that the subject did not come "directly" before the convention.

[27] Washington's vote was his signature, as President, on the Act of 1789 which enforced the Ordinance of 1787.

the two things alleged to be inconsistent, understood whether they really were inconsistent better than we—better than he who affirms that they are inconsistent?" The touch of sarcasm reveals a more aggressive attitude, but it is justified by the inductive process; Douglas' own criterion forces the conclusion that he does not comprehend the understanding of the fathers. Lincoln will become even more combative before he brings the first section to a close, but some comments on style are merited, and they will lead us into his conclusion.

The style of this section is entirely consistent with Lincoln's severely rational approach. The audience probably did not expect the "rhetorical fireworks of a Western stump-speaker,"[28] but Lincoln is most circumspect. There are none of the "many excuses" that made him a Uriah Heep to some of his opponents,[29] and he avoids all display, indulging neither in anecdotes nor figurative language. The syntax is complex at times, but the complexity is that of legal rather than literary prose, as is evidenced in the following sentence: "It, therefore, would be unsafe to set down even the two who voted against the prohibition as having done so because, in their understanding, any proper division of local from Federal authority, or anything in the Constitution, forbade the Federal Government to control as to slavery in Federal territory."

The preceding quotation, with its echo of the text, points to a noteworthy stylistic element: repetition. Lincoln includes fifteen extended citations of the issue and an equal number from the "text," repetitions that accentuate the single line of argument. He adds to the emphasis by stressing certain key words and phrases. For example, there are over thirty uses of the root "understand," usually in the participial "understanding," and Lincoln alludes to the "fathers" more than thirty-five times. None of these repetitions is blatant or forced because he weaves them into the fabric of the inductive process. Furthermore, the repetitions concomitantly reinforce and control the emotional association with the fathers and their understanding of the Constitution. This point is crucial to an appreciation of Lincoln's rhetorical method. Both the direction of the argument and the symbols expressing it are fiercely emotional; yet, all is enmeshed in an incisive logical and linguistic structure, and while the tone remains rationalistic and legalistic, it also creates a subtle emotive nexus between the Republican audience and the founding fathers.

As noted above, style and argument shift in the concluding paragraphs, after Lincoln already has established his logical credentials. The argument becomes bolder, and the style alters appropriately. When developing the induction, Lincoln refers to the framers of the Constitution as the "thirty-nine," but they become "our fathers" again in the conclusion of the long first section of the speech. And there periods become more polished and sophisticated:

> If any man at this day sincerely believes that a proper division of local from Federal authority, or any part of the Constitution, forbids the Federal Government to control as to slavery. in the Federal Territories, he is right to say so, and to enforce his position by all truthful evidence and fair argument which he can. But he has no right to mislead others, who have less access to history, and less leisure to study it, into the false belief that 'our fathers who framed the government under which we live' were of the same

[28] Nicolay and Hay, *Abraham Lincoln*, II, 220.
[29] See Hofstadter, p. 94; *Collected Works*, III, 396.

opinion—thus substituting falsehood and deception for truthful evidence and fair argument.

This passage completes the negative phase of Lincoln's argumentation. Both matter and manner drive a rational wedge between the speaker and his rivals. Clearly, Lincoln suggests that Douglas may be guilty of deliberate "falsehood and deception," and just as clearly, his own position represents "truthful evidence and fair argument." Lincoln, one of those with "access to history" and some "leisure to study it," attempts to set the record straight. Another direct slash at Douglas, the very source of the text and issue. At the same time, Lincoln indirectly differentiates himself from Seward and his radical posture. Lincoln's position is more to the right, closer to the demands of objective inquiry, closer also to the demands of political availability, and it is important to remark that he achieves this dissociation without recourse to divisive rhetoric. The foray against the man and his position is patent, but is is completely inferential.

Although less obtrusive than the refutation, an equally important constructive movement exists within this part of the oration. Not only does Lincoln distinguish himself from his opponents, he nurtures Republican unity because he makes himself and party the vessels for transmitting the faith of the fathers. Avoiding self-references, he presents himself as the voice of Republicanism, and he caps this appeal with words both to and from the party:

> But enough! Let all who believe that 'our fathers who framed the government under which we live understood this question just as well, and even better, than we do now,' speak as they spoke, and act as they acted upon it. This is all Republicans ask—all Republicans desire—in relation to slavery. As those fathers marked it, so let it be again marked, as an evil not to be extended, but to be tolerated and protected only because of and so far as its actual presence among us makes that toleration and protection a necessity. Let all the guarantees those fathers gave it be not grudgingly, but fully and fairly, maintained. For this Republicans contend, and with this, so far as I know or believe, they will be content.

At this point in the speech, Lincoln has associated himself and his audience with the spirit, the principles and the actions of the founding fathers, and in doing so, he has taken the first steps toward ingratiation.

Comprising nearly half the speech, this initial section is so clearly logical that it regularly is cited as a demonstration of Lincoln's powers as a reasoner, but to say no more is to grossly underestimate his achievement. The next section, too, is remarkable for its logical development, and all that follows in the speech is anticipated and controlled by the attack upon Douglas. Failure to appreciate this unity has confounded commentators, and their confusion is strikingly illustrated in the generally accepted conclusion that Lincoln follows his attack with remarks "conciliatory toward the South."[30]

The second section does begin with an ostensible change in audience: "And now, if they would listen—as I suppose they will not,—I would address a few words

[30] Randall, I, 136.

to the Southern people." But we learn more about the beholders than the object when we are told that the next twenty-six paragraphs are filled with "words of kindly admonition and protest,"[31] words of "sweet reasonableness to allay Southern fears."[32] Presuming that he will not be heard, Lincoln notes that "our party gets no votes" in the South, and he flatly asserts later that "the Southern people will not so much as listen to us." These are not idle reservations. They represent the realistic assessment of an astute politician who knows that the coming election will be won or lost in the North; it is hardly plausible that this man would detract from his ultimate purpose by directing nearly forty per cent of his speech to an unavailable audience.

In truth, the audience does not change. Lincoln merely casts the second section of the speech in the form of a *prosopopoeia,* a figure he had rehearsed five months earlier in Cincinnati.[33] The device suits his purposes admirably. It enables him to create a mock debate between Republicans and the South, a debate in which he becomes spokesman for the party. In this role, Lincoln can strengthen the identification between himself and the available Republican audience. He is careful to extend the refutation of Douglas into the second section and thus carry over the lines of association and disassociation begun earlier in the discourse. If Lincoln leaves Douglas with little ground on which to stand, he performs the same argumentative service for the South, and the debate he manufactures is far from being conciliatory.

The *prosopopoeia* develops into another *ad hominem* argument. This time, however, the presentation is complicated by the need to deal with the collective contentions of a collective opposition. To provide control, Lincoln again begins by stressing reason, saying to the South, "I consider that in the general qualities of reason and justice you are not inferior to any other people." Yet, in the specific case, rational discourse is stymied because the Southerners never refer to Republicans except "to denounce us as reptiles, or, at the best, as no better than outlaws." Such responses are unjust to both sides. The proper course would be to "bring forward your charges and specifications, and then be patient long enough to hear us deny or justify." Obviously, the South is unwilling and unable to follow this procedure, and becoming persona for both Republicanism and reason, Lincoln reconstructs the charges and specifications; these include sectionalism, radicalism, agitation of the slavery question, and slave insurrections.

The putative debate begins: "You say we are sectional. We deny it. That makes an issue; and the burden of proof is upon you." The crux of the matter is whether Republicans repel the South with "some wrong principle." Republican principle, however, is based in the beliefs and actions of the fathers, and Lincoln challenges the South to respond to this fact. "Do you accept the challenge? No! Then you really believe that the principle which 'our fathers who framed the government under which we live' thought so clearly right as to adopt it, and indorse it again and

---

[31] Nicolay and Hay, *Abraham Lincoln,* II, 220.

[32] Nevins, II, 186.

[33] *Collected Works,* III, 438–454. Speaking at Cincinnati, September 17, 1859, Lincoln directs so much of his speech across the river "to the Kentuckians" (p. 440.) that one listener complained aloud, "Speak to Ohio men, and not to Kentuckians!" (p. 445.) Interestingly, Nevins appreciates the *prosopopoeia* in this speech, noting that Lincoln was "ostensibly speaking to Kentuckians," II, 56.

again, upon their official oaths, is in fact so clearly wrong as to demand your condemnation without a moment's consideration." Closing and reinforcing this line of reasoning Lincoln refers to the pre-eminent father: "Some of you delight to flaunt in our faces the warning . . . given by Washington in his Farewell Address," but if he were to speak for himself "would he cast the blame of that sectionalism upon us, who sustain his policy, or upon you, who repudiate it? We respect that warning of Washington, and we commend it to you, together with his example pointing to the right application of it."[34] Thus, the South claims to be the injured party, but analysis of the charge proves that the wounds are self-inflicted.

Lincoln uses the same refutational method for each of the other issues; first defining the charge with a series of rhetorical questions, he then turns the argument against the adversary. The South proclaims itself the bastion of conservatism and denounces Republican radicalism, but "what is conservatism? Is it not adherence to the old and tried, against the new and untried? We stick to, contend for, the identical old policy . . . which was adopted by 'our' fathers who framed the government under which we live'; while you with one accord reject, and scout, and spit upon that old policy, and insist upon substituting something new." The South alleges that Republicans have made the slavery issue more prominent. True, the issue is more prominent, but this situation arose because the South "discarded the old policy of the fathers." Finally, Southerners complain that Republicans foment insurrection among the slaves, but they can adduce no evidence to support this allegation, cannot "implicate a single Republican" and ignore that "Republican doctrines and declarations are accompanied with a continual protest against any interference whatever" with the institution in the slave states. Indeed, were it not for the loud and misleading protestations of Southern politicians, the slaves would hardly know that the Republican Party existed. Worse yet, the South refuses to acknowledge a simple truth contained in Republican doctrine, a truth articulated "many years ago" when Jefferson indicated that the cause of slave insurrections was slavery itself. Like Jefferson, Republicans would not interfere with slavery where it exists, but Republicans do insist, as the fathers did, that the federal government "has the power of restraining the extension of the institution—the power to insure that a slave insurrection shall never occur on any American soil which is now free."

Finishing his treatment of specific charges, Lincoln builds to a more forceful and aggressive tone, just as he did at the end of the first section. His arrangement of responses to Southern allegations is itself climactic, the issue of insurrections being both last and most critical. Always volatile, this issue had become extremely explosive in the wake of the Harper's Ferry raid and the trial of John Brown, and Lincoln understandably chooses this matter as the instrument for his most extensive defense of party and principle. He is not content, however, to assume a merely defensive posture: the entire pattern of his argumentation reveals a movement from reply to attack that gathers momentum as the discourse proceeds. Thus, having dis-

---

[34] The varied interpretations of Washington's warning and their longevity are illustrated in debates, early in 1850, over the purchase of the Farewell Address manuscript for the Library of Congress. Much of the debate is reproduced in William Dawson Johnston, *History of the Library of Congress* (Washington: Government Printing Office, 1904), I, 326–340.

posed of the insurrection controversy, Lincoln assails the very character of the Southern position, and he concludes this section with an examination of threats emanating from the South.

The South hopes to "break up the Republican organization." That failing, "you will break up the Union rather than submit to a denial of your constitutional rights." This is a course of "rule or ruin"; the union will be destroyed unless people are permitted to take slaves into the federal territories. But no such right exists in the Constitution and Southern threats are fruitless. Neither the Constitution nor the Republican Party are so malleable as to bend at the touch of Southern fancy. Not even the Dred Scott decision offers a refuge. That verdict was made "in a divided court, by a bare majority of the judges, and they not quite agreeing with one another in the reasons for making it." The decision rests upon "the opinion that 'the right of property in a slave is distinctly and expressly affirmed in the Constitution,' " but careful analysis shows that this right is not even implied. Surely it is reasonable to expect the Court to retract "the mistaken statement" when apprised of its error. Furthermore, the verdict runs contrary to the judgment of the fathers, those who decided the same question long ago "without division among themselves when making the decision," without division "about the meaning of it after it was made," and without "basing it upon any mistaken statement of facts." Having thus contrasted the babel of the Court with the unity of the fathers and their lineal descendants, Lincoln builds to a striking analogy:

> Under these circumstances, do you really feel yourselves justified to break up this government unless such a court decision as yours is shall be at once submitted to as a conclusive and final rule of political action? But you will not abide the election of a Republican president! In that supposed event, you say, you will destroy the Union; and then, you say, the crime of having destroyed it will be upon us! That is cool. A highwayman holds a pistol to my ear, and mutters through his teeth, 'Stand and deliver, or I shall kill you, and then you will be a murderer!'

Adding that the highwayman's threat can "scarcely be distinguished in principle" from "the threat of destruction to the Union," Lincoln completes his *ad hominem* assault against the Southern position, and the *prosopopoeia* ends.

The parallels and interrelationships between the first and the second sections of the speech are evident. Some shifts in invention and style between the two sections are occasioned by the change of antagonist, but it is more significant that Lincoln elects to argue against adversaries in both and that he uses the same fundamental argument to dispatch them all. In both sections, he strives to become spokesman for the party by demonstrating that he is a man of reason and that this characteristic melds himself and party with the principles of the founding fathers. In addition, the same characteristic distinguishes him from other candidates. Finally, each section is based on a severely rational framework and builds to a terminal climax that unifies and heightens logical and emotional dimensions.

Merging style and argument within and between parts of the discourse, Lincoln unquestionably remains in touch with his immediate audience, and he unquestionably has his eye on ingratiation. In the first movement, he separates himself and party from Douglas and Seward; in the second, he favorably contrasts the position of the party with that of its most vociferous opponent.[35] But one further step remains. To this juncture, the identification of speaker, party, and principle has been closely tied to a series of negative definitions. A positive gesture seems necessary, and in the final section of the speech, Lincoln fuses his audience together through more directly constructive appeals.

He begins by saying he will address "a few words now to Republicans," and though he puts aside both text and issue, his remarks evolve naturally from what has proceeded. Once more reason is the point of departure. Having, in the highwayman metaphor, implied a contrast between cool reason and hot passion, Lincoln urges Republicans to "do nothing through passion and ill-temper" that might cause discord within the nation, and, as he draws out the ultimate implications of the Southern position, antithesis becomes the dominant mode of argument and style. The section centers on a contrast between the Republicans and the South (between "we" and "they"); it extends and amplifies the distinction between word and deed that is present throughout the speech; and the argument is couched in and reinforced by antithetical syntax.

Recognizing Southern intransigence, Lincoln still wants his party to "calmly consider their demands" and reach conclusions based on all "they say and do." Pursuing the inquiry, he asks, "Will they be satisfied if the Territories be unconditionally surrendered to them? We know they will not." And "will it satisfy them if, in the future, we have nothing to do with invasions and insurrections? We know it will not." It will not because past abstention has not exempted "us from the charge and the denunciation." To satisfy them, "we must not only leave them alone, but we must somehow convince them that we do let them alone." Experience shows that this is no easy task because Republican policy and actions have been misconstrued consistently. The only recourse seems to be "this and only this: cease to call slavery wrong, and join them in calling it right. And this must be done thoroughly—done in acts as well as words. Silence will not be tolerated—we must place ourselves avowedly with them." Republicans must suppress all "declarations that slavery is wrong," must return "fugitive slaves with greedy pleasure," and must pull down all free state constitutions "before they will cease to believe that all their troubles proceed from us."

Most Southerners, Lincoln admits, would not put the argument in this extreme form. Most would simply claim that they want to be left alone, but "we do let them alone." Consequently, it is apparent that "they will continue to accuse us of doing, until we cease saying." Given the nature of their arguments and the character of their actions, the Southerners cannot stop short of the demand that all Republicans desist from speaking and acting out of conviction. Those who hold that "slavery is morally right and socially elevating" must necessarily call for its recognition

<hr/>

[35] The second movement continues the implicit attack upon Seward, and all texts indicate a mimicking of Douglas' "gur-reat pur-rinciple." Buchanan also is a victim here, for he had championed popular sovereignty in his "Third Annual Message," December 19, 1859; *The Works of James Buchanan,* ed. John Bassett More (1908–1911; rpt. New York: Antiquarian Press Ltd., 1960), X, 342. Lincoln's efforts were not lost on a New York *Evening Post* reporter who wrote that "the speaker places the Republican party on the very ground occupied by the framers of our constitution and the fathers of our Republic" and that "in this great controversy the Republicans are the real conservative party." His report is reprinted in the *Chicago Tribune,* 1 Mar. 1860, p. 1.

"as a legal right and a social blessing." Stripped of its veneer and examined in the cold light of reason, the Southern position reveals the disagreement governing the entire conflict; it also underscores the principle from which Republicans cannot retreat. Lincoln expresses both points in a final antithesis that reduces the issue of slavery to a matter of right and wrong, to a matter of moral conviction:

> Their thinking it right and our thinking it wrong is the precise fact upon which depends the whole controversy. Thinking it right, as they do, they are not to blame for desiring its full recognition as being right; but thinking it wrong, as we do, can we yield to them? Can we cast our votes with their view, and against our own? In view of our moral, social, and political responsibilities, can we do this?

Providing no answers because they are only too obvious, Lincoln moves on to merge self and party with the fathers, and Washington is the exemplar.

Style changes appropriately as Lincoln makes his final call for unity. Antithetical elements appear in the penultimate paragraph, but the opposed clauses are subordinated within the long, periodic flow of the final sentence, a flow that builds emotionally to a union with Washington's words and deeds. Lincoln repeats that slavery can be left alone where it exists, but he insists that there can be no temporising when it comes to the extension of slavery:

> If our sense of duty forbids this, then let us stand by our duty fearlessly and effectively. Let us be diverted by none of those sophistical contrivances wherewith we are so industriously plied, and belabored—contrivances such as groping for some middle ground between the right and the wrong: vain as the search for a man who should be neither a living man nor a dead man; such as a policy of 'don't care' on a question about which all true men do care; such as Union appeals beseeching true Union men to yield to Disunionists, reversing the divine rule, and calling, not the sinners, but the righteous to repentance: such as invocations to Washington, imploring men to unsay what Washington said and undo what Washington did.
>
> Neither let us be slandered from our duty by false accusations against us, nor frightened from it by menaces of destruction to the government, nor of dungeons to ourselves. Let us have faith that right makes might, and in that faith let us to the end dare to do our duty as we understand it.

This short third section, constituting less than fifteen per cent of the text, is a fitting climax to Lincoln's efforts. Rational principle develops into moral conviction, and the resulting emotional intensity emerges from and synthesizes all that has gone before. Yet the intensity is controlled. Speaker and audience are resolute and principled, but at the same time, they are poised and logical. Others may indulge in "false accusations" and "menaces of destruction," but Lincoln and Republicans will have faith in right and in their understanding.

With this closing suggestion of antithetical behavior, Lincoln harks back to all he has said, and with it, he completes his exercise in ingratiation. Douglas is a pitiful example of one who argues misguided principle in maladroit fashion, and Seward's notion of an irrepressible conflict is at odds with the true spirit of the Republican Party, a party whose words and deeds follow from what the framers of the government said and did. Neither opponent measures up to the new and higher self-conception that the speaker has created for his audience. Furthermore, Lincoln has, by this very performance, demonstrated that he is the one who will best represent party and principle. Starting with reason and principle, he has shunted aside opposition, differentiated between Republicans and the South, and pushed on to unite the party in the faith that will "let us to the end dare to do our duty as we understand it."

The very wording of the concluding paragraphs reflects the organic quality of Lincoln's quest for unity. "Understand" echoes the "text"; Washington is a synecdochic reminder of the fathers; and the antithetical language recalls dissociations that are fundamental. In examining the discourse, we have attempted to explicate this internal coherence by tracing the sequence of arguments and images as they appear in the text, by dealing with the speech on its own terms. We are satisfied that the analysis has produced a reading that is more accurate than those previously available, a reading that goes farther toward explaining why the Cooper Union Address was one of Lincoln's most significant speeches.

Our interpretation is at odds, of course, with the conventional wisdom concerning his attitude toward the South. Where others have found him conciliatory, we argue that his position on slavery was calculated to win the nomination, not to propitiate an unavailable audience. That he had made "many similar declarations, and had never recanted any of them"[36] unquestionably contributed to the triumph of availability that was to be his, but his position ultimately pointed to an ideological conflict between North and South. Some Southerners took solace from Lincoln's assurances that slavery would be left alone where it existed, but extremists perceived him as the personification of Black Republicanism, even as the source of the irrepressible conflict doctrine.[37] The latter perceptions were distorted. So are ours, if we blink the realities of political rhetoric, and whatever else the speech might have been, it was certainly an oration designed to meet the immediate problems of a political campaign.

This perspective emphasizes that alternatives sometimes really do exclude and that rhetoric may nurture exclusion. Such a perspective may be uncomfortable for those who want to cast Lincoln as the Great Conciliator, but we are convinced that an accurate reading of the Cooper Union Address demands a frank recognition of the immediate rhetorical motives. Despite the mythology, the man was human, perhaps gloriously so, and it does him no disservice to accept this speech as evidence of his political skill, as evidence that "he was an astute and dextrous operator of the political machine."[38] Nor does this acceptance detract from the speech as literature and as logical exposition. The political artistry and the rhetorical artistry are functions of each other, and an appreciation of this coalescence can only enhance our understanding of the Cooper Union Address. And viewing the speech as a whole, we are quite content to close with a slightly altered evaluation from another context: 'The speech is—to put it as crudely as possible—an immortal masterpiece."[39]

[36] Abraham Lincoln, "First Inaugural Address," in *Collected Works*, IV, 263.

[37] Michael Davis, *The Image of Lincoln in the South* (Knoxville: Univ. of Tennessee, 1971), pp. 7–40; traces Southern views from nomination through inauguration. See *Southern Editorials on Secession,* ed. Dwight L. Dumond (1931; rpt. Gloucester, Mass.: Peter-Smith, 1964), pp. 103–105, 112–115, 159–162, *et passim.*

[38] David Donald, *Lincoln Reconsidered* (New York: Alfred A. Knopf, 1956), p. 65.

[39] The original is Randall Jarrell's comment on a poem, Robert Frost's "Provide Provide," in *Poetry and the Age* (New York: Vintage-Knopf, 1953), p. 41.

The Passionate Negation: The Chartist Movement in Rhetorical Perspective

James R. Andrews

In 1781 Abigail Adams wisely observed that "It is from a wide and extensive view of mankind that a just and true estimate can be formed of the powers of human nature."[1] Much recent research and criticism in rhetoric has attempted to take such a broad view, either to establish a theoretical framework or to produce insights which illuminate rhetorical transactions. Rhetorical scholars have recently concerned themselves, for example, with the study of movements and have become increasingly convinced of the fruitfulness of such a field of investigation.[2] In this paper, I propose to identify, clarify, and apply a rhetorical perspective on the study of an historical movement, for the recent literature in rhetorical studies suggests to me that there is a particular way in which the rhetorical critic can view such a phenomenon. Specifically, the essay will focus on an important working-class movement of nineteenth-century England: Chartism.

A RHETORICAL PERSPECTIVE

The sociologist Amitai Etzioni has recently written of the "iron law of sociology that states that the fate of all popular movements is determined largely by historical forces they do not control."[3] Etzioni probably overstates the case; Lloyd Bitzer provides balance when he argues that a myriad of factors interact to produce the context in which movements live, and from these interrelationships exigencies develop. An exigence, according to Bitzer, "is an imperfection marked by urgency," and becomes rhetorical "when it is capable of positive modification and when positive modification requires discourse or can be assisted by discourse."[4] Exigencies may or may not actually produce rhetoric, but the critic must understand and iden-

---

[1] *The Adams-Jefferson Letters*, 2 vols., ed. Lester J. Cappon (Chapel Hill, North Carolina: Univ. of North Carolina Press, 1959), II, 420.
[2] The rhetorical study of historical movements surely begins with Leland M. Griffin, "The Rhetoric of Historical Movements," *QJS*, 38 (Apr. 1952), 184–188. Professor Griffin's essay, "A Dramatistic Theory of the Rhetoric of Movements," in *Critical Responses to Kenneth Burke*, ed. William H. Rueckert (Minneapolis: Univ. of Minnesota Press, 1969) is a later statement which modifies his earlier views. Other studies which deal with various theoretical and methodological aspects of movements include: Dan F. Hahn and Ruth M. Gonchar, "Studying Social Movements: A Rhetorical Methodology," *Speech Teacher*, 20 (Jan. 1971), 44–52; Robert S. Cathcart, "New Approaches to the Study of Movements: Defining Movements Rhetorically," *Western Speech*, 36 (Spr. 1972), 82–88; and the particularly important study by Herbert W. Simons, "Requirements, Problems, and Strategies: A Theory of Persuasion for Social Movements," *QJS*, 56 (Feb. 1970), 1–11. Examples of studies of particular movements are: Leland M. Griffin, "The Rhetorical Structure of the 'New Left' Movement: Part I," *QJS*, 50 (Apr. 1964), 113–135; James R. Andrews, "Piety and Pragmatism: Rhetorical Aspects of the Early British Peace Movement," *Speech Monographs*, 34 (Nov. 1967), 423–436.
[3] "The Women's Movement—Tokens vs. Objectives," *Saturday Review*, 20 May 1972, p. 35.
[4] Lloyd F. Bitzer, "The Rhetorical Situation," *Philosophy and Rhetoric*, 1 (Jan. 1968), 3, 6–7.

tify *rhetorical imperatives* and *strategic indicators* that arise from the context. Rhetorical imperatives are situations or events which *compel* certain people to take some kind of concrete action. The isolation and examination of these imperatives can provide significant information regarding the ultimate goals of the movement and the nature of those who create and sustain it. Factors in the context which suggest the rhetorical form that the movement will take are strategic indicators. That is, the historic situation has imbedded within it group experiences, group perceptions, and a network of values which influence the way adherents of the movement will attempt to exploit communication channels and the ways in which they will identify crucial agents of change.[5]

Given the insight which the understanding of rhetorical imperatives and strategic indicators provide him, the critic then may turn to an investigation of *patterns of advocacy and reaction.* As the movement develops it identifies itself or becomes identified with a philosophy and with specific goals and thus may become itself a rhetorical imperative for others who are compelled to act in a hostile or conciliatory way, either through physical repression or discourse. Robert Cathcart has argued that a movement is defined rhetorically at this point. He describes as the "essential attribute" the "creation of a *dialectical tension growing out of moral conflict*" and maintains that "the formulation of a rhetoric proclaiming that the new order, the more perfect order, the desired order, cannot come about through the established agencies of change . . . in turn, produces a counter-rhetoric that exposes the agitators as anarchists or devils of destruction."[6] The moral nature of the conflict is emphasized since rhetorical imperatives are filtered through perceptions of the contemporary value system as well as being ordered in some hierarchical fashion by those involved according to their experience and the saliency of the imperatives. It is important, however, for the critic to recognize that patterns of advocacy and reaction may also include strong elements of the practical-impractical argument in that strategic choices may contribute to a rhetorical form that is susceptible to attack: the "sympathetic enemy" may abhor (or feign to abhor) the condition which gave birth to the movement, but dismiss the solution proposed (and, in consequence, most likely the movement itself, as visionary or impractical.[7] Furthermore, the patterns not only of advocacy but of reaction as well will be formed and modified by tensions within the movement itself. As Herbert Simons has observed, "Movements are as susceptible to fragmentation from within as they are to suppression from without."[8]

As the rhetorical patterns of the movement develop, as the movement itself matures, as it engages widespread attention, as it declines, as it ceases to exist as a recognizable, cohesive force, a series of *influential relationships* may be observed. The movement's rhetorical interpretation of imperatives influences a variety of concurrent actions throughout the life of the movement and after, but the success or

[5] Bitzer has defined the "rhetorical audience" as "those persons who are capable of being influenced by discourse and of being mediators of change" (*ibid.,* 8). I would be inclined to consider, in this connection, the agents of change as those who could be influenced by *action,* which may include discourse, but which may take other forms.
[6] "New Approaches to the Study of Movements: Defining Movements Rhetorically," 87.
[7] I have discussed the problem of impracticality and its relationship to strategy in "Piety and Pragmatism: Rhetorical Aspects of the Early British Peace Movement."
[8] "Requirements, Problems, Strategies: A Theory of Persuasion for Social Movements," 11.

failure of the movement to achieve specific goals at a particular point in history is not a sufficient measure of its rhetoric. It has already been argued that movements invite response in order to exist as movements at all. But the intrusion of problems or issues, reflecting both the imperatives and the strategies employed by the movement, have the potential to provide a continuing source of motivation and rationale for modifications within society at large. Furthermore, influential relationships are reciprocal: changes in the social condition may make the imperatives less important or less salient, new imperatives may take precedence, rival movements deriving from the same imperatives may sap the initial movement's energy and will. Moreover, the movement leaves behind it a rhetorical legacy: the strategies it employed, the values it embodied, the heroes and villains that it created, form some part of the historical-cultural heritage and may prove an important source of invention for future spokesmen, further causes.

I would suggest, then, that a critic could fruitfully examine an historical movement from a rhetorical perspective through an investigation of rhetorical imperatives, strategic indicators, patterns of advocacy and reaction, and influential relationships. An examination of the Chartist Movement, which must here be more suggestive than exhaustive, will hopefully serve to make this perspective more clear.

RHETORICAL IMPERATIVES OF THE CHARTIST MOVEMENT

To England the nineteenth century brought growth and change; it was an age of bustle, of unrest, of paradoxes. Industrialization was the great fact, and what Dr. Andrew Ure termed "the blessings [of] physico-mechanical society" were everywhere apparent. The railroads snaked their way throughout the countryside and travel and commerce benefited. The population boomed, particularly in the urban and industrial centers. It doubled in England and Wales between 1801 and 1851; London grew 145.5 percent during the same period, and the great manufacturing county of Lancashire, dominated by the smokestacks of Manchester, increased its population by 201.4 percent in the first half of the century.[9]

But with the blessings came the curse. Among the laborers who supported the industrial complex were great masses who faced, at best, a life of monotonous drudgery and, at worst, frightful privation. The Chartist, Thomas Cooper, was shocked to learn that weavers' earnings were four shillings and sixpence per day.[10] And even this sum was not always reached, for in 1837 the weavers declared in a petition that their income was but one and a half pence per day.[11]

Although living conditions had improved over those of the eighteenth century, squalor and disease still haunted the working classes. In 1842 the Poor Law Commission sponsored a *Report on the Sanitary Conditions of Labouring Population* which pointed out that in Leeds, for example, the drainage system was so poor that it was not uncommon for drains to back up repeatedly, once so badly that "many

[9] *Annual Register,* 93 (1851), 450–451.
[10] Thomas Cooper, *The Life of Thomas Cooper* (London: Hodder and Stoughton, 1882), pp. 137–139.
[11] Donald Read, "Chartism in Manchester," *Chartist Studies,* ed. Asa Briggs (London: Macmillan, 1959), p. 32.

of the inhabitants were floated in their beds"; many streets were without water or "out-offices"; inhabitants of some neighborhoods had to use cesspools constructed under their doors; streets were so badly paved, if paved at all, as to be hazardous.[12]

The working class did not accept its situation with equanimity. A song current in Manchester in the 30's demonstrates both the bitterness and the pathos of the laboring poor:

> *How little can the rich man know*
> *Of what the poor man feels*
> *When Want, like some dark demon foe,*
> *Nearer and nearer steals!*
>
> ....
>
> He *never saw his darlings lie*
> *Shivering, the flags their bed;*
> He *never heard that maddening cry*
> *'Daddy, a bit of bread!'*[13]

The situation in which the working classes found themselves gave rise to sporadic, violent response. Politically powerless, the lower orders often were prone to react through extra-legal means. During the early part of the century, before the Chartist movement came into being, erratic outbursts occurred throughout England. Before the end of the war with France, for example, the discontented "Luddites" smashed weavers' frames in Nottinghamshire, causing more troops to be quartered in the Luddite areas in 1812 than had gone to the Peninsula with Wellesley in 1808; in the midland and northern counties there were over 1200 regular horse and foot stationed.[14] In 1816 a mob in Loughborough attacked the Heathcote and Borden mill, smashing fifty-three frames and inflicting six thousand pounds damage. At the Nottingham Assizes six men were sentenced to death and three to transportation for their part in the assault, and Luddism seemed to subside.[15]

In spite of firm government repression, however, spontaneous uprisings continued to occur throughout the first years of the century. It is important to understand that these outbreaks, motivated though they were by hunger and distress had, nevertheless, strong rhetorical overtones. For the violence was directed not only at appropriating needed commodities, but also at defying, even cowing authority. In Brandon in 1816, for example, the mob protested against the high cost of bread and meat by levelling the house of the local butcher, Mr. Willit, to the ground. The Sheriff and a local banker testified that the unruly men had marched about the streets waving a banner inscribed, "Bread or Blood."[16] Such a direct ultimatum was implicit in all the disturbances; actions were meant to be seen as symbolic of what might result if authority did not move to change conditions. While the imperatives often did not produce discourse, they did call forth coercive rhetorical acts as perhaps the only discernible options open to the oppressed.

[12] Edwin Chadwick, "The Sanitary Condition of the Labouring Poor," *Society and Politics in England,* ed. J.F.C. Harrison (New York: Harper and Row, 1965), pp. 152–156.

[13] Cited by Read, p. 32.

[14] R. J. White, *Waterloo to Peterloo* (London: William Heinemann, 1957), 111.

[15] *Ibid.,* pp. 115–117.

[16] *Annual Register,* 58 (1816), 66–69.

Agitation by the working class for relief in the early nineteenth century did take other rhetorical forms. The famous demonstration at St. Peter's Fields, Manchester, the scene of the "Peterloo Massacre," was a peaceful attempt to promote parliamentary reform.[17] And in collaboration with the middle classes in the first years of the 1830's, the working classes worked for the reform of the House of Commons even though they seemed to play their most important role as bogeymen: their violent attacks on the enemies of parliamentary reform served as concrete evidence for the Whig claims that only reform would avert revolution.[18] There can be little doubt that the masses of workingmen believed that the Reform Bill of 1832 would do great things for them. Yet from the vantage point of the twentieth century it is difficult to understand the expectations of great feats from a parliament so moderately and mildly reformed. The middle classes had, indeed, enhanced their power in the national councils, but the working classes remained without an effective political voice. "A Reformed Parliament," Charles Greville observed in 1833, "turns out to be very much like any other parliaments."[19]

Not only was the Reformed Parliament to prove unresponsive to lower class demands, it was this same parliament that passed the hated Poor Law Amendment Act of 1834. To the lower classes, this act seemed a cruel, almost calculated attempt to deprive them of the means of even marginal subsistence. Its administration represents an undoubted imperative which lay beneath Chartist agitation.

Up until 1834 what was known as the Speenhamland System of poor relief was common in the southern and eastern parts of England and, to a lesser extent, existed in parts of the north. Under this plan wages were supplemented by outdoor relief so that the worker, in times of high prices and low wages, could count on some minimum income related to the price of bread and the size of his family. On the surface, the plan seemed a reasonable, humane one. In practice, such a scheme tended to depress wages even further and to impose a crushing burden on the local rate payer.

Parliament's action in 1834 was an attempt to remedy this situation by abolishing outdoor relief altogether except for the aged or infirm. A system of "unions," some 600 in number, was set up to receive the indigent, but the dreaded and often dreadful workhouses offered cold comfort to the needy. Indeed, they were not meant to, for the Poor Law Commissioners believed that any relief system must insure that the pauper was always worse off than the poorest labourer.[20] Cole and Postgate argue that the Commissioners were preoccupied with agricultural labourers and "forgot, or ignored, the fact that in the industrial districts the old Poor Law served quite a different purpose—that of relieving unemployment due to the fluctuations of trade, and also that of preserving from literal starvation the handloomweavers and other domestic producers whom the factory system was throwing rapidly upon the industrial scrap-heap. The removal of outdoor relief could not help unemployed factory workers or miners to find employment when the times were bad: nor could it do anything at all to raise the wages of the miserable

---

[17] For a detailed discussion of the St. Peter's Field meeting see White, 176–192. See also, Charles W. Lomas, "Orator Hunt at Peterloo and Smithfield," *QJS,* (Dec. 1962), 400–405.

[18] I have discussed this point in some detail in "The Rhetoric of Coercion and Persuasion: The Reform Bill of 1832," *QJS,* 56 (Apr. 1970), 187–195.

[19] *The Greville Memoirs,* ed. Roger Fulford (New York: Macmillan, 1963), p. 102.

[20] "The 1834 Poor Law Report," in *Society and Politics in England,* pp. 147–148.

handloom-weavers."[21] Well might Dickens' Christmas charity solicitors answer Scrooge's question, "Are there no workhouses?" with the horrified response, "Some cannot go there, others would rather die." The Unions were popularly known as "Bastilles" and symbolized for the poor the utter depths of human degradation and despair.

For those who formed and supported the Chartist movement these aspects of nineteenth-century English life were particularly salient. The laboring poor, suffering economic distress intensified by the new Poor Law and unmitigated by the Reformed Parliament from which so much was expected, were compelled to take some action.[22] Sir Charles Napier, who commanded the Northern district of the army took the measure of the problem: ". . . the doctrine of slowly reforming when men are starving is of all things the most silly; famishing men cannot wait."[23] From these imperatives the rhetoric of Chartism emerged. The ultimate goal of the movement, accordingly, had to be the alleviation of economic distress, and the context out of which it grew readily explains why the movement was the first almost exclusively working class movement. Furthermore, the needs and experiences of the working classes as well as the political realities which surrounded them, help to explain the rhetorical strategies which evolved.

STRATEGIC INDICATORS

The context that I have briefly and selectively reviewed suggests certain important features which help to explain the lines of strategy which the movement developed. The strategy was directly influenced by the Chartists' perception of the focus of power, their relationships with the middle class, and by lower class experiences with and perceptions of the role of violence in promoting change.

It was apparent in nineteenth-century England that the House of Commons was the seat of political power. The entire agitation for parliamentary reform had been predicated on the conviction that the alteration of the composition of parliament was the surest way to modify the condition of life generally. This was the message of the 1832 reformers and it had been absorbed and believed by the lower classes. And it was essentially a correct view. As Richard Cobden observed in discussing the strategy of the Anti-Corn Law League (the middle-class agitational rival of Chartism), ". . . the present construction of the House of Commons . . . forbids us hoping for success. *That House must be changed before we can get justice.*"[24]

The optimistic hopes that the lower classes placed in the 1832 Act proved illusory. So to bring about improvement of the quality of life for the lower classes, the

[21] G. D. H. Cole and Raymond Postgate, *The British People, 1746-1946* (London: Methuen, 1961), p. 278.

[22] A severe economic depression in the late '30s and '40s intensified the problem and made it even more imperative. The effects, circumstances, and degree of severity differed in different parts of England, but the industrial county of Lancashire was among the hardest hit. By June of 1837, in the Manchester area alone fifty thousand workers were unemployed or on short time. See Read, p. 31.

[23] Sir W. Napier, *The Life and Opinions of General Napier* (1857), II, 22. Cited in Asa Briggs, *The Age of Improvement, 1783-1867* (London: Longmans, Green, 1959), p. 309.

[24] Letter to J. B. Smith, 1840, cited in Norman McCord, *The Anti-Corn Law League, 1838-1846* (London: Allen and Unwin, 1958), p. 82.

Chartists proposed complete and radical reconstruction of the House of Commons. In effect, the strategy of parliamentary reconstruction became an end in itself, a secondary goal which was prerequisite to the ultimate goal. The movement took its very name from the "People's Charter," which set forth six demands: (1) universal manhood suffrage, (2) the ballot, (3) payment of members of Parliament, (4) elimination of the property qualifications for members of Parliament, (5) formation of equal electoral districts, and, (6) annual parliamentary elections. The experience of the past led Chartists to believe that democracy—and the Charter did embody what we have come to identify as basic elements of democratic government—was the only remedy for their ills. Paradoxically, their understanding of the focus of power also led the Chartists to try to influence as best they could the existing House of Commons drastically to reconstruct itself.

Their realization of the source of power, their experiences with the 1832 agitation, and their perceptions of their employers colored the Chartists' strategy with regard to the middle classes. The middle classes appeared to have betrayed them, yet the only spokesmen that working men had in the House were middle class radicals.[25] The uneasy relations with the middle class were aggravated by the variety within the ranks of Chartism itself. Asa Briggs points out in *Chartist Studies* that there were three major social groups who comprised the movement's membership.[26] First, there were the superior craftsmen who were in communication with the "respectables" of the middle classes, but who, at the same time, were somewhat suspect by the lower orders of the working class. Second, there were the factory operatives who were mainly concentrated in the northern centers of the textile industry. Third, there were the domestic outworkers such as handloom weavers, framework knitters, and nailmakers. The existence of subclasses within the working classes contributed to misunderstandings and outright feuds among the Chartists. The tensions between the working class and the middle class and within the working class itself indicate the serious strategic problems that the movement was to face, and it is understandable that contradictory strategies would develop. This was especially true with regard to the role of violence in promoting the movement's aims.

When a group is without political, social, or economic power, it is not surprising that they turn to physical violence. When only the hope of intimidation exists it will be exploited. Thus it had been with the disorganized, erratic outbreaks in the past. Certainly the lessons of 1832 would not have been entirely lost on the lower classes, nor would the more remote, but more potent, example of the French Revolution. But threat and action are not the same. What plagued the Chartists, who never, after all, advocated the outright overthrow of existing institutions, but, rather, their radical amendment, was when and under what circumstances to encourage violence, or at least threaten it, and how to control violence so that the whole repressive weight of government was not brought to bear to destroy the movement. Such considerations were bound to be a confounding factor in the development of a coherent strategy as the movement progressed.

[25] Men like Thomas Attwood and Thomas Duncombe were allies of the Chartists but were successful members of the middle class themselves. "Orator" Hunt was the only working class man to be elected to the unreformed House of Commons, and Feargus O'Connor, the only avowed Chartist to be elected, was not returned until 1847.

[26] Briggs, pp. 4–5.

PATTERNS OF ADVOCACY
AND REACTION

Various groups developed in the 1830's with the purpose of bettering the lot of the laboring poor, but it was with the writing of the Charter itself that the movement crystalized and became a more coherent force. In 1838 William Lovett, a leading figure in the London Workingmen's Association, drafted the Charter in the form of a parliamentary bill. The next year a convention, which brought supporters from all parts of the country, was called in London. The Convention drafted a petition which embodied the principles and program of the Charter and presented it to the House of Commons in May, 1839.

The basic goal seemed to be to impress parliament with the overwhelming support which the petition enjoyed, and a campaign to get great numbers of signatures was undertaken. Pressure on parliament was the key to action, and the demonstration of widespread support would intensify that pressure. Agitation for the Reform Bill seemed to Chartists an admirable model to follow. As one Chartist spokesman claimed, "in 1832 the working classes by their moral and physical organization beat the Tories for the sake of the Whigs—by the same means they can in 1837 beat both Whigs and Tories for the sake of themselves."[27] Thus agitation took the form of the canvassing and presentation of gigantic petitions, mass meetings in working class districts, and, to a limited and markedly unsuccessful extent, some attempts to influence parliamentary elections.[28]

Advocacy of the Charter, through petitions and mass meetings, were generally agreed upon tactics within the movement. But the strategic problems, which have already been discussed, distorted the patterns of advocacy and invited strong reactions. The conduct of the Convention of 1839 affords an example of the pattern that Chartist agitation followed and clearly indicates the internal dissension over means which were exploited by the opposition.

Even before the national meeting was convened in February of 1839, a serious rupture had occurred. The Chartists of Birmingham, London, and Scotland (more closely allied with the middle class and used to seeking the aid of middle-class parliamentary radicals) became alarmed at the pyrotechnics of their counterparts in the manufacturing districts of the north of England. In the fall of 1838, in Lancashire and Yorkshire, mass torchlight meetings heard speakers such as J. R. Stephens discourse on the virtues of an armed populace, a giant demonstration in Hartshead Moor listened while Feargus O'Connor, the "lion of the North," talked menacingly on the benefits of tyrannicide. In O'Connor's newspaper, *The Northern Star,* this strongly suggestive note appeared: "The National Guards of Paris have petitioned

[27] Quoted in the Lovett Scrapbook, Vol. I, cited by Briggs, *The Age of Improvement,* p. 305.
[28] Between 1837 and 1852 Chartist candidates did stand for election in several constituencies, particularly in the General election of 1841 and in the bi-elections in 1842, 1844, and 1845. The General election of 1847 saw a number of Chartists on the hustings and O'Connor won a seat at Nottingham. He, however, was the only Chartist ever returned, and the contesting of elections was never a major tactic of the Chartist movement. For details concerning this form of Chartist political activity see G. D. H. Cole, *British Working Class Politics, 1832-1914* (London: Routledge, 1941), pp. 19-24.

for an extension of the Suffrage, and they have done it with arms in their hands."[29] The moderates were aghast. The Edinburgh Chartists passed a resolution which structured the use of violent language and physical force. In turn, O'Connor and others denounced these "moral philosophers" while Stephens sneered at the Birmingham enemies of physical force as "old women."[30]

By the time the delegates assembled there were serious differences as to the scope and purpose of the Convention itself. J. P. Cobbett introduced a motion that attempted to limit the Convention to a body that would exist only to shepherd the National Petition through Parliament. Some of the more radical members, however, were already beginning to think of the Convention as a kind of legislative alternative to parliament itself, a body more truly representative of the people, and the motion was defeated. To imply that the Convention might be more than an agitational body was unacceptable to moderates, and Cobbett quit the Convention. His defection was the first of many by the moral force wing of Chartism, and the Convention gradually came under the sway of the less temperate delegates.

The Convention, racked by dissension, plagued by indecision, and torn between the Scylla of Government repression and the Charybdis of inaction, failed to provide decisive leadership. They moved their seat from London, where the proximity to the Home Secretary and the Metropolitan Police made members somewhat apprehensive, to Birmingham, and finally back to London again. They passed a resolution calling for a general strike without providing for any kind of strike fund; moderates vainly pointed out that such action was a direct invitation to the strikers to plunder for subsistence. Reports from the country that indicated that such a strike would be impossible to organize and carry out successfully caused them to rescind the action. There was much discussion of the Convention's right to adopt "any means whatsoever" to secure the demands set forth in the Petition, and one speaker pointed out that signatures on a petition meant nothing unless they were "the signatures of millions of fighting men who will not allow any aristocracy, oligarchy, landlords, cotton lords, money lords, or any lords to tyrannize over them longer."[31] From the Convention came strong words but no clear, well planned course of action. Mass meetings continued throughout the country. Some Chartist leaders were arrested. There were wild tales of general insurrections in the making, and doubtless many Chartists, particularly in the North, were busily arming themselves. Arrest of many of its leaders and defections among the moderates thinned the ranks of the Convention. In August of 1839, a month after Parliament had rejected the Petition, the "Peoples Parliament" finally dissolved itself amid bitter recriminations among the members.

Disagreements over physical force were an inevitable disintegrating factor within the movement. Given the right circumstances, the threat of violence may coerce ameliorative action even if it does not convince the opposition. Moderate

---

[29] *The Northern Star*, 8 Sept. 1838.

[30] Mark Hovell, *The Chartist Movement* (Manchester: Manchester Univ. Press, 1918), p. 120. Hovell's book is probably the best account of the earlier phases of the Chartist movement. His chapter on "The People's Parliament," 116–135, provides a wealth of detail based on contemporary sources.

[31] *Ibid.*, p. 127.

reformers may use the threat, even while deploring it, as a spur to reform.[32] But in the Chartists' case it alarmed authority without intimidating it and poisoned relations with the powerful middle-classes. In such a situation only out and out revolution held the promise of immediate success, and there was very little real revolutionary sentiment among the Chartists. As Hovell astutely observed in *The Chartist Movement*, ". . . there was little sincerity in the physical force party. To a large section of it . . . the appeal to arms was a game of bluff calculated to terrorize the governing classes into submission. To another section it was even less than this; it was simply a blatant device to attract attention."[33]

The pressures exerted on the movement by the physical-moral force conflict resulted in a number of rhetorical fissures and counter pressures. Moderate spokesmen had to devote some considerable energy and attention to disavowing violence and placating the middle and governing classes. The millionaire radical, Thomas Attwood, was a firm friend of the Chartists, and spoke in their behalf in the House of Commons. His speech on introducing the Petition on June 14, 1839 is typical of moderate attempts to keep the Chartist agitation on a legal and parliamentary footing. "Although he most cordially supported the petition, was ready to support every word contained in it, and was determined to use every means in his power in order to carry it out into a law," Attwood announced to the House, "he must say, that many reports had gone abroad, in regard to arguments said to have been used in support of the petition on different occasions, which he distinctly disavowed." Attwood asserted that "He never, in the whole course of his life, recommended any means, or inculcated any doctrine except peace, law, order, loyalty, and union." And, "he washed his hands of any idea, of any appeal to physical force." Attwood's declaration that "every argument which justice, reason, and wisdom dictate," would finally secure a favorable public reaction without physical force embodies the hope and the strategic philosophy which activated moderate Chartists and their allies.[34] It also exposes the kernel of the issues around which debate on and within the movement revolved. The Charter itself, with all its political and social ramifications, and the means to attain enactment of the Charter, define the real points of clash and not the conditions of the poor which brought about the agitation in the first place. Naturally, the miserable plight of the poor was discussed, but the situation is analogous to a debate in which the need was barely alluded to after the first constructive speech, and the debate became riveted on the plan.

The ruling classes reacted to the new imperatives created for them by the emergence of Chartism. In some cases they naturally responded repressively. Chartist leaders were arrested from time to time, the movement's activities were kept under police surveillance, and when actual rioting broke out the military was used deci-

---

[32] I have argued elsewhere that this was the case in 1832. See "The Rhetoric of Coercion and Persuasion: The Reform Bill of 1832," esp. 192–194.

[33] Hovell, p. 305. The tension between physical force and moral suasion seems to me to be one of the most striking of consistent characteristics of movements; certainly parallels with the Black Power movement, for example, seem apparent.

[34] *Hansard's Parliamentary Debates*, Third Series, LXVIII, 14 June 1839. In the debate on the petition in 1842 Duncombe also spent considerable time trying to establish the respectability of Chartism, linking the movement historically not only with radicals of the past, but also with aristocratic Whig reformers. *Hansard's Parliamentary Debates*, Third Series, LXIII, 3 May 1842.

sively. At other times, the Chartists were considered more eccentric than threatening, or at least of such insufficient importance to warrant serious retribution or rebuttal. For example, on Attwood's motion of July 12, 1839 to go into a committee of the whole House to consider the National Petition, scarcely anyone who *voted* against the motion, troubled to *speak* against it even though it was swamped by a vote of 235 to 46.[35]

But the masses could seriously disturb the equanimity of the governing classes. As Charles Kingsley observed, "young men believed (and not so wrongly) that the masses were their natural enemies, and that they might have to fight, any year or any day, for the safety of their property and the honour of their sisters."[36] The explicit democracy of the Charter called forth the most strenuous rhetorical reactions on the part of Chartism's enemies. The defense of property and traditional institutions, and the preservation of parliamentary independence were the principal thrusts of the counter-rhetoric.

In the debate in the House of Commons on May 3, 1842, may be seen the microcosm of anti-Chartist rhetoric.[37] Thomas Duncombe, the radical associate of the Chartists, moved that the petitioners be heard at the bar of the House. Thomas Babington Macaulay, the great Whig proponent of reform in 1832, led the attack on the Charter. He saw universal suffrage as "fatal to all purposes for which Government exists, and for which aristocracies and all other things exist, and that it is utterly incompatible with the very existence of civilization" (p. 46). And then Macaulay came to the heart of the argument: "I conceive that civilization rests on the security of . . . property" (p. 46). The conservative argument was based on the real conviction that those who did not hold property themselves would be most unlikely to protect it. Indeed, the effect of granting the franchise to the uneducated, easily influenced masses, would be governmental "spoliation," according to Macaulay (p. 50). Underlying the argument was the tacit recognition that there were social imperfections, but the means suggested by the Chartists to remedy them were attacked as horrendous. Lord John Russell continued and expanded Macaulay's theme. The condition of the poor, he argued, was not at issue, rather the existence of the ancient and venerable institutions of the country were at stake.

John Arthur Roebuck, while speaking in defense of the motion, had dismissed the Chartist leader Feargus O'Connor as a "malignant" and "cowardly demagogue." (p. 54). Opponents quickly seized on this untimely reference. Russell argued that if a cowardly, malignant demagogue could gain ascendance over the Chartist movement, would not he and his kind be likely to be elected to a democratic parliament? Sir Robert Peel asked who would speak at the bar if the motion carried? Would it be the cowardly and malignant demagogue? The Charter, according to Peel, was incompatible with the monarchial form of government which had, he asserted, brought to the people of England greater liberty and happiness than to any other people in the world.

The counter-rhetoric clearly labelled the Chartist spokesmen as despoilers of

[35] Hovell, p. 164.
[36] Cited by George Rude, *The Crowd in History, 1780-1848* (New York: London, Sydney: John Wiley and Sons, 1964), p. 182.
[37] Quotations are from *Hansard's Parliamentary Debates,* Third Series, LXIII, 3 May 1842, 39-88.

England's property and her greatness. It implied that mob rule, that is democratic rule, would make servile politicians who catered to every whim of a rapacious and uninformed electorate. The independence of Members of Parliament was a firmly entrenched value in early Victorian England. The historian Norman Gash maintains that "the highest respect . . . was reserved for the independent politician, in the sense not of one who was outside party but of one who was in party solely because of his conscientious opinion and perhaps traditional association." Gash goes on to explain, "Integrity was held to be inseparable from intellectual independence; and intellectual independence inseparable in the long run from financial independence. All members and all candidates claimed to be independent in their opinions and votes because it was the contemporary ideal of what a politician should be, however far removed from reality that ideal was."[38]   In the context of this ingrained value, the call for payment of members, annual parliaments, and members to be responsive to the whims of a large constituency, could easily be pictured as the destruction of the cherished traditions of English liberty.

Cast in this devil role, political Chartism was vulnerable. It could never realistically hope to achieve from the early Victorian House of Commons so sweeping a political change. Its own strategy was a weapon used by its enemies against it. Its own divisions made the accomplishment of its ultimate social goals exceedingly difficult. Mark Hovell has summed up the situation this way:

> They were well agreed in the diagnosis of the obvious social diseases of their time; they could unite in clamouring for the political reforms which were to give the mass of the people the means of saving themselves from their miseries. Beyond this, however, the Chartist consensus hardly went. It was impossible for them to focus a united body of opinion in favour of a single definite social ideal. The true failure of Chartism lay in its inability to perform this task. Political Chartism was a real though limited thing; social Chartism was a protest against what existed, not a reasoned policy to set up anything concrete in its place. Apart from machinery, Chartism was largely a passionate negation.[39]

The "machinery," from the rhetorical point of view, was what was crucial, however, for that is where the debate focused. Yet from the negation, from the protest against what existed, there were discernible influences.

INFLUENTIAL RELATIONSHIPS

Economic and social conditions both influenced and were influenced by the Chartist movement. As severe depressions reversed and the standard of living became better, support dwindled. On the other hand, agitation was most severe when times were harder. The basic evils persisted, but as legislation to limit working hours was passed, as increased world trade caused a rise in wages, and as the Anti-Corn Law movement drew off support, particularly from the better-off workers, the im-

[38] *Politics in the Age of Peel* (London: Longmans, Green, 1953), p. 109.
[39] *The Chartist Movement*, p. 303.

peratives became less salient.[40] G. D. H. Cole has observed that "the League's [the Anti-Corn Law League] success seemed to give the lie to the Chartist contention that without the Charter nothing could be done to improve the condition of the people. The passing of the Ten Hours Act carried the same moral; and during the 'fifties the Chartists decisively lost their hold on the main body of the working class."[41]

But the Chartists, if not successful in the impossible task of getting Parliament to adopt its political program, did infuse into the situation imperatives which demanded some kind of action. Cole and Postgate claim that Chartist rhetoric influenced other reforms. "These three great advantages," they wrote, "the repeal of the Corn Laws, the Ten Hours Act, and the softening of the Poor Law—were secured under the pressure of the torchlight meetings, the riots, insurrectionary plots and strikes of Chartism. To that extent Chartism was not a failure."[42]

The coercive threat of Chartism made other alternatives seem more attractive, yet Chartist influences may be observed in other areas as well. They left a rhetorical legacy, a memory of strategies which failed and hopes that did not materialize, a stock of arguments to be exploited in other ways and the example of working-class leadership and its problems and advantages. Some historians have seen in Chartism the seeds of Trade Unionism, indeed, of the British labor movement itself.[43] In regard to the influence of the movement Mark Hovell wrote: "In tracing the influence of Chartism on later ideals we must look to the individual rather than the system, to the spirit rather than the letter. But it would be unjust to deny the variety and the strength of the stimulus which the Chartist impulse gave towards the furtherance of the more wholesome spirit which makes even the imperfect Britain of today [1918] a much better place for the ordinary man to live in than was the Britain of the early years of Victoria. The part played by the Chartists in this amelioration is not the less important because, as with their political programme, the changes to which they gave an impetus were effected by other hands than theirs."[44]

In human history events crowd upon events, and the meaning we extract from collective experience is bound to the perspective from which we view the past. Rhetorical scholars, long interested in discrete transactions, are becoming increasingly convinced that we can apply our rhetorical perspective to a more diverse set of occurrences in order to uncover rhetorical meaning in history. If we view history in our own unique way, we may begin to understand not only the reciprocal shaping of rhetoric and events, but the impact of events-as-perceived on the course of history. As rhetorical critics examine movements we are compelled by the nature of our perspective to see that imperatives depend on perception and saliency and not on typicality. A "balanced" historical view, for example, may be necessary to paint an accurate picture of life in early Victorian England, but the rhetorical scholar

---

[40] Alfred A. Funk has recently shown how the Anti-Corn Law proponents increasingly focused their arguments on the injustice of high food costs for laborers, an attractive argument for the lower classes. See "Chain of Argument in the British Free Trade Debates," *QJS*, 58 (Apr. 1972), 152–160.
[41] *British Working Class Politics*, pp. 22–23.
[42] *The British People*, pp. 315–316.
[43] See Cole and Postgate, p. 316 ff.
[44] *The Chartist Movement*, p. 310.

looking at this period needs to understand the milieu of those who suffered in it; that is, to distill that which would truly be rhetorically imperative. What becomes relevant is not so much historical forces, trends, or even specific events; relevance for rhetorical critics depends on popular interpretations of phenomena. This exploratory study of Chartism suggests to me that rhetorical scholars who focus on man's perception and interpretation of his world may, indeed, be best equipped to understand and explain movements which have shaped our history.

The Image of the Right Honourable Margaret Thatcher

J. Jeffery Auer

In the British General Election on May 3, 1979, Mrs. Margaret Hilda Thatcher[1] retained her House of Commons seat as the member from Finchley by a margin of 7,878 votes out of 55,468 cast, just slightly more than double her majority of 3,911 in the last previous General Election in 1974. Because in this election there was a nationwide 5.2 percent swing to the Conservative Party, the Tories altogether received 339 seats (up from 282), against 268 for the Labour Party (down from 307), 11 for the Liberal Party (down from 14), and 17 for all other minor parties (down from 29). Thus Mrs. Thatcher, the Leader of the Opposition since her election in November 1974, as leader of the Conservative Party, became Prime Minister on May 5 for the "Forty-Eighth Parliament of the United Kingdom of Great Britain and Northern Ireland and the Twenty-Seventh Year of the Reign of Queen Elizabeth II." Incidentally, Mrs. Thatcher also thus became principal author of Queen Elizabeth's twelve-minute speech at the State Opening when the new Parliament was convened on May 15, 1979.

Since a parliamentary majority of 43 seats provides a substantial cushion against adverse results in any by-elections made necessary by the death or resignation of any Conservative member, and because traditional party discipline makes any significant loss by rebellion almost unthinkable, it appears likely that the Conservative Party will remain in office, and that Mrs. Thatcher will occupy No. 10 Downing Street for the maximum of five years that is permitted, under British law, between general elections. Therefore what we can know about the Right Honourable Margaret Thatcher—her political personality and her public persuasion, up to her assumption of the chief parliamentary role in Great Britain—should be recorded now.

As in the United States, so in Britain, the perceived images of parliamentary leaders are thought by voters to reveal true character and, in the case of candidates, qualification for office. An individual's image consists of a composite projection of a variety of inherent and acquired characteristics. Some of these may be strictly political and projected largely by oral messages: he believes in capital punishment, she

---

[1] Mrs. Thatcher prefers to be called Mrs. Thatcher, and that governs the style of this report. Only London tabloid headline writers call her "Maggie."

is opposed to abortion; he expresses liberal views, she is a fiscal conservative, and so on. Other characteristics reveal personality, typically projected in non-verbal communication: physical appearance, manner of speaking, projection of life style, manifestation of integrity, empathy, and so on. Collectively these characteristics seem to reveal an individual's style, the way in which as a leader he or she would make those necessary choices, identified by John F. Kennedy after seventeen months in office as choices "among men, among measures, among methods."[2] Thus the images of candidates provide perceptions that help determine how prospective voters think and feel about them.

It is possible, of course, that an individual's image may be projected differently in a variety of social contexts: in campaigning a person may not appear the same in public meetings, telecasts, and one-on-one conversations. Sometimes these differences may result from deliberate efforts to manipulate one's image (try to give the appearance of being more determined, more understanding, or more "plain folks," for example). At other times the media itself may make the difference (some people do well with formal addresses but are not facile in television interviews, for example). It is also true that images are viewed differentially by those who perceive them. An image might be constant, but be seen as more or less positive according to the influence on the beholder of such factors as education, experience, social aspirations and economic status.

Those who undertake to examine images in political communication must be aware of these differences both in the circumstances of projection and in the perceptions of their beholders. Where it is impossible to obtain adequate survey data for quantitative conclusions the most rewarding procedure is to attempt to observe as many elements as possible of an individual's image and in a variety of contexts, and then to identify and discuss, using whatever resources may be available, those constituents of the image that are judged to be most salient.

What follows is based upon a study of political communication in Britain over a period of approximately eight weeks prior to the May 3 General Election, supplementing observations of parliamentary debate and public persuasion by reading contemporary British newspapers, periodicals and books; and especially by a series of interviews with both Labour and Conservative members of Parliament, party political advisers and press secretaries, newspaper editors and broadcast journalists;[3]

[2] John F. Kennedy, Foreword, *Decision-Making in the White House: The Olive Branch or the Arrows* (New York: Columbia Univ. Press, 1963), p. xii.

[3] Interviewees are listed alphabetically and identified by positions held on the interview dates: Barbara Beck, secretary to Helene Hayman, Labour MP, March 9; Anthony Wedgewood Benn, Labour MP, Secretary of State for Energy, March 8: Patrick Cosgrave, historian, freelance political journalist, speechwriter for Mrs. Thatcher, March 14; Robin Day, BBC political interviewer, Radio 4 "Election Call" moderator, March 16; Barbara Hardy, Professor and Chairman, Dept. of Literature and Language, Birbeck College, University of London, March 15; Kenneth Harris, associate editor, *The Observer*, April 3; Derek Howe, press secretary to Mrs. Thatcher, March 8; Robert Rhodes James, Conservative MP, March 16, April 4; Bryan Magee, Labour MP, April 3; James D. McCaffery, press secretary to Mr. Callaghan, April 2; Thomas McNally, political adviser and speechwriter for Mr. Callaghan, April 4; Eric Parsloe, president Eric Parsloe Industrial Communications, April 2; Willam Rees-Mogg, editor, *The Times*, March 9; Peter Riddell, economics correspondent, *Financial Times*, March 15; Jo Ryder, secretary to Kenneth Harris and Douglass Cater, *The Observer*, March 12, 14. While I have drawn heavily and generally upon the education provided me in these interviews, I have tried to be discreet in ascribing quotations.

and by talking informally with a variety of British citizens, ranging from innkeepers and civil servants to pensioners and at least one sergeant-major in Her Majesty's Royal Marines.

As a representative of the Finchley constituency for twenty years, a government minister for seven years,[4] and Leader of the Opposition for four and a half years, the public eye has long enough been on Mrs. Thatcher to permit characterization of the five most salient elements of her political personality, as revealed in her public image.

CULTURAL IDENTIFICATION

Those who live in the public eye inevitably invite critical comment. Because so many of the criticisms of Mrs. Thatcher, even by her political friends, are at least indirectly related to her cultural background, it must be noted first of all.[5]

She grew up in Grantham, in Lincolnshire, a market town hitherto notable only as the home of King's School where Isaac Newton propounded the laws of gravity some three hundred years ago. One grandfather was a shoemaker, the other a railway guard. Her mother, Beatrice Stevenson, had a dress-making shop before her marriage. Her father, Albert Roberts, was a largely self-taught man whose formal education ended at age twelve when he became a grocer's apprentice. By the time Margaret, the Roberts' second daughter, was born on October 13, 1925, the family occupied a flat, without hot water or an indoor toilet, over the grocery shop that he by then owned. In due course Roberts acquired a second shop and found time to serve his community as mayor, justice of the peace, a member of the libraries committee, and on the governing board of the local girls' school and the boys' school. The family all were devout members of the Firkin Street Methodist Church; Albert was a lay preacher, and he also served as a trustee for some ten other churches in Lincolnshire. And he became a Rotarian. In short, Margaret Thatcher's father was a striver, and he strove successfully into the middle class society of Grantham.

Along with middle class membership in the pre-war East Midlands counties of England went middle class morality. Some of this was traditional Sabbath-keeping: there was no dancing in the Roberts home on Sunday, nor tennis, swimming, cinema, or walking in the parks. Some of it was grandmotherly admonition: "Cleanliness is next to Godliness." "If a thing's worth doing it's worth doing well." Some of it was religious instruction, as Margaret Thatcher recalled it: "Everything had to be clean and systematic. We were Methodists and Methodist means method. We were taught what was right and wrong in considerable detail. There were certain

[4] 1961–64, Minister of Pensions in Harold Macmillan's government; 1970–74, Minister of Education in Edward Heath's cabinet.

[5] Published sources with reasonably complete and biographical information are Patrick Cosgrave, *Margaret Thatcher: A Tory and Her Party* (London: Hutchinson, 1978); George Gardiner, *Margaret Thatcher* (London: Kimber, 1975); Russell Lewis, *Margaret Thatcher: A Personal and Political Biography* (London: Associated, 1975): Ernie Money, *Margaret Thatcher: First Lady of the House* (London: Frewin, 1975); Tricia Murray, *Margaret Thatcher* (London: W. H. Allen, 1978). Unless otherwise noted, biographical information used here is drawn from Cosgrave and from Murray.

things you just didn't do and that was that." Some of it was a closeness of the family: "most of the things we did we tended to do together," whether it was activity at the church, helping out in the grocer's shop, or going every Thursday evening to university extension lectures on current affairs. And always it was a sense of duty, "very, very strongly engrained into us. Duties to the church, duties to your neighbour and conscientiousness were continually emphasized." All in all, as Margaret Thatcher has said, her upbringing was "rather puritan," but if she ever regretted that fact there was no sign of it in her first message back home after being elected Leader of the Conservative Party: "I always believe that I was very lucky to be brought up in a small town with a great sense of friendliness and voluntary service."

Morality of the kind just suggested has, to some extent, gone out of fashion all around the world. To many it now has a distinctly rural and folksy cast, it seems old-fashioned. And of course it was before the high and family fractionating mobility of the automobile, and the substitution of the television tube as a conversational partner. Among the Thatchers conversation was highly regarded; at home after the Sunday evening service there were friends for supper and religious talk, in the grocer's shop proprietor and customers exchanged political views, and at school her classmates knew Margaret as a good debater. Out of all this talk came reinforcement for the middle class virtues of honesty, self-reliance, neighborliness compounded by real concern for others and, always, hard work. High on the list of chores was decision-making: "You make up your own mind," admonished her father, "you do not do something or want to do something because your friends are doing it." And one step further: "You do not follow the crowd because your're afraid of being different—you decide what to do yourself and if necessary you lead the crowd, but you never just follow."

Paul Johnson, former editor of *The New Statesman,* ticked off for Tricia Murray the virtues of Margaret Thatcher. "First of all and most important of all, she is a Christian. She *does* believe in the ten commandments. She *does* make very clear distinctions in her mind between what is morally right and wrong . . . with complete passionate intensity and conviction and I think it evokes a very definite response among ordinary people. . . . They like to hear someone at the top of public life speak out for these ordinary things that they were brought up on and regret seeing disappear in our rapidly changing society. . . ."[6] She would be, Johnson wrote elsewhere, "the first fully-committed Christian prime minister since Lord Salisbury." But this does not mean that Christianity is a matter of party politics:

> She emphasizes that neither Labour nor Conservatives have a private line to the deity (or, for that matter, to the devil). But she does claim . . . that the Judaeo-Christian system of ethics, its view of human conduct and the organization of society for nonmaterial ends, is a central element in the historical traditions which have shaped the British political system.[7]

Few graduates of the Grantham Girls School sought higher education at Oxford, but at age seventeen Margaret Roberts was enrolled in Somerville College, in the

---

[6] Interview with Murray, pp. 77–78.
[7] Paul Johnson, "Margaret Thatcher," *Illustrated London News,* May 1979, p. 45.

long run heading for a legal degree, but in the short run majoring in chemistry and, after graduation, securing a position in the development department of a plastics manufacturer in Essex.

Science majors, especially women whose male classmates were at least a year older, worked hard at their studies. But Margaret Roberts found time for one extra-curricular activity: the Oxford University Conservative Association. It is doubtful that she would have been more attracted to the Oxford Union, but in any case it was not for another twenty years that it saw fit to admit women. Men, meanwhile, were unrestricted. Edward Boyle, for example, became president of the Conservative club, and was succeeded by Margaret Roberts, but he was also a member of the first postwar Oxford debate team to tour America. It cannot be said that Margaret entered Oxford as a dedicated Conservative, though it is clearly the general imprint that Grantham might make. Indeed, as she told Murray, "I joined the Conservative Club right from the beginning simply because I was interested but it was really no more than that. Whatever club you joined, there was an eventful life evolving round it and most of the students joined one or more of the associations."[8]

Even though socializing may have been a part of the rationale for joining the Conservatives, Margaret Roberts threw herself into its political activities. In 1945, when the war ended she campaigned for Quintin Hogg, a successful candidate, though overall Labour overwhelmed the Conservatives and the heroic Churchill became ex-Prime Minister. It was not too long after, Mrs. Thatcher recalls, someone said to her, "I feel that what you would really like to do is to be a member of Parliament," and "that was the very first time that it had occurred to me that perhaps one day I could, if the chance ever came."[9] But first there was the Oxford degree to complete, then the research job with B X Plastics, residence in Colchester, membership in the local Conservative Association, and attendance at party conferences representing the Oxford Graduates Association.

"My ideas," said Margaret Thatcher, "took form at Oxford."[10] Aside from her education in chemistry, where she took respectable second class honors, the Oxford influences appear to have affected most of her views on politics and on religion. She had come from a home where her father was an Independent, but Conservative-leaning, and where both parents exemplified the Non-conformist work ethic that nourished the rising middle class. At Oxford, 1943–47, the forces of both scientism and socialism were strong and pervasive, and while the inductive and experimental methods of the former were professionally attractive, the collectivism of the latter was philosophically disturbing. Essentially her negative reaction to socialism had a stronger religious base than a political one. This was reflected in a speech at St. Lawrence Jewry, in London, on March 30, 1978:

> I never thought that Christianity equipped me with a political philosophy, but I thought it did equip me with standards to which the political actions must, in the end, be referred. It also taught me that, in the final analysis, politics is about personal relations, about establishing the conditions in

[8]Murray, p. 41.
[9]Murray, p. 42.
[10]Cosgrave, p. 138.

which men and women can best use their fleeting lives in this world to prepare themselves for the next. Now all this may sound rather pious. But I still believe that the majority of parents want their children to be brought up in what is essentially the same religious heritage as was handed to me. To most ordinary people, heaven and hell, right and wrong, good and bad, matter.[11]

From that base it seems an easy step for Margaret Roberts of academic Oxford to become the Margaret Thatcher of everyday politics and attack the socialist wing of the Labour party for wanting every decision a political one: "I hate the things which I believe deny each and every person's right to dignity and respect, and their right to live their own lives in their own way, provided it doesn't harm anyone else. . . . I dislike the way the party has sold itself to socialism, to nationalisation, to almost a Marxist philosophy."[12]

Because there is a strong Christian theme that runs through Thatcher's political thinking, it may be significant to identify its origins. In Grantham, as has been said, she and her family were staunch Methodists, and at Oxford she regularly attended meetings of a student Methodist group. But also at Oxford she began to read religious treatises, with special attention to C. S. Lewis; thus began, in one biographer's view, her gradual move away ("higher and higher," she said) from Methodism, from fundamentalist to sacerdotal views.[13] When Margaret Roberts married Denis Thatcher in 1951 it was in a Methodist church, but when the twins were born in 1953 they were baptized in an Anglican church.

The conception of Mrs. Thatcher as a middle class high achiever, with upper class affiliations through education, politics and religion should by no means suggest that she is not personally a warm, compassionate and decent person. Brian Walden, thirteen years a Labour MP, now chief presenter for the ITV Weekend World, but himself a product of a deprived background, is very emphatic:

> She isn't a snob–she really isn't. I know that traditionally by all appearances, she ought to be and I also know that successful people of lower class origin are often the worst snobs because they are insecure. For some reason, she isn't insecure and she isn't a snob. . . . She has as much or as little interest in Dukes as in housewives. There is no element of the English vice which is disliking people not for what they are but for what they seem to be. There is no element of that in her at all.[14]

Unfortunately the English vice of which Walden complains is still very much in evidence. As was said at the outset, much of the criticism of Mrs. Thatcher that is heard in conversation and from the platform, and that is read in the press, relates at least indirectly to her cultural background. She is criticized for what she seems to be, for the image that she indeed sometimes projects, and not necessarily for what she is. The focus is not so much upon substance as upon her style.

[11] Interview with Murray, pp. 148–150.
[12] Murray, p. 145.
[13] Cosgrave, p. 136.
[14] Interview with Murray, pp. 83–84.

THE SOUND OF "CLASS"

It is about matters of style that English snobbishness is most apparent. In his foreword to the 1978 volume that updates Nancy Mitford's 1956 *Noblesse Oblige,* H. B. Brooks-Baker, managing director of Debrett's Peerage, contends that "England is among the least snobbish and class-conscious countries," but "this does not mean that snobbishness is rare in England. On the contrary, it is prevalent to some degree in most areas of society," and can be observed in the way that middle-classes often imitate in vain "the peculiar characteristics of language and behavior which come naturally to the English upper-classes."[15] The class distinction is reflected in the categories of "U" (Upper Class) and "non-U" (not Upper Class); that "not only means that one speaks with the right accent, but . . . also means that a person must choose the right word or phrase." While these two matters of style are "vitally important," Brooks-Baker also notes that "clothes, clubs, vocations and hobbies are also U and non-U, as well as such things as the way in which a person walks."[16] Richard Buckle's essay in the same volume illuminates the general point with the specific complaint that "Mrs. Thatcher, who may or may not be our next Prime Minister, pronounces 'involved' with a long 'o', as in 'vote'."[17]

Whatever the exact accent and word choice patterns of lower middle class Grantham, those of Margaret Roberts were influenced by childhood elocution lessons and, during her first years out of Oxford, reported her plastics company employer Stanley Booth, "she tended to iron out of herself her human characteristics, trying hard even then to become a politician, teaching herself artificial speech."[18] If indeed she did try to sound like one of the elite by modifying her vocal behavior, including accent, emphasis patterns, inflections, and precision of phrasing, she did not bring it off, at least in the eyes of that elite. Over and over one hears and reads in England a common set of terms used by professional political commentators, and Members of Parliament from both parties, to describe Mrs. Thatcher's communication characteristics. To be sure that these terms are understood in the way that Englishmen use them, they are presented here along with definitions taken from the most recently published and up to date Oxford English dictionary.[19] According to these informants, all themselves members of the elite, Mrs. Thatcher's speech is:

> *Plummy*—"full of plums . . . sounding affectedly full and rich in tone"
> *Toffee-nosed*—"snobbish, pretentious"
> *La-di-da*—"having an affected manner of pronunciation"
> *Starchy*—"stiff and formal in manner"

And her words mark her as:

> *Suburban*—"having only limited interests and narrow-minded views"
> *Privet hedge personality*—see suburban

[15] Richard Buckle, ed., *U and non-U Revisited* (London: Debrett's Peerage, Ltd., 1978), p. xi.

[16] Buckle, p. xvi.

[17] Buckle, p. 86.

[18] *Newsweek* International Edition, May 14, 1979, p. 51.

[19] *The Oxford Paperback Dictionary,* Joyce M. Hawkins, compiler (Oxford: Oxford Univ. Press, 1979).

The thrust of these commonly used labels, of course, is to tax Mrs. Thatcher with *affectation*—"behavior that is put on for display and not natural or genuine, pretence." Specifically, of course, this means that as she engaged in upward social mobility she tried to sound more and more like the elite. It is not unnatural anywhere to want to fit the expectations of one's peers, though it is probably more common in America than in Britain that one moves from non-U to U.

The attitudes reflected in the terms just cited are of long standing as applied to Mrs. Thatcher, but they came most conspicuously into use at the time of her 1975 challenge to Edward Heath for the Leadership of the Conservative Party. As Patrick Cosgrave reported that contest, Ian Gilmour, owner of the *Spectator* and Secretary of State in the Heath cabinet, even carried his opposition outside the party conference and to his constituents who heard him phrase "a dig against what was rapidly coming to be thought of as Margaret Thatcher's suburban image." "We cannot," said Gilmour at Amhersham, "retreat behind the privet hedge into a world of narrow class interests and selfish concerns."[20] At the outset of the 1979 General Election campaign there were still notes of concern, as in a not unfriendly review of her career by Philip Rawstorne:

> The well-groomed appearance, the cultivated accent, suggested a Southern suburban outlook, a scale of values which would strike few sympathies outside its own trimly hedged world. Many Tories having taken a leap in the dark [by electing her as leader], were disturbed by the distance from their immediate past at which they had apparently landed. . . . [But] the aggression with which she won her position and the abrasiveness caused in part by the tensions of maintaining it have been softened.[21]

It may be appropriate to ask whether American journalists would find kindlier terms with which to describe Mrs. Thatcher's political personality insofar as it is reflected in her communicative behavior. Here are fair samples from the most widely circulated American reports on Mrs. Thatcher in the election campaign. For the International Edition of *Newsweek,* John Nielsen and Anthony Collings thought "Thatcher still suffers from a humorless, doctrinaire image."[22] Peter Webb and Collings later wrote of "her combative speeches and abrasive style."[23] And Angus Deming, Tony Clifton, Allan J. Meyer and Collings heard "a strong-willed, somewhat shrill and prickly suburban matron," though admittedly "she tried to alter her image, speaking softly and avoiding controversial details on just how she would make her new-right government work."[24] The *Time* team headed by Bonnie Angelo summed up the Thatcher campaign by saying that her "sometimes hectoring, sometimes condescending manner irritated many voters. . . . [She had] an upper-class accent acquired by elocution lessons. . . . She had, and still has, two faces that are startlingly different: prim and tart-tongued in public, she is also a homebody who delights in comparing prices with other housewives. . . . Because of

[20]Cosgrave, pp. 62–63. Gilmour speech in Trevor Russell, *The Tory Party: Its Policies, Divisions and Future* (Middlesex; Penguin, 1978), pp. 163–164.
[21]*Financial Times,* March 31, 1979, p. 30.
[22]*Newsweek* International Edition, April 9, 1979, p. 24.
[23]*Newsweek* International Edition, April 30, 1979, p. 10.
[24]*Newsweek* International Edition, May 14, 1979, p. 50.

her authoritarian air, she sometimes appears to be rather like a headmistress dealing sternly with rowdy students."[25]

To sum up this matter, Kenneth Hudson's perceptive volume on *The Language of Politics* is helpful. He cites the common English term "Officer Class" v. "Not Officer Class Material," used to identify those whose education and family background make it apparent that "command has been placed in the right hands." To sound like Officer Class requires distinctive accents and vocal subtleties. Among recent Prime Ministers only Edward Heath was a middle class product and he lacked the true U Officer Class voice. In common with Heath, says Hudson, Mrs. Thatcher acquired the upper class accents too late in life for them to sound genuine. "A connoisseur of such matters can spot the difference immediately and so, one suspects, can quite a large proportion of the electorate. The imitation is too perfect, yet the subtleties are missing." Although Hudson does not question her sincerity, he notes that "the main disadvantage of the accent which is not quite right is that it is liable to give an impression of insincerity, of an actor playing a part."[26] In short, there are grounds for viewing Mrs. Thatcher as "plummy" and putting on the "la-di-da," as one prominent journalist said of her.

Mrs. Thatcher is, of course, well aware of what many critics have said about her speech behavior and her political personality. In a widely read interview with Kenneth Harris, published in *The Observer,* he reported that "I sometimes hear it said [and from some Conservatives] that your manner, your voice, even your looks, have a kind of middle-class quality which diminishes your appeal to the electorate as a whole." Her reply:

Absolutely poppycock! Isn't it ridiculous? It would be far better if such critics got on with the job of putting across Conservative views and philosophy, and did a little more converting themselves. I am what I am, and I will stay that way. I just hope to improve in communicating as I go along.

Harris pursued the topic of communication: "What do you think about your image on television? Do you work on your image on television?" No, she said, she doesn't work on it, but just tries to be more relaxed. "You can't alter your own personality. You just can't. You don't try to. If you discovered some irritating mannerisms that you didn't previously know about, of course you'd try to get rid of them, because if you don't, people will be distracted by them and not listen to what you're saying."[27] There is some evidence that Mrs. Thatcher accepts criticism of her speaking. Brian Walden, former Labour MP and now a television presenter, has encouraged her to be more spontaneous, in part to loosen her up and shed some of her studio dignity. Monty Modlyn, a longtime BBC announcer and interviewer, and now with LBC, advised Mrs. Thatcher that her style "was too much like a grande duchess and that her rather high pitched speaking voice should be altered since she was giving the impression that she spoke posher than the Queen." And Janet Brown, a television and cabaret entertainer, one of whose popular impersonations has been of Mrs. Thatcher, gave her suggestions on more effective script read-

[25] *Time,* May 14, 1979, pp. 31, 32, 34.
[26] Kenneth Hudson, *The Language of Politics* (London: Macmillan, 1978), pp. 51-55.
[27] *The Observer,* February 16, 1979, p. 33.

ing and phrasing of lines. "One of her great strengths," concluded Brown, "is that whatever criticism is levelled at her, she tries so blooming hard to put it right."[28]

TORY PERSUASION

"The trouble with politicians," Mrs. Thatcher said in an interview with Anthony King, "is we have to speak more often than we have something to say. And by the time you've been speaking two, three, four or five times a week, while Parliament is sitting, not always in the House, but the many organizations you have to speak to, you feel a bit stale." The remedy, she proposed, is that "you must try to find in politics a different approach. There's not much new to say in politics, there hasn't been for years, but it's the approach that's individual and different."[29]

Margaret Thatcher has made a political career out of taking "a different approach."

Her 1959 maiden speech in the House of Commons violated the polite tradition of introducing one's self by a few noncontroversial remarks, perhaps on the features of one's constituency. Instead it was a twenty-seven minute speech, "delivered without a note,"[30] arguing for her Private Member's Bill that would require local council meetings to be open to citizens and to journalists (what has been called in America a "sunshine" law). It was reported to be "Front Bench quality" and it "drew plaudits from Ministers as well as Opposition spokesmen."[31]

Her 1975 speech to the National Press Club in Washington overturned the tradition that no one ever speaks ill of his or her own country when abroad, and laid out the problems of Britain and the spirit in which she approached them:

> In my country, at present, we have serious problems; it would be foolish to ignore them. We have, to a more intense degree than many other countries, a combination of rising prices, falling output and unemployment. And we have a sense of losing our way. The problem is not a technical one. It is one of the life and death of the national spirit. We are in the midst of a struggle for human dignity.
>
> It is not my job, nor the job of any politician, to offer people salvation. It is part of my political faith that people must save themselves. Many of our troubles are due to the fact that our people turn to politicians for everything.[32]

Her three speeches on foreign policy and defense (July, 1974, at Chelsea; January, 1976, at Kensington; and July, 1976, at Dorking) challenged not only the position of Roy Mason, the British Defense Secretary, but also the policy of Henry

---

[28] In interviews with Murray: Walden, pp. 89-90; Modlyn, p. 104; Brown, pp. 121, 123.
[29] Hudson, p. 105.
[30] Johnson, p. 45.
[31] Cosgrave, p. 114. Her bill did ultimately become law and made its contribution to overcoming government secretiveness, which has been called one of the two principal weaknesses in postwar Britain. Peter Calvocoressi, *The British Experience, 1945-1975* (New York: Pantheon, 1978), p. 228.
[32] Cosgrave, p. 191.

Kissinger, the American Secretary of State, and specifically the practice of *detente* at the Helsinki conference. For this the Russian press labelled her "The Iron Lady," and Warsaw radio shifted the figure to say "she flutters like an iron butterfly."[33]

Her impromptu speech to a group of journalists with whom she was touring a computer factory near London during the recent campaign was a surprise lecture on science. She volunteered to explain to her companions what they were looking at, because "if you don't know it'll be deadly dull." Then came a briefing on the use of silicone chips in making small computers that could be used in moving data for decision making into field units and away from the central corporate office, and this conclusion:

> The political point is that the age of centralization and massive Big Brother computers is going, and you can have small computers with microprocessors on the spot, so that decisions can be taken on the spot. That is very much more interesting than pumping it all up there, having a few powerful chaps up there, and not being able to use your nous [common sense] locally.

As one of the journalists started to move on, she called "I haven't finished with you chaps. Here we all are in a science factory. You've all been concentrating on the possibility of the first woman Prime Minister in Downing Street. What you have failed to observe, which I must point out to you in all modesty, is that I will be the first person in No. 10 Downing Street to have a science degree."[34]

Overall Mrs. Thatcher speaks with good effect. Because they are so often generalities, her arguments frequently sound like slogans, but they are theme-related and the linkages are always apparent. Kenneth Hudson suggests that the flavor of much Conservative speaking has always been non-ideological (in contrast with Labour), and characterized by "plain statement on topics where straightforward, direct language is out of fashion."[35] One can easily select examples from the Thatcher speeches: "I gather from the radio I am called a reactionary. Well, there is a lot to react against." "Free choice is ultimately what life is about ·. . . from saying we are all equal it is only a small step to saying that we cannot make any choice for ourselves." "The balance between power and responsibility in the trades union movement needs to be restored as between employer and employee."[36]

Her style is fairly undistinguished, other than by the square-jawed, uncompromising phraseology of her convictions. The style is seldom marked by the figures of speech, metaphors, and graphic phrases that seem to fit so smoothly together in speaking of British elites. Perhaps it is simply that the speaking experience in the Oxford Conservative Association is no match for that in the Oxford Union.

Whatever shortcomings there may be in Mrs. Thatcher's public speaking, they are not the result of inattention. Like all British politicians, she knows the importance of quality in public discourse. The distinguished academic student of politics,

---

[33] Cosgrave, pp. 198–208; Murray, pp. 9–10.

[34] *Christian Science Monitor,* May 3, 1979. p. B19.

[35] Hudson, p. 70.

[36] *International Herald Tribune,* April 23, 1979: *Financial Times,* March 31, 1979; *Financial Times,* March 30, 1979.

Jean Blondel, writes of the essential talents of politicians: "They must be able to grasp quickly the main points of a question with which they are not familiar . . . they must be able to speak reasonably fluently in public, they must be able to argue a case in debate with some cogency, they must be able to retort quickly and see the flaw in the other man's argument."[37] Few practitioners of communication could be less in agreement on political issues than William Rees-Mogg, editor of *The Times*, and Anthony Wedgewood Benn, MP and Labour Minister of Energy. But on at least one point they are agreed: both of these former presidents of the Oxford Union affirm that at least fifty percent of a politician's success in England depends upon his ability in public speaking.[38] This truth Margaret Thatcher also recognizes, and there is ample testimony from her associates that she works very hard indeed at anything she thinks is important, and speeches are in that category.

Like most political leaders in America, in England at least the top bracket people (Prime Minister, Leader of the Opposition, and cabinet members) receive some assistance in the preparation of their speeches. Some of Mrs. Thatcher's predecessors used very little help. Sir Harold Wilson, Prime Minister, 1964–70 and 1974–76, testified that "I never used any drafting, or speech contributions, until the 1974 elections, when I was faced with two or three or even five and six a day, plus a hand-out for each day's press conference."[39] Edward Heath, Prime Minister, 1970–74, however, had Michael Wolff on his staff as a speechwriter, and at least five other persons were regular aides in turning out complete speech drafts for him. Though he always intended to rework the drafts, there was never enough time, and so "at the last minute the adequate draft was looked at, reluctantly approved and unenthusiastically delivered."[40] The two political heroes of Margaret Thatcher are earlier Prime Ministers, Winston Churchill and Harold Macmillan, and she tends to follow their speechwriting practices. Churchill, for example, "relied on civil servants and other functionaries to provide briefing material, but preferred to actually compose [his speeches himself], often moving from draft to draft and taking several days over the polishing and revision."[41]

It is important to recognize in this matter that "the man in the street" in London, and even the average university intellectual, is unaware of the pervasiveness of the professional speechwriter in political and business circles; they take it for granted that the speaker himself writes what he speaks. Even politicians who may hire the services of ghostwriters keep very quiet about it for the practice is thought to be infra dig. The exception is understood to be the Prime Minister, the Leader of the Opposition, or a major spokesman; for such persons some speechwriting aid is understandable and acceptable, provided, as Roger Evans put it, "that you always sound like yourself; and Mrs. Thatcher always sounds like Mrs. Thatcher, whereas, unfortunately, Ted Heath, when he was in office—he really did sound like his

[37] Jean Blondel, *Voters, Parties and Leaders: The Social Fabric of British Politics* (Hammondsworth: Penguin, 1977 rev. ed.), p. 30.

[38] Interviews with Rees-Mogg and Benn.

[39] Harold Wilson, *The Governance of Britain* (London: Sphere, 1976), p. 114.

[40] Douglas Hurd, *An End to Promises: Sketch of a Government, 1970–74* (London: Collins, 1979), p. 76.

[41] Hudson, p. 124.

speechwriters."[42] To sum up the matter, it appears that Mrs. Thatcher's speech preparation procedure is something like this:[43]

1. She holds a general discussion, sometimes more like an informal seminar, on a subject, and having a speech rather than a policy paper or a policy decision as the goal. Outside experts frequently take part.

2. Her views are expressed (a) to a speech writing aide, or (b) to an expert on her shadow staff, and "she explains the destination she wants the argument to reach and the track along which it is to go." If instructing the former, the end product will probably be a draft of the speech; if the latter, the product will be a brief, similar to that used by a lawyer, including all of the relevant factual information, and organized but not phrased as it might be used in an oral presentation.

3. This product, first draft or brief, is now subjected to criticism and further discussion. If pertinent documentation is missing, it is asked for, and if an unfamiliar quotation is used, its context must be produced. Then the aide is asked to have another go at it, or Mrs. Thatcher may herself undertake the second draft.

4. Still another session, and until she is satisfied the draft continues to be amended. One speechwriter who worked with her recalls spending eight to ten hours getting the last three or four pages of a manuscript just right, when the subject was extremely controversial and the feelings of the audience unusually tender. In any case, when the speech is ready, it has on it the authentic stylistic stamp of the Leader.

There is some reason to believe that Mrs. Thatcher, as Prime Minister, will wish to make somewhat less use of civil servants for the preparation of briefs of facts and figures than some of her predecessors. It is expected that instead she will have a larger political staff at No. 10 Downing Street, and draw upon its members for any speechwriting help she may need. Interestingly enough, if that proves to be the case, it will be because prececessor Wilson in March 1974 initiated the practice of appointing political advisers, both in his own office and for his Cabinet ministers. In a list of seven examples of areas in which they would work, he designated one as "speech writing and research."[44]

As the 1979 General Election campaign got underway, Mrs. Thatcher's speech-writing team included a number of part-time aides, but only two regular members. One was Patrick Cosgrave, historian and biographer, political columnist, former staff member of the *Spectator* and now free lance writer, who has served off and on for the last few years as a writer for Mrs. Thatcher. The other was Professor Douglas C. Hague, deputy director of the Manchester Business School, former consultant to the National Economic Development Office, and member of the Price Commission. Now, he told the press, he would advise Mrs. Thatcher on economic developments and write some of her speeches.[45]

The substantive source for Mrs. Thatcher's campaign speeches was a party document, called a manifesto. Each party issues one, and generally it is shorter than the American party platform and cast in more general terms. It is written "in a very

[42] Transcript of William F. Buckley, Jr., "Firing Line's British Correspondents," broadcast taped in London, June 27, 1978.

[43] Based upon interviews with Cosgrave, Howe, Riddell and Hardy; Cosgrave, pp. 25–26.

[44] Wilson, pp. 245–246.

[45] Letter from Patrick Cosgrave, April 14, 1979; *Financial Times,* April 6, 1979.

216

woolly fashion," says one political scientist, because in recent years it has become a ritualistic enterprise, not so much to influence the electorate as to provide the party faithful with a compact reference work on policies, and to reassure them that "the party image" has not been changed.[46] Under the Thatcher leadership, however, the manifesto has taken on a new significance. Issues identified in it are the themes of campaign speeches, and policies it lays out are seriously intended to provide a blueprint for action by the Conservative government.[47] Mrs. Thatcher in some ways may strive to do the accepted thing in public life, but her personal style would seem to preclude performing rituals for their own sake. "If a thing is worth doing, it's worth doing well," her grandmother used to tell her.[48]

An overview of the substance of the Tory persuasion in the recent election is therefore provided by the manifesto that refused to accept the inevitability of Britain's decline and said so in language that might well have been Thatcher's: "We think we can reverse it, not because we think we have all the answers but because we think we have the one answer that matters most. We want to work with the grain of human nature, helping people to help themselves—and others. This is the way to restore that self-reliance and self-confidence which are the basis of personal responsibility and national success." Five tasks would be performed by an elected Tory government:

1. Control inflation and set a fair balance between rights and responsibilities of trade unions, to restore national economic health.
2. Reduce income taxes at all levels, to ensure that "hard work pays, success is rewarded and genuine new jobs are created."
3. Uphold Parliament and maintain law and order, to improve the nation's health.
4. Help people become home-owners, provide better education, and focus welfare services on the truly needy, to support family life.
5. Work with allies and strengthen national defense, to protect national interests in a world of turmoil.

It doubtless was not by chance that a major opinion poll on April 2 revealed that the electorate thought that these were the issues, and in this order, that the General Election should be about: Prices/inflation, Unemployment, Trade unions/strikes, Taxation, Law and order, Common Market. A breakdown of the responses revealed that exactly the same ranking was given to these issues by three significant groups: women, 18-24 year olds, and trade unionists.[49]

The strategy for making the Tory persuasion effective struck many English as too American in style, i.e., controlled exposure with less emphasis upon party rally speeches and more on formal television appearances, and wide coverage for "telly news" programs of personal appearances in shops and factories, chats with the elderly, and the informal strolls called "walkabouts" in shopping centers and residential neighborhoods. Indeed, its great reputation for television commercial work apparently led to the selection of the firm of Saatchi and Saatchi to handle

[46] Geoffrey Alderman, *British Elections* (London: Batsford, 1978), pp. 26-28.

[47] In the first months of her administration even some persons who know her well were not prepared for the faithfulness of her proposed legislation to manifesto promises.

[48] Murray, p. 17.

[49] *Financial Times,* April 14, 1979.

Tory publicity, and to the inevitable references to "The Marketing of Margaret Thaatchi."[50] Doubtless it was the agency's advice, agreed to by party publicity director Gordon Reece, himself formerly a television producer and marketing director of EMI, that led Mrs. Thatcher to decline an invitation to make a joint appearance with Prime Minister Callaghan. Labour was quick to try for a point: "We can only assume that the Opposition Leader does not believe Conservative policies will stand up to such detailed public scrutiny," said the party's general secretary, Ron Hayward; and the political editor of Labour's daily paper suggested that voters were thus denied an opportunity to see how Mrs. Thatcher would react under pressure. An editorial in the *Evening News* defended Mrs. Thatcher's decision. After all, it said, "Mr. Callaghan could probably sell a second-car to Richard Nixon if he had a mind to," and there was no point in facing that kind of competition. Besides, "issues and policies, rather than personalities decide elections," and "salesmanship or TV technique" is no basis for deciding upon the best Prime Minister, any more than a Callaghan-Thatcher "race around Smith Square, or a game of Scrabble."[51]

Whoever may have had the right on the issue of an American-style television confrontation, Labour strategy included no personal attacks upon Mrs. Thatcher. When Robert Mellish suggested, in the Prime Minister's "Question Time" in the House of Commons, that everything possible should be done to "ensure that Mrs. Thatcher appear as frequently as possible on television, because her appearances could only be of advantage to Labour," he was mildly rebuked by Mr. Callaghan. That same evening, in a campaign warmup speech to the Parliamentary Labour Party, Callaghan instructed his colleagues to resist any temptation to make a personal campaign against Mrs. Thatcher.[52] It was freely speculated that at base this gentlemanly approach was taken as a precaution against angering women voters by anything that might appear to be "male chauvinist piggery." More than that, however, it was based upon the assumption that nothing Labour could say would be as devastating to Mrs. Thatcher as the mistakes they were sure she would make before the campaign was over. "Maggie'll blow it," they were confident, perhaps with an intemperate public outburst about immigration, capital punishment, or some equally divisive topic.

In the campaign television did play, to the dismay of many, a greatly increased role. In keeping of course with the British tradition of even handedness, even the substantially greater financial resources of the Tories[53] could not purchase additional television programs, but only spend more money on the production of their "fair share" allotment. In an agreement worked out by the political parties, BBC and the independent broadcasters, the Labour and Tory parties were each allocated five ten-minute television broadcasts; seven radio broadcasts, matched schedules of five and ten minutes; and all television broadcasts were scheduled for the same hour and on all networks. Mr. Callaghan and Mrs. Thatcher were each scheduled for one forty-minute live television session when viewers could put their own questions to

[50] See Tom Baistow, *The Guardian,* April 30, 1979, p. 12.

[51] Hayward in *Evening News,* April 3, 1979; Terence Lancaster, *Daily Mirror,* April 5, 1979; editorial in *Evening News,* April 3, 1979.

[52] *The Guardian,* March 30, 1979; Alan Watkins, "Maggie's Nerve is the Target," *The Observer,* April 1, 1979, p. 14.

[53] *Financial Times,* March 15, 1979.

them. Unlike the American custom, there were no election eve political broadcasts.[54] Independently, of course, the candidates were free to accept invitations— and they did—to appear for interviews on the televised "Jimmy Young Show," and Robin Day's "Election Call" program of candidate responses to telephoned questions from listeners and Mr. Day's own firmly posed follow-ups.[55]

To the regret of Labour hopefuls, Mrs. Thatcher committed no blunders, and she did demonstrate an improved understanding of how to carry the Tory message effectively. In 1974 the party manifesto was entitled *Firm Action for a Fair Britain,* and it proclaimed that "The choice before the nation today, as never before, is a choice between moderation and extremism."[56] In 1979 the election was still a choice, but by now she created the feeling that it might be between two extremes, Labour's radical socialists and the right-wing Conservatives. "I seek confrontation with no one," she said in a speech at Swansea about curbing union power, "but I will always strenuously oppose those at home whose aim is to disrupt our society and paralyze our economy, just as I will always stand up to those who threaten our nation and its allies from abroad." In Birmingham she used another issue to make clear the contrast in party approaches when she recalled that she had a few years earlier warned her country about Soviet expansion and that the Russians had called her an "Iron Lady." As the audience shouted its approval she put a new line into her prepared speech: "Britain needs an Iron Lady!"[57] All of these things she communicated in her formal campaign speeches, and with gestures, as *Guardian* political reporter Simon Hoggart described how she suited the actions to the words in a speech at Nottingham:

A slapping hand indicated Government spending, cupped hands meant improved industrial output, and arms held up with the hand bent over signified the inflation rate. A fist clenched with the thumb up meant reduced taxation. When she got down to a complicated explanation of the theory of debased coinage and the money supply the gestures were so elaborate that if she held a ball of wool they would have knitted a Fair Isle jersey as she spoke.[58]

In general she ignored the subject of gender. Some women might say "it's time a woman got the chance to run the country," and some men might say "I'd 'a preferred a bloke," but she would make no issue of it. When one lady apologized for her husband who, she thought, felt so strongly that "woman's place is in the kitchen, not the House of Commons," that he would abstain sooner than vote for any woman, Mrs. Thatcher asked the lady to remind her husband that "one of our great success periods was under Queen Elizabeth I. Why, great heavens, if your husband had thought the same thing then, we might never have beaten the Spanish Ar-

[54]*Evening Standard,* April 4, 1979. Proportional allocations were also made to Mr. David Steel and the Liberal Party.
[55]*Evening Standard,* April 9, 1979; *Financial Times,* April 14, 1979.
[56]David McKie, Chris Cook and Melanie Phillips, *The Guardian/Quartet Election Guide* (London: Quartet, 1978), p. 13.
[57]*International Herald Tribune,* April 23, 1979.
[58]*Manchester Guardian Weekly,* April 29, 1979, p. 4.

mada."[59] On other occasions she also remembered Queen Victoria, and suggested that "Women in power have done very well for Britain."[60]

About half of her campaigning time was spent in her own constituency of Finchley; the rest was working the marginal constituencies, where a shift of one percent of the votes might rescue a seat from Labour, an effort that involved travelling over three thousand miles, delivering more than thirty speeches to local audiences, and spending days on walkabouts. She became increasingly skillful at explaining, sometimes in crisp teacherly fashion, what had gone wrong with Britain and how to right it. English political reporter James Lewis grumped that "it was not, on the whole, an edifying campaign, and the winning party will have to pay the penalty of living with its words until the voters forget, as they generally do, who said them." But when American reporter David S. Broder encountered her on the forty-minute "Ask Mrs. Thatcher" BBC television program, he found her no slouch. "She handled a series of pointed and probing questions from some obviously well-coached voters with a skill few U.S. politicians could match. Watching her, you could see why she was one of the youngest Tories elected to Parliament in the 1959 election and the first of her freshman class to achieve cabinet status."[61]

"KEN WHAT A WOMAN MAY BE?"

"Even your looks," said Harris to Thatcher, are thought by some to have "a kind of middle class quality." To discuss this topic here is not sexist; it is a recognition that a very real issue in the 1979 General Elections was how Margaret Thatcher looked—as a woman—in terms of common assumptions about a woman's ways of thinking, a woman's whims, a woman's sensitivity—and as a woman who might become Prime Minister. There was not a print or broadcast journalist, a Member of Parliament, or a political staff member who was unwilling to be interviewed on this issue; nor was there one who thought it unimportant. It was as freely discussed on the streets and in the press.[62]

It was about two centuries ago when Samuel Johnson assured Boswell that "a woman preaching is like a dog's walking on his hind legs. It is not done well; but you are surprised to find it done at all." The tolerance of Englishmen for women in public life is somewhat greater this century, but for each individual woman there is a predictable scrutiny.

Hardly anything is written or said about the appearance of avuncular James Callaghan, Labourite Prime Minister, 1974-79, but there has been much on "what

[59]*International Herald Tribune,* April 25, 1979.

[60]Interview with Bonnie Angelo, *Time,* May 14, 1979, p. 33.

[61]Lewis in *Manchester Guardian Weekly,* May 6, 1979, p. 3; Broder in *International Herald Tribune,* April 25, 1979, p. 4.

[62]Representative articles in the daily press: Ian Atkins, "Callaghan Vetoes Abuse of Thatcher," *The Guardian,* March 30, 1979; Leonard Downie, Jr., "Mrs. Thatcher Faces Issue of Being . . . Mrs. Thatcher," *International Herald Tribune,* April 23, 1979; Anne Edwards, "Will Men be Fair to the Lady?" *The Sunday Express,* April 1, 1979; George Gale, "Maggie's Double Challenge: She is something new and disturbing—not just because of her ideas, but because of her sex," *Daily Express,* March 29, 1979; Alan Rapheal, "Jim's Ray of Election Hope," *The Observer,* March 25, 1979.

does *'she'* look like?" Well, she is small but not petite, blonde and of fair complexion, carefully coiffed and immaculately dressed, often somewhat stern of visage but generally attractive, poised and seemingly self-confident. Whether Callaghan's checked tie clashes with his striped shirt was not commented on by journalists during the campaign, but it was reported regularly "what *'she'* is wearing." She often used to wear hats, and they were caricatured by London newspaper cartoonists, along with the pearls and swooping manner that had characterized so many Tory women, but a shorter hairstyle has outmoded her hats anyway. She eschews flashy jewelry; pictures show her wearing a variety of earrings, but almost always the same relatively simple bracelet, and one decorative ring. She also avoids fussy clothes; most often she appears in fairly simple dresses or well tailored suits. How Mrs. Thatcher looks and what she wears are, in the long run of history, and even today, trivial matters. But to the readers of the London daily tabloids and at least some of the women's magazines, they seem to be matters that matter, and they are duly reported. For example, when addressing an audience in her Finchley constituency she complimented the women present on wearing blue, although " 'I feel terribly guilty I am not wearing blue, but I am going to the television studios and the background is bright turquoise—so I have to wear brown. We girls must think about these things,' Mrs. Thatcher said with a smile."[63]

More significant than visual images in terms of developing a political personality is the impact upon candidates of public stereotypes and prejudices. Just being a woman, in England more than in America, jeopardizes a political career. Even though women gained complete voting equality in 1928, in the elections between the wars an average of only seven women were chosen for the House of Commons, and in the elections since 1945 an average of twenty-four.[64] During the Fifties the belief was that voters were less likely to vote for a woman than for a man, though this was more apparent among Conservative than among Labour candidates. In the two elections in the Sixties Conservative women candidates continued to be less successful than men of their party, but Labour women did somewhat better than the men. Studies of elections in the Seventies show that the bias against Conservative women candidates has disappeared, although the public myth of unequal treatment of women candidates persists.[65]

Where there is inequality, however, is in the selection of candidates. Given a knowledge of electoral history, of course, fewer women are inclined to seek nominations, and the persistence of the myth of male bias in the General Election reinforces them. Thus the proportion of women among all parliamentary candidates has never risen above 7 percent, and although the total number of women candidates increases, about the same total get elected (the high was 27 out of the 635 members of the House of Commons in the government that was dissolved in March 1979), and thus the percentage of those women who run and are elected has declined almost by half in the past decade.[66] The net result is that about 4 percent of the MPs are women, usually a majority being Conservative when that party is in control, and Labour when that party controls. In either case it is traditional for the

[63] *Daily Telegraph,* April 2, 1979.
[64] Richard Rose, *Politics in England Today* (London: Faber & Faber, 1974), p. 149.
[65] Alderman, pp. 84–85.
[66] Alderman, p. 84.

Prime Minister to appoint one woman member as a minister.[67] This gives women a fair proportion of their number in the House, but far less than in the electorate.

Among the voters at large women number slightly over half, and of those a majority—as in all democracies for which data is available—now regularly support the most conservative party. (Since women live longer than men, there is a special tilt toward the right, and it is thus estimated that the average Conservative lives long enough to take part in thirteen general elections, and the average Labour voter only in twelve.)[68] Nevertheless, as between the two major parties, women find it harder to be selected for nomination by Conservative constituency parties than do women seeking nomination by Labour constituencies.[69]

Political analysts in England attribute the low rate of participation by women to a mix of institutional influences that are political and social.[70] The political institutional barrier is simply that there has been skepticism about the potential of women for effectiveness in politics, and if any woman survives that basic male prejudice it is likely to be only in a constituency that is "safe" for the other party anyway. Margaret Roberts encountered this barrier in 1948. Her friend John Grant, manager of Blackwell's bookshop at Oxford, proposed to John Miller, chairman of the Dartford constituency, that she would make a good candidate. At first Miller was opposed to the suggestion, on the grounds that Dartford was an industrial south of London area with a traditional 20,000 vote majority for the Labour party candidate. A year later, nevertheless, and perhaps because of the bleakness of Conservative prospects, Margaret Roberts, the only female applicant, was given the nomination. As could have been expected, she lost in the general elections of both 1950 and 1951, but the youngest candidate in the country had the satisfaction of reducing the Dartford Labour majority by nearly half. In 1954 she put in for the seat at Orpington, but was not nominated, an outcome that did not greatly upset her since the year before, "with her usual efficiency," as one friend put it, she produced twins. When they were only four months old she sat for and passed her Bar finals; and it is not insignificant that she opted for legal work as a barrister (entitled to represent clients in higher courts) rather than as a solicitor (who ordinarily does not function as a courtroom advocate).

In 1957 Margaret Thatcher was ready to try politics again, and she applied for the nomination at Beckenham. Here she encountered the second of the institutional influences that tend to bar women from politics. While the selection committee at Dartford had seemingly welcomed a bright and attractive young woman, Beckenham saw no political virtue in motherhood: "You are a woman with young children, and we don't think you ought to contest an election."[71] At Maidenstone there was a similar response, but in 1958 success came at Finchley in north London, where in 1955 there had been a Conservative majority of over 12,000 votes. In that constituency she first stood for election in 1959 and was elected with an increased majority, to enter Parliament and the Conservative government of Harold Macmillan.

[67] Rose, p. 149.

[68] Iain McLean, *Elections* (London: Longman, 1976), pp. 58–59. Also see Alderman, p. 168.

[69] Alderman, pp. 83–84.

[70] Rose, p. 149. Also see Blondel, pp. 53–54, 58, 168.

[71] Johnson, p. 45.

Although Margaret Thatcher continuously held her seat in Finchley, and by an increased majority in the May 1979 General Election, her successes have not been typical of women in politics. In the House of Commons that was dissolved in March there were twenty-seven women, but there are only nineteen in the House that assembled in May. (Most of the losses, of course, were Labour members, including the greatly respected Mrs. Shirley Williams and the young and impressive Mrs. Helene Haymen.)[72] Among the Thatcher department ministers there is only the one obligatory woman, Mrs. Sally Oppenheimer.

Although private Conservative party polls by March, 1979, showed Mrs. Thatcher attracting 50 percent of the women, while Prime Minister Callaghan was favored by only 30 percent,[73] her special appeal to women is not that she is a feminist. In her first press conference after being selected Leader of the party in 1975 she responded to a question about "Women's Lib" by asking "What has it ever done for me?"[74] In 1979, at a press conference in Glasgow on April 26, she was unchanged: "I don't like strident females. I like people who have ability and who don't run the feminist picket too hard. If you get somewhere it is because of your ability as a person, not because of your sex."[75] One is left with the assumption that Margaret Thatcher believes that if she could achieve so can other women, and without special legal assistance. "I think the fact that a woman had become Prime Minister would do something that no amount of legislation could," she told Tricia Murray. "It's practice that matters now far more than law. I would think it would be a tremendous boost to many women, especially those trying to reach the top in whatever sphere."[76]

The feminists responded mainly by writing critical letters to the newspapers.[77] Although during her national campaign tour Thatcher was generally protected against heckling, the feminists succeeded in making their rebuttal in person when a small group surrounded an election day meeting in Finchley, carrying banners and chanting, "We want women's rights, not a Right wing woman."[78]

The women that Margaret Thatcher appeals to are clearly not the feminists, but they are the housewives who read the major women's magazines, notable in England for their large circulations and longtime retention. Traditionally these publications have avoided articles that were in any way political, and have refused political advertisements. In recent years, however, they have been willing (or persuaded) to carry extensive interviews with Mrs. Thatcher.[79] In general these pieces have been devoid of any outright political pitch, but concentrated on the Thatcher "philosophy" about such matters as running a home and raising a family, and also having a public career. As longtime press secretary Derek Howe put it, Mrs.

[72] The Conservatives fielded 31 women candidates, three fewer than in 1974, and increased their MPs from seven to eight; Labour fielded 52 women candidates, as against 38 in 1974, and had a net loss of seven, electing only eleven.

[73] Interview with Derek Howe.

[74] Cosgrave, p. 14.

[75] Reuters despatch, *International Herald Tribune*, April 27, 1979.

[76] Murray, p. 147.

[77] See representative anti-Thatcher feminist letters, *The Guardian*, May 3, 1979, p. 11.

[78] Michael White, "Thatcher Pushed and Jostled at Rally," *The Guardian*, May 3, 1979, p. 28.

[79] It should be noted that with typical British even-handedness there have also been interviews with Mrs. Callaghan, but of course she was not running for office.

Thatcher declines to give bread recipes, but she is happy to talk about the importance of bread.[80]

The image of Thatcher the housewife is also promoted in her formal speeches and in informal walkabouts. She at least appears to enjoy making forays into shopping centers (followed by television news cameras) and comparing products and prices with other housewives. Certainly she smiled generously for a picture that made the front page of the *Daily Express,* holding up a large bag of groceries representing what one Tory pound bought in 1974, and another small bag to show how little the Labour pound would buy in 1979.[81] An American reporter was surprised by a typical Thatcher exercise in Birmingham: at the Cadbury chocolate factory she chatted with a worker who was to be married in a few days, discussing how to set up a routine for running a home and still keeping her job. "You've got to dovetail in all your shopping and think ahead the whole time, haven't you? And when you've had a full day's work you don't want to go back to an untidy house." Household budgets and planned housekeeping could become a habit, she assured the young woman, just as they had in the Thatcher household.[82]

One final element of the Thatcher political personality that doubtless aggravates the fenimists, but seems not to bother her, is the way that her male colleagues refer to her as having male qualities of mind and male instincts for politics. From a series of interviews by Tricia Murray it is easy to find examples.[83]

Lord Pannell, an MP from 1949 to 1974, recalled that in the famous 1975 contest that replaced Heath as Conservative Leader, "when the chips were down, she was the only one man enough in the Conservative Party to stand for the leadership."

Sir Harold Wilson, an MP since 1945, and Labour Prime Minister, 1964–70 and 1974–76: "Women politicians vary a great deal, as indeed do men, but you occasionally find that a woman politician is more of a man than any of the men . . . and I would say it's probably true of Mrs. Thatcher . . . who obviously possesses a great deal of feminine charm and good looks but who at the same time is as determined and relentless as any male politician."

Andrew Faulds, a Labour MP who once referred to her as "that bloody woman" in a parliamentary debate: "I think she may need to put up a tough appearance to compensate for the fact that she's not a man . . . Politics is more naturally a man's world. I think some women hold their own very well but I think they lessen their femininity and womanhood by holding their own very well—she's one of them."

Within the Shadow Cabinet, Mrs. Thatcher assured Kenneth Harris, there are no men or women, just politicians. "I'm not conscious of them as men at all," she said. "Don't mistake me: I see A as taller than B; I see X as more handsome than Y. What woman wouldn't? What man wouldn't have such perceptions about women? But I don't see me and my colleagues in an 'I'm a woman, you are men relationship.' I'm conscious of my colleagues as different personalities. The differ-

[80] Interview with Howe.

[81] *Daily Express,* April 25, 1979, p. 1.

[82] Takashi Oka, *Christian Science Monitor,* May 3, 1979, p. B2. Also see Ferdinand Mount, *Spectator,* May 5, 1979, p. 4.

[83] In Murray: Pannell, p. 109; Wilson, pp. 112–13; Faulds, p. 138.

ences between them are so great that—it may sound strange—you hardly notice that they are men and you are a woman."[84]

A SENSE OF CONVICTION

In one respect, however, Mrs. Thatcher does differ markedly from most of her male colleagues. It is undoubtedly the most distinctive feature of her personal style and deserves specific though brief notice: she is a self-pronounced "conviction politician." For a long time she had described herself as a reformer, bent on reversing what she saw as the national decline resulting from the radicalism of the Labour Party. But there were many who doubted that in a real contest she would hold so staunchly to her equally radical conservative views; surely she would temper them under campaign fire. In the spring of 1979, with an election inevitable at least by fall, she reacted to the doubters in a statement given wide circulation in *The Observer:* "I'm not a *consensus* politician or a *pragmatic* politician. I'm a *conviction* politician. And it's my job to put forward what I believe and try to get people to agree with me."[85] Throughout the campaign she refused to waffle on her ultimate ends, though she was sometimes unclear about the means. The nation had had enough of consensus on the middle road, even though some of her right wing Conservative colleagues still travelled it. In a rousing campaign speech at Cardiff, in the Welsh country of Prime Minister Callaghan, and in her own sharp style, she said it all again: "I am a reformer and I am offering change." From the evangelical Welsh background she took her mission: "If you've got a message, preach it." Though she was in solid Labour territory she gave witness of the strength of her beliefs:

I am a conviction politician. The Old Testament prophets didn't say "Brothers, I want a consensus." They said: "This is my faith, this is what I passionately believe. If you believe it too, then come with me."[86]

No Prime Minister in more than three decades had been so blunt in staking out an uncompromising position; some Tory ones had supported capitalism only softly, and some Labour ones had talked socialism in mild terms. They were all male politicians. Impatience with consensus-seeking and intensity of conviction may not be sex-related qualities, but among her peers it is Margaret Thatcher who clearly has them both.

For some voters the Thatcher style has been refreshing and for others frightening. Within the customary margin of error, the public opinion polls from the dissolution of Parliament to the General Election told the story. Relying upon published reports of polls by MORI (Market and Opinion Research International), just before the campaign began in earnest (slow getting underway because of the death of Airey Neave and the Easter holiday), the fallen Labourites commanded only 38 percent, the Liberals 10 percent, and the Conservatives 51 percent, a substantial majority that would easily sweep them into office if it could be maintained.[87] With-

[84]Interview, *The Observer*, February 16, 1979, p. 33.
[85]Interview with Kenneth Harris, *The Observer*, February 25, 1979, p. 33.
[86]*Manchester Guardian Weekly,* April 22, 1979.
[87]*Daily Express, April 4, 1979.*

out much variation during the campaign Labour steadied into a final "day of election" poll figure of 39.8 percent, the Liberals increased substantially to 13.5 percent and the Conservatives gradually declined to 44.4 percent, still enough to provide an ample margin of victory.[88]

Meanwhile the Conservative Leader fared far less well than her party. Just before the campaign began, those polled on the question of who would make the better Prime Minister gave 42 percent to Callaghan and 40 percent to Thatcher.[89] (At the same time a separate poll revealed that 47 percent were satisfied with Thatcher's leadership of the party, and 38 percent dissatisfied, a healthy shift from the 43 percent–45 percent figures in early March.[90] By mid April the "better Prime Minister" question showed 45 percent for Callaghan, 37 percent for Thatcher.[91] The trend continued in a poll reported on April 25: 46 percent Callaghan, 33 percent Thatcher; by April 28 the report was 50 percent Callaghan, 31 percent Thatcher.[92] And in one final "day of election" poll that also offered the option of David Steel, the Liberal party Leader, Callaghan rose to 57 percent, Steel received 28 percent, and Thatcher fell sharply to 23 percent.[93]

One of the conclusions that may be drawn from these divergent figures, showing the Conservative party much stronger than its Leader, is that *Guardian* political columnist Peter Jenkins was correct when he told Robin Day on BBCI, as the election returns were being reported, that "she has fought less than a brilliant campaign."[94] The editor of *The Economist* looked at both sides of the coin: "Mrs. Thatcher has not had a good campaign, while Mr. Callaghan has had a very good one."[95] A derivative conclusion may also be drawn by saying that among the voters at large Mrs. Thatcher's political personality, the image that she projected, failed to generate a high degree of either confidence or enthusiasm.

Americans who reflect upon this matter must remember, however, that Mrs. Thatcher, wherever she may have campaigned, was not actually running for national office and did not solicit personal electoral support from the voters at large. The retention of her seat in the House of Commons depended only upon being "first past the post" (i.e., a plurality) in the five-candidate race in the 55,468 vote constituency of Finchley. The retention of her position as Leader of the Conservative party was not at stake at all, for it is dependent upon receiving a majority of votes of the parliamentary members of the party. And succeeding James Callaghan and becoming the new Prime Minister depended upon having enough other Conservative candidates winning election to constitute a House of Commons majority. Thus the question of how Mrs. Thatcher's personality was perceived by the voters at large was not a critical issue. What was important in the election was that the personality

---

[88] *Financial Times*, May 3, 1979. The official results showed Labour at 36.9 percent, Liberals at 13.8 percent, and Conservatives at 43.9 percent. See *Manchester Guardian Weekly*, May 13, 1979.

[89] *Daily Express*, April 4, 1979.

[90] *Daily Express*, April 4, 1979; *The Guardian*, March 9, 1979.

[91] *Daily Express*, April 25, 1979.

[92] *Daily Express*, April 25, 1979; *The Guardian*, April 28, 1979.

[93] *International Herald Tribune*, May 2, 1979. The MORI poll that day reported Callaghan at 46 percent, Thatcher at 38 percent, and "don't know" at 11 percent. See *Evening Standard*, May 3, 1979.

[94] BBCI election night broadcast, May 3–4, 1979.

[95] *The Economist*, May 5, 1979, p. 13.

of each competing candidate for 635 constituency seats—including Mrs. Thatcher in Finchley—be favorably perceived.

Americans should also be interested in the way Mrs. Thatcher dealt with the matter of political personality. It came up when she received an invitation to appear in a face-to-face confrontation with Prime Minister Callaghan on two peak time television broadcasts. A presidential style debate would be alien to British broadcasting traditions of "presenting the whole policy of a party to the nation. . . . Personally, I believe that issues and policies decide elections, not personalities. We should stick to that approach. We are not electing a president, we are choosing a government."[96]

Mrs. Thatcher was, of course, quite correct in her assessment. Had the election been American style, obliging her to seek voter approval nationwide, the results of the "who would be the better Prime Minister" polls show that she would still be Leader of the Opposition. Had the election turned upon the question of who projected the most compelling image, Mr. Callaghan would still be the Prime Minister. But of course Callaghan's relaxed and avuncular, familiar and comforting image, so well projected on television, was not at issue: and neither was Thatcher's intense and proper, reserved and deliberately disturbing image. If anything, it could be said that British voters at large were willing to gamble on Mrs. Thatcher's political personality. What they were betting on was that a set of Tory policies and proposals would be better than the perceived failures of the Labour government. The British voters often, so their politicians and political scientists say, vote against the government instead of for the opposition. They did it again in May 1979.

One might well conclude this report by saying that it is reassuring to see a democracy function so that it may truly be said that the great decision was made upon "issues and policies . . . not personalities." It is an affirmation of Edmund Burke's advice to his British countrymen more than two hundred years ago: "Not men, but measures."

[96]*Financial Times,* April 4, 1979, p. 10.

The Metaphoric Cluster in the Rhetoric of Pope Paul VI and Edmund G. Brown, Jr.

Kathleen Hall Jamieson

Frequently a lone metaphor's recurrence solicits a critic's interest but occasionally a skein of metaphors taken together weaves a pattern that is at least coherent and at best compelling. Black,[1] Osborn,[2] and Sontag[3] are among the critics who have offered provocative responses to the question—Of what significance is a recurrent metaphor? To their work, which persuasively justifies critical focus on a single recurrent metaphor, I wish to append a footnote illustrating what may be learned by dissecting the metaphoric lexicon of a single rhetor. By isolating a rhetor's range of metaphors and comparing them with other habitual rhetorical behaviors, critics can minimize the likelihood that they are generalizing from aberrant rhetorical cues.

Underlying this examination is the assumption that recurrent patterns observable in the surface language reflect deeper rhetorical consistencies, the understanding of which is important in explicating a person's rhetoric. In this essay, I shall examine the metaphoric networks created by California Governor Edmund G. Brown, Jr., during his run for the presidency in 1976 and Pope Paul VI during his fifteen-year reign.[4] I intend to argue that what is significant about the rhetoric of each is not the recurrence of a single metaphor but rather the appearance of clusters of related metaphors which reveal the rhetor's projected relationship with his audience and corroborate otherwise inconclusive rhetorical cues.

[1] Edwin Black, "The Second Persona," *Quarterly Journal of Speech*, 56 (1970), 109–19.

[2] Michael Osborn, "Archetypal Metaphor in Rhetoric: The Light-Dark Family," *Quarterly Journal of Speech*, 53 (1967), 115–26; Michael Osborn, "The Evolution of the Archetypal Sea in Rhetoric and Poetic," ibid., 63 (1977), 347–63.

[3] Susan Sontag, *Illness as Metaphor* (New York: Farrar, Straus and Giroux, 1978). See, also, John Alexander Sawhill, *The Use of Athletic Metaphors in the Biblical Homilies of St. John Chrysostom* (Princeton: Princeton Univ. Press, 1928); Marietta Conroy, *Imagery in the Sermons of Maximus, Bishop of Turin* (Washington, D.C.: Catholic Univ. Press, 1966); and Hermann G. Stelzner, "Analysis by Metaphor," *Quarterly Journal of Speech*, 51 (1965), 52–61. In addition, see J. Vernon Jensen, "British Views on the Eve of the American Revolution: Trapped by the Family Metaphor," *Quarterly Journal of Speech*, 63 (1977), 43–50; Jane Blankenship, "The Search for the 1972 Democratic Nomination: A Metaphorical Perspective," in *Rhetoric and Communication*, ed. Jane Blankenship and Hermann G. Stelzner (Urbana: Univ. of Illinios Press, 1976), pp. 236–60. Blankenship's analysis of "the metaphors used about and by the candidates in the print media" (p. 236) for the 1972 Democratic presidential nomination is a useful account of the lexicon of the press. Unlike Blankenship, I intend to focus directly on the unmediated rhetoric of the single speaker.

Studies of the metaphors inherent in a single work include: Christie Jeffries, "Metaphor in 'Sons and Lovers,'" *Personalist*, 29 (1948), 287–92; Barbara Hughes Fowler, "The Imagery of the *Prometheus Bound*," *American Journal of Philology*, 78 (1957), 173–84; Jackson I. Cope, *The Metaphoric Structure of* Paradise Lost (Baltimore: Johns Hopkins Univ. Press, 1962); Sigurd Burckhardt, "The Metaphorical Structure of Goethe's 'Auf dem See,'" *Germanic Review*, 31 (1956), 35–48.

[4] This paper is based, in part, on analysis of 63 audio-taped speeches delivered by Edmund G. Brown, Jr., between 5 May and 2 November 1976; eight interviews (ranging from three to twenty minutes) with Brown; texts of Brown's inaugural, his 1975 budget message, his 1975 state of the state address, and interviews published in the *Washington Post* and *Playboy*. The author attended the Democratic National Convention in 1976. Eleven hundred and forty-two of Paul VI's public speeches were read and analyzed.

The Rhetoric of Pope Paul VI and Edmund G. Brown, Jr.

I have chosen the rhetoric of a presidential hopeful and the rhetoric of a pope because Brown and Paul's uses of metaphor are both similar and different in significant ways. In his bid either for the governorship or the presidency Brown could have stressed his kinship to the liberal philosophy of his father, former California Governor Edmund G. (Pat) Brown, Sr., by adopting the metaphoric lexicon of the Great Society. Instead Jerry Brown's metaphoric network sets him apart not only from his father but from the other presidential contenders in 1976 and from other politicians as well. Paul VI's purpose is not differentiation but identification. By employing the metaphors in which Christ, the apostles, and nineteen centuries of popes have expressed Catholicism, Paul VI implies that he has preserved the tradition of the Church and, hence, is a legitimate heir of Peter. So, while Brown's metaphors may suggest a rejection of his father's philosophy, Paul's metaphors endorse ancestral doctrine.

Unlike Brown, Paul VI embraces both an established rhetorical repertoire and the mandate to conserve the doctrine that it expresses. Accordingly, Brown will be observed in the process of *discovering* the available means of persuasion and Paul in *choosing* from among means already discovered. Initially, for example, Brown contends, "I am not a Santa Claus": then, apparently realizing the rhetorical liabilities such a contention may carry, replaces it with, "The President is not a Santa Claus." Because the metaphors Paul adopts have been refined through centuries of use, he is unlikely to employ a counterproductive metaphor.

Paul inherits a publicly accessible rhetorical repertoire; consequently a critic can analyze and ascertain the significance of Paul's choices from among the known means of persuasion. For instance, Pope Innocent III's claim to be empowered to "uproot what must be uprooted" can function as a counterbalance against which to weigh Paul's description of himself as "a frail messenger . . . an ant on the world stage."

Scripture and other Church rhetoric school Paul's audience in the metaphors he employs. As a result, it is unlikely that Paul's metaphors will tantalize with their freshness, but likely that the audience will assign intended referents.

Yet, in an obvious demographic sense, Paul's audience is more heterogeneous than Brown's. Brown is addressing adult residents of the United States; Paul is speaking to Catholics throughout the world. It is not surprising, then, that Paul relies on archetypal metaphors that resonate across cultures while Brown's metaphors (e.g., wagon train, Santa Claus) are more specifically culture bound.

The cluster of associated elements implied by each metaphor is detailed clearly in Paul's speeches, but not in Brown's. In the language of Osborn and Ehninger, Paul employs more "contextual qualifiers"[5] than does Brown; Paul's metaphors are more fully extended. Paul's claim that the Church is a body is illustrative: Christ is its head; the pope is Christ's vicar; the faithful are members of the body; the body is enlivened by tradition; the faithful, by sinning, can sever themselves from the body. In contrast, when Brown likens politics to the House of Atreus, the House remains unpeopled. His listeners do not know, for instance, who, in the role of Thyestes, has cursed the House—or how, if at all, the curse can be lifted. Paul's use of metaphor illustrates Osborn and Ehninger's contention that "extensions add

[5]Michael M. Osborn and Douglas Ehninger, "The Metaphor in Public Address," *Speech Monographs*, 29 (1962), 228.

clarity, direction, and a certain pictorial quality to the metaphoric experience. . . .
They serve both to discipline the interpretations of the more freely imaginative
members of an audience and to stimulate the interpretations of the unimaginative."[6]

For Paul, the metaphor is a vehicle for teaching complex truths to a popular
audience. (Consequently metaphors abound in Paul's homilies but seldom appear
in his doctrinal encyclicals.) Metaphoric extensions are especially useful to one
whose object is education because "they increase for the entire audience the time
available for contemplating the sense and significance of a metaphoric assertion."[7]
Extensions are less appropriate for Brown, whose metaphors function most often
as illustrations.

Because they are elaborated, Paul's metaphors are able to serve as arguments.
It is by the "sort of internal alchemy" postulated by Osborn and Ehninger that
Paul metaphoric extensions, "by certifying through explication the appropriateness
of item of association to subject . . . serve . . . to make of the metaphor itself an
argument in its own behalf."[8] If the conscience is an eye and tradition is light, it
follows that tradition is indispensable to moral sight. Similarly, St. Paul's claim
(Ephesians 5:22–4) that the husband is head of the wife as Christ is head of the
Church solicits the conclusion that, "As the Church submits to Christ, so wives
should submit to their husbands in everything."

Although the metaphors employed by Brown and Paul presuppose different
audiences and functions, their use of metaphor is similar in many respects. Both
Brown and Paul assume that reality exists and is known by them; both posit metaphoric worlds in which they are invested with special responsibility; neither accepts
the responsible role eagerly; both see themselves buffeted by threats and frustrations; both rely on metaphors of passage—Brown urging his audience to abandon
"conspicuous consumption" for "an era of limits" and Paul pleading that Catholics
accept their doctrinal inheritance, safeguard it, and transmit it to the next generation. Paul assumes a paternal posture and assigns the Church a maternal role; Brown
implies a parental role for himself. Both argue from a posture of moral superiority
while casting members of their audiences as children. The metaphors employed by
both are redundant. For Brown, "Santa Claus," "rabbits from hats," and "magi-
cian with a magic wand" are functionally equivalent expressions. A passage written
by St. Cyprian demonstrates clearly the interchangeability of the metaphors employed by Paul:

> . . . the church is one, even though she embraces larger and larger multi-
> tudes in the course of her prolific growth. So, the sun has many rays but
> only one light; a tree has many branches, but one trunk rooted firmly in
> the soil; and when many streams originate in one source . . . yet there is but
> one source. . . . The Church extends her branches over the whole world
> . . . her full flowing streams course everywhere—but there is only one trunk,
> one source.[9]

[6] Ibid., pp. 228 and 233.
[7] Ibid., p. 233
[8] Ibid.
[9] *De Unitate Ecclesiae, Patrologiae Latinae cursus completus* . . . ed. J. P. Migne (Paris:
1844 et seq.), 4, 517 ff. Hereafter cited as *PL*. Translations from the Old and New Testaments
are from the St. Joseph's edition of *The New American Bible*.

The existence of interchangeable metaphors in a rhetor's lexicon enables the critic to clarify the meaning and function of individual metaphors by playing them against each other.

This essay presupposes that neither Paul or Brown nor their intended audiences perceive the analyzed figures of speech as statement of fact. The disclaimer is an important one, for Christianity has been sundered by believers who could not agree on whether a passage in Scripture ought to be read literally or figuratively. For example, Huldreich Zwingli, a leader of the Reformation in Switzerland, insisted that when Christ said of the bread at the Last Supper, "This is my Body," He was contending that the bread *represented* His body. The Church condemned claims such as Zwingli's as the distortions of "contentious men" who "deny the truth about the body and blood of Christ" by distorting Christ's words into "fictive and imaginary figures of speech (*tropos*)."[10] For Zwingli, the eucharist was a sanctified metaphor; for the popes it is the body of Christ.

This essay is grounded in the assumption that metaphors simultaneously create inventional possibilities and impose inventional constraints. Adopting one metaphor, for example, often entails abandoning others. Brown cannot liken himself both to Sisyphus and Hercules without sacrificing imagistic consistency. So, too, expressing content in a metaphor rather than a simile argues that a fundamental correspondence exists between the metaphor and the object it signifies. The metaphoric claim that the Church *is* a body entails the conclusion that the Church has a single head. Correlatively, an institution governed by triumvirs ought not metaphorically *em-body* itself. The Church as a two-headed body is a metamorphosed metaphor which is either menacing (i.e., a potential hydra) or a pitiable and freakish mutant. Indeed the papal bull *Unam sanctam* (1302) reinforces the conclusion that the Church has a single head by dismissing the "monstrous" alternative: "the one and only Church has one body, one head not two heads like a monster (*quasi monstrum*)."[11]

Popes have been quick to condemn those who contort false doctrine into a shape compatible with a fundamental metaphoric cluster. For example, Martin de Barcos sidestepped *Unam sanctam's* condemnation of the belief in a two-headed Church by arguing that Saints Peter and Paul "are two Supreme pastors and rulers who make but one head."[12] Nonetheless, in 1647, Pope Innocent X declared that proposition heretical if it is explained "so as to establish the complete equality of Saints Peter and Paul without subordinating and subjecting St. Paul to St. Peter in the ultimate power and governance of the Church."[13]

Use of any metaphor neccessitates suppression of those metaphoric elements that could subvert the rhetor's purposes. Consequently, skilled rhetors draw judi-

[10] Pope Julius III, "Decretum de ss. Eucharistia" (11 Oct. 1551) in *Enchiridion Symbolorum*, ed. Henricus Denzinger and Adolfus Schönmetzer (Rome: Herder, 1976), xxxvi, 1637, p. 385.

[11] Boniface VIII, "Unam sanctam" (18 Nov. 1302) in *Enchiridion Symbolorum*, 872, p. 280.

[12] "Decr. S. Officii" (24 Ian. 1647) in *Enchridion Symbolorum*, 1999, p. 445.

[13] Ibid. Dispute over the papal claim to head the Church continues. Maximos IV, Patriarch of Antioch, told the Second Vatican Council (*Council Speeches of Vatican II*, ed. Hans Küng, Yves Congar, and Daniel O'Hanlon [Glen Rock, N.J.: Paulist Press, 1964], p. 73): "It should be clear to all of us that the only head of the Church, the only head of the Body of Christ which is the Church, is our Lord Jesus Christ, and he alone. The Roman Pontiff is the head of the College of bishops just as Peter was the head of the College of Apostles."

ciously upon the inventional resources created by a metaphor. A pope, for example, is unlikely to analogize the armpits or anus of the Church's body. Opponents of the Church exploit such suppressed inventional resources, as Luther did in describing papal decrees as "the blasphemous hellish devil's filth and stench."[14]

Suborning papal metaphors to attack papal doctrine is a standard ploy of reformers and revolutionaries. Luther, for example, suggested that the popes had transformed the once virginal bride of Christ into the arch-whore of the devil while he and his followers "hold fast once more to the ancient church, the virgin and pure bride of Christ." Accordingly, he concluded, "we are certainly the true, ancient church, without any whoredom or innovation."[15]

Obviously, neither Brown nor the popes has an exclusive claim to any of the analyzed metaphors. Indeed the popes often have confronted adversaries who heard different meanings in stock papal figures. In his oration before Maximilian I (1501), the poet Heinrich Bebel envisaged "Mother Germany" instructing Maximilian that "he is his sorrowful mother's only refuge and consolation, having been my hope since the time when I harbored him in my womb." Mother Germany urged Maximilian to "have no pity on those whose condition has degenerated to the point of decay. They must be cut from my flesh if my body is to be saved."[16] The confrontation in the Reformation between Mother Church and Mother Germany created a number of rhetorical anomalies. Each "body" considered the other a decaying member that could not be healed and must be excised.

To some extent, then, explication of the metaphoric repertoires of Paul VI and Edmund G. Brown, Jr., is a study of the creation, exploitation, and sacrifice of inventional capital.

THE METAPHORS OF PAUL VI

The Church, declared Paul VI, "is a traditional institution."[17] The believer "is a man of tradition."[18] Since "tradition" is a concept central to the papacy, I shall employ it as a lens to focus my analysis of Pope Paul VI's metaphoric lexicon. The metaphors in which Paul VI enwrapped the concept "tradition" elucidate his insistence that he must uphold the Church's traditional teachings on birth regulation, celibacy, and exclusion of women from the priesthood. Paul expressed his view of tradition in five metaphoric clusters: a body metaphor, a fertility-sterility metaphor, a light-dark metaphor, a patrimony-treasure metaphor, and a water-journey metaphor. That these metaphors are part of the lexicon of the New Testa-

[14] Martin Luther, "Against the Roman Papacy, An Institution of the Devil," (1545) trans. Eric W. Gritsch in *Luther's Works* (Philadelphia: Fortress, 1966), 41, 332.

[15] Luther, "Against Hanswurst," (1541), *Works*, 41, 205.

[16] "Oratio Henrici Bebeli . . . " in *Rerum germanicarum scriptores varii*, ed. Simon Schard (Giessen: 1673), pp. 95 ff.

[17] 25 Sept. 1968, p. 153. Unless otherwise indicated the speeches of Paul VI's that are cited are found in volumes titled *The Teachings of Pope Paul VI* (Washington, D.C.: U.S. Catholic Conference). The volumes are published the year after that in which the speech is delivered. Speeches delivered in 1968 and 1975 are located in *The Teachings of Pope Paul VI* (Vatican City: Libreria Editrice Vaticana). All translations of Paul's speeches, unless otherwise indicated, are those authorized by the Vatican.

[18] 27 May 1970, p. 212.

ment argues subtly that the pope is a legitmate heir of Peter who has preserved the tradition of the Church.

Were it not for papal notation of their origin, one might conclude that Paul VI was extracting his metaphors directly from the Old Testament. In fact Christ drew His metaphoric clusters from the Jewish rhetorical tradition that He and His audience shared. By developing the images of the Old Testament, Christ rhetorically underscored His contention that He had not come to destroy the Jewish law but to fulfill it. Parallels between the metaphors of the Old Testament and Pope Paul's body, fertility, light, water, and patrimony metaphors are abundant. Recall that in Isaiah (27:2-3) the Lord speaks of Israel as a pleasant vineyard; in Hosea (2:21) God tells Israel "I shall espouse you to Me forever"; in Genesis (1:3) God says "Let there be light" and light was made; a flood cleanses the Earth but Noah and those in the ark with him are saved; both Jacob and Joseph are deprived of their patrimony; and Micah (7:18-20) credits God with removing the guilt and forgiving the sin of "the remnant of his inheritance?"

Both the anti-Semitic and the ecumenical rhetoric of the Catholic Church capitalize on this shared inventional resource. St. Bernard, for example, defended his claim that Jewish comprehension was "ox-like" by quoting Isaiah: "The ox knows his owner, and the ass knows his lord's crib: Israel has not known me, my people have no comprehension." "You see, Jew," Bernard observed, "I am milder to you than your own prophet. I have put you on a par with beasts; he subordinates you to them."[19] In contrast, Pope John XXIII previewed the ecumenism of his reign by drawing into his coronational sermon a statement of reconciliation from the New Testament: "I am Joseph, your brother."[20] Later, he would greet Jewish guests with the same declaration.[21]

Before explicating the body, fertility, light, water, and treasure metaphors employed by Paul VI, I shall trace each to the New Testament and shall note its subsequent use by notable rhetors in the Church's history.

The Body Metaphor

The body metaphor is deeply engrained in the Catholic Church's rhetorical tradition. In his first letter to the Corinthians (12:12) and in his letter to the Romans (12:5), St. Paul notes that "we, though many, are one body in Christ, and individually members one of another." The metaphor inheres in the works of Augustine and many of the Church fathers as well as in the writings of Thomas Aquinas. In his encyclical *Mystici Corporis* (1943) Pope Pius XII defended the belief that the Church is the mystical body of Christ.[22]

[19] "Sermones in cantica," *PL*, 183, 1068a.

[20] "Pope and Pastor" (4 Nov. 1958), in *The Encyclicals and Other Messages of John XXIII* (Washington, D.C.: TPS Press, 1964), p. 16. John stated: "For a new pontiff, in the trials of this life, is like the son of the patriarch Jacob, who welcomed his suffering brothers and showed his love and compassion for them, saying: 'I am Joseph . . . your brother.'"

[21] Edward A. Synan, *The Popes and the Jews in the Middle Ages* (New York: Macmillan, 1965), p. 4. This is the statement Joseph used to reveal his identity to his brothers who had earlier sold him into slavery. By casting his Jewish guests in the role of Joseph's brothers, John inadvertently may have alienated them.

[22] Plus XII, "Mystici corporis," (29 Iun. 1943) in *Enchiridion Symbolorum,* 3800ss, pp. 745-53.

The body metaphor characterizes the Church in vocabulary drawn from universal human experience. Like each of the papal metaphoric clusters, this metaphor simultaneously creates inventional resources and imposes inventional constraints. Is the Church male or female? Young or old? Healthy or infirm? Living or dead? Strong or frail? What nourishes, wounds, inspires the Church?

At one level, the faithful are the Church. They are her cells. At another level, the faithful are the "children" of the Church.[23] The Church's parental role expresses itself in the paternal tone of papal documents, which, in turn, implies an audience "docile" to Church commands.

The metaphor of "mother Church" permits Paul to turn the primal taboo of matricide against dissenters: "The sharpest pain which a mother's heart can feel is that caused by one of her children. . . . A mother's heart can have no sweeter comfort than that strong and delicate comfort which comes from her sincere children."[24]

The body metaphor provides a lexicon through which attacks on the Church can be filtered. Dissenters, for example, can be linked to the ultimate sacrilege: crucifixion of Christ. Thus Paul contends that attacks on traditional teachings "lacerate" the church; the church is "crucified" by dissent: "We must at least suffer at the sight of the lacerations that have taken place in the mystical and visible body of Christ—the one and only Church."[25] The Church "is suffering at the defection and scandal of certain ecclesiastics and religious, who are crucifying the Church today."[26]

Diagnoses and prognoses of the health of the Church are the inevitable by-product of the metaphor. Critics "delight in describing fanciful symptoms of decrepitude and predicting ruin."[27] Critics charge that the Church is a "dried up skeleton,"[28] that "sclerosis . . . crystallizes Christianity into rigid, outworn formulas."[29] The body metaphor defines change as "renewal, a continuous, vital process in a living organism like the Church [which] cannot be a metamorphosis."[30] The Church is sustained by adherence to her principles: "The Church is not old, she is ancient; time does not subdue her, and, if she is faithful to the intrinsic and extrinsic principles of her mysterious existence, it rejuvenates her."[31]

The danger of paralysis comes not from audience to authentic tradition but rather from attacks on the Church. In the wake of dissent over *Humanae Vitae*, the Church was afflicted with "internal and external maladies"[32]; "a feeling of uncertainty is running through the Church's body like a feverish shudder. Could it be

---

[23] Description of the faithful as children or as sons and daughters occurs frequently in the concluding exhortations of Paul's speeches: Cf. 1 July 1970, p. 273; 2 Sept. 1970, p. 309; 19 Mar. 1968, p. 58; 26 Apr. 1969, p. 90. For analysis of corporal metaphors in both secular and religious Latin literature, see Ernst Robert Curtius, *European Literature and the Latin Middle Ages*, trans. Willard R. Trask (New York: Pantheon, 1953), pp. 136–38.

[24] 29 Apr. 1970, p. 158.

[25] 22 Jan. 1969, p. 18.

[26] 2 Apr. 1969, p. 70.

[27] 20 Sept. 1972, p. 295.

[28] 3 Nov. 1971, p. 173.

[29] 2 July 1969, p. 181.

[30] 8 Nov. 1972, p. 161.

[31] 2 July 1969, p. 179.

[32] 8 Oct. 1969, p. 252.

possible that this might paralyze the Catholic Church's characteristic charism, her charism of sureness and vitality."[33] Half a decade later, Paul suggested that the Church had survived the buffeting inflicted by reaction to *Humanae Vitae*—"Today, the Church is alive."[34]

Three related but infrequently used metaphors underscore Paul's perception of both the relationship between and the interdependence of the pope and the Church: the Church as a building,[35] as a flock,[36] and as a symphony.[37] The Church analogized as a flock stresses both the dependence of the individual adherent and the pastoral role of the pope as shepherd; the Church as a building or temple emphasizes the pope's role as the foundation of the Church and his tie to the rock— Peter; the Church as symphony posits the need for individual adherents to work in concert with each other under the conductor—the pope.

The Fertility-Sterility Metaphor

The New Testament is suffused with metaphors of fertility and sterility. In order to demonstrate the power of faith (Matthew 21:18-22), Christ curses a fig tree causing it to wither. In Matthew 13 Christ develops three related fertility parables: the seed (part of which was eaten by birds, part choked by thorns, part lodged in good soil) is likened to reception of the word of God; the devil is identi-fied as an enemy who sows weeds in a field planted with good seed (24-30, 36-43); and the reign of God is compared to a mustard seed, which, though small, grows to be a large plant (31-32).

The metaphor of the vine and the branches (John 15:1-8) expresses content comparable to that expressed by the body metaphor: "I am the vine," Christ notes, "you are the branches. He who lives in me and I in him, will produce abundantly, for apart from me you can do nothing."

In papal rhetoric, the fertility-sterility metaphor typically expresses the genera-tion and degeneration of faith. Pope Boniface, for example, calls for an abundant "Harvest of faith" (*fructum fidei*).[38]

---

[33] 3 Dec. 1969, pp. 302-03.

[34] 23 June 1975, p. 319.

[35] The building metaphor generally develops the theme established in Matthew 16:18 ("On this rock I shall build my Church"). On 26 Aug. 1969 (p. 90), for example, Paul cited that passage and noted that visitors to the Vatican assure themselves that "the rock, the stone, on which [the Church] is built is not worn away by the centuries."

[36] 28 June 1972, p. 92. On 8 July 1970 (p. 275), Paul devoted an entire sermon to the pastoral character of the Second Vatican Council. In that speech Paul noted that the pastor's "authority is not conferred by the flock . . . He does not let himself be led by the flock, con-trary to what is favoured by a certain view of authority today."

[37] On 5 Nov. 1969 (pp. 276-77), Paul spoke of a spirit of rebellion which "has made more than a little headway into the symphony of the Church's life." In the same speech, he noted that "The Church is like a symphony; not even a leading instrumentalist in an orchestra may play as and what he wishes."

[38] Pope Boniface to Aethelburgh in Bede's *Ecclesiastical History*, ed. Bertram Colgrave and R. A. B. Mynors (Oxford: Clarendon, 1969), p. 175. By charging the popes with care for the faith (seed), the fertility metaphor enables popes to express their view of their relationship to the Church in this cluster. The decisive role Pope Innocent III arrogated to himself is evident in his statement that "we have been assigned by the Lord to uproot what must be uprooted and to plant what must be planted" (*PL*, 215, 1293 b). The metaphor of the faith as seed dominates Paul's apostolic letter on seminaries ("Summi Dei Verbum," 4. Nov. 1963 [Washington, D.C.: National Catholic Welfare Conference, 1963]).

Like the body metaphor, the fertility-sterility metaphor identifies the Church with life. In the rhetoric of Paul VI, the gnarled olive tree, a more apt image of the centuries old Church, replaced the New Testament's image of the fledgling Church as a vine and branches: "The Church is an age-old olive tree, with a scarred and twisted trunk. This might seem to be an image of age and suffering, rather than of springtime vitality, but you show that the Church of our times is capable of putting forth vigorous shoots and new promise of unthought of and abundant fruit."[39] The Holy Spirit is the sap which enlivens the tree (the Church). The Church is an "age-old institution which, still alive and consistent with its roots, receives as impulse the divine sap of the Holy Spirit always flowing through it towards the blossoming of a new spring."[40] Tradition is the "root"[41] which anchors the tree and which guarantees its nourishment. Tradition is "life giving."[42] "Like a tree whose roots are firm and spreading, she draws from herself her own spring-time in every period of history."[43] The Church cannot survive detached from tradition: "The necessary and opportune innovations, to which we must aspire, cannot come from an arbitrary detachment from the living root that Christ transmitted to us."[44] It is "only by faithfulness to its roots ... to its own centuries old, apostolic and evangelical tradition, that the Roman Church, and with it the Catholic Church, can preserve its perpetual and ever youthful vitality."[45] The word of God, preserved in Church tradition, "in its authenticity, is not for that reason dry and sterile, but fruitful and alive, and meant to be listened to not merely passively, but to be lived."[46]

The faithful face only two choices: Accept the traditional teaching of the Church or break with the source of their life: "The Church is Christ continued in time. We may not break away from her, just as a bough, wishing to burst into new flower in the springtime, may not separate itself from the tree and the root whence it draws its life ... It is a question of either belonging faithfully and fruitfully to the Church's authentic and authoritative tradition or of cutting off from it mortally."[47] Whether the Church formally acknowledges the break or not, the sinner "cuts off by himself the vital flow that kept him united to the living plant of the Church."[48]

The Light-Dark Metaphor

Christ identified with light throughout the New Testament. "I am the way the truth and the light," he tells the apostles. "No one comes to the Father but through me" (John 14:6). Those who embrace Christ's message become "the light of the world" (Matthew 5:14). The prologue to the Gospel of John identifies truth and God with light and identifies darkness with rejection of God: "The light shines on in darkness, a darkness that did not overcome it" (John 1:5). Accordingly, St. Paul

[39] 26 Sept. 1970, p. 321.
[40] 8 Nov. 1972, p. 161.
[41] 29 Apr. 1970, p. 157.
[42] 18 Sept. 1968, p. 147.
[43] 2 July 1969, p. 179.
[44] Ibid., p. 180.
[45] 24 June 1971, p. 278.
[46] 19 Jan. 1972, p. 13.
[47] 12 Aug. 1970, p. 295.
[48] 12 Mar. 1975, p. 34.

urges the Thessalonians (1:5:5) to be sons of light not darkness. Paul VI echoes that message:[49] "[S]ons of light, We want to call all of you, sons of day, not of the night or of darkness, as St. Paul says." Light is an unequivocally positive term.[50] Both the Church and Christ are *"lumen gentium"*—the light of peoples.[51] Employing this metaphor, Pope Boniface characterizes King Edwin's wife as "enlightened by the gift of eternal life."[52]

The light-dark metaphor is not unique to Christianity. Recall Plato's allegory of the cave and the deadly combat projected by Zoroastrianism between Light and Darkness.[53]

Osborn's analysis of the light-dark metaphor explains well the popes' use of that metaphor.[54] In the papal metaphoric network, darkness is identified with evil. Among the groups to whom Paul VI addresses his Christmas message in 1970, for example, are "you who are bewildered by the darkness of evil."[55]

Light is an apt analogue for tradition. A flame can be passed from candle to candle as it is in the Baptismal ritual. A beam of light is continuous.

In this network, conscience is an eye; an informed conscience is an eye guided by light. The conscience is an "eye which needs light"[56]; "subjective conscience is the first and immediate norm of our action, but it needs light to see what is the norm to follow, especially when the moral significance of an action is not self-evident."[57] Conscience not guided by the light may err: "But if conscience has lost its moral light, that is, its awareness of real good and real evil, an awareness that cannot be separated from the pole of the Absolute, from religious reference, where can it lead? What experiences may it wrongly authorize?"[58]

The metaphoric nexus between light and faith is underscored in Jesus' cure of the blind man possessed of the devil (Matthew 12:22-28); the blind men who expressed belief in Him (Matthew 9:27-31); and the blind men at Jericho, who, after being cured, became His followers (Matthew 20:29-34). The connection between sightedness and faith is clearest in the cure near the pool of Siloam. Before restoring a man's sight, Jesus declared, "I am the light of the world" (John 9:5-6). Consistent with this usage, those who reject the faith often are charged by the popes with blindness. In his famous tome to the Council of Chalcedon (451). for example, Pope Leo accused Eutyches of deliberately blinding himself to the "brightness of translucent truth."[59]

Those who reject the Church or her tradition are, in Paul VI's metaphoric network, blind: "The human eye does not see today even though the light is the

[49] 13 Nov. 1968, p. 187.
[50] 2 Mar. 1970, p. 95.
[51] 6 May 1970, p. 178.
[52] Pope Boniface to King Edwin of England in Bede's *Ecclesiastical History*, p. 169.
[53] Cf. Robert Zaehner, *Dawn and Twilight of Zoroastrianism* (London: London and Weidenfeld, 1961).
[54] Michael Osborn, "Archetypal Metaphor in Rhetoric: The Light-Dark Family," pp. 115-26.
[55] 25 Dec. 1970, p. 451.
[56] 7 Oct. 1970, p. 353.
[57] 28 Mar. 1973, p. 44.
[58] 12 Feb. 1975, p. 24.
[59] Pope Leo, "Tome of Leo" in "Collect. Novariem: de re Eutychis," *Acta conciliorum oecumenicorum* (Strasbourg: 1914-), II, V, ii.

same as before."[60] In fact, the Gospel suggests that some may prefer darkness to light (John 3:19). The notion reverberates in Paul VI's discourse: "Their eyes have been darkened, then blinded. They have dared to think that their own blindness was the death of God."[61] Modern men "walk like blind men: men who are deliberately blind, very often."[62] The image of self-inflicted blindness haunts classical tragedy and mythology. Paul draws on these associations when he likens modern humanity to a "blind giant."[63]

Treasure-Patrimony Metaphor

The body, fertility, and light metaphors implicitly argue the value of tradition by positing a world in which it is indispensable. The treasure-patrimony metaphor underscores both the value and the changelessness of tradition.

The parable of the prodigal son (Luke 15:11–32) details the story of a patrimony squandered and regained. In a related parable (Luke 20:9–17) tenants kill the heir of the owner of the vineyard thinking that by so doing they will inherit the property. Instead they are displaced.

A treasure metaphor also inheres in the New Testament. Jesus describes (Matthew 13:44) the "reign of God" in terms of a man who sold all he had in order to purchase the field in which he has found a treasure. Similarly, He advises (Luke 12:33), "Get . . . a never-failing treasure with the Lord which no thief comes near nor any moth destroys."

For Paul VI, tradition is an "impalpable treasure."[64] Tradition is "the wealth, the honour and the strength of our house, the Catholic Church."[65] The relationship between the Church and history does not "permit the Church to cast away the treasures of her march through time."[66] Transmission of tradition is described as receipt of an "inheritance,"[67] a "patrimony."[68] Tradition is valued; it is inherited; it must be preserved. The Church is defined by and draws her life from authentic tradition. Tradition "is not a weight to drag around, but it is a reserve of certainties and energies for the Church living in history."[69]

The person who rejects tradition spurns a patrimony and squanders a treasure. The desire to change everything risks "the squandering of the patrimony of tradition."[70]

The very nature of the Church is defined by faithful adherence to tradition: "it must be entirely founded upon the identical, essential, constitutional patrimony of the self-same teaching of Christ, as professed by the authentic and authoritative tradition of the one true Church."[71]

[60] 26 Aug. 1970, p. 304.
[61] 20 May 1970, p. 210.
[62] 12 Dec. 1973, p. 171.
[63] 3 Oct. 1973, p. 137.
[64] 11 Apr. 1970, p. 123.
[65] 5 Nov. 1969, pp. 277–78.
[66] 5 Mar. 1973, p. 233.
[67] 5 Nov. 1969, p. 276; 29 Oct. 1972, p. 303; 17 Sept. 1969, p. 239.
[68] 30 Aug. 1972, p. 125; 31 July 1969, p. 204.
[69] 11 Apr. 1970, p. 123.
[70] 30 Aug. 1972, p. 125.
[71] 31 July 1969, p. 203.

By safeguarding tradition, Paul VI legitimizes his claim to be the successor of Peter. For that reason, more than any other, a pope cannot break casually from past papal teaching. Tradition "is above all the vehicle which brings us doctrine and the Apostolic Succession. We cannot have Christ present today without acknowledgment of the historical and human channel which leads us back to the source of his appearance in the Gospel."[72] The argument that the legitimacy of the Church is certified by her transmission of tradition is a potent one. It is an argument suited to expression in a metaphor of conservation and inheritance. Tertullian, for example, argued that the Church is the "legitimate conservator of the inheritance of tradition" passed from God through Christ and from Christ through the apostles; heretics are "robbers."[73] The conviction that the pope is the successor of the apostles is implicit in the inheritance metaphor. St. Gregory of Nyssa, for instance, claims that "we have, as a more than adequate guarantee of our teaching, tradition, that is, the truth which has come down to us by succession from the apostles, as an inheritance."[74] Indeed, by insinuating the notion of succession into an argument, the inheritance metaphor subtly underscores the papal claim to primacy. Consequently, it is not surprising that Pope Clement VI's bull *Unigenitus*[75] (1343) and Sixtus IV's *Salvator noster*[76] (1476)—defenses of indulgences laced with treasurer-inheritance metaphors—were marshaled by subsequent popes to battle the Reformation.

The strength of the patrimony-treasure metaphor is its ability to suggest the transmission of something valuable from past to present. Two less developed metaphoric networks reinforce this notion: tradition as a "thread"[77] and tradition as a bridge spanning the centuries.[78]

Water-Journey Metaphor

Although Paul VI does contend that humanity lives in "the stream"[79] of the Church's tradition, tradition is not as focal an element in his development of the water-journey metaphor as it is in his other functionally similar metaphoric clusters. In the Bible as well as in contemporary papal rhetoric, water is an ambivalent symbol. The flood purged the world of evil by destroying all life not safeguarded by the ark. Yet many of the miracles of the New Testament (e.g., transforming water to wine, walking on water, calming the seas, guiding fishless nets to a catch) were associated with water. Water is a symbol of both transformation and cleansing. "No one can enter into God's kingdom," Christ tells Nicodemus, "without being begotten of water and spirit" (John 3:4). Christ's public life begins with His baptism in the river Jordan by John the Baptist. At the close of His public ministry, Christ washes the feet of the apostles.

[72] 5 Nov. 1969, p. 277.
[73] *De Praescriptionibus* 37, *PL*, 2, 50, b ff.
[74] *Contra Eunomium*, c. 4. *Patrologiae graecae cursus completus*, ed. J. P. Migne (Paris: 1857 et seq). n. pag.
[75] *Enchiridion Symbolorum*, 1025ss, p. 300.
[76] Ibid., 1398, p. 346.
[77] 6 Oct. 1971, p. 157.
[78] 28 Oct. 1970, p. 371.
[79] 10 Jan. 1973, p. 3. For an analysis of nautical metaphors in secular Latin literature, see Curtius, pp. 128–30.

Water both sustains life and signifies death in the New Testament. On the road to Calvary, Christ is offered water by sympathizers; the crucified Christ cries, "I thirst." Yet Christ's death is confirmed when water and blood issue from His pierced side.

The ambivalence of the metaphor is evident in the rhetoric of Pope Paul VI. Paul speaks of a "flood of repentence, of redemption, of rebirth in the paschal mystery,"[80] yet cautions that "In our times, both youth and adults stand in the path of a virtually ceaseless flood."[81] Similarly, evil is likened to "an ocean flooding in."[82] Water can cleanse, but it can also dilute. Paul notes that "Christian life begins with baptism" and asks, "Do we live our baptism?"[83] Yet in another section of the same address he observes, "We have so often watered down and emptied our specific title of Christian that we have deprived it of its vitality and lustre."

Symbolic antecedents of the metaphor of the Church as a ship can be found in both the Old and New Testaments. The ark shelters those spared by God. Christ transforms fisherman into "fishers of men." The image of a boat is imprinted on the coat of arms of Peter and impressed in the papal seal ("the fisherman's ring"). This seal authenticates the most important papal documents.

The water-journey metaphoric cluster creates a vocabulary to describe threats to the Church which is rivaled only by the body-disease cluster. Does the ship face a tempest or calm seas? Is shipwreck imminent? Is the ship caught in an irresistible current?[84]

The Church, Paul VI notes, "as an historical phenomenon is like Simon Peter's boat, tossed by the storm."[85] Will modern humanity permit the rudder of conscience to guide it to the harbor? The Church offers the shipwrecked "a secure foundation." "Without God, everything is cut adrift."[86]

Life, too, is likened to a ship whose rudder is "moral judgment"[87]: "A man without a conscience is like a ship without a rudder."[88] A person who rejects the Church is like a sailor who throws his compass overboard: "Man thinks he has got rid of a sense of sin, but in reality he has only cast away the compass guiding his own conscience and vital development."[89] Such a person "resembles a seafarer who has lost his way on the high seas, has lost contact with the shore."[90]

Like the body in a disease-ridden world, the light in darkness, and the seed on hard ground, the Christian in this metaphor faces a hostile environment—stormy seas. "Can a Christian, who wishes to be consistent and faithful to his adherence to

[80] 25 Mar. 1970, p. 97.
[81] 21 Apr. 1972, p. 239.
[82] 25 Mar. 1970, p. 95.
[83] 1 Apr. 1970, pp. 110-11.
[84] The metaphor also is able to express the Church's well-being and the pope-as-captain's relationship to the church-as-ship. For example, Pope Gregory the Great wrote [Epist. 1:4 *Monumenta Germaniae historica, Epistolarum* (Berlin: 1891-), 1, 5, 4 f.], "Unworthy and infirm I have taken charge of a ship that is old and battered."
[85] 22 Oct. 1969, p. 264.
[86] 18 Mar. 1971, p. 245.
[87] 12 July 1972, p. 97.
[88] 2 Aug. 1972, p. 108.
[89] 25 Mar. 1970, p. 96.
[90] 18 May 1970, p. 203.

the Catholic religion, plunge into the powerful, stormy sea of modern life?"[91] Paul asks. His answer is yes. However, those who abandon the faith, encapsulated in tradition, will "find themselves shipwrecked again in the mysterious sea of time, no longer having any notion of, or the capacity for the journey to be undertaken."

Interpretation

These self-consistent metaphoric networks communicate a world in which: (1) Authentic tradition is indispensable (as light is to seeing, as roots are to a tree, as a body is to its members, as patrimony is to heirs); (2) The Church and her tradition exist in a threatening environment (the body is plagued by illness, the tree by hard ground, the light by darkness, the boat by a storm, the treasure by potential squanderers); (3) The line carrying tradition must not be broken (as nourishment must be carried from the roots to the branches, life must be carried to the members of the body; a beam of light must be continuous to carry light to its destination; an inheritance must be transmitted from generation to generation); (4) Rejecting authentic tradition is self-destructive (a branch severed from a tree, self-inflicted blindness, a child who rejects an inheritance). Rejecting tradition brings death, darkness, and poverty. Accepting tradition brings life, light, and wealth.

These metaphors dispose those Catholics who find them compelling to accept the teaching authority of the Church. In each cluster the role assigned auditors entails free will; Catholics may cast away the compass of conscience, cut themselves from the life-giving tree or life-sustaining body, blind themselves, or spurn their patrimony. If they are not to destroy themselves, however, Catholics in each cluster must be receptive to and willing to act in accordance with the teaching of the Church.

Although in important respects each metaphoric cluster mirrors the others, each cluster more cogently than the others expresses some facet of the papal concept of tradition: the fertility-sterility metaphor—generation and degeneration; the body metaphor—the organic interconnectedness of the Church's members; the water-journey metaphor—the function of conscience; the light-dark metaphor—the portentous freedom to reject tradition; the patrimony-treasure-metaphor—the value of tradition and the need to preserve and transmit it. Expressing tradition in five distinct metaphoric clusters or networks enables popes to transcend the inventional limitations imposed by one cluster by electing to communicate through a more apt one.

Occasionally, however, no single self-consistent cluster is able to convey a pope's intended message. Pope Paul VI's mixed metaphors simply draw expressive elements from different metaphoric clusters. Paul declares, for example, that those who abandon tradition "could lose the *treasure* of faith, which has its human *roots* in certain moments of past history, to find ourselves *shipwrecked* again in the mysterious *sea* of time, no longer having any notion of, or the capacity for the *journey* to be undertaken."[92] Paul VI's mixed metaphors reveal the strengths

---

[91] 15 Oct. 1975, p. 121.
[92] 29 Oct. 1972, p. 303. Emphasis added.

of the elements he adopts and the limitations of the elements he abandons.[93] In the example cited, the water-journey metaphor dominates. The "anchor," that cluster's equivalent of "roots," cannot communicate and in fact precludes the notion that tradition transmits life. Hence, Paul mixes the metaphor by interposing into it "roots" from the fertility-sterility complex. Paul also alloys the treasure and water complexes. Of itself, the water-journey metaphoric complex lacks a term with which to express the value of tradition. Since a ship could safeguard a treasure, the water-journey and treasure-patrimony clusters, in this instance, complement one another.

When the vision of the Church expressed in these five clusters is overlaid on Pope Paul VI's self-expressive metaphors, a graphic picture of the papacy emerges.

In the papal metaphoric universe, the popes' function is tutelary. The Church does "not invent her doctrine; she is a witness, a custodian, an interpreter, a transmitter."[94] Christ speaks through tradition. In the voice of the Church is the "echo of Christ's voice."[95] Consequently, Catholics should be docile to tradition.[96]

In a sermon commemorating the ninth anniversary of his election, Paul confessed that, confronted by challenges to his traditional stands, he consoled himself with a passage from his predecessor Pope Leo I: *"dabit virtutem, qui contulit dignitatem"* (he who conferred that dignity will provide the strength).[97] Paul expressed the conviction he shared with Leo in a nautical and a theatrical metaphor that argued explicitly that the pope is Christ's surrogate. Employing a nautical metaphor struck by another of his predecessors, Paul reminded himself and his audience that the Church had weathered storms before: "It brings to Our mind the sorrowful words of Our great predecessor, St. Gregory; 'At one moment the waves beat against us, at another from the side the foaming mountains of the sea swell up, at another from the stern the storm pursues us. In the midst of all this with troubled mind I am driven at times to steer into the very heart of the storm, at times, turning the ship aside, to steer away from the menacing waves. I groan.'" Before rehearsing Gregory's agony, Paul affirmed his conviction that Christ would save the Church just as He saved Apostle's fishing boat: "this symbolical ship, the

---

[93] See Paul's observation (18 Oct. 1975, pp. 382–83), that "if the evangelical values are too often cut adrift from their moorings, geared to purely earthly objectives, they remain rooted in the soul of most of these European peoples." Note also Paul's contention (21 Apr. 1971, p. 59) that, "As the bearer of inexhaustible treasures, she [Church] must be always eagerly engaged in the fruitful outpouring of her truths and charisms." Or note Paul's observation (20 Sept. 1972, p. 295), "This venerable Mother of ours, whom some people today, even among her sons, take as the butt of harsh pitiless criticism; about whom some delight in describing fanciful symptoms of decrepitude, and predicting ruin: here we see her, on the contrary, bursting continuously into bud and blossoming." The theory offered in the text of this essay explains the mixed metaphors of other popes as well. In his preview of *Mater et Magistra*, for example, Pope John XXIII observed, "Pope Leo . . . wanted to dig into the treasures of the age-old teaching of the Church and bring forth the just and holy doctrine, the enlightening truth that would supply direction to the social order according to the needs of his time" (in *The Encylicals and Other Messages of John XXIII*, p. 228).

[94] 19 Jan. 1972, p. 13.

[95] 17 Feb. 1972, p. 225.

[96] 30 Oct. 1968, p. 179: "Lord, let my faith . . . not have any better guarantee than in docility to Tradition and to the authority of the magisterium of holy Church."

[97] 21 June 1972, p. 87. The passage of Leo's is in "Sermo II," *PL*, 54, 143.

Church, feels the buffeting of the storm characteristic of our time, which sometimes draws from our lips the imploring cry of the terrified disciples: "Save us, Lord; we are perishing' (Mt. 8:25.)"[98] Paul explicitly assured the audience that Christ safeguards the Church when he invited his listeners to "enjoy the tranquility that we ourself experience at the thought that it is not our weak and inexpert hand that is at the helm of Peter's boat, but that of the Lord Jesus, invisible but strong and loving."[99]

Before embarking on his trip to the Far East in 1970, Paul developed a metaphor, comparable to the nautical one, which—more clearly than any other in his papacy—detailed his relationship to the Church, Christ, and the modern world.[100] That speech described a "drama" whose "scene is history, our own history, our own time, today." The scene is "full of light and darkness." Three actors control the stage: the people of today, who are "giants yet they totter weakly and blindly, in agitation and fury in search of rest and order"; the pope, who is "the apostle, the messenger of the Gospel"; and Christ, "the actor who stands above it all and fills the whole stage wherever He is welcomed, by a distinct yet not uncustomary way for human knowledge: The way of faith."

By labeling themselves "the servants of the servants of God" and by emphasizing their personal unworthiness to succeed Peter, popes traditionally have downplayed their own significance. Such commonplace expressions of papal humility stress that Christ, not the pope, is the source of papal power. The passage from Paul's speech that follows is consistent with but more pronounced than the ritualized expressions of humility characteristic of his predecessors. In Paul's scenario he is

> small, like an ant, weak, unarmed as tiny as a *quantite negligeable*. [*Piccolo come una formica, debole, inerme, minimo fino alla quantite negligeable*.] He tries to make his way through the throng of peoples; he is trying to say something. He becomes unyielding [*ostinato*], and tries to make himself heard; he assumes the appearance [*aspetto*] of a teacher, a prophet. He assures them that what he is saying does not come from himself, but is a secret [*arcana*] and infallible [*infallibile*] word, a word with a thousand echoes, resounding in the thousand languages of mankind. But what strikes us most in the comparison we make between this personage and his surroundings, is disproportion: in number, in quality, in power, in means, in topicality . . . But that little man—you will have guessed who he is: the apostle, the messenger of the Gospel—is the witness. In this case it is the Pope, daring to pit himself against mankind. David and Goliath? Others will say Don Quixote . . . A scene irrelevant, outmoded, embarrassing, dangerous, ridiculous. This is what one hears said: and the appearances

[98] 15 Dec. 1969, p. 313. The passage of St. Gregory's is in his forty-third epistle (*PL*, 77, 497).

[99] 21 June 1972, p. 86.

[100] 25 Nov. 1970, pp. 410–13. The speech in the original Italian is located in *L'Osservatore Romano*: Pope Paul VI, "Messaggero del Vangelo il papa in Estremo Oriente," *L'Osservatore Romano*, 26 Nov. 1970, p. 1. As Curtius contends (pp. 138–44), theatrical metaphors inhere in the vocabulary of both Churchmen and secular writers in the Middle Ages. The passage cited is Paul's most extended use of the metaphor.

seem to justify these comments. But, when he manages to obtain a little silence and attract a listener, the little man speaks in a tone of certainty which is all his own.

The pope argues metaphorically that his power resides in the message he carries. Yet many fail to comprehend that message. He utters "inconceivable things, mysteries of an invisible world which is yet near us . . . Some laugh; others say to him: we will hear you another time, as they said to Paul (Acts 17:32-33) . . . Some perceive [correctly] that the word is the speaker's only in the sense that he is an instrument": It is the Word of Another. The other is the third actor on the stage: Christ. The pope is His representative, His spokesman. By implication then the pope must be David and not Don Quixote. If the metaphor were extended, one might ask, "Will the pope slay the giant which is mankind?" Armed by Christ, the pope undoubtedly could. But Paul neither asks nor answers that question. Indeed Paul suggests that if humankind adopts a proper role—that of an innocent child—the conflict between David and Goliath will be transformed into the loving encounter of a parent and child. The world, according to Paul, is "so corrupt and cruel [so like Goliath?] when it decides to be content with itself, and so innocent and so lovable when it is evangelically childlike (*evangelicamente bambino*)."

In the conclusion of the narrative, Paul suggested that the drama which he had described transcends his papacy: "This is the perennial drama [*la scena perenne*] which develops over the centuries, and which finds in our journey an instant of indescribable reality."

Paul's self-decriptive nautical and theatrical metaphors complement each other. In both, Paul VI is a weak, tormented person in a hostile environment who draws both his significance and his strength from Christ. The theatrical metaphor argues that humankind ought to attend to Paul because he speaks for Christ. The nautical image contends that Catholics ought to accept Paul's leadership because his actions are guided by Christ.

In the metaphoric universe Paul creates, the pope is not a tyrant imposing his will on the Church. Although the pope appears to be a teacher and a prophet, he is instead a frail messenger who believes that Christ speaks through him. When viewed against the backdrop created by the five examined clusters and his self-expressive metaphors, Paul's contention that he, for example, *could not* approve artificial methods of birth regulation is clarified. In the metaphoric world which Paul projects, change in a doctrinal tradition defended throughout the Church's history is not merely unlikely, it is inconceivable.

THE METAPHORS OF EDMUND G. BROWN, JR.

Like human beings in general, politicians root their perception of the present in the past. The historical analogues which politicians forge reveal their interpretation of themselves in a given historical context. But while politicians generally compare themselves to actual historical figures, Edmund G. Brown Jr., pictures himself in metaphors drawn primarily from fiction and myth.

Gerald Ford's presidency was calculated in its development of a Truman analogue;[101] and, in 1972, Edmund Muskie ran in Lincolnesque images.[102] Occasionally the press and politicians cast an event in antagonistic analogues, creating competing claims on the collective consciousness. While the Republican leaders, for example, were casting the 1976 Republican convention in terms of the ultimate harmony of 1960, the press was casting it in the ruins of 1964. Brown's campaign opened in a scenario of competing analogues. The press labeled him "Lochinvar,"[103] but, in contrast, Brown described himself in deterministic, isolative metaphors which, in the main, were either classical or fictive.

The president "is not a Santa Claus with a bag of tricks,"[104] does not have a "magic wand,"[105] cannot "pull a rabbit—a technological fix—out of the hat,"[106] does not dispense "patent medicines."[107] "He is not a 'superman.'"[108] The president is "just a human being"[109] who wakes up in the morning and goes to bed at night. The de-mythologizing metaphors of the presidency began in the Maryland primary in the first person ("I am not a Santa Claus")[110] but extended in the Rhode Island primary to anyone who is or would be president (a more effective rhetorical posture since Brown could not then be cast in the role of Scrooge play-

---

[101] Ford sought opportunities to forge a link between his presidency and Truman's. In his first State of the Union address (15 Jan, 1975, text provided by White House Press Office) Ford quoted from the State of the Union address Truman had delivered the year Ford was sworn in as a freshman Congressman. A bust of Truman was displayed in the Oval Office during Ford's tenure. In a speech dedicating a statue of Truman in the Independence Square Courthouse (8 May 1976, text provided by the White House Press Office), Ford rehearsed his relationship with Truman and drew themes of Truman's into his own presidential campaign (i.e., "[H]e often said the president was the only person in Washington whose job is to lobby on behalf of all of the American people"; "[H]e was never afraid of the heat in the kitchen"). The analogy to Truman was intended to transform perceptions of Ford's incompetence into perception of him as a plainspoken, common man who, like Truman, would be vindicated by history.

[102] Robert Squier, who produced the Muskie election eve broadcast in 1970 and the televised commercials run on Muskie's behalf in the early primaries of 1972, noted that parallels between Muskie and Lincoln were deliberately underscored. (Speech to Political Communication Seminar, University of Maryland, 14 Oct. 1974).

[103] Cf. Lloyd Shearer, "Hi! My Name's Jerry Brown, and I'm Running for President," *Parade*, 6 June 1976, p. 4. Shearer described Brown as "the bachelor Lochinvar from the Far West."

[104] Speech at the University of Maryland, College Park, 5 May 1976. See, also, *Face the Nation*, 9 May 1976 (transcript from audiotape): "I'm not trying to say that I have a secret bag of tricks that will solve all the problems."

[105] Question and Answer, Bowie, Maryland, 15 May 1976.

[106] Question and Answer after speech to Pennsylvania delegates at the Democratic National Convention, 13 July 1976. The author attended the Democratic National Convention where she functioned as a radio reporter. All speeches cited from the Convention were transcribed from audiotapes.

[107] Speech to non-California delegates for Brown, McAlpin Hotel, 13 July 1976, at the Democratic National Convention.

[108] Speech at rally for Prince George's County Delegates, College Park, Maryland, 11 Aug. 1976. Transcript from audiotape.

[109] University of Maryland, 5 May 1976.

[110] Brown used the metaphor in speeches in Baltimore before a blue collar audience (3 May 1976), in College Park before a student audience (5 May 1976), in Bowie before a white collar middle aged audience (15 May 1976), and in Silver Spring before an audience of businessmen and women (17 May 1976).

ing to someone else's Santa Claus). The metaphors are deprivative: They describe what he and the president are not and what they cannot do. Underlying these analogues is a metaphor of passage. Santa Claus, magic wands, bags of tricks, rabbits pulled from hats are part of the fantasy world of children. Brown consistently pairs "fantasy and unreality"[111] in his descriptions of policies to be disavowed. His metaphors disavow fantasy as well. He speaks of the decisions that mark "a mature individual and a mature nation"[112] and rejects "a child-like faith"[113] in technology and expertise. Brown assumes a parental role—shattering belief in childhood fantasies. That role is rendered clear in his description of his function as overseer of the cookie jar—who must make certain that everyone gets a fair share.[114]

Brown's metaphors argue that he, not his audience, ought to define the nature of the office he seeks. If the metaphors succeed, Brown, rather than the audience, will have defined the relationship into which it will have elected him.

In place of Santa Claus, Brown gives us Sisyphus. The metaphors in which he describes his present are sterile images of persons confronting overwhelming odds (including the unreasoning forces of fate or nature) and bordering on failure. He describes himself as one who is pushing a boulder up a hill (Sisyphus),[115] as a potential member of the Greek chorus,[116] as a little Dutch boy holding his finger in the dam.[117] Governmental corruption is described in terms of the curse on the House of Atreus,[118] political and educational degeneration in terms of monads.[119] Government in California is likened to a "beleaguered wagon train assaulted by

---

[111] The pairing is found in most of the speeches Brown delivered during the campaign. Although Brown claims that he is not an expert and that there are no certainties in politics, he clearly believes that reality exists, that he is in touch with it, and that he is obliged to communicate it to audiences. In a Platonic fashion, Brown advises audiences to "look behind the rhetoric for the reality" (Bowie, Md., 15 May 1976). See, also, *Face the Nation*, 9 May 1976: "I think that that is a very interesting issue because of the inherent inconsistency between what appears to be and what is." Reality is a God-term for Brown. He spoke in 1976 of political "realities," social "realities," ecological "realities," and "planetary realism." Infeasible political acts were "not real." For Brown, "reality" apparently is extrinsic, objective, and knowable.

Brown charges the president with responsibility for articulating a statement capable of permitting people to "see their own lives in terms of a greater vision and a future that fits into the reality of the changing balance of power in this country." (*Thoughts* [San Francisco: City Lights, 1976], p. 67.) At times, Brown's notion of "reality" seems to entail temporal participation in the Platonic forms: The work at hand "is to carry on the teaching, and get the young people working, and create some beauty and harmony and strength and stability" ("Caring and Clarity: Conversation with Gregory Bateson and Edmund G. Brown, Jr., Governor of California," *Co-Evolution Quarterly* [Fall 1975], p. 44.)

[122] Nationally televised address, 25 June 1976. Transcript obtained from Office of Governor, State of California. Contents of transcript checked by comparing them to audiotape of the speech.

[113] Speech to the Overseas Press Club, 13 July 1976. Transcript from audiotape.

[114] Speech at rally for Representative Herb Harris in Falls Church, Virginia, 12 Aug. 1976. Transcript from audiotape.

[115] Ibid.: "It's like rolling the stone up the hill everyday and it tends to roll back when you're finished."

[116] Jerry Brown, "Interview: Jerry Brown," *Playboy,* Apr. 1976, p. 187.

[117] Quoted by "USA: People and Politics," WETA (PBS) TV, 11 June 1976.

[118] Brown, *Playboy*, p. 187.

[119] Brown, *CoEvolution Quarterly*, p. 37.

special interests."[120] These metaphors are consonant with the philosophy of a governor who claims that the people will have to try harder just to slip back a little more slowly.[121] But as important is the self-portrait of Brown they paint. The role he assigns himself in these metaphors is an indispensable one; yet his metaphoric counterparts are powerless to change drastically their environment. They are responding to exigencies not creating them; they are filled with a stubborn, almost foolish, resolve; they face enormous odds, alone; if they fail, catastrophe follows. These uncluttered images, struck in sharp relief against a bleak background, suggest that in 1976, at least, Brown saw himself as an isolated individual, under siege. And to the extent that the metaphors in which he cast himself were metaphors describing the times, they graphically underscored his central theme by envisioning an era of limits.

Brown did not claim to be able to change reality but rather the ability to articulate it and to actualize already existing potential. He likened his role in the farm workers' bill to that of a midwife; "And I don't think I did anything other than—like a midwife—bring things along that were already there. At least that's the way I perceive. . . . You can't force things against nature."[122]

One who feels constrained by an uncontrollable reality must be viewed as a tragic figure. One who naively attempts to change the unchangeable has both comic and tragic potential. One who realizes that reality is unalterable but attempts to alter it anyway is a fool. However, the role each assigns rhetoric would differ.[123] A person, such as Brown, who feels constrained by an uncontrollable reality will test premises carefully to determine that they comport with reality and will move from those premises to a rhetoric of explication. Brown's rhetoric of an era of limits, difficult choices, lowered expectation, and a choice from among competing goods is consistent with this view.

Brown's vision of reality clashes with the role traditionally assigned politicians. Politicians are expected to effect social and economic change. Brown must redefine the role of the politician or fail. Hence, his attack on the view of the president as Santa Claus. In the world posited by Brown, rhetoric is not a vehicle for changing reality, because that is impossible, but rather for explaining the options reality presents. Thus rhetoric becomes expository, hence didactic. The politician becomes an educator.

By framing political experiences as lessons learned, Brown provided support for

[120] "Good-Morning America" ABC-TV, 26 Aug. 1976.

[121] Speech at a rally for Congressional Candidate Lanny Davis, Montogmery County, Md., 11 Aug. 1976. Transcript from audiotape.

[122] Brown, *CoEvolution Quarterly*, p. 44. Although Brown indicated that he used the term "midwife" in a Platonic sense, he was, at the time it was used, not aware of the rich role Plato assigned the midwife. Consequently, Brown's use of that metaphor does not undercut the contention that he viewed himself as unable drastically to alter events. His use of the midwife metaphor is consistent with his other self-expressive metaphors because Brown, who had not read the *Theatetus* at the time he employed the midwife metaphor (interview, Philadelphia airport, 25 Oct. 1976) was unaware of the midwife's responsibility for selecting the parents, hastening the delivery, and determining whether the fetus ought to be aborted. When asked to define the way in which his political actions resemble midwifery, Brown responded simply, "I draw things out. That's all politics is about—drawing things out" (ibid.).

[123] I am indebted to Karlyn Kohrs Campbell, who suggested these distinctions.

the interpretation that he viewed himself as an educator. The second sentence of his 6 Jan. 1975 inaugural asked, "What have we learned?"[124] During the primaries he repeatedly observed that the country was "ready to learn some new lessons."[125] For Brown, leadership is a didactic process: "You have to have some way to *explain* where the country is to those who live in it. Like theodocy, you have to *explain* history to those who are living it."[126] When used by politicians, the word "vision" is usually accompanied by an "ought" statement about the future. But if reality is inexorable, then the world of "ought" is the province of poets not politicians. In 1976 Brown consistently spoke of a vision of where the country *is* going not of where it *ought* to go. This suggested that his function was not suasory but expository: "When I say people are going to have to accept less, that's not a recommendation. It's description of reality."[127]

Brown's view that neither he nor government can drastically alter reality insulated him from failure. When a bill or idea which he had championed failed to win popular or legislative approval, he described what in any other lexicon would be a failure as "an idea whose time has not come."[128] (Even that notion presupposes special access to reality, for how else would he know that it was not instead an idea whose time had passed?)

The level of redundancy in Brown's addresses was symptomatic of their didactic nature as well. Brown's pairings of synonyms and closely related words suggest that he is attempting to ensure audience comprehension:[129] "big, whopping tax break," "the earth, the planet," "first and foremost," "swift, certain and sure," "finished to a conclusion," "effective, productive," "fantasy and unreality," "the linkage, the interconnectedness," "open, honest, candid," "break the continuity, the tradition," "risk and peril," "despair and hopelessness," "respect and reverence." When a less common term is paired with a more common synonym, the couplings assume a patronizing tone: "bandaids and palliatives," "exemplar and model," "bankruptcy and failure," "malaise, scepticism, cynicism," "scrutinize and analyze," "arcane . . . difficult to understand," "equality and egalitarianism," "pragmatism and a tradition of practicality," "wastes, pollutants," "mundane, day-to-day," "the interaction . . . the dialectic."

The lecture is the proper rhetorical outlet for Brown's vision of the presidency.

---

[124] Brown, "Inaugural Address," 6 Jan. 1975. Transcript provided by the Office of the Governor, State of California. Lew Werner, LeRoy Chatfield, and Elise Flynn of the Office of the Governor supplied me with copies of material by and about Brown.

[125] For instances of the theme "we are ready to learn new lessons" see the speech delivered at the rally for candidate Lanny Davis in Maryland, 11 Aug. 1976; and the speech delivered in Bowie, Md., 15 May 1976.

[126] Brown, *Thoughts*, p. 61, emphasis added. See, also, an interview with Brown published under the title "'The Chemistry Has Changed,'" *Time*, 31 May 1976, p. 10: "There's been a lot of flimflam. The role of the President is to describe what's possible and what isn't."

[127] George Skelton, "Brown Sounds Warning: Prepare to Work More, Receive Less," *Los Angeles Times*, 2 Sept., 1975, p. 24.

[128] Brown used the phrase in interviews with the press pool at the Governors' Conference in Washington, D.C., 27 Feb. 1978. The conference, held at the Hyatt Regency Hotel, was attended by the author.

[129] These examples are drawn from the 17 May 1976 speech in Silver Spring, Md., the televised address to the nation delivered on 25 June 1976, the speech to the National Press Club on 18 June 1976, and the speech to the Overseas Press Club on 13 July 1976. Transcript from audiotapes.

The Rhetoric of Pope Paul VI and Edmund G. Brown, Jr.

Brown's stock speeches during the 1976 campaign were lectures on government and politics. They contained *pensées* on the nature of the presidency (the president is not a Santa Claus), the nature of power (it is transitory), the nature of the vice-presidency (a frustrating office because one cannot avoid "turf battles"), the impact of Watergate and Vietnam on the nation's consciousness (they changed the way we view political reality), the way a governor approaches a budget (not line-by-line), the hazards of speaking of the moral and immoral (the words summon an emotional response which is potentially counterproductive), the nature of current political discourse (it is unclear, filled with cant, debased), the role of the press (it is the press's role, not his, to label and define), and the drawbacks of political campaigning (recycling rhetoric is boring). He issued monitions to audiences, prefacing statements about the "future of the planet" or the "survival of the species" with the instruction, "think about it."

Consequently, it is not surprising that Brown was described as a lecturer. "Brown was his usual self last night," noted an article in the *Washington Post*, "lecturing to the audience rather than begging for applause. At one point, while he was answering questions, someone asked him about his vision for the nation's future. After a five minute dissertation, the former seminarian concluded that ... "[130] When Brown said that he was not prepared to place his *imprimatur* on the BI bomber, audiences laughed. Yet, given his philosophy of the presidency, "imprimatur" may have been an appropriate word choice.

The tendency to lecture and the tendency to patronize are kindred. Despite such egalitarian symbolic acts as rejecting the governor's mansion, driving a Plymouth rather than a limousine, staying in a run-down hotel at the Democratic Convention, and flying tourist class during the campaign, a patronizing tone occasionally seeped from the public and interpersonal rhetoric of Edmund G. Brown, Jr. Brown, for example, closed his second state of the state address with a benediction that implied a superior-subordinate relationship with the legislature and evinced a paternal tone. He told them that he was proud of them and that the people could be proud of them.[131] Since Brown wrote that speech ("no speechwriters")[132] in advance of delivery, one may assume that he feels comfortable in a paternal rhetorical role. The uneasy sense that Brown views others as his intellectual inferiors was also present in an interchange with a reporter for a Maryland newspaper who criticized his 25 June televised address, noting that she was more impressed by his campaign speeches during the Maryland primary: "You didn't watch it all the way through. You must have turned it off before it was over," Brown said, and then added almost teasingly, "You just didn't understand it."[133] Taken together, the didactic tendencies in his speeches and the occasional patronizing tone corroborate the inference drawn from Brown's metaphoric networks—he views himself as an educator.

[130] Milton Coleman, "Jerry Brown Helps Davis' Md. Campaign," *Washington Post*, 12 Aug. 1976, p. E9.
[131] Edmund G. Brown, Jr., "Report to the Legislature," p. 5. Transcript provided by Office of the Governor, State of California.
[132] "Interview," 10 Aug. 1976, following a speech delivered by Brown on behalf of the candidacy of William Green for Senate in the Bellevue Stratford Hotel.
[133] Speech delivered at a rally on behalf of the candidacy of Congresswoman Gladys Spellman, College Park, Md, 11 Aug. 1976.

CONCLUSION

In addition to corroborating otherwise inconclusive verbal cues and revealing the rhetor's projected relationship with the audience, analysis of a rhetor's metaphoric lexicon enables a critic to ask four potentially fruitful questions: Do the metaphors which characterize a speaker or the rhetoric of institutions change over time, and, if so, how and by what apparent pressures? What sorts of metaphors are absent from the examined lexicon? Are the verbal and nonverbal metaphors of a rhetor consistent? To what extent, if at all, are the descriptive metaphors applied to rhetors consistent with their self-descriptive metaphors?

Analysis of a rhetor's metaphoric lexicon opens a means of monitoring symptomatic changes in the rhetoric over time. A critic unfamiliar with the traditional range of papal metaphors may not realize, for example, that "the people of God," a democratizing metaphor legitimized by the Second Vatican Council, is supplanting the "body" metaphor in the official rhetoric of Pope John Paul II.[134]

Indeed the absence of certain types of metaphors may be as significant and occasionally more significant than habitual use of other metaphors. For example, it is noteworthy that the pope who banned the pill as an artificial (*artificiose*) means of regulating birth[135] relied on metaphors coined in a prescientific agrarian age. The few technological metaphors Paul VI did employ tended to be negative. He warned, for example, that man "must be prevented from becoming only the mechanized caterer to a blind machine which devours the best of himself,"[136] worried that man could be "swept along by irrestible current of his inventions,"[137] condemned the "anaesthesia of moral conscience,"[138] and cautioned against "surgical simplifications, that sometimes destroy the traditional heritage of ecclesial life."[139] It is not surprising that a rhetor whose vocabulary prized fertility and scorned technology would ban the birth control pill. The lexicon expressed, enforced, and to some extent eventuated assumptions compatible with such a ban.

A focus on the metaphoric lexicon of a rhetor permits the critic to probe the consistency of those metaphors that have both verbal and nonverbal components. Some verbal and nonverbal metaphors mirror one another. For example, in 843 the patriarch of Constantinople employed a nonverbal light-dark metaphor when he cut the eyes from an icon to protest the Empress Theodora's reinstitution of iconolatry.[140] Even when the correspondence between verbal and nonverbal metaphors is inexact, it is possible to corroborate otherwise inconclusive rhetorical cues by comparing the consistency of verbal and nonverbal metaphoric behavior. For example, by donating the proceeds of his papal tiara to the poor and by stipulating that his funeral be simple, Pope Paul VI increased the credibility of his other metaphoric expressions of personal insignificance. Similarly, by accompanying the

---

[134]Where Paul VI would have employed a body metaphor, Pope John Paul II employs a metaphor of "the people of God." (Cf. *Redemptor hominis*. 21. in *The Pope Speaks*, 24 [1979], 141.)

[135]*Humanae Vitae* (Washington, D.C.: U.S. Catholic Conference, 1968), 17.1.

[136]10 June 1969, p. 147.

[137]Ibid.

[138]28 June 1971, p. 116.

[139]7 May 1969, p. 112.

[140]Bamber Gascoigne, *The Christians* (London: Johathan Cape, 1977), p. 47.

traditional papal blessing with a request that the assembled Cardinals bless each other, Pope John Paul II behaved in a manner consistent with his metaphor of the Church as "the people of God."

Whether or not the images or the invitation they imply are consciously intended, a rhetor's self-expressive metaphors do invite auditors to adopt their perspective. The existence of this invitation raises questions: What rhetorical behaviors call into being the metaphors employed by others to describe a rhetor? And to what extent are such characterizing metaphors consistent with a rhetor's self-description? For instance, by responding to questions with questions, by labeling his style "dialectical,"[141] by dividing the rhetorical universe into "reality" and "appearances," and by likening himself to a midwife, Jerry Brown solicits the characterization, "Socratic."[142] Such an ascetic image is compatible with Brown's self-expressive metaphors. By contrast, a credible characterization of Brown as Bacchic or Dionysian could subvert both Brown's self-description and his ability convincingly to champion an "era of limits."

In addition to facilitating a number of potentially productive critical moves, a focus on the metaphoric lexicon of rhetors may illumine understanding of the nature and function of metaphor. Questions awaiting answers include: Can the metaphoric options of a rhetor—the as yet unarticulated units in a cluster—be defined by a critic who understands the constraints operating in a situation? When a rhetor's lexicon includes a number of metaphoric clusters, does one cluster exercise esemplastic power over the others? What is the relationship among the metaphoric clusters in a rhetor's lexicon?

[141] Brown, *Playboy*, p. 80. When I termed his style "dialogic" instead, Brown rejected the label insisting that "dialectical" was the proper term (interview 10 Aug. 1976). In fact, Brown's "method" is not sufficiently vigorous to be considered "dialectical" in either a Platonic or Hegelian sense.
[142] Cf. "The Newest Face of '76," *Newsweek*, 31 May 1976, p. 24: "His basic approach to correcting the excess is a Socratic one of posing brilliant questions—and mourning the death of concrete answers."

Select Bibliography of Recent Critical Studies

Although the following Bibliography is quite extensive, it is not exhaustive. The bibliography represents a generous sample of critical studies published over the last decade and clearly demonstrates the rich variety of critical purposes, approaches and objects for study that are open to the rhetorical critic.

Amntson, Paul. "The Seventh of March Address: A Mediating Influence." *Southern Speech Communication Journal,* 40 (1975), 288–301.

Anderson, Floyd. "Hugh Latimer, Spokesman for a Christian Commonwealth." *Central States Speech Journal,* 21 (1970), 146–153.

Anderson, Ray Lynn. "The Rhetoric of the 'Report from Iron Mountain.'" *Speech Monographs,* 37 (1970), 219–231.

Andrews, James R. "The Rhetoric of Coercion and Persuasion: The Reform Bill of 1832." *Quarterly Journal of Speech,* 56 (1970), 187–195.

——. "Reflections of the National Character in American Rhetoric." *Quarterly Journal of Speech,* 57 (1971), 316–324.

——. "Spindles vs. Acres: Rhetorical Perceptions on the British Free Trade Movement." *Western Speech,* 38 (1974), 41–52.

Auer, J. Jeffery. "Special Report: Tom Corwin's 'Reply to General Crary': The Speech That Launched the Campaign of 1840 and Immortalized the Tippecanoe Legend." *Central States Speech Journal,* 30 (1979), 368–373.

Backes, James G. "J. S. Mill and His Preposterous Motion." *Western Speech,* 34 (1970), 90–99.

Baird, John E. "The Rhetoric of Youth in Controversy Against the Religious Establishment." *Western Speech,* 34 (1970), 53–61.

Barclay, Martha Thomson. "Distaff Campaigning in the 1964 and 1968 Presidential Elections." *Central States Speech Journal,* 21 (1970), 117–122.

Barefield, Paul A. "Republican Keynoters." *Speech Monographs,* 37 (1970), 232–239.

Bennett, W. Lance; Patricia Dempsey Harris; Janet K. Laskey; Alan H. Levitch; and Sarah E. Monrad. "Deep and Surface Images in the Construction of Political Issues: The Case of Amnesty." *Quarterly Journal of Speech,* 62 (1976), 109–127.

Benson, Thomas W. "Rhetoric and Autobiography: The Case of Malcolm X." *Quarterly Journal of Speech,* 60 (1974), 1–13.

Berens, John F. " 'Like a Prophetic Spirit': Samuel Davies, American Eulogists, and the Deification of George Washington." *Quarterly Journal of Speech,* 63 (1977), 290–297.

Berthold, Carol A. "Kenneth Burke's Cluster-Agon Method: Its Development and an Application." *Central States Speech Journal,* 27 (1976), 302–309.

Bezayiff, David. "Legal Oratory of John Adams: An Early Instrument of Protest." *Western Speech,* 40 (1976), 63–71.

Black, Edwin. "Electing Time." *Quarterly Journal of Speech,* 59 (1973), 125–129.

Bormann, Ernest G. "Fetching Good Out of Evil: A Rhetorical Use of Calamity." *Quarterly Journal of Speech,* 63 (1977), 130–139.

Bosmajian, Haig A. "The Sources and Nature of Adolph Hitler's Techniques of Persuasion." *Central States Speech Journal,* 25 (1974), 240–248.

Boyd, Newell D. "Gladstone, Midlothian and Stump Oratory." *Central States Speech Journal,* 30 (1979), 144–155.

Bradley, Bert E. "Refutation Techniques of John C. Calhoun." *Southern Speech Communication Journal,* 37 (1972), 413–423.

Brown, William R. "Will Rogers: Ironist as Persuader." *Speech Monographs,* 39 (1972), 183–192.

——. "The Prime-Time Television Environment and Emerging Rhetorical Visions." *Quarterly Journal of Speech,* 62 (1976), 389–399.

Brownlow, Paul C. "Winston Churchill and Fraternal Association: The History of a Phrase." *Central States Speech Journal,* 21 (1970), 242–247.

——. "The Pulpit and Black America: 1865–1877." *Quarterly Journal of Speech,* 58 (1972), 431–440.

——, and Beth Davis. "A Certainty of Honor: The Eulogies of Adlai Stevenson." *Central States Speech Journal,* 25 (1974), 217–224.

——. "The Northern Protests Pulpit and Andrew Johnson." *Southern Speech Communication Journal,* 39 (1974), 248–259.

Brummett, Barry. "Presidential Substance: The Address of August 15, 1973." *Western Speech,* 39 (1975), 249–259.

——. "Gary Gilmore, Power, and the Rhetoric of Symbolic Forms." *Western Speech,* 43 (1979), 3–13.

——. "Symbolic Form, Burkeian Scapegoating, and Rhetorical Exigency in Alioto's Response to the 'Zebra' Murders." *Western Speech,* 44 (1980), 64–73.

Burgchardt, Carl R. "Two Faces of American Communism: Pamphlet Rhetoric of the Third Period and the Popular Front." *Quarterly Journal of Speech,* 66 (1980), 375–391.

Butler, Sherry D. "The Apologia, 1971 Genre." *Southern Speech Communication Journal,* 37 (1972), 281–289.

Bytwerk, Randall L. "Rhetorical Aspects of the Nazi Meeting." *Quarterly Journal of Speech*, 61 (1975), 307–318.
——. "The Rhetoric of Defeat: Nazi Propaganda in 1945." *Central States Speech Journal*, 29 (1978), 44–52.
——. "The SST Controversy: A Case Study of the Rhetoric of Technology." *Central States Speech Journal*, 30 (1979), 187–198.
Callahan, Carole Riester. "Stevenson of Illinois: Identification in the 1970 Senatorial Campaign of Adlai E. Stevenson, III." *Central States Speech Journal*, 24 (1973), 272–277.
Campbell, J. Louis III. "Jimmy Carter and the Rhetoric of Charisma." *Central States Speech Journal*, 30 (1979), 174–186.
Campbell, John Angus. "Charles Darwin and the Crisis of Ecology: A Rhetorical Perspective." *Quarterly Journal of Speech*, 60 (1974), 442–449.
——. "The Polemical Mr. Darwin." *Quarterly Journal of Speech*, 60 (1974), 442–449.
Campbell, Karlyn Kohrs. "The Rhetoric of Radical Black Nationalism: A Case Study in Self-Conscious Criticism." *Central States Speech Journal*, 22 (1971), 151–160.
——. "The Rhetoric of Women's Liberation: An Oxymoron." *Quarterly Journal of Speech*, 59 (1973), 74–86.
——. "Stanton's 'The Solitude of Self': A Rationale for Feminism." *Quarterly Journal of Speech*, 66 (1980), 304–312.
Campbell, Paul Newell. "The Personae of Scientific Discourse." *Quarterly Journal of Speech*, 61 (1975), 391–405.
Carpenter, Ronald H., and Robert Seltzer. "Situational Style and the Rotunda Eulogies." *Central States Speech Journal*, 22 (1971), 11–15.
——."The Rhetorical Genesis of Style in the 'Frontier Hypothesis' of Frederick Jackson Turner." *Southern Speech Communication Journal*, 37 (1972), 233–248.
——. "Alfred Thayer Mahan's Style on Sea Power: A Paramessage Conducing to Ethos." *Speech Monographs*, 42 (1975), 190–202.
——. "Frederick Jackson Turner and the Rhetorical Impact of the Frontier Thesis." *Quarterly Journal of Speech*, 63 (1977), 117–129.
Carter, David A. "The Industrial Workers of the World and the Rhetoric of Song." *Quarterly Journal of Speech*, 66 (1980), 365–374.
Chaly, Ingeborg. "John Adams and the Boston Massacre: a Rhetorical Reassessment." *Central States Speech Journal*, 28 (1977), 36–46.
Chambers, Stephen, and G. P. Mohrmann. "Rhetoric in Some American Periodicals, 1815–1850." *Speech Monographs*, 37 (1970), 111–120.
Chapel, William Gage. "Christian Science and the Nineteenth Century Women's Movement." *Central States Speech Journal*, 26 (1975), 142–149.
Cheathem, Richard. "An Overview of Contemporary Gubernatorial Inaugurals." *Southern Speech Communication Journal*, 40 (1975), 191–203.
Chesbro, James. "Rhetorical Strategies of Radicals." *Today's Speech*, 20 (1972), 371.
Clark, E. Culpepper. "Henry Grady's New South: A Rebuttal from Charleston." *Southern Speech Communication Journal*, 41 (1976), 346–358.
Clark, Thomas. "Rhetorical Image-Making: A Case Study of the Thomas Paine-William Smith Propaganda Debates." *Southern Speech Communication Journal*, 40 (1975), 248–261.
——. "An Exploration of Generic Aspects of Contemporary American Christian Sermons." *Quarterly Journal of Speech*, 63 (1977), 384–394.

——. "An Exploration of Generic Aspects of Contemporary American Campaign Orations." *Central States Speech Journal*, 30 (1979), 122–133.

——. "Rhetoric, Reality, and Rationalization: A Study of the Masking Function of Rhetoric in the London Theosophical Movement." *Communication Quarterly*, 26 (1978), 24–30.

Connelly, F. Marlin Jr. "Some Questions Concerning Lyndon Johnson's Rhetoric in the 1964 Presidential Campaign." *Southern Speech Communication Journal*, 37 (1971), 11–20.

Cox, J. Robert. "Perspectives on Rhetorical Criticism of Movements: Antiwar Dissent, 1964–1970." *Western Speech*, 38 (1974), 254–268.

——. "The Rhetoric of Child Labor Reform: An Efficacy-Utility Analysis." *Quarterly Journal of Speech*, 60 (1974), 359–370.

Cragan, John F. "Foreign Policy Communication Dramas: How Mediated Rhetoric Played in Peoria in Campaign '76." *Quarterly Journal of Speech*, 63 (1977), 274–289.

Crocker, James W. "A Rhetoric of Encounter Following the May 14th, 1970 Disturbances at Kent State University." *Communication Quarterly*, 25 (1977), 47–55.

Dees, Diane. "Bernadette Devlin's Maiden Speech: A Rhetoric of Sacrifice." *Southern Speech Communication Journal*, 38 (1973), 326–339.

de Spain, Jerry Lynn. "A Rhetorical View of J. R. R. Tolkein's *The Lord of the Rings.*" *Western Speech*, 35 (1971), 88–95.

Dickens, Milton, and Ruth E. Schwartz. "Oral Argument Before the Supreme Court: Marshall *v.* Davis in the School Segregation Cases." *Quarterly Journal of Speech*, 57 (1971), 32–42.

Doolittle, Robert J. "Riots as Symbolic: A Criticism and Approach." *Central States Speech Journal*, 27 (1976), 310–317.

Dorgan, Howard. "The Doctrine of Victorious Defeat in the Rhetoric of Confederate Veterans." *Southern Speech Communication Journal*, 38 (1972), 119–130.

——. "A Case Study in Reconciliation: General John B. Gordon and 'The Last Days of the Confederacy.'" *Quarterly Journal of Speech*, 60 (1974), 83–91.

Douglas, Donald G. "Cordell Hull and the Implementation of the 'Good Neighbor Policy.'" *Western Speech*, 34 (1970), 288–300.

Duncan, Roger Dean. "Rhetoric of the Kidvid Movement: Ideology, Strategies, and Tactics." *Central States Speech Journal*, 27 (1976), 129–135.

Ehrlich, Larry G. "Ambassador in the Yard." *Southern Speech Communication Journal*, 38 (1972), 1–12.

Eich, Ritch K., and Donald Goldmann. "Communication, Confrontation, and Coercion: Agitation at Michigan." *Central States Speech Journal*, 27 (1976), 120–128.

Enos, Richard Leo. "Cicero's Forensic Oratory: The Manifestation of Power in the Roman Republic." *Southern Speech Communication Journal*, 40 (1975), 377–394.

——. "Rhetorical Intent in Ancient Historiography: Herodotus and the Battle of Marathon." *Communication Quarterly*, 24 (1976), 24–31.

Erickson, Keith V. "Black Messiah: The Father Divine Peace Mission Movement." *Quarterly Journal of Speech*, 63 (1977), 428–438.

——. "Jimmy Carter: The Rhetoric of Private and Civic Piety." *Western Speech*, 44 (1980), 235–251.

Erlich, Howard S. "'. . . And by Opposing, End Them.' The Genre of Moral Justification for Legal Transgressions." *Today's Speech*, 23 (1975), 13–16.

——. "Populist Rhetoric Reassessed: A Paradox." *Quarterly Journal of Speech*, 63 (1977), 140–151.

Farrell, Thomas B. "Political Conventions as Legitimation Ritual." *Communication Monographs,* 25 (1978), 293–305.

Fischli, Ronald. "Anita Bryant's Stand Against 'Militant Homosexuality': Religious Fundamentalism and the Democratic Process." *Central States Speech Journal,* 30 (1979), 262–271.

Fisher, Jeanne Y. "A Burkean Analysis of the Rhetorical Dimensions of a Multiple Murder and Suicide." *Quarterly Journal of Speech,* 60 (1974), 175–189.

Fisher, Walter R. "Reaffirmation and Subversion of The American Dream." *Quarterly Journal of Speech,* 59 (1973), 160–167.

Foss, Sonja K. "Equal Rights Amendment Controversy: Two Worlds in Conflict." *Quarterly Journal of Speech,* 65 (1979), 275–288.

Freeman, Patricia Lynn. "An Ethical Evaluation of the Persuasive Strategies of Glenn W. Turner of Turner Enterprises." *Southern Speech Communication Journal,* 38 (1973), 347–361.

Frentz, Thomas S., and Thomas B. Farrell. "Conversion of America's Consciousness: The Rhetoric of *The Exorcist.*" *Quarterly Journal of Speech,* 61 (1975), 40–47.

——, and Janice Hocker Rushing. "The Rhetoric of 'Rocky': Part Two." *Western Speech,* 42 (1978), 231–240.

Fulkerson, Gerald. "Frederick Douglass and the Kansas-Nebraska Act: A Case Study in Agitational Versatility." *Central States Speech Journal,* 23 (1972), 261–269.

Fulkerson, Richard P. "The Public Letter as a Rhetorical Form: Structure, Logic, and Style in King's 'Letter from Birmingham Jail.' " *Quarterly Journal of Speech,* 65 (1979), 121–136.

Funk, Alfred A. "Chain of Argument in the British Free-Trade Debates." *Quarterly Journal of Speech,* 58 (1972), 152–160.

——. "A Durkheimian Analysis of the Event at Masada." *Speech Monographs,* 41 (1974), 339–347.

Gibson, Chester. "Eugene Talmadge's Use of Identification During the 1934 Gubernatorial Campaign in Georgia." *Southern Speech Communication Journal,* 35 (1970), 342–349.

Gilbert, R. A. "John Bright's Contribution to the Anti-Corn Law League." *Western Speech,* 34 (1970), 16–20.

——. "A Canadian Case Study in Confrontation Rhetoric." *Central States Speech Journal,* 22 (1971), 118–122.

Goodman, Richard J., and William I. Gorden. "The Rhetoric of Desecration." *Quarterly Journal of Speech,* 57 (1971), 23–31.

Gregg, Richard B., and Gerard A. Hauser. "Richard Nixon's April 30, 1970 Address on Cambodia: The Ceremony of Confrontation." *Speech Monographs,* 40 (1973), 167–181.

——. "A Rhetorical Re-Examination of Arthur Vandenberg's 'Dramatic Conversion,' January 10, 1945." *Quarterly Journal of Speech,* 61 (1975), 154–168.

Gribbin, William. "The Juggernaut Metaphor in American Rhetoric." *Quarterly Journal of Speech,* 59 (1973), 297–303.

Griffin, Keith H. "The Light That Failed: A Rhetorical Analysis of Walter Hines Page as a Ceremonial Orator." *Southern Speech Communication Journal,* 46 (1980), 228–250.

Gronbeck, Bruce E. "Government's Stance in Crisis: A Case Study of Pitt the Younger." *Western Speech,* 34 (1970), 250–261.

——. "Rhetorical Invention in the Regency Crisis Pamphlets." *Quarterly Journal of Speech,* 58 (1972), 418–430.

——. "John Morley and the Irish Question: Chart-prayer-Dream." *Speech Monographs,* 40 (1973), 287–295.

Gross, Nicolas P. "Alcestis and the Rhetoric of Departure." *Quarterly Journal of Speech,* 60 (1974), 296–305.

Gunter, Mary F., and James S. Taylor. "Loyalist Propaganda in the Sermons of Charles Inglis, 1770–1780." *Western Speech,* 37 (1971), 47–55.

Hahn, Dan F. "One's Reborn Every Minute: Carter's Religious Appeal in 1976." *Communication Quarterly,* 28 (1980), 56–62.

Hammerback, John C. "The Rhetoric of a Righteous Reform: George Washington Julian's 1852 Campaign Against Slavery." *Central States Speech Journal,* 22 (1971), 85–93.

——. "Barry Goldwater's Rhetoric of Rugged Individualism." *Quarterly Journal of Speech,* 58 (1972), 175–183.

——, and Richard J. Jensen. "The Rhetorical Worlds of Cesar Chavez and Reies Tijerina." *Western Speech,* 44 (1980), 176–189.

Hancock, Brenda Robinson. "Affirmation by Negation in the Women's Liberation Movement." *Quarterly Journal of Speech,* 58 (1972), 264–271.

Harrell, Jackson, B. L. Ware, and Wil Linkugel. "Failure of Apology in American Politics: Nixon on Watergate." *Speech Monographs,* 42 (1975), 245–261.

Harris, Barbara Ann. "The Zionist Rhetoric of Louis Dembitz Brandeis." *Western Speech,* 35 (1971), 199–209.

Harris, Thomas E., and Patrick C. Kennicott. "Booker T. Washington: A Study of Conciliatory Rhetoric." *Southern Speech Communication Journal,* 37 (1971), 47–59.

Hart, Roderick P. "The Rhetoric of the True Believer." *Speech Monographs,* 38 (1971), 249–261.

——. "Absolutism and Situation: Prolegomena to a Rhetorical Biography of Richard M. Nixon." *Communication Monographs,* 43 (1976), 204–228.

——. "An Unquiet Desperation: Rhetorical Aspects of 'Popular' Atheism in the United States." *Quarterly Journal of Speech,* 64 (1978), 33–46.

Harte, Thomas B. "The Rhetoric of Pox: Invention in George Wallace's Speech at Cape Girardeau, Missouri." *Central States Speech Journal,* 23 (1972), 202–205.

Hazel, Harry Jr. "Images of War, Guilt and Redemption in the First Crusade Speech of Urban II." *Communication Quarterly,* 26 (1978), 24–30.

Heath, Robert L. "Dialectical Confrontation: A Strategy of Black Radicalism." *Central States Speech Journal,* 24 (1973), 168–177.

——. "A Time for Silence: Booker T. Washington in Atlanta." *Quarterly Journal of Speech,* 64 (1978), 385–399.

Heisey, D. Ray. "The Rhetoric of the Arab-Israeli Conflict." *Quarterly Journal of Speech,* 56 (1970), 12–21.

Hemmer, Joseph J. Jr. "The Charleston Platform Debate in Rhetorical-Historical Perspective." *Quarterly Journal of Speech,* 56 (1970), 406–416.

Hensley, Carl Wayne. "Harry S. Truman: Fundamental Americanism in Foreign Policy Speech-making 1945–1946." *Southern Speech Communication Journal,* 40 (1975), 180–190.

——. "Rhetorical Vision and the Persuasion of a Historical Movement: The Disciples of Christ in Nineteenth Century American Culture." *Quarterly Journal of Speech,* 61 (1975), 250–264.

Hill, L. Brooks. "David Lloyd George as Minister of Munitions: A Study of His Speaking Tour of Industrial Centers." *Southern Speech Communication Journal,* 36 (1971), 312–323.

Hillbruner, Anthony. "Archetype and Signature: Nixon and the 1973 Inaugural." *Central States Speech Journal,* 25 (1974), 169–181.

Hoban, James R. Jr. "Solzhenitsyn on Detente: A Study of Perspective by Incongruity." *Southern Speech Communication Journal,* 42 (1977), 163-177.

Hogan, Michael R. "Roe v. Wade: The Rhetoric of Fetal Life." *Central States Speech Journal,* 27 (1976), 192-199.

Holtan, Orlay I. "A. C. Townley, Political Firebrand of North Dakota." *Western Speech,* 35 (1971), 24-29.

Hope, Diane Schaich. "Redefinition of Self: A Comparison of the Rhetoric of the Women's Liberation and Black Liberation Movements." *Today's Speech,* 23 (1975), 17-26.

Howe, Roger J. "The Rhetoric of the Death of God Theology." *Southern Speech Communication Journal,* 37 (1971), 150-162.

Hudson, Lee. "Belting the Bible: Madalyn Murray O'Hair vs. Fundamentalism." *Western Speech,* 34 (1972), 233-240.

Hunsaker, David M. "The Rhetoric of *Brown v. Board of Education:* Paradigm for Contemporary Social Protest." *Southern Speech Communication Journal,* 43 (1978), 91-109.

Hynes, Thomas J. Jr. " 'McGovern, Come Down' : An Analysis of Senator George McGovern's Confrontation with Demonstrators, Doral Beach Hotel, July 12, 1972." *Southern Speech Communication Journal,* 39 (1974), 269-278.

Hyres, Sandra Sarkela. "Dramatic Propaganda: Mercy Otis Warren's 'The Defeat,' 1773." *Today's Speech,* 23 (1975), 21-28.

Ilkka, Richard J. "Rhetorical Dramatization in the Development of American Communism." *Quarterly Journal of Speech,* 63 (1977), 413-427.

Ivie, Robert L. "William McKinley: Advocate of Imperialism." *Western Speech,* 36 (1972), 15-23.

——. "Presidential Motives for War." *Quarterly Journal of Speech,* 60 (1974), 337-345.

Jablonski, Carol J. "Richard Nixon's Irish Wake: A Case of Generic Transference." *Central States Speech Journal,* 30 (1979), 164-173.

——. "Promoting Radical Change in the Roman Catholic Church: Rhetorical Requirements, Problems, and Strategies of the American Bishops." *Central States Speech Journal,* 31 (1980), 282-289.

Jamieson, Kathleen Hall. "Interpretation of Natural Law in the Conflict Over Humanae Vitae." *Quarterly Journal of Speech,* 60 (1974), 201-211.

——. "Antecedent Genre as Rhetorical Constraint." *Quarterly Journal of Speech,* 61 (1975), 406-415.

Jensen, J. Vernon. "British Voices on the Eve of the American Revolution: Trapped by the Family Metaphor." *Quarterly Journal of Speech,* 63 (1977), 43-51.

Jensen, Richard J., and Carol L. Jensen. "Labor's Appeal to the Past: The 1972 Election in the United Mine Workers." *Central States Speech Journal,* 28 (1977), 173-184.

——, and John C. Hammerback. "Radical Nationalism Among Chicanos: The Rhetoric of Jose Angel Gutierrez." *Western Speech,* 44 (1980), 202-212.

Johnson, Robert C. "Kinsey vs. Christianity: A Clash of 'Paradigms' on Human Nature." *Quarterly Journal of Speech,* 61 (1975), 59-70.

Johnson, Samuel R. "The Non-Aristotelian Nature of Samoan Ceremonial Oratory." *Western Speech,* 34 (1970), 262-273.

Johnstone, Christopher L. "Thoreau and Civil Disobedience: A Rhetorical Paradox." *Quarterly Journal of Speech,* 60 (1974), 313-322.

Kallan, Richard A. "Style and the New Journalism: A Rhetorical Analysis of Tom Wolfe." *Communication Monographs,* 46 (1979), 52-62.

Kaplan-Tuckel, Barbara. "Disraeli on Jewish Disabilities: Another Look." *Central States Speech Journal,* 30 (1979), 156–163.

Katula, Richard A. "The Apology of Richard M. Nixon." *Today's Speech,* 23 (1975), 1–6.

Kaufer, David S. "The Ironist and Hypocrite as Presidential Symbols: A Nixon-Kennedy Analog." *Communication Quarterly,* 27 (1979), 20–26.

Kendall, Kathleen Edgerton, and Jeanne Y. Fisher. "Francis Wright on Women's Rights: Eloquence Versus Ethos." *Quarterly Journal of Speech,* 60 (1974), 58–68.

Kennicott, Patrick C. "Black Persuaders in the Antislavery Movement." *Speech Monographs,* 37 (1970), 15–24.

King, Andrew A., and Floyd Douglas Anderson. "Nixon, Agnew, and the 'Silent Majority': A Case Study in the Rhetoric of Polarization." *Western Speech,* 35 (1971), 243–255.

——. "The Rhetorical Legacy of the Black Church." *Central States Speech Journal,* 22 (1971), 179–185.

——. "Booker T. Washington and the Myth of Heroic Materialism." *Quarterly Journal of Speech,* 60 (1974), 323–327.

Klumpp, James F. "Challenge of Radical Rhetoric: Radicalization at Columbia." *Western Speech,* 37 (1973), 146–156.

——, and Thomas A. Hollihan. "Debunking the Resignation of Earl Butz: Sacrificing an Official Racist." *Quarterly Journal of Speech,* 65 (1979), 1–11.

Kosokoff, Stephen, and Carl W. Carmichael. "The Rhetoric of Protest: Song, Speech, and Attitude Change." *Southern Speech Communication Journal,* 35 (1970), 295–302.

Larson, Barbara A. "Samuel Davies and the Rhetoric of the New Light." *Speech Monographs,* 38 (1971), 207–216.

——. "The Election Eve Address of Edmund Muskie: A Case Study of the Televised Public Address." *Central States Speech Journal,* 23 (1972), 78–85.

——. "Criticism and the Campaign Concept of Persuasion: A Case Study Analysis of Method." *Central States Speech Journal,* 24 (1973), 32–59.

Larson, Charles U. "The Trust Establishing Function of the Rhetoric of Black Power." *Central States Speech Journal,* 21 (1970), 52–56.

Lazenby, Walter. "Exhortation as Exorcism: Cotton Mather's Sermons to Murderers." *Quarterly Journal of Speech,* 57 (1971), 50–56.

Levison, Gayle Lewis. "The Rhetoric of the Oral Argument in *The Regents of the University of California v. Bakke.*" *Western Speech,* 43 (1979), 271–277.

Ling, David A. "A Pentadic Analysis of Senator Edward Kennedy's Address to the People of Massachusetts, July 25, 1969." *Central States Speech Journal,* 21 (1970), 81–86.

Linkugel, Wil A. "Lincoln, Kansas, and Cooper Union." *Speech Monographs,* 37 (1970), 172–179.

——, and Dixie Lee Cody. "Nixon, McGovern and the Female Electorate." *Today's Speech,* 21 (1973), 25–32.

Litfin, A. Duane. "Senator Edmund Muskie's 'Five Smooth Stones': An Analysis of Rhetorical Strategies and Tactics in his 1970 Election Eve Speech." *Central States Speech Journal,* 23 (1972), 5–10.

——. "Eisenhower on the Military-Industrial Complex: Critique of a Rhetorical Strategy." *Central States Speech Journal,* 25 (1974), 198–209.

Logue, Cal M. "Rhetorical Ridicule of Reconstruction Blacks." *Quarterly Journal of Speech,* 62 (1976), 400–409.

——. "The Rhetorical Appeals of Whites to Blacks During Reconstruction." *Communication Monographs,* 44 (1977), 241–251.

Lucas, Stephen E. "The Man with the Muck Rake: A Reinterpretation." *Quarterly Journal of Speech,* 59 (1973), 413–422.

Macksoud, S. John, and Ross Altman. "Voices In Opposition: A Burkeian Rhetoric of *Saint Joan.*" *Quarterly Journal of Speech,* 57 (1971), 140–146.

Makay, John J. "The Rhetoric of George C. Wallace and the 1964 Civil Rights Law." *Today's Speech,* 18 (1970), 26–33.

Mandel, Jerry E. "The Presentation of Image in Charles H. Percy's Whistlestop Tour of 1966." *Central States Speech Journal,* 21 (1970), 209–216.

Mansfield, Dorothy M. "Abigail S. Dumiway: Suffragette with Not-so-common Sense." *Western Speech,* 35 (1971), 24–29.

Mark, Dale W. "Sacred Rhetoric of Gipsey Smith." *Western Speech,* 37 (1973), 103–110.

Martin, Howard H. "A Generic Exploration: Staged Withdrawal, The Rhetoric of Resignation." *Central States Speech Journal,* 27 (1976), 247–257.

McCants, David A. "The Role of Patrick Henry in the Stamp Act Debate." *Southern Speech Communication Journal,* 46 (1981), 205–227.

McCracken, David. "The Development of Edmund Burke's *Reflections.*" *Western Speech,* 40 (1976), 156–167.

McGee, Michael C. "The Fall of Wellington: A Case Study of the Relationship Between Theory, Practice and Rhetoric in History." *Quarterly Journal of Speech,* 63 (1977), 28–42.

McGuire, Michael D. "Rhetoric, Philosophy, and the Volk; Johann Gottlieb Fichte's *Addresses to the German Nation.*" *Quarterly Journal of Speech,* 62 (1976), 135–144.

——. "Mythic Rhetoric in Mein Kampf: A Structuralist Critique." *Quarterly Journal of Speech,* 63 (1977), 1–13.

——, and John H. Patton. "Preaching in the Mystic Mode: The Rhetorical Art of Meister Eckhart." *Communication Monographs,* 44 (1977), 263–272.

McKerrow, Ray E. "Truman at Korea: Rhetoric in the Pursuit of Victory." *Central States Speech Journal,* 28 (1977), 1–12.

Measell, James S. "William Pitt and the Suspension of Habeas Corpus." *Quarterly Journal of Speech,* 60 (1974), 468–476.

Medhurst, Martin J. "McGovern at Wheaton: A Quest for Redemption." *Communication Quarterly,* 25 (1977), 32–39.

Merriam, Allen H. "Symbolic Action in India: Gandhi's Nonverbal Behavior." *Quarterly Journal of Speech,* 61 (1975), 290–306.

Minnick, Wayne C. "A Case Study in Persuasive Effect: Lyman Beecher on Duelling." *Speech Monographs,* 38 (1971), 262–276.

Mohrmann, G. P., and F. Eugene Scott. "Popular Music and World War II: The Rhetoric of Continuation." *Quarterly Journal of Speech,* 62 (1976), 145–156.

Murray, Michael D. "Persuasive Dimensions of See It Now's 'Report on Senator Joseph R. McCarthy.' " *Today's Speech,* 23 (1975), 13–20.

——. "To Hire a Hall: An Argument in Indianapolis." *Central States Speech Journal,* 26 (1975), 12–20.

Newman, Robert P. "Lethal Rhetoric: The Selling of the China Myths." *Quarterly Journal of Speech,* 61 (1975), 113–128.

Nickel, Sandra. "The Rhetoric of Union: Stylized Utterance." *Central States Speech Journal,* 24 (1973), 137–142.

Nordvold, Robert O. "Rhetoric as Ritual: Hubert H. Humphrey's Acceptance Address at the 1968 Democratic National Convention." *Today's Speech,* 18 (1970), 34–38.

Norton, Robert Wayne. "The Rhetorical Situation Is the Message: Muskie's Election Eve Broadcast." *Central States Speech Journal,* 22 (1971), 171–178.

Patterson, J. W. "Arthur Vandenberg's Rhetorical Strategy in Advancing Bipartisan Foreign Policy." *Quarterly Journal of Speech,* 56 (1970), 284–295.

Patton, John H. "Rhetoric at Cantonsville: Daniel Berrigan, Conscience and Image Alteration." *Today's Speech,* 23 (1975), 3–12.

——. "A Government as Good as Its People." *Quarterly Journal of Speech,* 63 (1977), 249–257.

Phelps, Lynn A., and Edwin Cohen. "The Wilberfore-Huxley Debate." *Western Speech,* 37 (1973), 56–64.

Polisky, Jerome B., and Frances R. Wolpaw. "Jewish Statehood Legitimated: Abba Hillel Silver at the American Jewish Conference." *Quarterly Journal of Speech,* 58 (1972), 209–216.

Pollock, Arthur. "Stokely Carmichael's New Black Rhetoric." *Southern Speech Communication Journal,* 37 (1971), 92–94.

Porter, Laurinda W. "The White House Transcripts: Group Fantasy Events Concerning Mass Media." *Central States Speech Journal,* 27 (1976), 272–284.

Powers, Lloyd, D. "Chicano Rhetoric: Some Basic Concepts." *Southern Speech Communication Journal,* 38 (1973), 340–346.

Pratt, James W. "An Analysis of Three Crisis Speeches." *Western Speech,* 34 (1970), 194–202.

Quimby, Rollin W. "Agnew, the Press and the Rhetorical Critic." *Western Speech,* 39 (1975), 146–154.

Rarick, David L. "The Carter Persona: An Empirical Analysis of the Rhetorical Visions of Campaign '76." *Quarterly Journal of Speech,* 63 (1977), 258–273.

Raum, Richard D., and James S. Measell. "Wallace and His Ways: A Study of the Rhetorical Genre of Polarization." *Central States Speech Journal,* 25 (1974), 28–35.

Reed, Robert Michael. "The Case of Missionary Smith: A Crucial Incident in the Rhetoric of the British Anti-Slavery Movement." *Central States Speech Journal,* 29 (1978), 61–71.

Reid, Loren. "John Bright; Spokesman for America." *Western Speech,* 38 (1974), 233–243.

——. "Bright's Tribute to Garrison and Field." *Quarterly Journal of Speech,* 61 (1975), 169–177.

Reid, Ronald F. "New England Rhetoric and the French War, 1754–1760: A Case Study in the Rhetoric of War." *Communication Monographs,* 43 (1976), 256–286.

Reinsdorf, Walter D. "'This Nation Will Remain Neutral:' Franklin D. Roosevelt Uses Inclusive and Exclusive Terms to Justify a Policy." *Today's Speech,* 22 (1974), 17–21.

Reynolds, Beatrice K. "Context of Girandist Rhetoric." *Western Speech,* 35 (1971), 256–263.

——. "The Rhetorical Methods of Pierre Vergniaud." *Southern Speech Communication Journal,* 39 (1973), 174–184.

——. "Mao-Tse Tung: Rhetoric of a Revolutionary." *Central States Speech Journal,* 27 (1976), 207–211.

Rickert, William E. "Horace Greeley on the Stump: Presidential Campaign of 1872." *Western Speech,* 39 (1975), 175–183.

——. "Winston Churchill's Archetypal Metaphors: A Mythopoetic Translation of World War II." *Central States Speech Journal,* 28 (1977), 106–112.

Ritter, Ellen M. "Elizabeth Morgan: Pioneer Female Labour Agitator." *Central States Speech Journal,* 22 (1971), 242–251.

Ritter, Kurt W. "The Myth-Making Functions of the Rhetoric of the American Revolution: Francis Hopkinson as a Case Study." *Today's Speech,* 23 (1975), 25-32.

——. "Confrontation as a Moral Drama: The Boston Massacre in Rhetorical Perspective." *Southern Speech Communication Journal,* 42 (1977), 114-136.

——. "American Political Rhetoric and the Jeremiad Tradition: Presidential Nomination Acceptance Addresses, 1960-1976." *Central States Speech Journal,* 31 (1980), 153-171.

Rogers, Jimmie N. "John Adams' Summation Speech in *Rex v. Wemms, Et Al.*: A Delicate Art of Persuasion." *Southern Speech Communication Journal,* 39 (1973), 134-144.

Rosenfeld, Lawrence B. "The Confrontation Policies of S. I. Hayakawa: A Case Study in Coercive Semantics." *Today's Speech,* 18 (1970), 18-22.

Rosenfield, Lawrence W. "Politics and Pornography." *Quarterly Journal of Speech,* 59 (1973), 413-422.

——. "August 9, 1974: The Victimage of Richard Nixon." *Communication Quarterly,* 24 (1976), 19-23.

Rosenwasser, Marie D. "Rhetoric and the Progress of the Women's Liberation Movement." *Today's Speech,* 20 (1972), 45-56.

Ross, David. "The Projection of Credibility as a Rhetorical Strategy in Anwar el-Sadat's Address to the Israeli Parliament." *Western Speech,* 44 (1980), 74-80.

Rushing, Janice Hocker, and Thomas S. Frentz. "The Rhetoric of 'Rocky': A Social Value Model of Criticism." *Western Speech,* 42 (1978), 63-72.

——, and Thomas S. Frentz. " 'The Deer Hunter': Rhetoric of the Warrior." *Quarterly Journal of Speech,* 66 (1980), 392-406.

Sanbonmatsu, Akira. "Darrow and Rorke's Use of Burkeian Identification Strategies in *New York* vs. *Gitlow (1920)." Speech Monographs,* 38 (1971), 36-48.

Saxon, John D. "Contemporary Southern Oratory: A Rhetoric of Hope Not Desperation." *Southern Speech Communication Journal,* 40 (1975), 262-274.

Schmidt, Patricia L. "The Role of Moral Idealism in Social Change: Lord Ashley and the Ten Hours Factory Act." *Quarterly Journal of Speech,* 63 (1977), 14-27.

Schneider, Valerie. "Parker's Assessment of Webster: Argumentative Synthesis Through the Tragic Metaphor." *Quarterly Journal of Speech,* 59 (1973), 330-336.

Scholten, Pat Creech. "Exploitation of Ethos: Sarah Winnemucca and Bright Eyes On Lecture Tour." *Western Speech,* 41 (1977), 233-244.

Schweck, Robert C. "Rhetorical Art and Literary Form in Mill's *The Subjection of Women." Quarterly Journal of Speech,* 61 (1975), 23-30.

Scott, F. Eugene. "The Political Preaching Tradition in Ulster: Prelude to Paisley." *Western Speech,* 40 (1976), 249-259.

Scott, Robert L. "Rhetoric That Postures: An Intrinsic Reading of Richard M. Nixon's Inaugural Address." *Western Speech,* 34 (1970), 46-52.

——. "Diego Rivera at Rockefeller Center: Fresco Painting and Rhetoric." *Western Speech,* 41 (1977), 70-82.

Sedano, Michael Victor. "Chicanismo: A Rhetorical Analysis of Themes and Images of Selected Poetry from the Chicano Movement." *Western Speech,* 44 (1980), 190-201.

Sharf, Barbara F. "Rhetorical Analysis of Nonpublic Discourse." *Communication Quarterly,* 27 (1979), 21-30.

Shields, Evelyn. "The Rhetoric of Emerging Nationalism: A Case Study in Irish Rhetorical Failure." *Central States Speech Journal*, (1974), 225–232.

Sillars, Malcolm O. "The Rhetoric of the Petition in Boots." *Speech Monographs*, 39 (1972), 92–103.

Simons, Herbert W., James W. Chesebro, and C. Jack Orr. "A Movement Perspective on the 1972 Presidential Campaign." *Quarterly Journal of Speech*, 59 (1973), 168–179.

Sinzinger, Richard A. "Henry Clay, Master Propagandist for Latin American Revolutionists." *Today's Speech*, 18 (1970), 27–32.

Smith, Arthur L. "Henry Highland Garnet: Black Revolutionary in Sheep's Vestments." *Central States Speech Journal*, 21 (1970), 93–98.

Smith, Craig R. "Nixon's 1968 Acceptance Speech as a Model of Dual Audience Adaptation." *Today's Speech*, 19 (1971), 15–21.

——. "The Republican Keynote Address of 1968: Adaptive Rhetoric for the Multiple Audience." *Western Speech*, 39 (1975), 32–39.

——. "Ronald Reagan's Attempt to Build a National Majority." *Central States Speech Journal*, 30 (1979), 98–102.

Smith, F. Michael. "Rhetorical Implications of the 'Aggression' Thesis in the Johnson Administration's Vietnam Argumentation." *Central States Speech Journal*, 23 (1972), 217–224.

Smith, Ralph R., and Russell R. Windes. "The Innovational Movement: A Rhetorical Theory." *Quarterly Journal of Speech*, 61 (1975), 140–153.

——, and Russell R. Windes. "The Rhetoric of Mobilization: Implications for the Study of Movements." *Southern Speech Communication Journal*, 42 (1976), 1–19.

Smith, Robert R. "Raymond Swing's Broadcasts 'In the Name of Sanity.' " *Quarterly Journal of Speech*, 56 (1970), 369–377.

Smith, Stephen A. "Rhetorical Strategies in the Courtrooms of Territorial Arkansas." *Southern Speech Communication Journal*, 42 (1977), 318–333.

——. "Sounds of the South: The Rhetorical Saga of Country Music Lyrics." *Southern Speech Communication Journal*, 45 (1980), 164–172.

Solomon, Martha. "The Rhetoric of STOP ERA: Fatalistic Reaffirmation." *Southern Speech Communication Journal*, 44 (1978), 42–59.

——. "The 'Positive Woman's' Journey: A Mythic Analysis of the Rhetoric of STOP ERA." *Quarterly Journal of Speech*, 65 (1979), 262–274.

——. "Redemptive Rhetoric: The Continuity Motif in the Rhetoric of Right to Life." *Central States Speech Journal*, 31 (1980), 52–62.

Speer, Diane Parkin. "Milton's *Defensio Prima: Ethos* and Vituperation in a Polemic Engagement." *Quarterly Journal of Speech*, 56 (1970), 277–283.

Speer, Richard. "The Rhetoric of Burke's Select Committee Reports." *Quarterly Journal of Speech*, 57 (1971), 306–315.

Sproule, J. Michael. "Newspapers as Political Persuaders: The Campaign Against James G. Blaine." *Central States Speech Journal*, 24 (1973), 310–318.

Starosta, William J. "Roots for an Older Rhetoric: On Rhetorical Effectiveness in the Third World." *Western Speech*, 43 (1979), 278–287.

Starr, Douglas P. "Succession Speeches of Four Deep South Governors Who Would Rather Fight Than Switch." *Southern Speech Communication Journal*, 38 (1972), 131–141.

Stelzner, Hermann G. "Humphrey and Kennedy Court West Virginia, May 3, 1960." *Southern Speech Communication Journal*, 37 (1971), 21–33.

——. "Ford's War on Inflation: A Metaphor That Did Not Cross." *Communication Monographs*, 44 (1977), 284–297.

Stewart, Charles J., and Joseph P. Zima. "The Congressional Case for a School Prayer Amendment." *Central States Speech Journal,* 21 (1970), 9–17.

Stocker, Glenn. "Charles Sumner's Rhetoric of Insult." *Southern Speech Communication Journal,* 38 (1973), 223–234.

Stuart, Charlotte L. "Mary Wollstonecraft's *A Vindication of the Rights of Men:* A Rhetoric Reassessment." *Western Speech,* 42 (1978), 83–92.

Sudol, Ronald A. "The Rhetoric of Strategic Retreat: Carter and the Panama Canal Debate." *Quarterly Journal of Speech,* 65 (1979), 379–391.

Thompson, Wayne N. "Barbara Jordan's Keynote Address: Fulfilling Dual and Conflicting Purposes." *Central States Speech Journal,* 30 (1979), 272–277.

——. "Barbara Jordan's Keynote Address: The Juxtaposition of Contradictory Values." *Southern Speech Communication Journal,* 44 (1979), 223–232.

Trent, Judith S. "Richard Nixon's Methods of Identification in the Presidential Campaigns of 1960 and 1968: A Content Analysis." *Today's Speech,* 19 (1971), 22–30.

Turner, Kathleen J. "Comic Strips: A Rhetorical Perspective." *Central States Speech Journal,* 28 (1977), 24–35.

Valley, David B. "Significant Characteristics of Democratic Presidential Nomination Acceptance Speeches." *Central States Speech Journal,* 25 (1974), 46–62.

Vatz, Richard E., and Theodore Otto Windt, Jr. "The Defeats of Judges Haynsworth and Carswell: Rejection of Supreme Court Nominees." *Quarterly Journal of Speech,* 60 (1974), 477–488.

Vickrey, James Frank. "The Lectures on 'Discoveries and Inventions'–A Neglected Aspect of the Public Speaking Career of Abraham Lincoln." *Central States Speech Journal,* 21 (1970), 181–190.

Volpe, Michael. "The Persuasive Use of Humor: Cicero's Defense of Caelius." *Quarterly Journal of Speech,* 36 (1977), 311–323.

Walker, Harold L. "Social Change Through Rhetoric: A Study of the Public Address of Abraham Jacobi." *Central States Speech Journal,* 24 (1973), 14–21.

Wander, Philip C. "The John Birchers and Martin Luther King Symbols in the Radical Right." *Western Speech,* 35 (1971), 4–14.

——. "The Rhetoric of Science." *Western Speech,* 40 (1976), 226–235.

Ware, B. L., and Wil A. Linkugel. "They Spoke in Defense of Themselves: On the General Criticism of Apologia." *Quarterly Journal of Speech,* 59 (1973), 273–283.

Warnick, Barbara. "The Rhetoric of Conservative Resistance." *Southern Speech Communication Journal,* 42 (1977), 256–273.

Weatherly, Michael. "Propaganda and the Rhetoric of the American Revolution." *Southern Speech Communication Journal,* 36 (1971), 352–363.

Weaver, Bruce J. "Debate and the Destruction of Friendship: An Analysis of Fox and Burke on the French Revolution." *Quarterly Journal of Speech,* 67 (1981), 57–68.

Weaver, Richard L. "The Negro Issue: Agitation in the Michigan Lyceum." *Central States Speech Journal,* 22 (1971), 196–201.

Weidhorn, Manfred. "Churchill the Phrase Forger." *Quarterly Journal of Speech,* 58 (1972), 161–174.

——. "Churchill as Orator, Wish and Fulfillment." *Southern Speech Communication Journal,* 40 (1975), 217–227.

Wiethoff, William E. "Machiavelli's *The Prince:* Rhetorical Influence in Civil Philosophy." *Western Speech,* 33 (1974), 98–107.

——. "Guns or Butter: The American Revolution as a Parliamentary Ploy." *Central States Speech Journal,* 26 (1975), 244–253.

——. "Rhetorical Strategy in the Brimingham Political Union, 1830–1832." *Central States Speech Journal,* 29 (1978), 53–60.
——. "Rhetorical Enterprise in the Ministry of 'Reverend Ike.'" *Communication Monographs,* 44 (1977), 52–59.
Wilson, Gerald L. "A Strategy of Explanation: Richard M. Nixon's August 8, 1974 Resignation Address." *Communication Quarterly,* 24 (1976), 14–20.
Windt, Theodore Otto. "The Rhetoric of Peaceful Coexistence: Krushchev in America, 1959." *Quarterly Journal of Speech,* 57 (1971), 11–22.
——. "The Diatribe: Last Resort for Protest." *Quarterly Journal of Speech,* 58 (1972), 1–14.
Winn, Larry James. "The War Hawks' Call to Arms: Appeals for a Second War With Great Britain." *Southern Speech Communication Journal,* 37 (1972), 402–412.
Woodward, Gary C. "Mystifications in the Rhetoric of Cultural Dominance and Colonial Control." *Central States Speech Journal,* 62 (1975), 298–303.
Wooten, Cecil W. "The Ambassador's Speech: A Particularly Hellenistic Genre of Oratory." *Quarterly Journal of Speech,* 59 (1973), 209–212.
Zacharis, John C. "Emmeline Pankhurst: An English Suffragette Influences America." *Speech Monographs,* 38 (1971), 198–206.
Zarefsky, David. "President Johnson's War on Poverty: The Rhetoric of Three 'Establishment' Movements." *Communication Monographs,* 44 (1977), 352–373.
——. "The Great Society as a Rhetorical Proposition." *Quarterly Journal of Speech,* 65 (1979), 364–378.

Select Bibliography of Works on Critical Theory and Practice

The following bibliography samples work on the theory and practice of rhetorical criticism.

Andrews, James R. *A Choice of Worlds: The Practice and Criticism of Public Discourse*. New York: Harper Row, 1973.
——. "Disintegration and Liberation in Rhetorical Studies." *Today's Speech*, 20 (1972), 39–44.
Baskerville, Barnet. "Must We All Be 'Rhetorical Critics'?" *Quarterly Journal of Speech*, 63 (1977), 107–116.
Bitzer, Lloyd F. "Functional Communication: A Situational Perspective." In *Rhetoric in Transition: Studies in the Nature and Uses of Rhetoric*. Ed. by Eugene E. White. University Park: Pennsylvania State Press, 1980. pp.21–38.
——. "The Rhetorical Situation." *Philosophy and Rhetoric*, 1 (1968), 1–14.
Black, Edwin. *Rhetorical Criticism: A Study in Method*. New York: Macmillan, 1965; rpt. Madison, Wisconsin: University of Wisconsin Press, 1978.
Bock, Douglas G. "Axiology and Rhetorical Criticism: Some Dimensions of the Critical Judgment." *Western Speech*, 37 (1973), 87–96.
Booth, Wayne C. *The Rhetoric of Fiction*. Chicago: University of Chicago Press, 1961.
Bormann, Ernest H. "Fantasy and Rhetorical Vision: The Rhetorical Criticism of Reality." *Quarterly Journal of Speech*, 58 (1972), 396–407.

The Practice of Rhetorical Criticism

Brockriede, Wayne. "Rhetorical Criticism as Argument." *Quarterly Journal of Speech,* 60 (1974), 165–174.
Bryant, Donald C. *Rhetorical Dimensions of Criticism.* Baton Rouge: Louisiana State University Press, 1973.
Burgess, Parke. "The Rhetoric of Moral Conflict: Two Critical Dimensions." *Quarterly Journal of Speech,* 56 (1970), 120–130.
Burke, Kenneth. *A Grammar of Motives.* Englewood Cliffs, N.J.: Prentice-Hall, 1946.
———. *A Rhetoric of Motives.* Englewood Cliffs, N.J.: Prentice-Hall, 1950.
Campbell, Karlyn Kohrs. "Criticism: Ephemeral and Enduring." *Speech Teacher,* 23 (1974), 9–14.
———, and Kathleen Hall Jamieson, eds. and intro. essay. *Form and Genre.* Falls Church, Va.: Speech Communication Association, n.d.
———. "The Nature of Criticism in Rhetorical and Communicative Studies." *Central States Speech Journal,* 30 (1979), 4–13.
Chesebro, James W., and Caroline D. Hamsher. "Contemporary Rhetorical Theory and Criticism: Dimensions of the New Rhetoric." *Speech Monographs,* 42 (1975), 311–334.
Clark, Robert D. "Biography and Rhetorical Criticism" (A Review Essay). *Quarterly Journal of Speech,* 44 (1958), 182–186.
———. "Lesson from the Literary Critics." *Western Speech,* 21 (1957), 83–89.
Corbett, Edward P. J., ed. *Rhetorical Analyses of Literary Works.* New York and London: Oxford University Press, 1969.
Crable, Richard E. "Ethical Codes, Accountability, and Argumentation." *Quarterly Journal of Speech,* 64 (1978), 23–32.
Cragen, John F. "Rhetorical Strategy: A Dramatistic Interpretation and Application." *Central States Speech Journal,* 26 (1975), 4–11.
Crandell, S. Judson. "The Beginnings of a Methodology for Social Control Studies in Public Address." *Quarterly Journal of Speech,* 32 (1947), 36–39.
Croft, Albert J. "The Functions of Rhetorical Criticism." *Quarterly Journal of Speech,* 42 (1956), 283–291.
Ellingsworth, Huber W. "Anthropology and Rhetoric: Toward a Culture-Related Methodology in Speech Criticism." *Southern Speech Communication Journal,* 28 (1963), 307–312.
Ericson, Jon M. "Evaluative and Formulative Functions in Speech Criticism." *Western Speech,* 32 (1968), 173–176.
Eubanks, Ralph T. "Axiological Issues in Rhetorical Inquiry." *Southern Speech Communication Journal,* 44 (1978), 11–24.
Fisher, Walter R. "Method in Rhetorical Criticism." *Southern Speech Communication Journal,* 35 (1969), 101–109.
Gregg, Richard. "A Phenomenologically Oriented Approach to Rhetorical Criticism." *Central States Speech Journal,* 17 (1966), 83–90.
Griffin, Leland M. "The Rhetoric of Historical Movements." *Quarterly Journal of Speech,* 38 (1952), 184–188.
Gronbeck, Bruce E. "Rhetorical History and Rhetorical Criticism: A Distinction." *Speech Teacher,* 24 (1975), 309–320.
Grossberg, Lawrence. "Marxist Dialectics and Rhetorical Criticism." *Quarterly Journal of Speech,* 65 (1979), 235–249.
Hagen, Michael R. "Kenneth Burke and Generative Criticism of Speeches." *Central States Speech Journal,* 22 (1971), 252–257.
Hahn, Dan F., and Ruth M. Gonchar. "Studying Social Movements: A Rhetorical Methodology." *Speech Teacher,* 20 (1971), 44–52.

Harrell, Jackson, and Wil A. Linkugel. "On Rhetorical Genre: An Organizing Principle." *Philosophy and Rhetoric,* 11(1978), 262–281.

Hendrix, J. A. "In Defense of Neo-Aristotelian Rhetorical Criticism." *Western Speech,* 32 (1968), 246–252.

Hillbruner, Anthony. "Creativity and Contemporary Critics." *Western Speech,* 24 (1960), 5–11.

——. "Criticism as Persuasion." *Southern Speech Communication Journal,* 28 (1963), 260–267.

——. "The Moral Imperative of Criticism." *Southern Speech Communication Journal,* 40 (1975), 228–247.

Hunt, Everett Lee. "Rhetoric and Literary Criticism." *Quarterly Journal of Speech,* 21 (1935), 564–568.

Jamieson, Kathleen M. Hall. "Generic Constraints and the Rhetorical Situation." *Philosophy and Rhetoric,* 6 (1973), 162–170.

Leff, Michael C., ed. "Rhetorical Criticism: The State of the Art," *Western Speech,* 44 (1980). This symposium contains the following essays: G. P. Mohrmann, "Elegy in a Critical Grave-Yard"; Suzanne Volmar Riches, and Malcolm O. Sillars, "The Status of Movement Criticism"; Walter R. Fisher, "Genre: Concepts and Applications in Rhetorical Criticism"; Thomas B. Farrel, "Critical Models in the Analysis of Discourse"; Bruce E. Gronbeck, "Dramaturgical Theory and Criticism: The State of the Art (or Science?)"; Edwin Black, "A Note on Theory and Practice in Rhetorical Criticism"; Michael C. Leff, "Interpretation and the Art of the Rhetorical Critic."

Lomas, Charles W. "Rhetorical Criticism and Historical Perspective." *Western Speech,* 32 (1968), 191–203.

Maloney, Martin. "Some New Directions in Rhetorical Criticism." *Central States Speech Journal,* 4 (1953), 1–5.

Mohrmann, G. P., Charles J. Stewart, and Donovan J. Ochs, eds. *Explorations in Rhetorical Criticism.* University Park, Penn.: The Pennsylvania State University Press, 1973.

Murphy, James J., ed. *Demosthenes' "On the Crown."* New York: Random House, 1967.

Murphy, Richard. "The Speech as Literary Genre." *Quarterly Journal of Speech,* 44 (1958), 117–127.

[Nichols], Marie Hochmuth. "The Criticism of Rhetoric." In her *A History and Criticism of American Public Address.* Vol. III. New York: Longmans, Green, 1955, pp. 1–23.

Nichols, Marie Hochmuth. *Rhetoric and Criticism.* Baton Rouge: Louisiana State University Press, 1963.

Nilsen, Thomas R. "Criticism and Social Consequences." *Quarterly Journal of Speech,* 42 (1956), 173–178.

——, ed. *Essays on Rhetorical Criticism.* New York: Random House, 1968.

——. "Interpretive Functions of the Critic." *Western Speech,* 21 (1957), 70–76.

Rathbun, John W. "The Problems of Judgment and Effect in Historical Criticism." *Western Speech,* 33 (1969), 146–159.

Redding, W. Charles. "Extrinsic and Intrinsic Criticism." *Western Speech,* 21 (1957), 96–102.

Reid, Loren. "The Perils of Rhetorical Criticism." *Quarterly Journal of Speech,* 30 (1944), 416–422.

Riches, Suzanne Volmar, and Malcolm O. Sillars. "The Status of Movement Criticism." *Western Speech,* 44 (1980), 275–287.

Rosenfield, Lawrence W. "The Anatomy of Critical Discourse." *Speech Monographs,* 35 (1968), 50–69.

———. "The Experience of Criticism." *Quarterly Journal of Speech*, 60 (1974), 489–496.

Rueckert, William H., ed. *Critical Responses to Kenneth Burke*. Minneapolis: University of Minnesota Press, 1969.

Scott, Robert L., and Bernard L. Brock. *Methods of Rhetorical Criticism: A Twentieth Century Perspective*. New York: Harper & Row, 1972; rev. ed. Detroit: Wayne State University Press, 1980.

Simons, Herbert W. "Doing Rhetorical Criticism." *Persuasion: Understanding, Practice, and Analysis*. Reading, Mass.: Addison-Wesley, 1976, pp. 269–317.

Thonssen, Lester, A. Craig Baird, and Waldo W. Braden. *Speech Criticism*. 2d ed. New York: Ronald Press, 1970.

Wander, Philip, and Steven Jenkins. "Rhetoric, Society, and the Critical Response." *Quarterly Journal of Speech*, 58 (1972), 441–450.

Wichelns, Herbert A. "The Literary Criticism of Oratory." *Studies in Rhetoric and Public Speaking in Honor of James A. Winans*. New York: Century, 1925, pp. 181–216.

Wrage, Ernest J. "The Ideal Critic." *Central States Speech Journal*, 8 (1957), 20–23.

———. "Public Address: A Study in Social and Intellectual History." *Quarterly Journal of Speech*, 33 (1947), 451–457.

Index

Index